Lecture Notes in Computer Science 13264

More information about this series at https://link.springer.com/bookseries/558

Osslan Osiris Vergara-Villegas ·
Vianey Guadalupe Cruz-Sánchez ·
Juan Humberto Sossa-Azuela ·
Jesús Ariel Carrasco-Ochoa ·
José Francisco Martínez-Trinidad ·
José Arturo Olvera-López (Eds.)

Pattern Recognition

14th Mexican Conference, MCPR 2022
Ciudad Juárez, Mexico, June 22–25, 2022
Proceedings

 Springer

Editors
Osslan Osiris Vergara-Villegas ⓘ
Universidad Autónoma de Ciudad Juárez
Ciudad Juárez, Mexico

Vianey Guadalupe Cruz-Sánchez ⓘ
Universidad Autónoma de Ciudad Juárez
Ciudad Juárez, Mexico

Juan Humberto Sossa-Azuela ⓘ
Instituto Politécnico Nacional
Mexico City, Mexico

Jesús Ariel Carrasco-Ochoa ⓘ
Instituto Nacional de Astrofísica, Óptica y
Electrónica
Puebla, Mexico

José Francisco Martínez-Trinidad ⓘ
Instituto Nacional de Astrofísica, Óptica y
Electrónica
Puebla, Mexico

José Arturo Olvera-López ⓘ
Autonomous University of Puebla
Puebla, Mexico

ISSN 0302-9743   ISSN 1611-3349 (electronic)
Lecture Notes in Computer Science
ISBN 978-3-031-07749-4   ISBN 978-3-031-07750-0 (eBook)
https://doi.org/10.1007/978-3-031-07750-0

This Springer imprint is published by the registered company Springer Nature Switzerland AG
The registered company address is: Gewerbestrasse 11, 6330 Cham, Switzerland

Preface

The Mexican Conference on Pattern Recognition 2022 (MCPR 2022) was the 14th event in the series organized by the Institute of Engineering and Technology of the Universidad Autónoma de Ciudad Juárez (UACJ) and the Computer Science Department of the Instituto Nacional de Astrofísica, Óptica y Electrónica (INAOE) of Mexico. The conference was auspiced by the Mexican Association for Computer Vision, Neurocomputing, and Robotics (MACVNR), a member society of the International Association for Pattern Recognition (IAPR). MCPR 2022 was due to be held in Ciudad Juárez, Chihuahua, Mexico, during June 22–25, 2022, but was instead held virtually due to the COVID-19 pandemic.

MCPR aims to provide a forum for exchanging scientific results, practice, and new knowledge, promoting collaboration among research groups in pattern recognition and related areas in Mexico and worldwide.

In this edition, as in previous years, MCPR 2022 attracted not only Mexican researchers but also worldwide participation. We received 66 manuscripts from authors in 13 countries including Chile, Colombia, Cuba, Ecuador, Germany, Mexico, Moldova, the Netherlands, Pakistan, South Africa, Spain, the USA, and Vietnam. Each paper was strictly peer reviewed by at least two members of the Program Committee. All the members of the Program Committee are experts in many fields of pattern recognition. As a result of peer review, 34 papers were accepted for presentation at the conference and included in this excellent conference proceedings.

We were very honored to have as invited speakers such internationally recognized researchers as

- Rama Chellappa, Departments of Electrical and Computer Engineering (Whiting School of Engineering) and Biomedical Engineering (School of Medicine), Johns Hopkins University, USA.
- Raúl Rojas, Department of Mathematics and Statistics, University of Nevada, Reno, USA.
- Maria de Marsico, Department of Computer Science, Sapienza University of Rome, Italy.

We would like to thank all the people who devoted so much time and effort to the successful running of MCPR 2022. Particularly, we extend our gratitude to all the authors who contributed to the conference. In addition, we give special thanks to the invited speakers, who shared their keynote addresses on various pattern recognition topics during the conference. We are also very grateful for the efforts and the quality of the reviews of all Program Committee members and additional reviewers. Their work allowed us to maintain the high quality of the contributions to the conference and provided a conference program of a high standard.

Finally, but no less important, our thanks go to the Institute of Engineering and Technology of the Universidad Autónoma de Ciudad Juárez (UACJ) for providing key support to this event.

We are sure that MCPR 2022 provided a fruitful forum for Mexican pattern recognition researchers and the broader international pattern recognition community.

June 2022

Osslan Osiris Vergara-Villegas
Vianey Guadalupe Cruz-Sánchez
Juan Humberto Sossa-Azuela
Jesús Ariel Carrasco-Ochoa
José Francisco Martínez-Trinidad
José Arturo Olvera-López

Organization

MCPR 2022 was sponsored by the Institute of Engineering and Technology of the Universidad Autónoma de Ciudad Juárez (UACJ) and the Computer Science Department of the Instituto Nacional de Astrofísica, Óptica y Electrónica (INAOE).

General Conference Co-chairs

Osslan Osiris Vergara-Villegas	UACJ, Mexico
Vianey Guadalupe Cruz-Sánchez	UACJ, Mexico
Juan Humberto Sossa-Azuela	CIC-IPN, Mexico
Jesús Ariel Carrasco-Ochoa	INAOE, Mexico
José Francisco Martínez-Trinidad	INAOE, Mexico
José Arturo Olvera-López	BUAP, Mexico

Local Arrangement Committee

Cervantes Cuahuey Brenda Alicia
Dominguez Guerrero Josué
Noriega Armendáriz René
Robledo Portillo Ivonne H.
Santiago Ramírez Everardo

Scientific Committee

Alexandre, L. A.	Universidade da Beira Interior, Portugal
Araujo, A.	Universidade Federal de Minas Gerais, Brazil
Benedi, J. M.	Universidad Politécnica de Valencia, Spain
Borges, D. L.	Universidade de Brasília, Brazil
Cabrera, S.	University of Texas at El Paso, USA
Dos-Santos, J. A.	Universidade Federal de Minas Gerais, Brazil
Escalante-Balderas, H. J.	INAOE, Mexico
Facon, J.	Pontifícia Universidade Católica do Paraná, Brazil
Fierrez, J.	Universidad Autonoma de Madrid, Spain
Fumera, G.	University of Cagliari, Italy
García-Borroto, M.	Cuban Society of Pattern Recognition, Cuba
García-Hernández, R. A.	Autonomous University of the State of Mexico, Mexico
Godoy, D.	UNICEN, Argentina

Grau, A.	Universitat Politécnica de Catalunya, Spain
Gregorová, M.	HEG, HES-SO, Switzerland
Gutierrez-Garcia, J. O.	ITAM, Mexico
Heutte, L.	Université de Rouen, France
Hurtado-Ramos, J. B.	CICATA-IPN, Mexico
Jiang, X	University of Münster, Germany
Kampel, M.	Vienna University of Technology, Austria
Kim, S. W.	Myongji University, South Korea
Kober, V.	CICESE, Mexico
Körner, M.	Technical University of Munich, Germany
Lazo-Cortés, M. S.	ITTLA, TecNM, Mexico
Levano, M. A.	Universidad Católica de Temuco, Chile
Loyola-González, O.	Altair Management Consultants, Spain
Martínez-Carranza, J.	INAOE, Mexico
Mendoza, M.	Universidad Técnica Federico Santa María, Chile
Montes-Y-Gomez, M.	INAOE, Mexico
Montoliu, R.	Universidad Jaume I, Spain
Morales-Reyes, A.	INAOE, Mexico
Oliveira, J. L.	Universidade de Aveiro, Portugal
Palagyi, K.	University of Szeged, Hungary
Pedrosa, G. V.	Universidade de Brasília, Brazil
Penaloza, C.	Advanced Telecommunications Research Institute International, Japan
Perez-Suay, A.	Universitat de València, Spain
Pina, P.	Instituto Superior Técnico, Portugal
Real, P.	University of Seville, Spain
Ruiz-Shulcloper, J.	UCI, Cuba
Salas, J.	CICATA-IPN, Mexico
Sanchez-Cortes, D.	Groupe Mutuel Holding SA, Switzerland
Sánchez-Salmerón, A. J.	Universitat Politècnica de València, Spain
Sansone, C.	Università di Napoli, Italy
Sossa-Azuela, J. H.	CIC-IPN, Mexico
Subbarayappa, S.	M. S. Ramaiah University of Applied Sciences, India
Sucar, L. E.	INAOE, Mexico
Tolosana, R.	Universidad Autónoma de Madrid, Spain
Valev, V.	Institute of Mathematics and Informatics, Bulgaria
Valle, M. E.	Universidade Estadual de Campinas, Brazil
Wang, C.	University of Geneva, Switzerland
Wario, F.	ISTC-CNR, Italy

Additional Referees

Aragon, M. Ezra	INAOE, Mexico
Lopez, J.	UACH, Mexico
Barella, V. H.	University of Sao Paulo, Brazil
Samper-Escalante, L. D.	ITESM, Mexico
Coelho, T.	University of Campinas, Brazil
Solorio-Fernández, S.	INAOE, Mexico
Guerrero, R.	Universidade de Aveiro, Portugal
Steniner, K.	University of Fribourg, Switzerland

Sponsoring Institutions

Institute of Engineering and Technology of the Universidad Autónoma de Ciudad Juárez (UACJ)

Instituto Nacional de Astrofísica, Óptica y Electrónica (INAOE)

Mexican Association for Computer Vision, Neurocomputing and Robotics (MACVNR)

National Council of Science and Technology of Mexico (CONACYT)

Contents

Natural Language Processing and Recognition

Robotics and Remote Sensing Applications of Pattern Recognition

Pattern Recognition Techniques

Hot Spots & Hot Regions Detection Using Classification Algorithms in BMPs Complexes at the Protein-Protein Interface with the Ground-State Energy Feature

O. Chaparro-Amaro[✉] [iD], M. Martínez-Felipe [iD], and J. Martínez-Castro [iD]

Centro de Investigación en Computación, Instituto Politécnico Nacional, Av. Juan de Dios Bátiz s/n, Esq. Miguel Othón de Mendizábal, Col. Nueva Industrial Vallejo, Gustavo A. Madero, CDMX C.P. 07738, Mexico
ochaparroa2019@cic.ipn.mx

Abstract. We present the results of the application of some machine learning algorithms to predict the hot spots & hot regions residues in protein complexes at the protein-protein interface between their polypeptide chains. The dataset consisted of twenty-nine bone morphogenetic proteins (BMPs) obtained from the Protein Data Bank (PDB). The training features were selected from biochemical and biophysical properties such as B-factor, hydrophobicity index, prevalence score, accessible surface area (ASA), conservation score, and the ground-state energy (using Density Functional Theory (DFT)) of each amino acid of these interfaces. Also, we implemented parallel CPU/GPU hardware acceleration techniques during the preprocessing in order to speed up the ASA and DFT calculations with more efficient execution times. We evaluated the performance of the classifiers with several metrics. The random forest classifier obtained the best performance, achieving an average of 90% of well-classified residues in both the true negative and true positive rates.

Keywords: Hot spots · Hot regions · BMPs · DFT

1 Introduction

Bone morphogenetic proteins (BMPs) form a group of similar-structure proteins with short-length amino acids chains and low molecular weight, which configure functional growth factors [6]. A protein-ligand binding and signaling occur on the molecular protein interfaces; this is why, characterizing and locating these residues that mainly contribute to the binding processes, is of particular interest [21]. Protein complexes are compounded of several amino acids chains binding by non-covalent protein-protein interactions [31]. A protein interface is a set of residues that form a region where two or more protein chains link themselves

© The Author(s), under exclusive license to Springer Nature Switzerland AG 2022
O. O. Vergara-Villegas et al. (Eds.): MCPR 2022, LNCS 13264, pp. 3–14, 2022.
https://doi.org/10.1007/978-3-031-07750-0_1

by interactions such as Van der Waals, electrostatic, hydrogen bonding, ionic, or a combination of these [19]. A well-known strategy to find the residues that mainly contribute to and mediate the protein-protein interactions at the interface is to measure the stability of the protein complex through their free energy change [10]. These residues are called hot spots, which get more than $\Delta\Delta G$ 2 kcal/mol, where the binding free energy is calculated when a particular residue is changed or mutated [1]. Alanine scanning mutagenesis (ASM) is a method to predict $\Delta\Delta G_{bind}$ values using alanine mutation between two non-covalent bonded chains at their interface. Robetta server is a protein-structure prediction service that calculates the free energy function ΔG and also calculates the binding-mutation function $\Delta\Delta G_{bind,n}$ of a specific residue n between two different chains [10, 11]. This procedure has been used to classify and to discover hot spots residues previously [17]. The connection between residues is established when the distance between their C_α atoms is ≤ 6.5 Å and either one of these residues or both results in a hot spot as defined before, forming hot regions [7]. In this sense, several machine learning classification models such as neuronal networks, support vector machines and random forest have been implemented for the prediction and detection of hot spots residues following different strategies and using different dataset sizes [13, 14, 29]. Besides, another type of biomolecules such as small peptides of interest are been searching by their sequences using similar strategies [28].

2   Materials and Methods

The general implementation for manipulating and preprocessing the Protein Data Bank (PDB) structures files (.pdb extension) was developed and performed within a C++ framework. The ASA calculation was supported by GPU GeForce 840M with CUDA (Compute Unified Device Architecture 8.0) API [22]. Part of the DFT calculation and the training process were performed in CPU Intel® Core TM i7-4510U 2.00 GHz (CPU 1), the rest of DFT calculations were performed in CPU processors Intel® Core TM and Intel® Core TM2 Quad Processor Q8200 2.33 GHz. To constitute the dataset, we fetched twenty-nine BMP complexes files from the Protein data bank [3] (three-dimensional crystallized structures described in Table 1).

2.1   Preprocessing (Feature Obtaining)

As a first proceeding, the Hydrogen atoms were added through the server tool called Mol Probity [9] with the flip method (Asn/Gln/His) using electron-cloud $x - H$ bond lengths and Van der Waals radii. HETATM and NAG molecules were excluded from the analysis. We consider a statistical prevalence to be more likely hot spots such as valine, leucine and serine considering the biochemical properties described in [1] as an input feature. Usually, hot spots & hot regions are excluded to have contact with the solvent [31]. So, a quantitative measurement of hydrophobicity was taken from [12] for each amino acid type. Another essential feature is the conservation score, which reflects the evolutionary changes under several steps in the linear sequence formed by amino acids (protein chain), and is also used to predict hot spots in some learning classification models [24]. We used the server ConSurf tool to calculate this feature by selecting the homolog search algorithm (HMMER) with 0.0001 as E-value of cut-off, using the MAFFT-L-INS-i alignment method and Bayesian calculations [2]. On the other hand, the B-Factor represents the average of the flexibility of the crystallized molecules and has been used to predict hot spots in previous works [30]. The B-factor value is included in the PDB file for each atom and it is calculated for each the residue using the standardized function from [5].

ASA Calculation. The ASA of each amino acid is one of the most important features that can describe some biochemical properties of proteins as in the case of hot spots [31], so we chose the Shrake & Rupley approximation algorithm to calculate the whole ASA protein complex. The precision of the method depends on the number of points used to cover the surface of the Van der Waals atomic spheres. We set from one-hundred to one-thousand points for each atomic sphere. To evaluate the solvent exposure, each atomic sphere is in contact with a spherical solvent probe with standard water Van der Waals radii $d_w = 1.4$ Å. Then, the more occluded the atoms and residues are from the solvent probe, the fewer points in the atomic surface are in contact with the solvent probe [25]. To better performance in execution time, the implementation was parallelized with the CUDA (Compute Unified Device Architecture) API on the GPU hardware [22].

DFT Calculation. Density Functional Theory (DFT) is a method that can be used to approximate the ground-state energy of a molecular many-particle system using its three-dimensional electronic conformation. It has been reported to be efficient and well-correlated results for calculating binding free energies for proteins [26]. To estimate the ground-state energy of the individual amino acids, we used the python module PyQuante2 [18], which will be an input feature to the machine learning model, disregarding effects from neighbor residues. We implemented the STO-3G minimal basis sets to model atomic orbitals, using SVWN functional solver and 0.00001 as tolerance value. In terms of computational performance, the execution time of the DFT calculation could be more complex and slower for customary scalar processors (one data at a time), especially for large macromolecules formed by amino acids chains. So, as part of the data preprocessing, we combined and accelerated the PyQuante2 implementation with the Multiprocessing python module [15]. This module allows running the parallel subprocesses concurrently between multiple CPU cores.

2.2 Training of the Models

The chosen classification algorithms are based on supervised machine learning. The inputs of these algorithms for training and testing correspond to each residue and the features selected previously. In total, it was fetched and processed roughly 12100 entries (one per amino acid that constitutes each protein in the dataset). The dataset of the protein complexes presents 24% of the interface residues, from which 32.4% of these residues are hot spots & hot regions. Then, for training, we used only the interface residues (around 2920 entries). These entries describe each interface residue, which is constituted by six numerical type variables: B factor, ASA, hydrophobicity index, prevalence, conservation score, and ground-state energy. Since hot spots & hot regions are mandatory residues from the interface, we filtered them for the training and testing datasets using the rules given in [19]. There, p is defined as $p = V_1\ _{radii} + V_2\ _{radii} + 0.5$ Å, where $V_{1,2}\ _{radii}$ are the Van der Waals radius of the first and second atom compared to each different residue respectively. The dataset was filtered using the interface residues that are in contact with the polypeptide chains. Hot spots residues were labeled using the ASM computational method [10,11] from the Robetta server. Alternatively, the hot regions were labeled using the server of the HotRegion database [7]. Joining the results of the Robetta server and the HotRegion database, a binary label dataset was conceived following the preprocessing described above.

The first algorithm used was "logistic regression algorithm" with a liblinear solver, the second was a "random forest classifier" with five-hundred trees, the third was a "support vector classifier" with a radial basis function (rbf): $e^{-\gamma\|x-x'\|^2}$, which $\gamma = 0.01$ in this kernel and regularization parameter of $\rho = 10$. The last classifier was a "neural network" based on multilayer perceptron model with five layers, $tanh(x)$ activation function, Adam optimization and binary cross-entropy as loss function; the training was performed using three-hundred epochs with extra data scale preprocessing [8]. A hyperparameter-grid search optimization was performed over the parameters of the models. Then the whole dataset was randomly split (hold-out technique with ten-folds), where 70% and 30% of this dataset were for training and testing respectively. The training data was validated using K-Fold Cross-Validation using ten splits repeated ten times (one-hundred in total) by each algorithm with the parameters selected by the grid search optimization. Consequently, the logistic regression algorithm was dismissed due to it got the worst results. Therefore, the three remaining models were evaluated using the test data, which results are discussed below (described in Fig. 1). All these models were implemented in scikit-learn and keras.

3   Results and Discussion

3.1   Preprocessing Performance

We compared our parallel ASA implementation, that improves the performance in contrast with the scalar method proposed by Pdbremix python API [23], reducing the execution time considerably as the protein complexes become larger (see Fig. 2). This algorithm presents roughly $O(n^2)$ complexity by each protein with n atoms. Our parallel strategy allow us to distribute the load in every available core. With this, we can locally calculate the ASA between adjacent atoms and residues inside a spatial three-dimensional box.

Table 1. Description of the twenty-nine BMPs that conforms the dataset in the training and evaluation processes.

PDB complex	Code	Number of atoms	PDB complex	Code	Number of atoms
1. BMP-2 and two BMP receptors	1ES7	5711	2. BMP-7 and secreted antagonist Noggin	1M4U	4968
3. BMP-2 and its receptor	1REW	5742	4. BMP-2 bound with BMPR and ActRII	2GOO	8635
5. BMP-2 and ligand-receptor	2H62	5698	6. BMP-2 ligand-receptor II	2H64	4414
7. BMP-2 with BMPR-IA variant B1	2QJ9	5827	8. BMP-2 with BMPR-IA variant B12	2QJA	5805
9. BMP-2 with BMPR-IA variant IA/IB	2QJB	5752	10. BMP-2 and the first Von Willebrand domain type C	3BK3	5054
11. Inhibitor BMP with mutant oro- tidine 5' - monophosphate decarboxylase	3LTY	6527	12. RGMA-BMP-2 with BMP-2	4UHY	4107
13. RGMA-BMP-2 form 1	4UHZ	2636	14. RGMA-BMP-2 form 2	4UI0	3945
15. BMP-2 with RGMC-BMP	4UI1	5376	16. BMP-2-inducible kinase with an Indazole inhibitor	5I3O	9494
17. RGMB-BMP2-NEO1	4UI2	8413	18. BMP-9	4YCG	9549
19. BMP-2-inducible Indazole kinase with inhibitor	5I3R	9424	20. Orotidine 5' phosphate decarboxy- lase with hydroxyuridine 5' BMP	1DQX	1 6539
21. Orotidine 5' monophosphate decarboxylase with BMP-2	1X1Z	6281	22. Orotidine 5' monophosphate decarboxylase with inhibitor BMP	4DF1	6208
23. BMP-1 with reverse hydroxymate compound 22	6BSL	6270	24. BMP-1 with reverse hydroxymate compound 1	6BTN	6292
25. BMP-1 with hydroxamate	6BTP	6262	26. BMP-1 with hydroxamate comp. 2	6BTQ	6431
27. BMP-10 with activin receptor ALK1	6SF1	2797	28. BMP-9 with activin receptor ALK1	6SF2	8210
29. BMP-10 with activin receptor ALK1 AT 2.3 Å	6SF3	2849	–	–	–

In addition to the performance comparison, we contrasted the accuracy of our parallel implementation with the scalar python implementation Pdbremix and the values obtained from the FreeSASA library [16] for each protein complex using the relative error. The relative error average between parallel implementation and the scalar Pdbremix implementation was 0.0773%, whereas the FreeSASA implementation was 0.4985% for the whole dataset. For the scalar implementation, the greater the number of points used in the ASA calculation, the more complex is the computation for the scalar processes on the CPU. On these terms, the parallel GPU implementation gets a speed-up ratio between three to twenty-two times. In the case of DFT performance, the execution time for the whole protein by the DFT method is the sum of the individual residue's execution times. The DFT calculation was performed by each core in a multiprocessing module, showing a general speed improvement of 3.5 to 4 times (according to the number of CPU cores).

3.2   Evaluation and Testing of the Classification Models

To assess the prediction performance, we counted the true positives, false positives, true negatives and false negatives. The classification models were evaluated with the Accuracy, Precision, Recall and F_1-score rates using both micro-average and macro-average methods, respectively (taken from [13]).

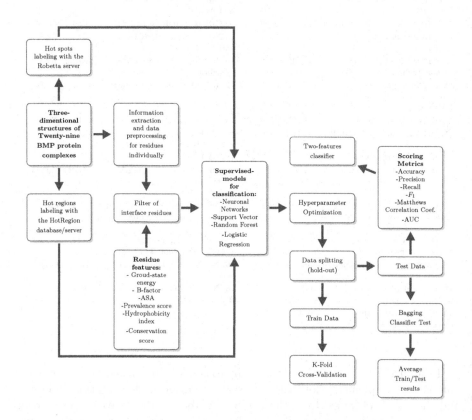

Fig. 1. General training processes.

Using the optimized parameters and the whole training data, the random forest, support vector and neuronal network classifiers were trained (ten complete processes) and then tested with the testing data (see Table 2). The best classifier was the random forest method with a very low outputs variance. In the case of the support vector classifier, we got better performance than the neuronal network in all metrics, and almost the same response in the mean of the recall metric for hot spots & non-hot regions class. To check the effects of the imbalanced data, we trained the algorithms using just 1328 (50% for each class), in which, for the random forest, we obtained an average of F_1-score for the hot spot & hot region class of 0.814 and for the complementary class 0.893. The proportion between the true negative and true positive was roughly 86.44% of the test data, which were worse than the imbalanced training dataset with the same $AUC = 0.95$. Besides, we used the Matthews correlation coefficient (MCC) from [4], which obtained an average of 0.7476, 0.66 and 0.5517 for the random forest, support vector and the neuronal network respectively. The MCC for the random forest trained with the balanced dataset was 0.72, so a general better performance was not observed with this training. Based on all these metrics, the random forest classifier was the best scored and obtained an average of OOB = 0.87445 (Out-of-bag) error (see its confusion matrix in Fig. 4). The feature importance for this classifier from the most to the least important was: ASA, ground-state, energy, conservation score, B-factor, hydrophobicity index and prevalence score. The average AUC and ROC curves between the classification models are compared in Fig. 3.

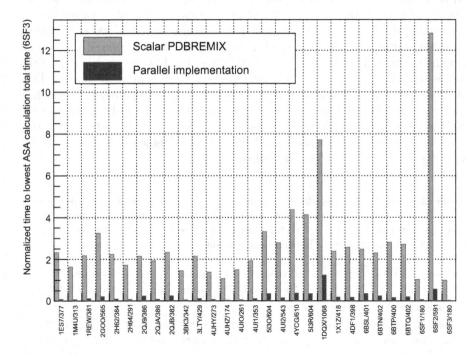

Fig. 2. Average (CPU 1)/GPU execution time of ten measurements of the parallelization (red bar) vs scalar implementation (blue bar). The X-axis shows the protein PDB code/(number of amino acids). The performance is normalized to ASA calculation of 6SF3 complex (the fastest in terms of scalar implementation with 200 points per atom). (Color figure online)

To verify if the random forest can improve its performance based on a bagging ensemble (decision trees on subsets of the dataset with the sum of each contribution), we combined the random forest and a Bagging predictor with different sizes of estimators. However, this technique does not improve the performance of the whole classifiers neither adding more trees to the random forest. To understand how the classifier divides the decision space of the inputs as a function of the labeled classes, we trained a separate sub-random forest classifier with five-hundred trees to get a two-dimensional decision surface projection using just the best two scored features (ASA and ground-state energy) by the random forest classifier (plotted in Fig. 5). The sub-random forest classifier obtained an average accuracy or micro-F_1-score of ≈ 0.79, OOB $= 0.805$ and MCC ≈ 0.513, with Std. Dev. of 0.00256, 0.001827 and 0.0058 respectively. The projection shows that we can find almost all hot spots & hot regions residues clustered at lower ASA values (<50 Å^2) as was expected [20,27], and between 200, 270, 300, and 580 E_h of ground-state energies. We should emphasize that the hydrophobicity index and prevalence features were the worst features scored. However, including this information, in combination with the other features, improved the general results, in contrast to using only the two best-scored features. In the case of the whole-random forest classifier, the conservation score is kept as the third and the B-factor as the fourth in feature importance in the training process. Hence, this indicates that the evolutionary conservation and low structural flexibility of the residues at a specific position in the interface correspond to occluded and buried residues from the solvent molecules. The behavior of these residues is consistent with properties of hot regions, described in [19,30].

Table 2. Rates for the classifiers. The mean of the accuracy or micro-F_1-score were $\approx 0.8893, 0.7856, 0.844$ with Std. Dev. $\approx 0.0017, 0.0158$ and 0.0 for the random forest, neuronal networks and support vector algorithms respectively. The Std. Dev. equal to 0 indicates the same outputs in each classification.

Class	Precision		Recall		F_1-score	
	Mean	Std. Dev.	Mean	Std. Dev.	Mean	Std. Dev.
Random forest classifier						
Non-hot spot & non-hot region	0.9232	0.00136	0.913	0.00227	0.918	0.0013
Hot spot & hot region	0.82	0.0038	0.839	0.00313	0.83	0.0025
Support vector classifier						
Non-hot spot & non-hot region	0.9163	0	0.8484	0	0.8811	0
Hot spot & hot region	0.722	0	0.8357	0	0.7748	0
Neural network (multilayer perceptron)						
Non-hot spot & non-hot region	0.894	0.01437	0.776	0.019	0.8311	0.0132
Hot spot & hot region	0.6298	0.0216	0.804	0.03	0.706	0.0209

In this sense, the random forest algorithm is suitable for being adapted and scaled to different sub-proteins families as long as the number of available three-dimensional structures of protein complexes increases. The main disadvantage of this method is still the long execution time for DFT calculation. This problem can be tackled by developing deeper parallel implementations, combined with machine learning and hardware speed-up techniques.

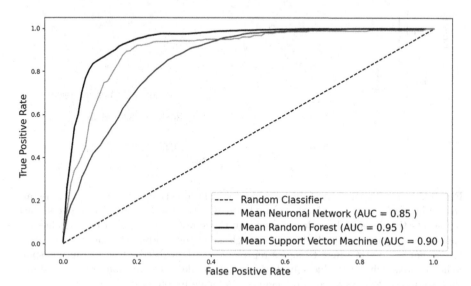

Fig. 3. Average performance of the ROC curves (ten complete processes) of each classifier using interpolation. Their respective average AUC values of the hot spots & hot regions classifiers of the interface residues denote better results for the random forest.

		Predicted values	
		Negative	Positive
	Non-hot spot/ hot region	TN 62.2%	FP 5.77%
Actual values	Hot spot/ hot region	FN 5.13%	TP 26.91%
		Non-hot spot/ hot region	Hot spot/ hot region

Fig. 4. Confusion matrix of the average-random forest classifier. Combining both the true negative (TN) and true positive (TP) values we obtained roughly 90% (correct prediction) of the total evaluation.

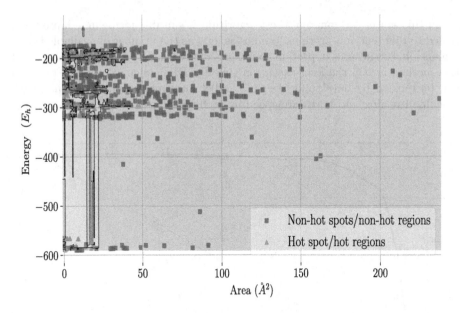

Fig. 5. Average hyperplane of the two-dimensional projection between the ground-state energy in the Y-axis (E_h) (Hartrees) and ASA (Å^2) in the X-axis. The orange surface represents the decision boundary formed by the sub-random forest that classifies hot spots & hot regions, while the blue surface classifies the residues that are not hot spots & non-hot regions. Orange triangles represent the data distribution of the hot spots & hot regions, while the blue squares represent the data distribution of those residues that are non-hot spots & non-hot regions. (Color figure online)

4   Conclusions

Nowadays, the amount of protein complex data has been increasing fast. So, strategies that can accelerate the data processing in both software and hardware levels should be explored. Because of this, the execution time of the ASA calculation was improved by a ratio from four to sixty-five times depending on the number of points and numbers of amino acids that use parallel computing via GPU hardware. Therefore, a single random forest classifier was the best algorithm to detect and classify the hot spots & the hot regions according to the rates of the metrics obtained. Consequently, we found that the ground-state energy was the second most important feature (considering ASA as the first one), scored by this classifier, which indicates that this feature can describe the nature of protein-protein interactions of BMPs. Finally, the main contribution of this work was to show that only six features could be used as input to the classifier to describe hot spots & hot regions at the protein-protein interface with appropriate computational performance. This fact can set up our understanding of the nature of the protein complexes and how the oligomers assemble themselves in non-covalent protein-protein interactions.

Author Disclosure Statement

The authors declare that no competing financial interests exist.

Acknowledgments. This study was supported by: "Programa de desarrollo tecnológico e innovación para alumnos del IPN. México 2021" and by CONACYT (Consejo Nacional de Ciencia y Tecnología).

References

1. Bogan, A.A., Thorn, K.S.: Anatomy of hot spots in protein interfaces. J. Mol. Biol. **280**(mb981843), 1–9 (1998)
2. Ashkenazy, H., et al.: ConSurf 2016: an improved methodology to estimate and visualize evolutionary conservation in macromolecules. Nucleic Acids Res. **44**, 344–350 (2016). https://doi.org/10.1093/nar/gkw408
3. Berman, H., Henrick, K., Nakamura, H., Markley, J.: The worldwide protein data bank (wwPDB): ensuring a single, uniform archive of PDB data. Nucleic Acids Res. **35**, D301–D303 (2007)
4. Boughorbel, S., Jarray, F., El-Anbari, M.: Optimal classifier for imbalanced data using Matthews correlation coefficient metric. PLoS ONE **12**(6), 1–17 (2017). https://doi.org/10.1371/journal.pone.0177678
5. Carugo, O.: How large b-factors can be in protein crystal structures. BMC Bioinf. **19**(61), 1–9 (2018). https://doi.org/10.1186/s12859-018-2083-8
6. Chen, D., Zhao, M., Mundy, G.R.: Bone morphogenetic proteins. Growth Factors **22**(4), 233–241 (2004)
7. Cukuroglu, E., Gursoy, A., Keskin, O.: HotRegion: a database of predicted hot spot clusters. Nucleic Acids Res. **40**(22080558), 829–833 (2011)
8. Haykin, S., Haykin, S.: Neural Networks and Learning Machines, vol. 10. Prentice Hall, New York (2009)
9. Hintze, B.J., et al.: MolProbity ultimate rotamer-library distributions for model validation. Proteins Struct. Funct. Bioinf. **84**, 1177–1189 (2016)
10. Kortemme, T., Baker, D.: A simple physical model for binding energy hot spots in protein-protein complexes. PNAS **99**(22), 14116–14121 (2002). https://doi.org/10.1073/pnas.202485799
11. Kortemme, T., Kim, D.E., Baker, D.: Computational alanine scanning of protein-protein interfaces. Sci. STKE Protoc. 1–8 (2004). https://doi.org/10.1126/stke.2192004pl2
12. Kyte, J., Doolittle, R.F.: A simple method for displaying the hydropathic character of a protein. J. Mol. Biol. **5**(157), 105–132 (1982). https://doi.org/10.1016/0022-2836(82)90515-0
13. Lise, S., et al.: Prediction of hot spot residues at protein-protein interfaces by combining machine learning and energy-based methods. BMC Bioinf. **10**(365), 1–17 (2009). https://doi.org/10.1186/1471-2105-10-365
14. Liu, S., Liu, C., Deng, L.: Machine learning approaches for protein-protein interaction hot spot prediction: progress and comparative assessment. MDPI Mol. **23**(10), 2535 (2018). https://doi.org/10.3390/molecules23102535
15. McKerns, M.M., et al.: Building a framework for predictive science. In: Proceedings of the 10th Python in Science Conference, vol. 1, pp. 1–11 (2011). https://doi.org/10.48550/arXiv.1202.1056

16. Mitternacht, S.: FreeSASA: an open source C library for solvent accessible surface area calculations. F1000 Res. **5**(189), 1–10 (2016). https://doi.org/10.12688/f1000research.7931.1
17. Morrow, J.K., Zhang, S.: Computational prediction of hot spot residues. Curr. Pharm. Des. **18**, 1255–1265 (2012). https://doi.org/10.2174/138161212799436412
18. Muller, R.: PyQuante2. PyQuante Sourceforge Project Page (2013). https://github.com/rpmuller/pyquante2
19. Tuncbag, N., Keskin, O., Gursoy, A.: Hotpoint: hot spot prediction server for protein interfaces. Nucleic Acids Res. **38**(20444871), 402–406 (2010). https://doi.org/10.1093/nar/gkq323
20. Nguyen, Q.T., Fablet, R., Pastor, D.: Protein interaction hotspot identification using sequence-based frequency-derived features. IEEE Trans. Biomed. Eng. **60**(11), 2993–3002 (2013). https://doi.org/10.1109/TBME.2011.2161306
21. Nussinov, R., Schreiber, G.: Computational Protein-Protein Interactions. CRC Press, Boca Raton (2009). https://doi.org/10.1201/9781420070071
22. NVIDIA, Vingelmann, P., Fitzek, F.H.: CUDA, release. Accessed 10 Feb 1989 (2020). https://developer.nvidia.com/cuda-toolkit
23. PDBremix: Calculating the solvent accessible surface area (2014)
24. Qiao, Y., et al.: Protein-protein interface hot spots prediction based on a hybrid feature selection strategy. BMC Bioinf. **14**(19), 1–16 (2018). https://doi.org/10.1186/s12859-018-2009-5
25. Shrake, A., Rupley, J.A.: Environment and exposure to solvent of protein atoms. lysozyme and insulin. J. Mol. Biol. **2**(79), 351–371 (1973). https://doi.org/10.1016/0022-2836(73)90011-9
26. Stephen, F., et al.: Density functional theory calculations on entire proteins for free energies of binding: application to a model polar binding site. Proteins Struct. Funct. Bioinf. **82**(12), 3335–3346 (2014). https://doi.org/10.1002/prot.24686
27. Tuncbag, N., Gursoy, A., Keskin, O.: Identification of computational hot spots in protein interfaces: combining solvent accessibility and inter-residue potentials improves the accuracy. J. Bioinf. **25**(12), 1513–1520 (2009). https://doi.org/10.1093/bioinformatics/btp240
28. Cavalcante, J.P.U., Gonçalves, A.C., Bonidia, R.P., Sanches, D.S., de Carvalho, A.C.P.L.F.: MathPIP: classification of proinflammatory peptides using mathematical descriptors. In: Stadler, P.F., Walter, M.E.M.T., Hernandez-Rosales, M., Brigido, M.M. (eds.) BSB 2021. LNCS, vol. 13063, pp. 131–136. Springer, Cham (2021). https://doi.org/10.1007/978-3-030-91814-9_13
29. Wang, L., et al.: Prediction of hot spots in protein interfaces using a random forest model with hybrid features. Protein Eng. Des. Sel. **25**(3), 119–126 (2012). https://doi.org/10.1093/protein/gzr066
30. Xia, J.F., et al.: APIS: accurate prediction of hot spots in protein interfaces by combining protrusion index with solvent accessibility. BMC Bioinf. **174**(11), 1–14 (2010). https://doi.org/10.1186/1471-2105-11-174
31. Yan, C., et al.: Characterization of protein-protein interfaces. Protein J. **27**(1), 59–70 (2008). https://doi.org/10.1007/s10930-007-9108-x

Clustering of Twitter Networks Based on Users' Structural Profile

Marisol Flores-Garrido[(⊠)] [ID], Luis Miguel García-Velázquez [ID], and Rodrigo Sebastian Cortez-Madrigal [ID]

Escuela Nacional de Estudios Superiores unidad Morelia, Universidad Nacional Autónoma de México, Antigua carretera a Pátzcuaro No. 8701, C.P. 58190 Morelia, Michoacán, Mexico
{mflores,luism_garcia,rcortez}@enesmorelia.unam.mx
https://www.enesmorelia.unam.mx/

Abstract. Twitter's ability to connect users around a given topic provides an insight into the complex mechanisms that grant positions of influence to a subset of users. This work focuses on clustering a collection of Twitter topic networks through an interpretable approach centered on the asymmetric relations on the platform. We create a network representation based on directed graphlet-orbits, using graphlets with 2–4 nodes. Our method has two main steps; first, we identify structural profiles for the network users. Then, we create network embeddings using the previous profiles and establish groups within the collection. We show the applicability of the proposed method by analyzing 50 real networks generated around trending topics in Mexico and discussing the identified user profiles from the viewpoint of the social power dynamics they reflect.

Keywords: Clustering · Graphlets · Twitter · Social roles

1 Introduction

Twitter is a microblogging service and social network in which users publish and interact through posts known as *tweets*. Tweets are publicly visible by default, and any user can reply to others; this creates a public discussion that can be thought of as a directed network.

There is a growing interest from different disciplines to understand the dynamics of the distribution of information on Twitter through the characterization of the roles of users; for example, identifying primary disseminators of information related to medical therapy or science articles in social media to characterize the content of the information that these users provide [9].

This work was supported by the Universidad Nacional Autónoma de México through the project DGAPA-PAPIIT IA106620 *Ciencia de datos para las humanidades digitales.*

The way information is propagated on Twitter resembles how information is propagated in real life. Human communications are usually characterized by an asymmetry between information producers (media, companies, influencers, among others) and content consumers [4]. Understanding the role users play in information propagation through the network can provide valuable insights into public discussions on the platform.

Given a collection of Twitter networks defined by users' interactions on particular topics, we aim at identifying groups within the collection according to the type and number of users that show a particular profile in the conversation.

To this end, we propose a representation of the topic networks based on the profile of their users. The profiles are built using the orbit signature assigned to each node in a graphlet-based analysis of the networks.

Graphlets are non-isomorphic small graphs that can describe the local structure of a network's node subsets. Much like degree distribution, counting the number and type of graphlets incident on each node could be valuable for establishing similarity between networks.

Our graphlet-based approach fulfills a double purpose. First, it provides a method to group Twitter networks in an explainable way, capturing differences among them that go beyond general network metrics. Second, it produces a characterization of the networks' users that can help to understand the structure, relations, and latent patterns created by the complex dynamics in Twitter.

We show the usefulness of our analysis by exploring 50 real networks associated with Twitter trending topics in Mexico during 2020 and discussing the different user profiles encountered in the process in terms of the behavioral patterns suggested by their components.

2   Related Work

The problem of clustering Twitter topic networks has been approached before by Himelboim et al. [6], who proposed to categorize the networks by using features like centrality, density, modularity, and the number of isolated users.

Their work, developed outside the machine learning paradigm, suggests a network taxonomy with six structures: divided, unified, fragmented, clustered, inward hub-and-spoke, and outward hub-and-spoke. Although this classification is useful to understand different communication patterns, the proposed categories are predefined - not data-driven. Consequently, the categories may be insufficient to capture the differences between networks in a given collection, assigning the whole set to the same category.

Regarding the use of graphlets, Charbey and Prieur use them to analyze the structure of collections of Facebook ego networks [3]. However, they do not consider directed networks nor focus on the users' role according to their position.

3   Graphlets and Social Roles

Clustering a collection of graphs is a challenging problem. Popular clustering algorithms, like KMeans, require embedding the graphs in a vectorial space.

This task can be accomplished by methods that range from feature extraction to more sophisticated embeddings generated through neural networks; among them, graphlets have been proposed to capture the overall network topology [10].

Graphlets were first introduced in a biological context and are defined as connected non-isomorphic subgraphs of a network. Przulj et al. introduce them, motivated by the idea of generalizing the degree distribution in order to effect a comparison between graphs [8]. They considered a dictionary of all the possible graphs with 2–5 nodes.

Graphlets proved successful at graph classification [1,13], and they were later extended to directed graphs [10]. Furthermore, Sarajlic et al. [10] proposed to represent each node u in a directed graph through a vector in $\mathbb{R}^{129}$, whose ith component represents the number of times that u appears in the ith automorphism orbit enumerated in the graphlet set, as listed by the authors. Orbits distinguish between the different roles that a node could have within the same graphlet. Therefore, computing the orbit signature of a node provides information on its generalized graphlet-based degree and the different ways it interacts with its neighbors.

Identifying the role that a node plays, given its structural position, is significant when analyzing social networks. Different works in social sciences focus on patterns of network ties to understand processes within a system; to name an example, Lusher and Robins [7] suggest the presence of configurations along the lines of *archeological traces* imprinted in the social mechanisms through time (see Fig. 1).

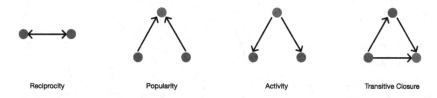

Reciprocity   Popularity   Activity   Transitive Closure

Fig. 1. Some of the patterns proposed by Lusher and Robins to describe social configurations in broader collective processes [7].

4   Proposed Approach

We aim at grouping a collection of Twitter networks where nodes represent users and edges describe the interaction among them, defined in the form of likes, replies, or retweets.

Twitter allows a dynamic flow of information that is not bidirectional, i.e., the platform is designed to follow others without a mutual acknowledgment of the relationship. In terms of our model, this translates into a directed network. In terms of the configuration of a social sphere, the one-way follow scheme creates four different types of relationships among every pair of users u and v: they can be *friends* when they follow each other, they can be in an *asymmetrical relationship* with u or v following the other without being followed back, or they can be *alienated*, when neither of them follows the other.

The different configurations give way to notions of authority and influence that significantly affect how ideas travel the *twittersphere* [5]. Furthermore, asymmetric relations favor the emergence of social ranking. The methodology proposed in this work is designed to make visible the different roles that a user can have in this information ecosystem.

Our approach has two main stages. First, we use clustering to identify different user profiles according to their orbit signature. Then, we cluster the networks in the collection using a network representation based on the frequency of the different profiles identified in the previous step. Each of these stages is described next.

4.1   Profiling Users

We propose that similar user profiles can be identified in the networks despite the specific topic giving rise to the conversation community. However, the frequency of each profile could vary depending on the interest elicited by a subject and the resulting collective behavior.

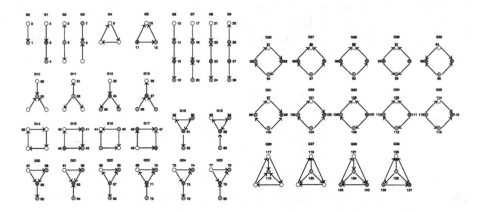

Fig. 2. There are 40 different directed graphlets with 2–4 nodes and 129 possible orbits within them.

To explore the different roles that users show in the collection, we start by performing a graphlet analysis of each network and characterize each user according to their graphlet-orbit count. When the graphlets have up to four nodes, 129 different orbits are possible (see Fig. 2). Therefore, each node is represented by a vector in $\mathbb{R}^{129}$ that indicates the number of times that the node appears in each of the roles defined by the orbits.

Next, we use clustering to partition the set of users and characterize the different profiles that appear in the topic networks. The value of k can be chosen using any of the methodologies available to evaluate the clustering quality observed at different values [12].

To characterize the role of users within the identified profiles, we consider the topological properties of the groups' dominant orbits, analyzing the role they play in the graphlets. Moreover, we also review orbits that are absent in all of the users in the group.

Each directed edge indicates a relationship between two nodes, where the starting node represents a user who has mentioned, replied, or retweeted the user represented by the ending node. A node n with $indegree(n) = 0$ will be called source. A node n with $outdegree(n) = 0$ will be called sink. Notice that each maximal path in a graphlet starts in a source and ends in a sink.

Since a node's indegree and outdegree are invariant under automorphisms, we can extend the definitions of sink and source from nodes to orbits. We will say that a source orbit $\mathcal{O}$ is a *listener* if, for each node $n \in \mathcal{O}$, the length of each maximal path that contains an edge starting in n is 1. Orbits 0, 6, 7, 21, 23, and 29 are examples of listener orbits, but orbits 11 and 17 are not.

We will say that an orbit $\mathcal{O}$ is an *audience* if, for each node $n \in \mathcal{O}$, n is a listener and every other node m in an edge that starts in n is a sink with $indegree(m) > 1$. The orbits 7, 21, and 29 are examples of audience orbits, but the orbit 23 is not.

Every node n participates in different graphlets within a network; each graphlet gives information about a local neighborhood of 2, 3, or 4 nodes in which n participates. Furthermore, the information provided by different graphlets is different from that given by the indegree and the outdegree alone.

Also, we remark that if nodes n and m are in the same orbit, an automorphism that interchanges these nodes preserves any given maximal path and the role that n and m play in it. Thus, roles and profiles of the orbits are well defined.

4.2   Network Clustering

After the main profiles have been established, we represent networks in terms of the frequency of each user type. Thus, each network is represented through a vector in $\mathbb{R}^k$ where the i-th component is the number of users with the ith profile identified in the previous stage.

Then, we use these profile-based embedding to explore the structure of the network dataset through hierarchical clustering.

Networks in our study are not defined by the follower-following relation at a given time but, instead, in terms of the interactions triggered by a conversation. Therefore, the structured data in which we identify user roles is a particular subgraph of the more general follow-based network and is defined by the topic's specific interactions. We propose that using the role-based profiles of the users as the central point of the network grouping task could bring insight into the latent relations and hierarchies that take part in the diffusion processes related to specific topics.

Regarding the time complexity of the proposed approach, the most expensive stage is identifying profiles. The most popular algorithm to estimate graphlet-orbits [10] has a time complexity in $\mathcal{O}(nd^{g-1})$, where n are the nodes, d is the maximum degree of a node in the network, and g is the size of the graphlets considered. On the other hand, k-means has a time complexity in $\mathcal{O}(Ikmn)$ where I is the bound on allowed iterations, k is the number of groups, n are the instances (nodes in our problem), and m is the dimension of the points. We have a fixed value for $m = 129$; the time complexity of our approach is in $\mathcal{O}(nd^3 + Ikn)$.

5   Experiments and Results

Data. A dataset with 50 Twitter trending-topic networks was created using NodeXL Software. The chosen topics were among the first five trending topics reported by Twitter, with more than 20k tweets in Mexico within November 2020. The networks were preprocessed to remove self-loops and isolates.

Each network comprises a set of users (nodes) and directed edges that correspond to the actions reply (including mentions) and retweet. Since we do not use labels in the networks, both interactions are equally represented by a directed edge. The order and size of the networks were within the range of $[1952, 24876]$ and $[9515, 35508]$, respectively; we worked with a total of 925896 nodes (users) in the collection.

Users' Profile. Graphlet orbit signatures were computed using the software developed by Anida Sarajlic et al. [10]. Since the networks have different order and sizes, the total orbit count for each node was normalized.

We analyzed the data focusing on the sum of square errors (SSE) with different numbers of groups, trying to identify the point with maximum curvature (elbow method); we selected $k = 5$. To cluster the orbit signatures across the whole network dataset, we used the scikit-learn implementation of MiniBatch KMeans – a modification of the KMeans algorithm proposed to address scalability in challenging scenarios [11]. We used a batch size of 100 instances, with initialization points selected through the algorithm k-means++ [2].

Since stability is a concern in our problem, we used 50 runs of the task to estimate the robustness of the identified groups. The average value of the pairwise Normalized Mutual Information of the runs was 0.9.

The k centroids corresponding to the best result, considering the SSE, were used as group representatives. Figure 3 shows the main orbits for each group. Table 1 expands the description of each profile by showing all the orbits above a general threshold $\Delta = 0.06$.

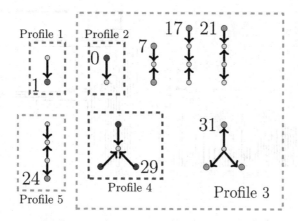

Fig. 3. Main graphlet-orbits (above threshold $\Delta = 0.06$) in each of the identified user profiles, according to the magnitude of their associated vector component.

Table 1. Identified profiles according to their graphlet orbits. For the main orbits (second column), we show only the components with magnitude above the threshold $\Delta = 0.06$.

Profile	(Orbit, score)	Absent orbits
1	(1, 0.85)	2, 3, 6, 7, 9, 11–18, 20, 21, 23–29, 31–62, 64, 65, 67–90, 92–124, 126–128
2	(0, 0.96)	1, 3–5, 7–10, 12–128
3	(29, 0.13), (7, 0.11), (31, 0.11), (17, 0.09), (0, 0.08), (21, 0.08)	None
4	(29, 0.94)	None
5	(24, 0.83)	111

Network Clusters. After grouping the users, we used the different profiles to create an embedding of each network in $\mathbb{R}^5$. Figure 4 shows the composition identified for each network in terms of their users' profiles.

We used agglomerative hierarchical clustering with the cosine distance and single linkage to explore the differences between networks. Results are shown in Fig. 4; a nonlinear scale has been used for clarity purposes regarding network groups.

6 Discussion

Regarding users, four of the profiles (1, 2, 4, 5) are distinguished by the presence of a dominant orbit in the representative centroid vector. By contrast, the remaining group (3) has a more balanced orbit distribution in the signature vector of its centroid.

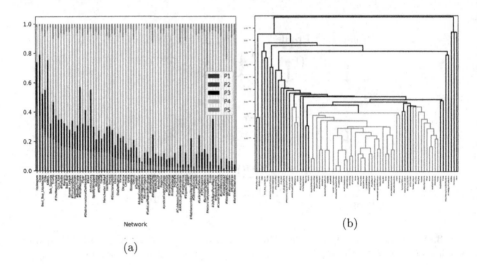

(a)

(b)

Fig. 4. (a) Percentage of the composition of each network according to the identified profiles in the dataset, (b) Network clustering obtained with the embedding based on user profiles. A nonlinear scale has been used in the x-axis to appreciate the groups better.

To exemplify the analysis derived from our methodology, we next present a characterization for each profile identified in our dataset. These profiles are different from those obtained by exclusively analyzing the notions of indegree and outdegree.

- *Profile 1, Broadcaster.* The dominant orbit is 1, which plays the role of a sink in the graphlet composed of a single arc. Orbits 2, 6, and 11 (sources) never appear. It is reasonable to assume that these users produce information that motivates readers to respond.
- *Profile 2, Repeater.* The dominant orbit is 0, which plays the role of a listener in an arc graphlet. If we look at all the neighborhoods with two and three nodes, this profile is never retweeted or mentioned by another user. Furthermore, the user does not participate in size four or larger graphlets. We could say that these users tend to repeat the messages in most of their interactions without significantly impacting the conversation.
- *Profile 3, Converser.* The main orbits of this profile include dominant source orbits of others. Furthermore, it contains orbits 7, 17, 21, and 31. The first three are sources, but the last one is a sink. The variety of roles that this user can take, reflected in the balanced composition of its signature vector, suggests that this profile allows the information to flow to and from the other predominant profiles.
- *Profile 4, Reporter.* The dominant orbit is 29, which performs all the listener roles in the graphlet of a triode. This dominant orbit plays the role of an audience. Analyzing the neighborhoods with three nodes, it is infrequent that this profile participates in paths with a length greater than one or responds

to tweets from two different nodes, but it is common for the user to reply to tweets being answered by one or two other people. Thus, we could say that this type of user tends to respond to popular tweets and users. Since this profile includes any listed orbit, we could say that these users have more impact on the conversation than repeaters.
- *Profile 5, Nonconformer.* The dominant orbit is 24, a sink in a 4-node graphlet. The particular architecture of this graphlet suggests the presence of nodes that gather information from different sources that do not respond to each other. The behavior indicates a node that participates in a more extensive discussion with a partial point of view.

Network Clustering. The composition of each network in terms of the five user profiles reveals different dynamics within the networks. They are mainly composed of users with profile 4 or *reporters*, which indicates highly hierarchical dynamics where a few users have authority and set the ideas that circulate on the topic. The second most common profile was the number 3 (*conversers*), followed by profiles 1 (*broadcasters*), 5 (*nonconformers*) and 2 (*repeaters*).

The analyzed collection evidences an asymmetry in Twitter communication dynamics, with a large group of users being engaged in the conversation mainly through responding/endorsing what a few established voices propose.

Regarding the clustering of networks, the proposed methodology can order the collection and define interpretable groups that provide an insight into the dynamics created by the different topics. Groups do not match a thematic differentiation, reinforcing the idea that diffusion processes in Twitter do not depend only on the content.

Our analysis reveals differences among the networks, with some showing an evident variation regarding the distribution of users' role in the circulation of ideas. The group of the networks that show a high inequity in the opinions propagated (leftmost networks in Fig. 4a), with a few authoritative voices (broadcasters) being echoed by other profiles (reporters), includes some government initiatives (#SalarioRosa, #OfrendaEdoMex, #TarjetaRosa). It could be the case that a few tweets are launched and strategically managed to increase their importance.

On the other side of the spectrum (rightmost instances in Fig. 4a), we find topic networks relating to movies and general topics (Coco, Karol, FelizMiercoles) that span a more distributed information exchange, suggesting a topic with a higher engagement level and fewer predominant voices on the subject.

7   Conclusions

Clustering network collections remains a challenging task, and not all the existing methods provide results that can be easily translated into new insights into the data. In this work, we present an alternative to cluster Twitter networks. Our proposed approach is both interpretable and able to capture the network structure through graphlets.

We showed the usefulness of our analysis by exploring 50 real Twitter topic networks. Besides providing information on the similarity between the networks, the users' profiles - established in an intermediate step of the process - give valuable information on the networks' structures and their associated social dynamics.

The results obtained suggest the presence of asymmetries that occur due to particular interactions on a specific topic. Thus, our approach could be more convenient than categorically labeling users as influencers or followers without considering their changing roles in the different conversations in which they participate.

Work remains to be done on a detailed analysis of user profiles, enhancing the discussion with conceptual tools from social sciences and structural theory.

References

1. Ahmed, N.K., Neville, J., Rossi, R.A., Duffield, N.G., Willke, T.L.: Graphlet decomposition: framework, algorithms, and applications. Knowl. Inf. Syst. **50**(3), 689–722 (2017). https://doi.org/10.1007/s10115-016-0965-5
2. Arthur, D., Vassilvitskii, S.: k-means++: The advantages of careful seeding. Technical report, Stanford (2006)
3. Charbey, R., Prieur, C.: Stars, holes, or paths across your Facebook friends: a graphlet-based characterization of many networks. Netw. Sci. **7**(4), 476–497 (2019)
4. Gabielkov, M., Rao, A., Legout, A.: Studying social networks at scale: macroscopic anatomy of the twitter social graph. In: The 2014 ACM International Conference on Measurement and Modeling of Computer Systems - SIGMETRICS 2014, pp. 277–288. ACM Press, Austin (2014)
5. Gilpin, D.R.: Working the Twittersphere: microblogging as professional identity construction. In: A networked self, pp. 240–258. Routledge (2010)
6. Himelboim, I., Smith, M.A., Rainie, L., Shneiderman, B., Espina, C.: Classifying twitter topic-networks using social network analysis. Soc. Media+ Soc. **3**(1), 2056305117691545 (2017)
7. Lusher, D., Robins, G.: Formation of social network structure. Exponential random graph models for social networks pp. 16–28 (2013)
8. Pržulj, N.: Biological network comparison using graphlet degree distribution. Bioinformatics **23**(2), e177–e183 (2007)
9. Rahimy, E., Sandhu, N.K., Giao, D.M., Pollom, E.L.: #trendingnow: Instagram versus twitter activity among radiation oncology patients and providers. Practical Radiation Oncology (2021)
10. Sarajlić, A., Malod-Dognin, N., Yaveroğlu, Ö.N., Pržulj, N.: Graphlet-based characterization of directed networks. Sci. Rep. **6**(1), 1–14 (2016)
11. Sculley, D.: Web-scale k-means clustering. In: Proceedings of the 19th International Conference on World Wide Web, pp. 1177–1178 (2010)
12. Yuan, C., Yang, H.: Research on k-value selection method of k-means clustering algorithm. J-Mult. Sci. J. **2**(2), 226–235 (2019)
13. Zhang, L., Han, Y., Yang, Y., Song, M., Yan, S., Tian, Q.: Discovering discriminative graphlets for aerial image categories recognition. IEEE Trans. Image Process. **22**(12), 5071–5084 (2013)

Lane Changing Model from NGSIM Dataset

Erik Martínez-Vera$^{(\boxtimes)}$ (iD), Pedro Bañuelos-Sánchez$^{(\boxtimes)}$ (iD),
and Gibran Etcheverry$^{(\boxtimes)}$ (iD)

Departamento de Computación, Electrónica y Mecatrónica,
EDEI Universidad de las Américas Puebla - UDLAP, Ex Hacienda Sta. Catarina
Mártir SN, CP. 72810 San Andrés Cholula, Mexico
{erik.martinezva,pedro.banuelos,gibran.etcheverry}@udlap.mx

Abstract. Autonomous driving systems aim to reduce traffic related
accidents; hence, lane changing models need to be developed to accurately represent the driving behaviour during this complex manoeuvre. In
this work, extensive pre-processing of real-world detailed vehicle trajectory information from the Next Generation Simulation (NGSIM) dataset
was performed in order to derive a suitable feature space to be used as
the input data to train and test a lane changing model. State-of-the-art
algorithms use the relative velocities and gaps of vehicles in adjacent
lanes to derive accurate prediction of the intention to move from one
lane to another. Two new feature spaces were developed based on these
data and four classification models were implemented by using Logistic
Regression, Adaptive Boosting and Extreme Boosting algorithms obtaining accuracies up to 98%.

Keywords: Lane change · NGSIM · Data Modeling

1 Introduction

The National Highway Traffic Safety Administration (NHTSA) reported that 9
per cent of all motor-vehicle crashes belonged to two-vehicle lane change col-
lisions, which amounted to 539,000 events in 1999. Seven crash scenarios are
defined as frequent with the most prevalent being the "typical lane change"
scenario, i.e. when two vehicles are travelling in parallel trajectories and one of
them changes lanes [1]. Autonomous driving systems aim to reduce traffic related
accidents; therefore, lane changing models need to be developed for accurately
represent the driving behaviour during this complex manoeuvre. The lane change
decision is considered very complex to model since it is not possible to observe
the decision making process or to assess all the variables that the driver considered before changing lane. Only the final action of changing lanes is observable
without even being able to ascertain the exact moment when the decision was

Supported by the Intelligent Systems PhD program at UDLAP.

taken. Additionally, it is also important to consider that a driver may perform tactical lane changing, that is, move to a lane with lower average speed in order to reach a desired lane with higher speeds. This is a simple example and unfortunately, speed is not the only feature evaluated when selecting lanes: speed, gaps, traffic signals, police presence, destination, desired arrival time, vehicle occupancy, individual driving behaviour, previous road knowledge are some of the variables that influence the decision. From all the above, the complexity of implementing an accurate lane changing model can be inferred. Several variables are involved in the procedure and many of them are not observable. At any given time, a different number of drivers will be interacting in the road, each one with different driving styles and destinations, adding difficulty to the model.

2   Literature Review

According to Ahmed, the principal approach to model lane change is through the gap acceptance phase [2]. That is, the driver evaluates the available gaps between his vehicle and the adjacent vehicles in the target lane; if they fall within an approved limit, the lane change process can continue. Figure 1 allows to better appreciate this process where the subject, lead and lag vehicles are identified and the lead and lag gaps are defined. Based on this model, Choudhury et al. [3] developed an algorithm that treats explicitly cooperative merging into another lane: drivers of adjacent lanes allowing lane changing when heavy traffic prevents suitable gaps formation. The lane selection process is also included in the model developed in [4] where the possibility of moving more than one lane in order to reach a desired target lane is evaluated. Also using the gaps estimation, a model for lane change decision-making is presented in [5] using Support Vector Machine with Bayesian optimization using real world data from the Next Generation Simulation (NGSIM) vehicle trajectories dataset. Their procedure to identify lane change vehicles uses a threshold in the lateral velocity and excludes mandatory lane changes. Their lane model is trained and tested with a Support Vector Machine and Bayesian optimization reporting accuracies up to 86% after 100 iterations. However, they also reported experimental validation with a vehicle. A fuzzy neural network with an adaptive learning algorithm is proposed to predict the lane changing in [6] using data from a driving simulator. Though performance metrics are reported using the root mean squared error, they mention higher prediction accuracies against linear regression and support vector machine algorithms. Finally, the approach developed by Zhang et al. [7], proposed a control method based on intention prediction with Hidden Markov Models and Gaussian Mixture Models that estimate online the probability of lane change behaviour by using a maximum likelihood methodology. The I-80 and US 101 locations of the NGSIM dataset served as the training data for this model: segmented scenarios lasting seven seconds on average recording the lane change or lane keeping behaviour. They reported accuracies up to 92% with cross-validation schemes.

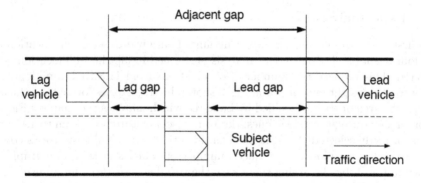

Fig. 1. Subject, lead, lag and front vehicles with lead and lag gaps [3].

3   Experiments

3.1   Dataset

The NGSIM dataset is provided by the U.S. Department of Transportation and consists of 11.8 million rows and 25 columns describing vehicle trajectories obtained through video cameras positioned at different roads: US 101, Lankershim Boulevard and I-80 in California and, Peachtree Street in Atlanta, Georgia [8]. Figure 2 displays a schematic of the location for the vehicle trajectories from the I-80 highway. It consists of six lanes with an on-ramp; each lane has 3.6 m width and a total length of 503 m. Merging is observed for vehicles entering the on-ramp which is labelled as lane number 7 in the figure. The dataset consists of 45 min of observations divided in three 15-min segments with 100 ms resolution.

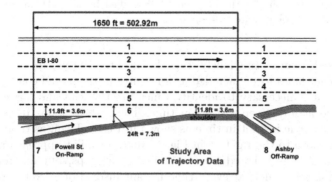

Fig. 2. Schematic of study area for vehicle trajectory data. Location belongs to I-80 highway, CA [3].

3.2   Data Analysis

The first step in processing this large amount of data was to select one location of the four available. Following the analysis performed in [3], the I-80 location was selected. This reduced the number of observations from 11.8 to 4.5 millions. In order to gain insight into the data, Fig. 3 shows the trajectories for all the vehicles in the I-80 area of study classified by Lane ID, which matches the shape of Fig. 2. In order to reduce processing times, the 15-min segment from 4:00 pm to 4:15 pm was arbitrarily selected. Next, it was identified that individual trajectories could be observed when plotting a reduced number of vehicles in the same graph as shown in Fig. 4, by classifying them with the variable $Vehicle_{ID}$ for 100 vehicles (upper graph) and 10 vehicles (lower graph). By comparing the initial and final lanes in the variable $Lane_{ID}$, it was found that 544 vehicles changed at least one lane while 1181 started and ended the path in the same lane.

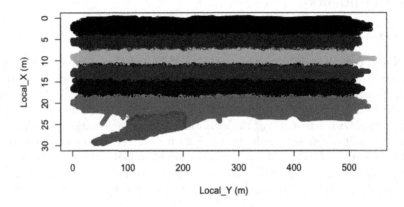

Fig. 3. Vehicle positions for the i-80 dataset classified by lane ID, merging vehicles appear in yellow. (Color figure online)

The models referred previously state the need to use the gaps of the vehicles in the adjacent lanes to be included as a features in the model construction [2–5]. For this, it is necessary to identify which are the lead and lag vehicles for every vehicle at any given instant in time. The first step was to plot all the vehicles for a single instant in time as shown in Fig. 5. Then, as time advances, the vehicles move to the right as in Fig. 6. Next, a similar approach as the one presented in [9] was followed here to estimate the gaps, but differences were calculated for one vehicle at every time instant instead of all vehicles at every time instant. To estimate the gaps, filtering was performed to the dataset to leave only the positions in the lane of the subject vehicle (central lane) and the possible target lanes to the right and to the left as displayed in Fig. 7. Further filtering was needed to leave only one subject vehicle at each time with its lead and lag vehicles to the left and to the right. This was implemented by estimating the vehicles with minimum higher velocity than the subject for the lead vehicles and the maximum lower velocity for the lag vehicles in both adjacent lanes. The lead vehicle in the current lane was obtained from the Preceding variable in the dataset. With this approach of the subject, lead and lag vehicles were identified for every vehicle at each instant in time and the gaps and relative velocities calculated. Figure 8 displays an example of a subject vehicle progressing in time and changing lane with its lead and lag vehicles to the left and right and the lead vehicle in the same lane. Notice that the centre frame is when the subject vehicle changes lanes and the lead and lag vehicles are updated. This process is repeated for every vehicle and the differences evaluated at every instant. New variables were created and added to the dataset in order to estimate these differences: lead and lag relative velocities to the right and left lanes, lead and lag gaps to the right and left lanes and, relative velocity and gap to the front vehicle. These new variables were the feature space used for the lane change model implementation.

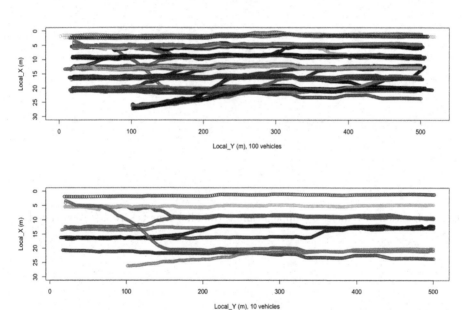

Fig. 4. Vehicle trajectories for 100 vehicles (upper) and 10 vehicles (lower).

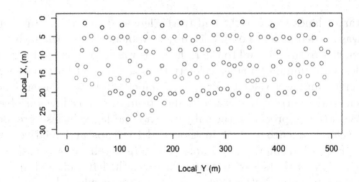

Fig. 5. Position of all vehicles at time t.

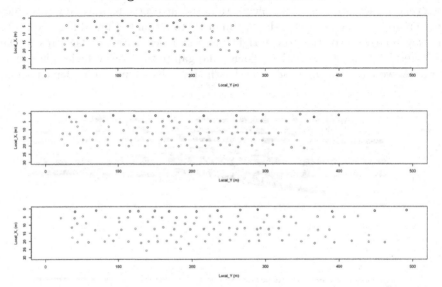

Fig. 6. Position of vehicles at (upper) time t, (middle) time t + 10 s, (lower) time t + 20 s.

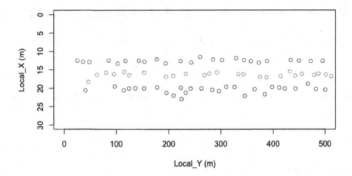

Fig. 7. Filtering of Fig. 5 showing position of all vehicles in central lane and possible target lanes to the right and to the left.

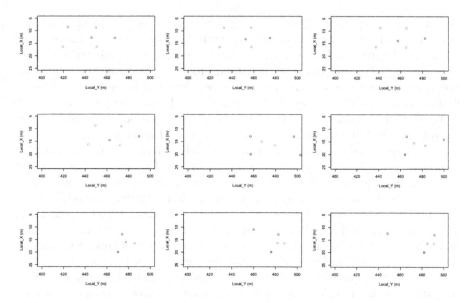

Fig. 8. Position of subject vehicle with lead and lag in the adjacent lanes advancing in time. Starting from the top left each frame shows the vehicle at instant t+ increments of 1 s.

4   Lane Change Model

The classification models selected for this work were the Logistic Model and the ADABoost model, which derivations have been reviewed before [10,11]. More recently, the Extreme Gradient Boosting algorithm has been developed as an improved version of the boosting methods by providing parallel boosting algorithms [12]. The first model implemented in R was the Logistic Regression following the procedure described in [10]. 80% data was selected for training and the rest for testing. A new conditioned variable LaneChangeLR in the model was used to store the label values 0,1 for same lane and lane change, respectively. Once the model was trained, predictions were obtained using the test data partition with a threshold probability of 50% for lane change. The accuracy of this model was 65.78118%. The next model implemented was the AdaBoost one from the library JOUSBoost following the procedures from [11,13]. Again, data was divided in 80% training and 20% testing. A new variable LaneChangeAB contained the labels −1,1 for same lane and lane change was included. This model uses decision tree classifiers as the weak algorithm to be boosted and tree depth was randomly choosen as 20 with only 2 iterations due to large processing times. The yielding accuracy with this model was 80.2799%. The last models implemented were the Extreme Gradient Boosting (xgboost) and its advanced version (xgb.train). Both models are included in the xgboost library available at [12]. With the former, an accuracy of 95.86343% was obtained with only 20 iterations and at much faster speed compared to using the AdaBoost algorithm. The obtained accuracy with the latter increased to 96.92964% with 20 iterations at higher speed than when using the AdaBoost algorithm as well and with the same dataset as the one used for Logistic Regression. Even though obtained accuracies were high, training times were also high. For this reason, as an attempt to reduce training times, the averages of each variable in the feature space were calculated for every vehicle in the dataset as in [14]. Then, a new feature space was obtained keeping the same 10 variables with a reduced dimension of only 1725 observations: one observation per vehicle. The four classification models were trained again and tested with this reduced dataset and training times were effectively reduced to seconds instead of several minutes. However, accuracies were also drastically reduced. The XGBoost algorithm had the highest accuracy with 80.28986%. During data pre-processing, it was observed that vehicle trajectories were tracked for 2-min intervals on average. Yet, the lane change manoeuvre would only take seconds to happen. Then, most of the data for a vehicle staying in the same lane and another changing lane would be almost the same, except for only a short period of time. Examples of this can be detected in Fig. 4 where whole trajectories are plotted and the lane change is spotted only for a short fraction of the sequence. This situation added complexity to the classification task by making the features for both classes similar. In order to solve this issue, the dataset was re-processed and only 20 s of data were selected for every vehicle. As the size of the dataset was reduced from 1 to 0.2 million observations, training times were also reduced; yet, this time accuracy increased from 96.9% to 98.9%.

5   Results and Discussion

The Logistic Regression, AdaBoost and extreme gradient models were re-trained with the new dataset described in the previous section. A summary of all the accuracies obtained with all the models is presented in Table 1. With the initial dataset, a 15% difference in accuracy can be observed between the Logistic Regression and AdaBoost models, which was further increased up to 31% with the XG models for 20 iterations. The accuracy with AdaBoost might increase by increasing the number of iterations, but due to high training times, this test was avoided. When using the averages dataset, the number of observations was reduced to 1725 and training times were also reduced; thus, the iterations were increased to 100 for both models by showing closer results between them. With the third dataset (20 s), only ten iterations were enough to obtain 97.9% of accuracy for AdaBoost, which is little less than 1% difference than the highest accuracy obtained with the XGBoost Advanced model. From this, data pre-processing can greatly affect the performance of the model either to improve or degrade it. The iterative algorithms performed generally better than the logistic model one. Extra tuning of this model might yield better results by appropriate selection of the most influential variables.

Table 1. Accuracies for different lane change models and datasets. (*2 iterations, **10 iterations, ***20 iterations, ****100 iterations).

Model	Full dataset	Averages	20 s datasets
Logistic Regression	0.6578118	0.7333333	0.7104603
AdaBoost	0.802799*	0.7362319****	0.9799163**
XGBoost	0.9586343***	0.8028986****	0.9877107****
XGBoost Advanced	0.9692964***	0.7710145****	0.9890496****

6   Conclusions

In this work, a lane changing model was developed using the real world data from the NGSIM dataset. Lane change is a complex manoeuvre that involves many variables that are not observable. The NGSIM dataset provides detailed information about vehicle trajectories in real world locations and pre-processing is necessary before feeding the data for model training. Extensive pre-processing was performed based on state-of-the-art algorithms to consider the gaps and relative velocities of the vehicles in adjacent lanes to serve as the new feature space. Four binary classifying models were implemented in R: Logistic Regression, Adaptive Boosting and Extreme Bosting in its simple and advanced versions. Accuracies up to 96% were obtained but with large training times. Two new feature spaces were proposed: one using averages for data of every vehicle and the second selecting only 20 s of data per vehicle. The former approach decreased training times, but with a large decrease in accuracy; whereas the latter resulted in lower training times with accuracies increased up to 98.9%, which compares to the ones reported in literature.

References

1. Sen, B., Smith, J.D., Najm, W.G.: Analysis of Lane Change Crashes. Technical report, U.S. Department of Transportation National Highway Traffic Safety Administration, DOT-NHTSA Cambridge, MA (2003). https://www.nhtsa.gov/sites/nhtsa.gov/files/doths809571.pdf
2. Ahmed, K.I.: Modeling drivers' acceleration and lane changing behavior - PhD Thesis, Massachusetts Institute of Technology (1999). https://dspace.mit.edu/handle/1721.1/9662
3. Choudhury, C., Ben-Akiva, M., Toledo, T., Rao, A., Lee, G.: NGSIM Cooperative Lane Changing and Forced Merging Model. Technical report, US DOT Federal Highway Administration, Washington, DC (2006). https://data.transportation.gov/Automobiles/Next-Generation-Simulation-NGSIM-Vehicle-Trajector/8ect-6jqj
4. Choudhury, C., Toledo, T., Ben-Akiva, M.: NGSIM Freeway Lane Selection Model. Technical report, US DOT Federal Highway Administration, Washington, DC, December 2004. https://data.transportation.gov/Automobiles/Next-Generation-Simulation-NGSIM-Vehicle-Trajector/8ect-6jqj

5. Liu, Y., Wang, X., Li, L., Cheng, S., Chen, Z.: A novel lane change decision-making model of autonomous vehicle based on support vector machine. IEEE Access **7**, 26543–26550 (2019). https://doi.org/10.1109/ACCESS.2019.2900416

6. Tang, J., Liu, F., Zhang, W., Ke, R., Zou, Y.: Lane-changes prediction based on adaptive fuzzy neural network. Expert Syst. Appl. **91**, 452–463 (2018). https://doi.org/10.1016/j.eswa.2017.09.025

7. Zhang, Y., Lin, Q., Wang, J., Verwer, S., Dolan, J.: Lane-change intention estimation for car-following control in autonomous driving. IEEE Trans. Intell. Veh. (2018). https://doi.org/10.1109/TIV.2018.2843178

8. USDOT: U.S. Department of Transportation Federal Highway Administration. Next Generation Simulation (NGSIM) Vehicle Trajectories and Supporting Data. [Dataset]. Provided by ITS DataHub through Data.transportation.gov (2016). https://data.transportation.gov/Automobiles/Next-Generation-Simulation-NGSIM-Vehicle-Trajector/8ect-6jqj

9. Ben-Akiva, M., et al.: Traffic simulation with MITSIMLab. In: Barceló, J. (eds.) Fundamentals of Traffic Simulation. International Series in Operations Research & Management Science, vol. 145, pp. 233–268. Springer, New York (2010). https://doi.org/10.1007/978-1-4419-6142-6_6

10. James, G., Witten, D., Hastie, T., Tibshirani, R.: An Introduction to Statistical Learning. STS, vol. 103. Springer, New York (2013). https://doi.org/10.1007/978-1-4614-7138-7

11. Hastie, T., Tibshirani, R., Friedman, J.: The Elements of Statistical Learning. SSS, Springer, New York (2009). https://doi.org/10.1007/978-0-387-84858-7

12. XGBoost: XGBoost: Scalable and Flexible Gradient Boosting. https://xgboost.ai/

13. RDocumentation: adaboost function - RDocumentation. https://www.rdocumentation.org/packages/JOUSBoost/versions/2.1.0/topics/adaboost

14. Valencia-Rosado, L.O., Rojas-Velazquez, D., Etcheverry, G.: Driver intent data analysis and classification. In: 28th International Conference on Electronics, Communications and Computers, CONIELECOMP 2018, pp. 207–211, March 2018. https://doi.org/10.1109/CONIELECOMP.2018.8327200

A Robust Fault Diagnosis Method in Presence of Noise and Missing Information for Industrial Plants

Francisco Javier Ortiz Ortiz[1]([⊠]) [iD], Adrián Rodríguez-Ramos[2] [iD],
and Orestes Llanes-Santiago[2] [iD]

[1] Programa de Maestría en Electrónica y Automatización,
Universidad Politécnica Salesiana, Cuenca, Ecuador
`fortizor@est.ups.edu.ec`

[2] Dpto. de Automática y Computación, Universidad Tecnológica de La Habana
José Antonio Echeverría, CUJAE, La Habana, Cuba
`adrian.rr@automatica.cujae.edu.cu, orestes@tesla.cujae.edu.cu`

Abstract. Fault diagnosis systems are necessary in industrial plants to reach high economic profits and high levels of industrial safety. For achieving these aims, it is necessary a fast detection and identification of faults that occur in the plants. However, the performance of the fault diagnosis systems, are affected by the presence of noise and missing information on the measured variables from the industrial systems. In this paper, a novel methodology for fault diagnosis in industrial plants is proposed by using computational intelligence tools. The proposal presents a robust behavior in the presence of missing data and noise in the measurements by achieving high levels of performance. The imputation process prior to the diagnosis of failures is carried out online, this being one of the advantages.

Keywords: Fault diagnosis · Missing data · Noise · Data imputation · Industrial plants · Computational intelligence

1 Introduction

Industrial systems are in a constant evolutionary process, and the use of terms such as intelligent industry and industry 4.0 is already commonplace [21]. These terms refer to the interconnection of all the components of an industry to achieve effective automated operation for obtaining high economic returns, continuous increase in the quality of final products and high levels of industrial safety. To achieve the above, early detection and location of faults that commonly appear in industrial systems is needed, since they translate directly into safety problems for operators, economic losses and possible effects on the environment. These reasons have motivated the development of a large number of investigations in the field of fault diagnosis in industrial processes in recent decades [1,19]. Scientific literature divides the methodologies for fault diagnosis into two groups, in the first group,

© The Author(s), under exclusive license to Springer Nature Switzerland AG 2022
O. O. Vergara-Villegas et al. (Eds.): MCPR 2022, LNCS 13264, pp. 35–45, 2022.
https://doi.org/10.1007/978-3-031-07750-0_4

it is necessary to use models that represent the different modes of operation of processes. The difficulty in the application of model-based methodologies is that a high level of knowledge of the characteristics of the process, its parameters and operating conditions is required, and this is currently difficult to achieve due to the high complexity of modern industrial plants. On the other hand, data-based methods do not need a precise mathematical model and do not require a high initial knowledge of the process parameters [5,17]. In this sense, there are multiple proposals that use computational and mathematical tools such as: fuzzy logic [18], clustering [19], statistical tools [17] and neural networks [20] just to mention a some of them.

Among the main factors that seriously affect fault diagnosis methodologies based on historical data are noise in measurements and missing data being both very common in industrial plants. From that comes the necessity to take into account these factors to obtain a robust behaviour, avoiding false alarms and loss of reliability of the system [2,13]. Despite the number of papers present in the scientific literature on fault diagnosis, most of them do not jointly analyze the robustness against noise in the measurements and the missing data.

Observations with incomplete values can be due to several issues such as sensor failures, occasional malfunctions of data acquisition systems, possible errors in data transmission networks and communication protocols, just to mention the most common sources. A review of the used techniques to treat missing data in the scientific literature indicate that ignore and delete incomplete data and impute missing data are the most used techniques. However, the missing information can be important to discover possible abnormal operating conditions and relationships between the variables. For this reason, the second method is the most recommended for using in industrial plants [2,13].

In recent years, deep learning neural networks have been increasing in popularity due to their ability to learn complex nonlinear features that significantly improve the discriminative power in classification processes. Some recent examples can be reviewed in [6,11,15].

The objective of this paper and its main contribution is to propose a robust fault diagnosis methodology against noise and missing data in industrial plants. For this, a hybrid scheme that combines easy-to-implement imputation algorithms with deep learning tools is presented. The proposed methodology performs online imputation of the missing data observation by observation achieving high levels of performance in the fault classification by using a deep learning neural network of the LSTM (Long Short Term Memory) type. The proposal presents a very robust behavior in the presence of noise and the possible deviations that the imputation of the missing data can introduce.

2   Materials and Methods

2.1   Missing Data Imputation

In [12] are analyzed the three types of information loss mechanism that can occur: Missing Completely at Random (MCAR), Missing at Random (MAR), Misssing

Not at Random (MNAR). In industrial plants, it is the MCAR mechanism that fundamentally occurs, therefore, it will be used in this paper [2,13].

Several techniques are presented in the scientific literature for data imputation [2]. However, all methods perform the imputation using the entire data set or part of it without strict time requirements. In the operation of industrial plants the time requirements are very important. The imputation of the missing variables in an observation obtained from the plant must be done online and with strict time requirements determined by the sampling period that has been established in the data acquisition system. In addition, it must be taken into account that all these measurements are affected by the noise that is characteristic of industrial processes.

2.2 Proposed Methodology for the Diagnostic System

Figure 1 presents the methodology proposed for fault diagnosis in this paper. It is composed of two stages: offline and online.

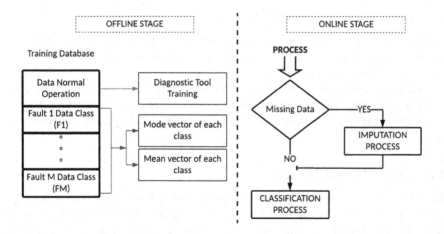

Fig. 1. Proposed methodology for fault diagnosis with noisy measurements and missing data

In the off-line stage, the training of the LSTM neural network is performed by using a training database which contains an enough quantity of observations corresponding to each class in the system (normal operation and faults) [22]. In addition, the mean vectors $(\bar{X}_{C_l})$ and the mode vectors (X_{MC_l}) for the l classes present in the system are obtained. To avoid the effect of the outliers for obtaining the mean vectors, the training database must be treated prior to its use with one of the well-known methods for the elimination of this type of data.

In the online stage, when an observation is received, it is analyzed. If there are no missing data, the classification process is carried out. If missing variables are detected, the imputation will be carried out.

Imputation Process. When a new observation with missing variables is received, the following procedure is carried out to impute online:

1. An observation $X \in R^{1 \times p}$ is received with r lost variables. The r missing variables in the observation and in the mean vectors of each class obtained in the off-line stage are eliminated. The distance from the observation $X \in R^{1 \times p-r}$ to the vectors $\bar{X}_{C_l} \in R^{1 \times p-r}$ $(d_l = X - \bar{X}_{C_l})$ of the classes represented in the training database is calculated. The minimum distance $(min(d_l))$ is determined and with this, the class to which the new observation will be assigned. The distance measure used in this paper is the Euclidean distance.
2. The imputation process is carried out with the method that has been decided to use.
3. Once all missing values have been estimated, the observation is classified using the classification tool of the diagnostic system. It is possible that the diagnostic tool classifies the observation with the estimated data in a different class than the one used for the imputation due to the degree of overlap that some classes may have in the space of the observations.

2.3 Imputation of Missing Data

In this paper, two imputation methods will be used: the arithmetic mean and the mode. These methods were chosen for their proven effectiveness and the simplicity of their implementation.

When an observation with missing variables is classified in a class, the value of the missing variables is obtained from the vector of mean values $(\bar{X}_{C_l})$ or the vector with the mode values (X_{MC_l}) of the corresponding class depending on the used method.

2.4 LSTM Neural Network

The LSTM neural network belongs to the family of Recurrent Neural Networks (RNN). It was proposed by Hochreiter and Schmidhuber in [9] and later Gers [8] proposed a variation that improved its performance. LSTM network overcomes the issue of exponential disappearance of error gradients present in backpropagation training of RNNs. For this, it uses gates to selectively retain information that is relevant and forget information that is not relevant. Lower sensitivity to time gap makes LSTM networks better for sequential data analysis than RNNs. Typically, an LSTM block has a memory cell, input gate, output gate, and a forget gate. The operation of a cell of a LSTM network is defined by the following equations [15]:

$$f_t = \sigma \left(W_f \cdot [h_{t-1}, x_t] + b_f \right) \tag{1}$$

$$i_t = \sigma \left(W_i \cdot [h_{t-1}, x_t] + b_i \right) \tag{2}$$

$$C'_t = \tanh \left(W_c \cdot [h_{t-1}, x_t] + b_c \right) \tag{3}$$

$$C_t = f_t \cdot C_{t-1} + i_t \cdot C'_t \tag{4}$$

$$h_t = O_t \cdot \tanh \left(C_t \right) \tag{5}$$

where σ denotes the sigmoid function, W represents the weights and b the deviation or *bias*.

The proposed LSTM network uses the optimization algorithm ADAM (Adaptive Moment Estimation) [10] which is an extension of the SGD (Stochastic Gradient Descent) algorithm and allows updating the weights of the network iteratively based on the training data.

2.5   Case Study: *DAMADICS*

To validate the methodology proposed in this paper, the known DAMADICS test problem will be used. It represents an intelligent electro-pneumatic actuator widely used in industries [3]. All information related to this testing process and the data used can be found at http://diag.mchtr.pw.edu.pl/damadics/.

The five faults diagnosed in the actuator and the measured variables used for that are shown in the Table 1.

Table 1. Diagnosed faults and measured variables in DAMADICS.

Fault	Description	Variable	Description
F1	Valve clogging	CV	Process control external signal
F7	Critical flow	P1	Pressure on inlet valve
F12	Electro-pneumatic transducer fault	P2	Pressure on outlet valve
F15	Positioner spring fault	X	Valve plug displacement
F19	Flow rate sensor fault	F	Main pipeline flow rate
		PV	Process value

These faults were chosen because they are representative of different parts of the actuator and in the case of faults F15 and F19 they are faults whose patterns overlap, making the correct classification difficult.

2.6   Performance Indices

In this paper, the robustness is considered from achieving a high performance of correct classification with a low percentage of false alarms as defined in [16]. Therefore, the robustness is evaluated by using the following indices:

Accuracy (Acc): This index evaluates the general performance of the classifier. It is defined as:

$$Acc = \frac{TP + TN}{TP + TN + FP + FN} \tag{6}$$

where **TP** (True Positives) represents the number of correctly classified observations belonging to a class, **FP** (False Positives) represents the number of observations wrongly classified as belonging to a class, **TN** (True Negatives) represents the number of observations not belonging to a class correctly classified as not belonging to it and **FN** (False Negatives) represents the number of observations belonging to a class and classified as not belonging to it.

False Alarm Rate (FAR): This index indicates the reason for observations corresponding to normal operation that are erroneously classified as fault and it is defined as:

$$FAR = \frac{FP}{TN + FP} \cdot 100\% \tag{7}$$

2.7   Design of Experiments

LSTM Network Architecture. For evaluating the methodology proposed in this paper, a LSTM network with several layers connected in cascade was designed as follow: an input layer that receives the 6 variables that are measured in the process; an LSTM layer with 500 hidden units with the output format set to full stream mode; a dropout layer to reduce overtraining and improve network generalization; a fully connected layer of 6 classes (corresponding to the 6 operating states of the system); a layer with the normalized exponential function or softmax function [4] and a classification layer at the output. The designed LSTM network was trained in a supervised manner in the off-line stage by using a set of training sequences. In the training, a combination of the ADAM optimization algorithm with parameters $\beta_1 = 0.9$ and $\beta_1 = 0.999$ as it is proposed in [10] with the BPTT (backpropagation through time) algorithm to calculate the necessary gradients during the optimization process was used, in order to change each weight of the LSTM network in proportion to the derivative of the error in the output layer with respect to the corresponding weight. As activation function to update the cell and the hidden state, the hyperbolic tangent activation function ($tanh$) was used. The maximum number of epochs used for training was 500 and a gradient threshold equal to 2. To prevent network overtraining, the dropout layer was included with a probability of discarding input elements, specified as a numerical scalar equal to 0.1. The learning rate (LR) is an important parameter that influences the adjustment of weights and the convergence of errors. By choosing an appropriate learning rate, it is possible to speed up the convergence of the LSTM network and improve its accuracy. In this experiment, the learning rate used was $LR = 0.001$.

In the training database, $k = 1000$ observations with the $p = 6$ measured variables of each one of the $nc = 6$ classes were used(NO: Normal Operation, F1: Fault 1, F7: Fault 7, F12: Fault 12, F15: Fault 15, F19: Fault 19). This indicates that the training database is made up of $n = 6000$ observations free of outliers, noise and missing variables.

For the training and validation of the proposed LSTM neural network in the off-line stage, the K-cross-validation process was used [7]. In this case $K = 5$ was selected (800 observations for training and 200 for validation). The results obtained in the training process are shown in Table 2.

Table 2. Confusion matrix for cross validation. Accuracy: 97,583%

	F1	F12	F15	F19	F7	Normal	Acc (%)	FAR (%)
F1	195	0	0	0	0	5		
F12	0	199	0	0	1	0		
F15	0	4	194	2	0	0		
F19	0	0	2	198	0	0		
F7	1	0	0	0	199	0		
Normal	3	0	0	0	0	197		
GEN							98,5	1,5

Experiments: In the experiments related to the online stage, a database with 400 observations different from those used in the training was used for each state of operation of the system, so the database for the experiments consisted of 2400 observations. To guarantee the repeatability of the results, each experiment was repeated 100 times and the average of the results obtained in those 100 repetitions was obtained as the final result.

The following experiments were carried out to evaluate the performance of the diagnostic system with the following characteristics in the data:

1. Observations without missing information
2. Observations with 1 randomly missing variable per observation
3. Observations with a random number of missing variables between 0 and 2

In each experiment were obtained results for a) the data without noise, b) with 2% of white noise with mean of zero and c) with 5 % of white noise with mean of zero. In the experiments with missing variables the imputation process was developed.

3   Results and Discussion

3.1   Results of the Experiments by Using Mean Values in the Imputation Process

Table 3 presents the results of the experiments.

Table 3. Results of % performance and % false alarms

Experiment	% Acc	% FAR
1) Without missing variables		
Without noise	98,17	0
2 % of noise	98,42	0
5 % of noise	98,54	0
2) 1 randomly missing variable, imputation with mean values		
Without noise	98,17	0
2 % of noise	98,54	0
5 % of noise	98,46	0
3) Random number of missing variables between 0 and 2, imputation with mean values		
Without noise	98,58	0
2 % of noise	98,38	0
5 % of noise	98,46	0
2) 1 randomly missing variable, imputation with mode values		
Without noise	97,15	0
2 % of noise	97,78	0
5 % of noise	97,59	0
3) Random number of missing variables between 0 and 2, imputation with mode values		
Without noise	97,60	0
2 % of noise	98,24	0
5 % of noise	98,17	0

As can be seen, the diagnosis system achieves a high performance in the classification process and there are not false alarms (FAR = 0%). These results indicate a high level of robustness against noise and missing variables of the proposed methodology. To find out if the used imputation method influences the results achieved, the Wilcoxon non-parametric statistical test was applied with a significance level of $\alpha = 95\%$ to compare similar experiments [14]. The results obtained indicate that there are no significant differences between the results, which indicates that either of the two methods can be used to impute. It should only be clear that if the mean value is used, the out-of-range data must be eliminated from the training database.

3.2 Comparison with Other Results Presented in the Scientific Literature

To compare with other algorithms present in the scientific literature, it is necessary to develop experiments with similar characteristics. In the scientific literature reviewed, there are few works that address the diagnosis of faults in the presence of noise and missing variables and in those found, the experiments were developed for other types of systems. Table 4 presents the results of diagnosis techniques in mechanical systems published in the last 5 years with excellent performances. In any case the missing variables in the observations were considered. In the comparison of the results of those algorithms with the proposed methodology in this paper no significant differences were found which indicates the robustness of the methodology presented here.

Table 4. Results of the comparison between algorithms in the literature

Algorithm	Noise	Missing variables	Accuracy
[20]	X		99,00%
[15]			96,60%
[11]			98,66%
[6]	X		98,46%

4   Conclusions

In this paper, a robust methodology against noise and missing variables in the measurements for fault diagnosis is proposed. It achieves high levels of performance in the classification and very low levels of false alarms which indicate a high level of robustness. The proposed methodology performs the on-line imputation observation by observation in case there are missing variables in the observations obtained from the plant. This is an advantage with respect to many of the proposals present in the scientific literature where it is necessary to accumulate a group of observations before carrying out the imputation. The used imputation methods are very simple to implement and due to their low computational complexity they allow their application in processes with high sampling frequencies, which represents another advantage. For the classification process, a LSTM deep learning neural network was used, which is trained in the off-line stage, achieving a high generalization capacity, demonstrated in the results of the experiments. The obtained results were compared with other methodologies presented in the current scientific literature that show very high percentages of satisfactory performance but whose results do not take into account the missing variables in the observations. The results of the comparison showed that there were no significant differences in the high levels of satisfactory classification achieved. This indicates the high level of robustness of the proposal made in this paper and therefore the advantages it offers with respect to other methods present in the scientific literature.

References

1. Ahmed, Q., Raza, S.A., Al-Anazi, D.M.: Reliability-based fault analysis models with industrial applications: a systematic literature review. Qual. Reliab. Eng. Int. **37**(4), 1307–1333 (2021). https://doi.org/10.1002/qre.2797
2. Askarian, M., Escudero, G., Graells, M., Zarghami, R., Jalali-Farahani, F., Mostoufi, N.: Fault diagnosis of chemical processes with incomplete observations: a comparative study. Comput. Chem. Eng. **84**, 104–116 (2016). https://doi.org/10.1016/j.compchemeng.2015.08.018
3. Bartyś, M., Patton, R., Syfert, M., de las Heras, S., Quevedo, J.: Introduction to the DAMADICS actuator FDI benchmark study. Control Eng. Pract. **14**, 577–596 (2006). https://doi.org/10.1016/j.conengprac.2005.06.015
4. Bishop, C.M.: Pattern recognition. Mach. Learn. **128**(9) (2006)
5. Cerrada, M., et al.: A review on data-driven fault severity assessment in rolling bearings. Mech. Syst. Signal Process. **99**, 169–196 (2018). https://doi.org/10.1016/j.ymssp.2017.06.012
6. Chen, X., Zhang, B., Gao, D.: Bearing fault diagnosis base on multi-scale CNN and LSTM model. J. Intell. Manuf. **32**(4), 971–987 (2020). https://doi.org/10.1007/s10845-020-01600-2
7. Devijver, P.A., Kittler, J.: Pattern Recognition: A Statistical Approach. Prentice Hall, London (1982)
8. Gers, F.A., Schmidhuber, J., Cummins, F.: Learning to forget: Continual prediction with LSTM. Neural Comput. **12**(10), 2451–2471 (2000). https://doi.org/10.1162/089976600300015015
9. Hochreiter, S., Schmidhuber, J.: Long short-term memory. Neural Comput. **9**(8), 1735–1780 (1997). https://doi.org/10.1162/neco.1997.9.8.1735
10. Kingma, D.P., Ba, J.: Adam: a method for stochastic optimization. arxiv: 1412.6980. Retrieved from the arXiv database (2014)
11. Lee, J.H., Pack, J.H., Lee, I.S.: Fault diagnosis of induction motor using convolutional neural network. Appl. Sci. **9**(15) (2019). https://doi.org/10.3390/app9152950
12. Little, R.J., Rubin, D.B.: Statistical Analysis with Missing Data, vol. 793. Wiley, Hoboken (2019)
13. Llanes-Santiago, O., Rivero-Benedico, B., Gálvez-Viera, S., Rodríguez-Morant, E., Torres-Cabeza, R., Silva-Neto, A.: A fault diagnosis proposal with online imputation to incomplete observations in industrial plants. Revista Mexicana de Ingeniería Química **18**(1), 83–98 (2019)
14. Luengo, J., García, S., Herrera, F.: A study on the use of statistical tests for experimentation with neural networks: analysis of parametric test conditions and non-parametric tests. Expert Syst. Appl. **36**(4), 7798–7808 (2009). https://doi.org/10.1016/j.eswa.2008.11.041
15. Medina, R., et al.: A LSTM neural network approach using vibration signals for classifying faults in a Gearbox. Proceedings - 2019 International Conference on Sensing, Diagnostics, Prognostics, and Control, SDPC 2019, pp. 208–214 (2019). https://doi.org/10.1109/SDPC.2019.00045
16. Patan, K.: Artificial Neural Networks for the Modelling and fault Diagnosis Of Technical Processes. Lecture Notes in Control and Information Sciences, Springer, Heidelberg (2008). https://doi.org/10.1007/978-3-540-79872-9

17. Prieto-Moreno, A., Llanes-Santiago, O., García-Moreno, E.: Principal components selection for dimensionality reduction using discriminant information applied to fault diagnosis. J. Process Control **33**, 14–24 (2015). https://doi.org/10.1016/j.jprocont.2015.06.003

18. Rodríguez Ramos, A., et al.: An approach to multiple fault diagnosis using fuzzy logic. J. Intell. Manuf. **30**(1), 429–439 (2016). https://doi.org/10.1007/s10845-016-1256-4

19. Rodríguez Ramos, A., Bernal de Lázaro, J.M., Prieto-Moreno, A., da Silva Neto, A.J., Llanes-Santiago, O.: An approach to robust fault diagnosis in mechanical systems using computational intelligence. J. Intell. Manuf. **30**(4), 1601–1615 (2017). https://doi.org/10.1007/s10845-017-1343-1

20. Saufi, S.R., Ahmad, Z.A.B., Leong, M.S., Lim, M.H.: Gearbox fault diagnosis using a deep learning model with limited data sample. IEEE Trans. Industr. Inf. **16**(10), 6263–6271 (2020). https://doi.org/10.1109/TII.2020.2967822

21. Ustundag, A., Cevikcan, E.: Industry 4.0: Managing the Digital Transformation. Springer, Cham (2018). https://doi.org/10.1007/978-3-319-57870-5

22. Watanabe, K., Matsuura, I., Abe, M., Kubota, M., Himmelblau, D.M.: Incipient fault diagnosis of chemical processes via artificial neural networks. AIChE J. **35**(11), 1803–1812 (1989). https://doi.org/10.1002/aic.690351106

A Preliminary Study of SMOTE on Imbalanced Big Datasets When Dealing with Sparse and Dense High Dimensionality

A. Bolívar[1]($\boxtimes$)(iD), V. García[2](iD), R. Florencia[2](iD), R. Alejo[3](iD), G. Rivera[2](iD), and J. Patricia Sánchez-Solís[2](iD)

[1] Doctorado en Ciencias de la Ingenería Avanzada,Instituto de Ingeniería y Tecnología, Universidad Autónoma de Ciudad Juárez, Chihuahua, Mexico
al198665@alumnos.uacj.mx

[2] División Multidisciplinaria en Ciudad Universitaria, Universidad Autónoma de Ciudad Juárez, Chihuahua, Mexico
{vicente.jimenez,rogelio.florencia,gilberto.rivera,julia.sanchez}@uacj.mx

[3] Tecnológico Nacional de México, IT Toluca, Metepec, Mexico
ralejoe@toluca.tecnm.mx

Abstract. The interest in exploiting big datasets with machine learning has led to adapting classic strategies in this new paradigm determined by volume, speed, and variety. Because data quality is a determining factor in constructing a classifier, it has also been necessary to adapt or develop new data preprocessing techniques. One of the challenges of most significant interest is the class imbalance problem, where the class of interest has a smaller number of examples concerning another class called the majority. To alleviate this problem, one of the most recognized techniques is SMOTE, which is characterized by generating instances of the minority class through a process that uses the nearest neighbor rule and the Euclidean distance. Various articles have shown that SMOTE is not appropriate for datasets with high dimensionality. However, in big data, datasets with high dimensionality have contained many zeros. Therefore, in this article, our objective is to analyze the SMOTE-BD behavior on imbalanced big datasets with sparse and dense dimensionality. Experimental results using two classifiers and big datasets with different dimensionalities suggest that sparsity is a predominant factor than the dimensionality in the behavior of SMOTE-BD.

Keywords: Big data · SMOTE · Class imbalance · High dimensionality · Dense dataset · Sparse dataset

1 Introduction

There are several definitions of what big data means. A well-known description is focused on the exponential data size generated for several areas like medicine,

O. O. Vergara-Villegas et al. (Eds.): MCPR 2022, LNCS 13264, pp. 46–55, 2022.
https://doi.org/10.1007/978-3-031-07750-0_5

business, transport, energy, and those devices connected to the Internet [12]. Another one suggests that if a dataset can not be stored, preprocessed, and analyzed in standard hardware and software, it can be considered Big Data [15]. The fact is that the matter of big data does not lie in the volume of data but in the hidden knowledge that can be extracted from it using artificial intelligence techniques [1,6,11,13,16,21,22].

Machine learning (ML) techniques are widely used to obtain valuable insights from standard and massive data. However, building thriving learning algorithms may depend on the intrinsic characteristics presented in the datasets, such as missing values, redundant and noisy data, and class imbalance [19]. Therefore, the data preprocessing step is crucial to obtain quality data and, consequently, successful classifiers.

A recurrent and complex problem is the well-known class imbalance problem. Class imbalance is presented when the number of examples between two or more data classes is not equal. In standard and big data problems, the solutions for this issue can be classified into three large groups [17]: 1) data level, 2) algorithm level, and 3) hybrid approaches. Of these approaches, the most exploited strategy is the former because it can be applied to any imbalanced class problem, regardless of the classifier used, either by undersampling the majority classes or oversampling the minority classes [5].

A renowned oversampling approach is the Synthetic Minority Oversampling TEchnique (SMOTE), which generates new artificial minority instances by interpolation [10]. Since its conception, this technique has given good results in several problems with a high imbalance ratio. Despite this, various weaknesses have been documented, which has caused great interest in the scientific community in developing a plethora of proposals based on SMOTE [16]. In this sense, we can classify the approaches into two groups [10]: 1) proposals applied on alternative learning paradigms such as semi-supervised learning, active learning, multi-label, multi-instance, streaming data, and 2) algorithms that take into account some intrinsic data characteristics as class overlapping, noisy data, small disjuncts, small sample, and high dimensionality.

SMOTE has been adapted for big data scenarios for both two-class and multi-class problems in the last years [23]. One of the characteristics of big data is the volume of data, which usually is defined as a dataset with a large number of samples. However, big datasets characterized by a high dimensionality have also been reported [7]. SMOTE uses a distance metric, usually the Euclidean distance, to find similarities between examples. However, it is well known that the Euclidean distance may not be suitable when the dataset shows a high dimensionality [9,20,24]. In high dimensions, the distances between examples are almost the same, making it impossible to determine the similarity between one example or other. This phenomenon is known as *the curse of dimensionality*. In [4] is showed that SMOTE, when the dataset has 1,000 attributes, their performance is diminished, being the random oversampling (ROS) the approach that presents the best results.

Although it has claimed that SMOTE is not suitable on high dimensionality datasets [20], it is important to mention that high dimensional sets can be characterized as dense or sparse (many features have mostly zero values). Therefore, SMOTE could be affected by other factors. Taking into account the just mentioned, in this paper, we analyze the behavior of an alternative SMOTE version, called SMOTE-BD, when an imbalanced big dataset shows a sparse or dense high dimensionality. More specifically, this work aims to investigate how and whether SMOTE-BD when given a high number of features with zero values, suffers as the dataset has features with non-zero value.

The paper is organized as follows: Sect. 2 provides a summary of SMOTE-BD for big data problems. Section 3 describes the experimental set-up that we have adopted in this study. Next, Sect. 4 discuss the experimental results. Finally, Sect. 5, remarks the main conclusions and avenues for future work.

2　Big Data Oversampling

The most straightforward oversampling technique is based on random duplication of examples of the minority class. This is called Random Oversampling or ROS. This technique is known for overfitting models because it creates identical copies of the examples [8].

Oversampling algorithms in big data use the paradigm of divide and conquer. This helps to preprocess datasets that may be impossible in a single computer. However, dividing data also represents an issue for algorithms designed to process the complete dataset in one computer. SMOTE is one of the affected techniques, where the k-nearest neighbor is calculated over the whole dataset, and not just in the data partition that is being processed [3].

In [18] the authors propose a solution of the nearest neighbor computation in Spark with the algorithm kNN-IS that is also used by [2] to create SMOTE-BD, which uses the Euclidean distance to determine similarity among examples.

The technique proposed by [2] can be seen in Algorithm 1 and 2. Nearest neighbors are obtained using kNN-IS [18] which is an exact kNN calculation that splits the training dataset into several partitions, calculates neighbors in each partition and creates a final list of k nearest neighbors in the reduction phase.

3　Dataset and Experimental Settings

As the main purpose of this paper is to evaluate the SMOTE's behavior considering the sparse and dense high-dimensionality in a context of class imbalance, two groups of experiments were performed on the KDD 2010 dataset taken from the LIBSVM repository (https://www.csie.ntu.edu.tw/~cjlin/libsvmtools/datasets/). The dataset contains the records of every time a student interacts with an algebra learning software. It has been used in international competitions, where the aim is to build machine learning models for predicting students' performance. Note that the original dataset is a balanced two-class problem with $1,163,024$ attributes (with zero values-sparse) and $19,264,097$ examples. Therefore, several transformations were carried out to perform an experimental comparison between two oversampling methods according to the two issues of

Algorithm 1. SMOTE-BD algorithm.

Require: Tr, Ts, ratio, k, nP, nR, nIt, minClassLabel
  $origData \leftarrow textFile(Tr)$
  $minData \leftarrow origData.filter(labels == minClassLabel)$
  $minData \leftarrow minData.map(normalize).repartition(nP)$
  $neighbors \leftarrow kNNIS.setup(Tr, Tr, k, nR, nI).calculatekNeighbours()$
  $crFactor \leftarrow (nMaj - nMin)/nMin$
  $neighbors \leftarrow broadcast(neighbors)$
  $balancedData = null$
  $synData = null$
  for $i < nIt$ **do**
    $synTmp \leftarrow minData.mapPartitionsWithIndex(createSynthData(index, partData, neighbors, crFactor, k))$
    if $synData == null$ **then**
      $synData \leftarrow synTmp$
    else
      $synData \leftarrow synData.union(synTmp)$
    end if
  end for
  $synData \leftarrow synData.map(denormalize)$
  $balancedData \leftarrow synData.union(origData)$

Algorithm 2. Function to create synthetic instances between the minority class examples and their neighbors.

procedure CREATESYNTHDATA(index,partData,neighbors,crFactor,k)
  $artificialData = null$
  for $firstInstance \leftarrow partitionData; nc = 0$ to $crFactor$ **do**
    $selNeighbor \leftarrow newRandom().nextInt(k)$
    $secondInstance \leftarrow neighbors(selNeighbor)$
    $newIntance \leftarrow interpolation(firstInstance, secondInstance)$
    $artificialData.add(newInstance)$
  end for
  return $artificialData$
end procedure

interest pointed out: 1) to generate a class imbalance problem with a ratio of 1:10 (for each minority sample, there are 10 in the majority class), we randomly removed samples from a class, 2) to get a dense dataset a PCA was employed, 3) to analyze the effect of high dimensionality, we created datasets with different attributes ranging from $50, 100, 200, 300, \ldots 900$, and 4) since the dataset cannot be processed in one single computer with the characteristics of our test infrastructure, we used a reduced dataset with $40,601$ examples by running a *shuffle* function in Spark[1].

---

[1] Although this medium-high dimensional dataset may not represent a big data problem in terms of volume, we believe it can be treated as such since it may not be processed and analyzed on standard hardware.

In both experiments on sparse and dense datasets, a hold-out strategy to evaluate the model's performance was employed, using 70% for training and 30% for testing (Table 1).

Table 1. Summary of the datasets used in the experiments.

Dataset	Partition	# Attributes	# Min	# Maj
KDD-2010-Sparse	Train	$[100, \dots, 900]$	2583	25838
KDD-2010-Sparse	Test	$[100, \dots, 900]$	1107	11073
KDD-2010-Dense	Train	$[100, \dots, 900]$	2583	25838
KDD-2010-Dense	Test	$[100, \dots, 900]$	1107	11073

SMOTE-BD and ROS were applied in all big datasets to reach a balance among classes. We have used the decision tree classifier (DT) and a SVM implementation included in the Apache Spark toolkit (https://spark.apache.org/mllib/).

A popular platform for big data problems used in this paper was the Apache Spark toolkit version 3.1.1, which includes different libraries for machine learning. As hardware, The Azure cloud was the service used to run Spark, where three different virtual servers were configured as follows: a) a virtual server with 2vCPUs and 16 GB of memory as the master and the executor node, and b) two additional executor nodes with two vCPU and 8 GB of memory. The software used was Linux Debian 10.8, Java 11, and Scala.

3.1 Evaluation Metrics

For a two-class problem, a classifier can be evaluated using a 2×2 confusion matrix (see Table 2), where each input (i, j) represents the number of correct and incorrect predictions [14]. In this matrix, the columns represent the output estimated by the classifier, and the rows are the real classes. The correct predictions can be obtained from the main diagonal; the wrong predictions are in the lower and upper diagonal elements.

From the confusion matrix, several performance metrics can be obtained. Accuracy is the most used metric to evaluate the performance of a classifier ($A = (TP + TN)/(TP + FN + TN + FP)$). However, this metric is not suitable when the dataset is imbalanced. For this reason, other metrics are used as an alternative [14] such as those that evaluate the performance in each class: the

Table 2. Confusion matrix for a binary class problem.

	Positive prediction	Negative prediction
Real Positive	True Positives (TP)	False Negatives (FN)
Real Negative	False Positives (FP)	True Negatives (TN)

True Positive Rate $(TPR = TP/(TP + FN))$ that is the proportion of the positive examples classified correctly; and (2) the True Negative Rate $(TNR = TN/(TN+FP))$ that the proportion of the negative examples classified correctly. As the main goal of this paper is to analyze the behavior of SMOTE in each class, we have omitted any performance metric that summarizes several performance metrics in a single value.

4   Results and Discussion

We focused our study on two oversampling methods, SMOTE-BD and ROS, comparing their behavior on sparse and dense high dimensionality datasets with an imbalance ratio 1:10. Two classifiers were built using the default parameters.

Fig. 1 and 2 show the plot between TPR/TNR rates and the number of attributes for each dataset. On the left side of both figures are the classification results on imbalanced and balanced sparse datasets, while on the right side are the results on the dense datasets.

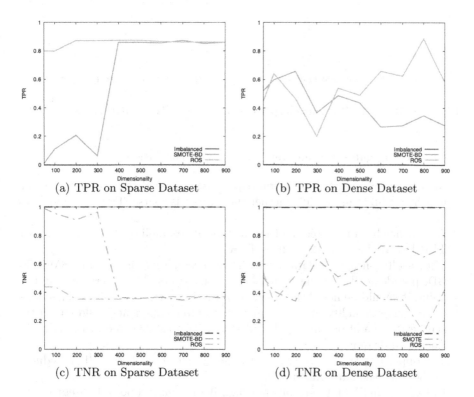

(a) TPR on Sparse Dataset

(b) TPR on Dense Dataset

(c) TNR on Sparse Dataset

(d) TNR on Dense Dataset

Fig. 1. TPR and TNR results on sparse and dense imbalanced datasets with DT.

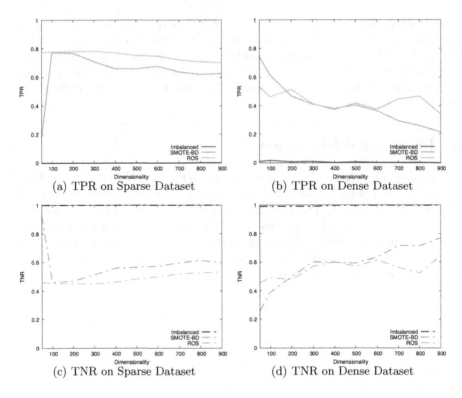

(a) TPR on Sparse Dataset   (b) TPR on Dense Dataset

(c) TNR on Sparse Dataset   (d) TNR on Dense Dataset

Fig. 2. TPR and TNR results on sparse and dense imbalanced datasets with SVM.

From both figures, we can draw the following conclusions:

- As it has been reported in several papers, regardless of the high dimensionality, the classifier used, and whether the dataset is sparse, TPR ≈ 0 and TNR ≈ 1.
- Also, it has been reported in other works that resampling algorithms increase TPR but at the same time affect TNR.
- The results on sparse datasets with DT reveal that, in general, SMOTE-BD, paradoxically, as the dimensionality increases, TPR increases. At this point, it should be noted that few attributes have non-zero values. Therefore, as the dimensionality increases, more non-zero components could enrich the synthetic generation process based on the nearest neighbor rule with the Euclidean distance.
- The opposite situation occurs on the dense datasets where TPR is reduced as the dimensionality increases.
- Unlike DT, in SVM, the results are slightly different. In both datasets, sparse and dense, TPR with SMOTE-BD a decrease is observed, with the difference that in the sparse datasets, the decrease is not as drastic as in the case of dense datasets.

– ROS has been reported in big data experiments as the winner compared as SMOTE-BD [3]. In both plots, this statement also has been demonstrated. However, in SMOTE-BD, complexities such as high dimensionality or sparsity have been predominant in yielding a low TPR.

5   Conclusions and Future Work

As been claimed, SMOTE on high dimensionality datasets shows a weakness caused by the use of the Euclidean Distance. Therefore, in this study, we have analyzed the effect of Imbalanced Big Datasets with sparse and dense high dimensionality when resampled using an alternative SMOTE called SMOTE-BD. To this end, two classifiers have been built on sparse and dense datasets with several dimensionalities ranging from 100 to 900. In all cases, the imbalance ratio was 10.

The SMOTE-BD results showed that as the dimensionality increases on sparse datasets, the TPR increases. We expected to see a tendency to have worse TPR in SMOTE-BD as the dimensions increased, as reported in previous works. However, the experimental results of this work cannot support these affirmations. Experimental results on dense datasets show what was expected, as dimensionality increases, TPR decreases. This allows us to conclude that although dimensionality plays an important role, the amount of information (non-zero values) present in the dataset seems to have the most influence in the Euclidean Distance.

Future works will focus on introducing, as the previous step of SMOTE-BD, a methodology capable of reducing the dimensionality and producing a dense dataset. Also, we are going to use more datasets, including artificial ones, in which we can experiment with modifying specific parameters of the datasets while all the others remain the same. Furthermore, we will expand the infrastructure, i.e., cloud resources, to run the experiment with more dimensions and samples. Lastly, other classifiers will be evaluated to better understand the impact of the different complexities in the dataset, like class overlapping.

References

1. Ali, A., Shamsuddin, S.M., Ralescu, A.: Classification with class imbalance problem: a review. Int. J. Adv. Soft Comput. Appl. **7**(3), 176–204 (2015)
2. Basgall, M.J., Hasperué, W., Naiouf, M., Fernández, A., Herrera, F.: SMOTE-BD: an exact and scalable oversampling method for imbalanced classification in big data. In: VI Jornadas de Cloud Computing & Big Data (JCC&BD) (La Plata 2018) (2018)
3. Basgall, M.J., Hasperué, W., Naiouf, M., Fernández, A., Herrera, F.: An analysis of local and global solutions to address big data imbalanced classification: a case study with SMOTE preprocessing. In: Naiouf, M., Chichizola, F., Rucci, E. (eds.) JCC&BD 2019. CCIS, vol. 1050, pp. 75–85. Springer, Cham (2019). https://doi.org/10.1007/978-3-030-27713-0_7

4. Blagus, R., Lusa, L.: SMOTE for high-dimensional class-imbalanced data. BMC Bioinform. **14**(106), 1–16 (2013)
5. Branco, P., Torgo, L., Ribeiro, R.P.: A survey of predictive modelling under imbalanced distributions. CoRR abs/1505.01658 (2015). http://arxiv.org/abs/1505.01658
6. Brennan, P.: A comprehensive survey of methods for overcoming the class imbalance problem in fraud detection. Master's thesis, Institute of Technology Blanchardstown, Dublin, Ireland (2012)
7. Chang, C.C., Lin, C.J.: LIBSVM. ACM Trans. Intell. Syst. Technol. **2**(3), 1–27 (2011)
8. Chawla, N.V., Bowyer, K.W., Hall, L.O., Kegelmeyer, W.P.: SMOTE: synthetic minority over-sampling technique. J. Artif. Intell. Res. **16**, 321–357 (2002)
9. Elreedy, D., Atiya, A.F.: A comprehensive analysis of synthetic minority oversampling technique (SMOTE) for handling class imbalance. Inf. Sci. **505**, 32–64 (2019)
10. Fernández, A., García, S., Herrera, F., Chawla, N.V.: SMOTE for learning from imbalanced data: progress and challenges, markin the 15-year anniversary. J. Artif. Intell. Res. **51**, 863–905 (2018)
11. García, V., Alejo, R., Sánchez, J.S., Sotoca, J.M., Mollineda, R.A.: Combined effects of class imbalance and class overlap on instance-based classification. In: Corchado, E., Yin, H., Botti, V., Fyfe, C. (eds.) IDEAL 2006. LNCS, vol. 4224, pp. 371–378. Springer, Heidelberg (2006). https://doi.org/10.1007/11875581_45
12. Hassib, E.M., El-Desouky, A.I., Labib, L.M., El-kenawy, E.S.M.: WOA + BRNN: an imbalanced big data classification framework using whale optimization and deep neural network. Soft. Comput. **24**(8), 5573–5592 (2020)
13. Jain, A., Ratnoo, S., Kumar, D.: Addressing class imbalance problem in medical diagnosis: a genetic algorithm approach. In: 2017 International Conference on Information, Communication, Instrumentation and Control (ICICIC), pp. 1–8 (2017)
14. Japkowicz, N., Shah, M.: Evaluating Learning Algorithms: A Classification Perspective. Cambridge University Press, Cambridge (2011)
15. Joyanes Aguilar, L.: Big Data: Análisis de grandes volúmenes de datos en organizaciones. Alfaomega (2013)
16. Kovács, G.: SMOTE-variants: a python implementation of 85 minority oversampling techniques. Neurocomputing **366**, 352–354 (2019)
17. Leevy, J.L., Khoshgoftaar, T.M., Bauder, R.A., Seliya, N.: A survey on addressing high-class imbalance in big data. J. Big Data **5**(1), 1–30 (2018). https://doi.org/10.1186/s40537-018-0151-6
18. Maillo, J., Ramírez, S., Triguero, I., Herrera, F.: kNN-IS: an iterative spark-based design of the k-nearest neighbors classifier for big data. Knowl.-Based Syst. **117**, 3–15 (2017)
19. Maillo, J., Triguero, I., Herrera, F.: Redundancy and complexity metrics for big data classification: towards smart data. IEEE Access **8**, 87918–87928 (2020)
20. Maldonado, S., López, J., Vairetti, C.: An alternative SMOTE oversampling strategy for high-dimensional datasets. Appl. Soft Comput. **76**, 380–389 (2019)
21. Pengfei, J., Chunkai, Z., Zhenyu, H.: A new sampling approach for classification of imbalanced data sets with high density. In: 2014 International Conference on Big Data and Smart Computing (BIGCOMP), pp. 217–222 (2014)
22. Saez, J.A., Galar, M., Krawczyk, B.: Addressing the overlapping data problem in classification using the one-vs-one decomposition strategy. IEEE Access **7**, 83396–83411 (2019)

23. Sleeman, W.C., IV., Krawczyk, B.: Multi-class imbalanced big data classification on spark. Knowl.-Based Syst. **212**, 106598 (2021)
24. Suárez, J.L., García, S., Herrera, F.: A tutorial on distance metric learning: mathematical foundations, algorithms, experimental analysis, prospects and challenges. Neurocomputing **425**, 300–322 (2021)

A Novel Survival Analysis-Based Approach for Predicting Behavioral Probability of Default

Cuauhtémoc Daniel Suárez-Ramírez⬤, Juan-Carlos Martínez, and Octavio Loyola-González$^{(\boxtimes)}$⬤

Altair Management Consultants, Calle de José Ortega y Gasset, 22-24, 5th floor, 28006 Madrid, Spain
{csr,jcm,olg}@altair.consulting

Abstract. Obtaining an accurate model for predicting the probability of default is a critical requirement for financial institutions. Nowadays, COVID19 has produced high economic instability bringing borrowers' delinquencies as well as moratorium regulations. During the KYC process for applicants, it is essential to estimate the probability of default for avoiding write-offs. However, there are several borrowers who, due to the pandemic, could have lost their jobs or decreased their income, producing several borrowers' delinquencies, even write-offs by frequent delinquencies. Consequently, having a behavioral model for estimating the probability of default during the loan lifetime is vital for financial institutions. Hence, in this paper, we propose the first survival analysis-based approach for predicting the behavioral probability of default. We collected two real financial databases from different countries with different borrowers' characteristics. From our experimental results, we can conclude that Logistic Hazard provides better results than Deep Hit for predicting the behavioral probability of default. Based on our experimentation and the risk analysis experts, Deep Hit provides inconsistent results for forecasts greater than six months while considering the financial changes due to the COVID19. Otherwise, Logistic Hazard is more accurate in forecasting the behavioral probability of default for a year, and it shows results more appropriate to risk analysis experts.

Keywords: Risk analysis · Probability of default · Survival analysis · Deep learning

1 Introduction

Nowadays, several borrowers are applying for loans. Consequently, financial institutions must have an accurate credit risk scoring model. Probability of default (PD) is one of the essential measures into the credit risk under Basel III regulations (Regulation 575/2013), which is used in advanced approaches (IRB) for the calculation of expected loss (EL) and risk-weighted assets (RWA)[1]. PD is computed by

---

[1] https://bit.ly/3g5dgAR.

© The Author(s), under exclusive license to Springer Nature Switzerland AG 2022
O. O. Vergara-Villegas et al. (Eds.): MCPR 2022, LNCS 13264, pp. 56–69, 2022.
https://doi.org/10.1007/978-3-031-07750-0_6

using the borrower's characteristics and its similarity with history data (previous borrowers), then, it provides the probability that the applicant could violate the contract conditions, such as the inability to pay the loan back [1].

Obtaining an accurate model for predicting good borrowers is vital for financial institutions because the loan payment depends on two main factors. On the one hand, the first is an objective factor; it is largely determined by the borrower's income (ability to pay). The second is a subjective factor, and it is more psychological because the borrower can choose to pay their balances and reduce funds available to spend on other items, or default on their loans and keep their current level of liquidity, accruing penalties and credit bruises in the process [1]. For the first one, as it is an objective factor, it is easier to compute by financial institutions because they can corroborate the borrower's saving and debit accounts as well as the borrower's bills. However, the second factor is more complicated to predict due to the subjective nature and even more complicated for those applicants without a credit history. For example, impulsive individuals are likely to have difficulty resisting the temptation to borrow for buying and, as a consequence, they are more likely to fail to pay their loans [1].

Usually, PD is computed during the Know Your Customer (KYC) process, and it has shown accurate results for effectively filtering out the riskiest borrowers. However, after a few months of approving loan applications, some borrowers begin to default. Therefore, financial institutions must apply behavioral PD models to monitor borrowers' repayment behaviors. However, it is not a common practice in financial institutions [13].

Behavioral PD models include borrower's additional characteristics than provided during the KYC process, which some are related to the borrower's behavior (e.g., receivable loan amount or delinquencies during the loan term), and others are related to the updated KYC data (e.g., occupation, income, and debt ratio after the loan) [13]. Nowadays, behavioral PD models are more necessary because of the COVID 19, which has produced high economic instability. Due to the pandemic, during 2021, several countries issued a moratorium regulation, which forced financial institutions to stop Prearranged Payment and Deposit (PPD). This situation raises more uncertainty for financial institutions because when the moratorium regulation is lifted, borrowers could have lost their jobs or decreased their incomes, producing several borrowers' delinquencies, even write-offs by frequent delinquencies. Hence, it is necessary to provide behavioral PD models to estimate the borrowers' PD during their credit life cycles, which can be updated monthly with the borrowers' PPDs and pandemic regulations. Hence, in this paper, we propose a novel survival analysis-based approach for predicting the behavioral probability of default. In this approach, several borrower behavior characteristics are considered monthly, such as PPDs and moratorium regulations. As far as we know, our proposal is the first behavioral probability of default model using survival analysis jointly with deep learning.

The remainder of this paper is organized as follows. In Sect. 2, we analyzed previous works for estimating probability of default. After, in Sect. 3, we introduced our proposal for predicting the behavioral probability of default by using borrower history data as well as we defined all our experimental setup. Next, in

Sect. 4, We presented the experimental results and a discussion of them. Finally, in Sect. 5, we provided our conclusions and future work.

2 Related Work

The probability of Default (PD) is usually computed by using the institution's historical data. This data is previously classified into two classes of borrowers, good and bad. After that, a mathematical model is commonly trained by using the classified data. Finally, a probability of default is given for an applicant [14].

One of the first approaches used for modeling PD by using Machine Learning was regression. The main idea is to relate a subset of characteristics of previous borrowers, which were classified as 1 for those without presenting delinquencies and 0 for those having write-off. Then, a regression model is trained, and a probability is given for new applicants [8,10]. The significant advantage of using regression-based approaches is that they can produce a simple probabilistic score, which can be interpretable jointly with the weight assigned to each characteristic used at the training stage. Otherwise, the weaknesses are that these models cannot correctly deal with the problems of non-linear and interactive effects of explanatory characteristics [14].

Based on the advantages of deep learning and avoiding the weakness mentioned above, the authors of [8] proposed using a deep neural network model for behavioral credit rating. This deep neural network model was compared against four machine learning models, such as logistic regression, Linear SVM, Random forest, and XGBoost, by using two databases. These databases contain information on loans between 2009 and 2018, including more than 1.5 million examples. The main problem of these compared approaches is that they do not consider the modeling of time on the analyzed data. For example, it is worse for borrowers who default in the first months of the loan term than those who default in the last months.

Survival analysis-based (a.k.a, time-to-event analysis) is a popular approach widely used in several fields, such as medicine, engineering, economics, and banking, to analyze an event's time distribution. The rationale is to understand the relationship between the (distribution of) times and the covariates [5]. Survival analysis-based is one of the most prominent approaches used on credit risk due to the high obtained accuracy and its analysis for modeling time to event data. However, it is still a novel and growing approach leaving room for improving it. The first idea of introducing survival analysis for building personal credit-scoring models was proposed by [9]. The core of this proposal is to use the Kaplan-Meier method and fitting exponential regression models.

In 2018, a regression-based model and a survival-based Cox model were compared on a real sample of Czech banking data [10]. From experimental results, the author claims that the survival-based Cox model outperforms the regression model in terms of the Gini coefficient and lift curves. Also, the survival-based Cox model shows a better predictive power in extrapolating the last observable default vintages [10]. After, in the same year, the authors of [13] proposed an ensemble mixture random forest model for estimating the probability of default over time. Their proposal was compared against Cox proportional hazards, a logistic regression model, and the mixture cure model [11]; the latter is a survival analysis that utilizes logistic regression and Cox proportional hazard regression. Their experimental results show that the ensemble mixture random forest model is competitive compared to the other models.

The survival analysis-based approach was considerably improved over the years by introducing new machine learning techniques, which gave the emergence of keystones, where the combination of survival analysis jointly with deep learning is considered a keystone [4,6]. However, as far as we know, there is no proposal of using survival analysis jointly with deep learning for predicting the behavioral probability of default.

The papers reviewed above are based on traditional techniques or keystone approaches for predicting the probability of default from a given applicant based on the historical data of previous borrowers. The survival curves are projected to obtain an estimated time during the loan term through a survival analysis-based approach and the characteristics obtained from the KYC process. However, the problem of this way of computing the probability of default is that these curves do not evolve through time based on the borrower's history considering the monthly data after the loan is granted, such as debt ratio and delinquencies. This is known as the behavioral probability of default [13].

In [13], the authors proposed a behavioral scoring model for estimating the probability of default. The proposal is based on an ensemble mixture random forest and was tested on a Chinese P2P loan database. They compared their proposal against three state-of-the-art algorithms, such as Cox proportional hazards, a logistic regression model, and the mixture cure model [11]. The ensemble, proposed in [13], showed results similar to the other compared algorithms. However, their results are based on a database from only one P2P institution in China, which lacks more databases to corroborate these results. Also, the authors did not provide information on excluding important survival analysis-based algorithms from their experimental setup, such as DeepHit [6].

As we have reviewed, only one paper proposes an algorithm for predicting the behavioral probability of default. However, the proposal is based on an ensemble of decision trees, and the authors did not include new approaches based on deep learning to Survival Analysis, such as Logistic Hazard [3] or Deep Hit [6]. Also, the authors did not provide a discussion jointly with risk analysis experts to corroborate the obtained results. Hence, in the next section, we introduce a novel deep learning and survival analysis-based approach for predicting the behavioral probability of default. Our approach will be corroborated jointly with risk analysis experts.

3 Our Approach for Predicting Behavioral Probability of Default

In this section, we introduce our approach for predicting the behavioral probability of default. Also, we provide our experimental setup and the rationale of our proposal to face the problem of estimating the behavioral probability of default.

For testing our proposal, we collected two loan databases, which provide historical payment information from different countries. On the one hand, Panama's database includes payments information from 363,184 borrowers considering loans from 2010 to 2021. One exceptional condition should be considered on this database because the government was forced to apply a moratorium regulation during 2021 due to the COVID19. Then, it contains several months where payments were not made, and consequently, borrowers' delinquency months were not increased. In this database, 23% of historical loans are labeled as write-offs. On the other hand, Trinidad & Tobago's database includes payments information from 316,293 borrowers considering loans from 2010 to 2021. In contrast to the Panama database, the government did not apply any moratorium regulation. This database is highly imbalanced because it contains only 8.5% of the historical loans labeled as write-offs.

As was stated before, both databases contain imbalanced data where write-offs are not the most common cases (a.k.a, minority class). A data level solution (resampling) was used to deal with the class imbalance problem by subsampling the majority class (paid-off). Also, it is important to comment that both databases contain several features, but after several discussions with financial institutions experts, we selected the 22 features shown in Table 1. Notice that there are six categorical features and 16 numerical features, which were selected and discussed jointly with experts in risk analysis from both countries. For each feature, in Table 1, the name used in the database system, the feature type, and a brief description are provided. There is one special feature to take into account: CUR_DLQ, which refers to the number of months the borrower is behind the DLQ (a.k.a delinquencies). After a borrower has seven delinquencies, the borrower's loan is considered as a write-off. Moreover, another extra feature is used in the Panama database due to applying government-enforced moratorium regulation to financial institutions; the payment made at each month PMT_X. Typically, when a payment is not made, the delinquency (CUR_DLQ) is increased by one. In this case, during the first years of the pandemic, this was not the case as borrowers were given a grace period where they will not be paying, and delinquency was not increasing. Thus, knowing if the borrower paid that month and if delinquency increased is necessary to detect this period.

An intrinsic data condition is that, usually, loans are given with certain pre-defined terms ranging from 12 months to 72 months; this would indicate that analyzing each of the discrete types of terms would be the best approach. The problem is that the government-enforced moratorium regulation or internal action as granting deferments change the actual terms, and there are no longer well-defined bins of terms. Therefore, the tested algorithms were trained considering only a specific amount of months before the event (paid-off or write-off).

Table 1. Features describing the two databases used in our experimentation.

Name	Type	Description
SCORE	Numerical	The borrower's credit history value issued during the onboarding process. It ranges from 300 to 850
LOAN_NBR	Numerical	Current number of loan from the same borrower
CUSTOMER_TYPE_CD	Categorical	Borrower type: new (NB), present (PB), or former (FB)
EMPLOYMENT_MONTHS	Numerical	Number of months in current employment of the borrower. It ranges from 0 to 1200
EMP_MTHLY_AMT_USD	Numeric	Borrower's monthly payment
DEBT_RATIO	Numeric	Borrower's debt ratio, according to the monthly payment
DINCOME_RATIO	Numeric	Borrower's income ratio ()
ORIG_SECTOR	Categorical	Employment sector at the moment of the application
SECTOR	Categorical	Current borrower 's employment sector
ACC_TERM	Categorical	Loan term (duration in months)
ACC_RATE	Numerical	Loan rate (percentage)
ACC_EXTN	Numerical	Moratorium in months for the loan
CUS_AGE	Numerical	Borrower's age
LOAN_AMT_USD	Numerical	Loan's total amount in US dollars
PMT_AMT_USD	Numerical	Amount to pay at each month in US dollars. This is used for normalizing other features
PAYOFF_AMT_USD	Numerical	Paid-off amount in US dollars
CUR_DLQ	Numerical	Current number of delinquency months
MAX_DLQ	Numerical	Maximum number of delinquency months until current date
DLQ_DIF_X	Numerical	Difference between CUR_DLQ and CUR_DLQ X months before current date. These group of features varies depending on the defined time window
PMT_X	Numerical	Payment amount done X months before current date divided by PMT_AMT_USD
PAYMENT_TYPE	Categorical	Payment type: Payroll deduction (PD)
ACUM_PERCENT	Numerical	Elapsed months divided by the ACC_TERM
WRITE_OFF	Categorical	It is the target feature (class). It labels whether the borrower's loan was considered as write-off or paid-off

For example, 24 months before the event is the cut-off for selecting borrowers' historical data to be used at the training stage. After several discussions with risk analysis experts, we test with two sets of borrower's historical months; 24 and 36. Also, these sets represent the most common terms for the given loans.

The deep learning architectures used for survival analysis can be divided into continuous-time and discrete-time models. The problem to solve in this paper needs a prediction in discrete time as the expected result is the probability of write-off at each month. Consequently, we select two survival analysis-based algorithms because they have shown promising results in several contexts [3, 8, 10, 12]. On the one hand, Logistic Hazard (NNnet-survival) [3], which parametrizes the discrete hazards and optimizes the survival likelihood. On the other hand, DeepHit [2], which parametrizes the Probability Mass Function (PMF) and optimizes the survival likelihood. It is important to comment that the survival analysis-based approach as well as the selected algorithms can deal with single or competing events, for which our problem could be formulated as a competing one (write-off vs. paid-off). However, after several experiments, the accuracy for write-offs decreases and the focus must be on predict with high accuracy the write-off events.

Table 2. Example of six rows from Trinidad database considering some of the features before normalization and before considering a time window.

MONTH	ACC_TERM	ACC_EXTN	PMT_AMT_USD	PMT_0	CUR_DLQ
1	48	0	105	105	0
2	48	0	105	105	0
3	48	0	105	0	1
4	48	0	105	157.5	1
5	48	0	105	157.5	0
6	48	2	105	105	0

Table 3. Example of six rows from Trinidad databases considering some of the normalized features and a time window of two months.

MONTH	ACC_TERM	ACC_EXTN	PMT_AMT_USD	PMT_0	PMT_1	PMT_2	CUR_DLQ	DLQ_DIF_1	DLQ_DIF_2	MAX_DLQ	ACUM_PERCENT
1	48	0	105	1	0	0	0	0	0	0	1/48
2	48	0	105	1	1	0	0	0	0	0	2/48
3	48	0	105	0	1	1	1	1	1	1	3/48
4	48	0	105	1.5	0	1	1	0	1	1	4/48
5	48	0	105	1.5	1.5	0	0	−1	−1	1	5/48
6	48	2	105	1	1.5	1.5	0	0	−1	1	6/50

For considering the evolution across time, a time window of x months is considered to create the new features DLQ_DIF_X and PMT_X $(x, x-1, x-2, \ldots, 1$ months before the current one). After testing with different time windows, we selected five months for Trinidad and six for Panama as they proved to obtain the best results. Table 2 shows an example of how the rows are presented in the original database, and Table 3 shows these rows and computed features after considering a time window of two months.

We use the PyCox framework (https://github.com/havakv/pycox) as support for implementing our approach. For both Logistic Hazard and DeepHit, we have set the same neuronal network backbone but varied the input depending on the database (41 for Trinidad and 43 for Panama) as this depends on the chosen time window. Also, as we tested the models with information from 24 and 36 months before the event, the output corresponds to these (25 or 36 outputs). After an analysis jointly with risk analysis experts, we only focused on the first 13 outputs corresponding to a 1-year prediction (see Fig. 1).

Figure 1 shows an example of the output of our approach showing write-off probability curves for five borrowers during a forecast year. Notice that the warning threshold is set to 0.5, and any borrower crossing this threshold is considered a potential write-off. Consequently, in this example, borrowers 1–3 are labeled as write-offs while borrowers 4–5 are stables. The warning threshold can be configured over or under 0.5, but it should be discussed with risk analyst experts. Different warning thresholds could be established depending on the borrowers' characteristics, such as occupation, type of payment, and age.

Our neuronal network structure consists of three hidden layers containing 128 neurons each, obtained after using a linear grid search for different numbers of layers and neurons. Also, for the learning rate, we executed the function

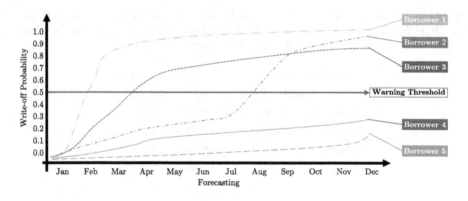

Fig. 1. An example of the output of our approach showing write-off probability curves for five borrowers.

lrfind.get_best_lr() in PyCox for obtaining the best initial value. Finally, we used an optimizer Adam with an alpha value of 0.005, which was obtained after testing different values.

For assessing the performance of the selected survival analysis-based algorithms on the tested databases, we use the number of write-offs predicted regarding the actual write-offs reported in the database. Also, we discuss together risk analysis experts the classification results and the trends of write-offs reported in the databases yearly.

In summary, our approach is an extension of the survival analysis approach in which every month's payment information is included as a new initial condition of the loan. Consequently, the payment information from previous months and the remaining borrower's on-board information are included as input.

4   Results and Discussion

In this section, we provide the obtained experimental results and a discussion of them. Firstly, we show the result using training data from January 2010 to 2018 and predict each month of 2019. After, we show the result using training data from January 2010 to June 2021 and predict from July 2021 to June 2022.

It is important to highlight that the tested databases have the characteristic that a loan is declared as write-offs after not paying for seven months (a.k.a seven delinquencies). Hence, risk analysis experts want to have a forecast of 12 months. The rationale is to discover those borrowers who start to default and consequently use internal actions to recover them before write-offs.

The summarized backtesting results obtained by the selected survival analysis-based algorithms on the tested databases are shown in Table 4 when 24 and 36 borrower's historical months are used. Table 4 shows the total of predicted write-offs and the actual values achieved during Jan-Dec 2019 for both countries. Notice that Logistic Hazard (36 months) achieved the best result (9,343) compared to the real value (9,304) for Panama. On the other hand, Deep Hit

Table 4. Backtesting of the different models and setups when historical data is used up December 2018. This table shows the total of predicted write-offs and the actual values achieved during Jan-Dec 2019 for both countries.

Model/Real values	Panama	Trinidad
Logistic Hazard (24 months)	9,002	3,921
Logistic Hazard (36 months)	9,343	3,875
Deep Hit (24 months)	9,946	3,851
Deep Hit (36 months)	9,705	3,929
Real Values	9,304	3,733

(24 months) reached the best result (3,851) compared to the real value (3,733) for Trinidad. Although, Logistic Hazard (36 months) also archived a close result (3,875) for Trinidad. It is important to highlight that all tested models accurately predict 2019 on both databases; the highest error value is 7%. However, detailed and monthly results of the backtesting executed are shown in Fig. 2 for Panama and Fig. 3 for Trinidad.

Figure 2 shows the results of the backtesting executed for the different tested combinations when using historical data of Panama until December 2018. This figure shows how Logistic Hazard (36 months) obtains the predicted values close to actual values during January-December 2019. Otherwise, notice how both combinations of Deep Hit (24 and 36 months) provide lower peaks in February while high peaks in October and November. Note that all combinations provide zero in December because the Panama government regulations dictate that borrowers must not pay in December. Then, all models are considering this law.

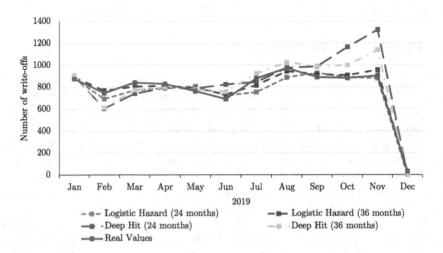

Fig. 2. Results of the backtesting executed for the different setups when using historical data of Panama until December 2018. This chart shows the number of predicted write-offs and the actual values achieved during Jan-Dec 2019 on a monthly basis.

In a similar way, Fig. 3 shows the results of the backtesting executed for the different tested combinations when using historical data of Trinidad until December 2018. This figure shows how Logistic Hazard (36 months) obtains predicted values close to actual values in March, September, November, and December. Also, it provides acceptable values for the remaining analyzed months, except October. On the other hand, notice how both combinations of Deep Hit (24 and 36 months) provide lower values from January to April while they provide high values from June to August. It is important to comment that the Trinidad database is more complicated for predicting the write-offs because, during the first pandemic wave, the financial institution was applying deferments to several and diverse borrowers without a clear rule to follow, complicating the learning of the models. Also, notice that the Trinidad database contains only 8.5% of the historical loans labeled as write-offs; consequently, it is an imbalanced database.

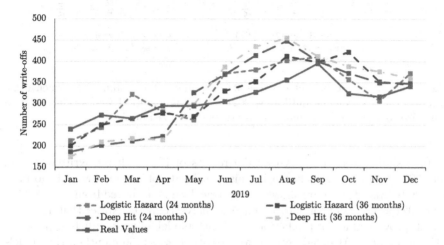

Fig. 3. Results of the backtesting executed for the different setups when using historical data of Trinidad & Tobago until December 2018. This chart shows the number of predicted write-offs and the actual values achieved during Jan-Dec 2019 on a monthly basis.

After a discussion with experts in risk analysis of both countries, they proposed to test all combinations for predicting the number of write-offs from July 2021 to June 2022 monthly when using historical data of each country until June 2021. The rationale behind these experts is to compare the trend of the tested models from July 2021 to June 2022 regarding their internal forecasting and the trend of the last 12 months having historical data.

Figure 4 shows the results of the predicted write-offs from July 2021 to June 2022 when using historical data of Panama until June 2021. Also, this figure shows the historical values achieved from July 2020 to June 2021 as points of comparison for risk analysis experts. Notice how both Logistic Hazard (24 and 36 months) models provide a similar trend to historical data. However, both

Deep Hit (24 and 36 months) models provide higher peaks and disproportionate values, classified as erratic values by experts in risk analysis.

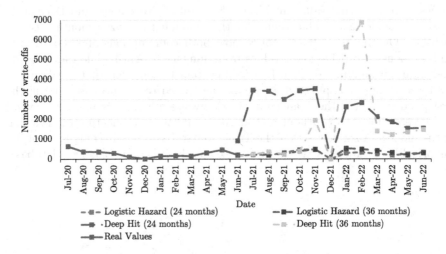

Fig. 4. Results of the predicted write-offs from July 2021 to June 2022 when using historical data of Panama until June 2021. Also, the historical values achieved from July 2020 to June 2021 are informed as points of comparison.

In a similar way, Fig. 5 shows the results of the predicted write-offs from July 2021 to June 2022 when using historical data of Trinidad & Tobago until June 2021. Also, this figure shows the historical values achieved from July 2020 to June 2021 as points of comparison for risk analysis experts. Notice that all tested models provide different predictions, and each model forecasts different peaks on different months. Although, except for Logistic Hazard (36 months), the models predict a high number of write-offs since February 2022. After discussing with the risk analysis experts and an in-depth analysis of the historical data, Logistic Hazard (36 months) is the most appropriate for them. Experts' rationale is that the highest peak in the historical data is 524 and Logistic Hazard (36 months) forecasts the highest peak (584) of write-offs in October 2021.

Table 5 shows the summarized results of the predicted write-offs from July 2021 to June 2022 for both countries. Compared with the real values, Logistic Hazard (24 months) is the most appropriate for Panama and Logistic Hazard (36 months) is the most appropriate for Trinidad. Notice that Deep Hit provides more than seven times the total of write-offs in Panama regarding the provided real values. For this reason, risk analysis experts in Panama agree to use Logistic Hazard instead of Deep Hit. On the other hand, compared with the trend and behavior of Trinidad's real values, the experts agree to use Logistic Hazard (36 months) instead of the remaining tested models.

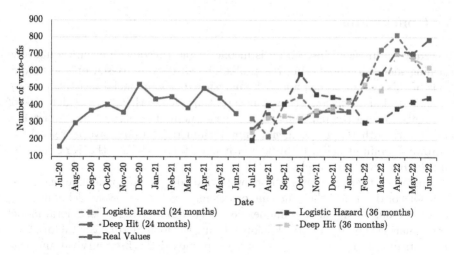

Fig. 5. Results of the predicted write-offs from July 2021 to June 2022 when using historical data of Trinidad & Tobago until June 2021. Also, the historical values achieved from July 2020 to June 2021 are informed as points of comparison.

Table 5. Total of predicted write-offs from July 2021 to June 2022 when historical data is used up June 2021. The historical values achieved for both countries, from July 2020 to June 2021, are informed as points of comparison.

Model/Real values	Panama	Trinidad
Logistic Hazard (24 months)	3,324	5,803
Logistic Hazard (36 months)	3,852	4,801
Deep Hit (24 months)	29,403	5,642
Deep Hit (36 months)	21,102	2,421
Real Values	3,225	4,696

As concluding remarks, based on the tested borrower databases, Logistic Hazard provided better results than Deep Hit for predicting the behavioral probability of default. After several experiments, we noticed that Deep Hit achieved good forecasting for up to 6 months. Otherwise, Deep Hit provided inconsistent results with high peaks, even using different borrower's historical months. On the other hand, Logistic Hazard achieved accurate forecasting results for more than six months, which can be corroborated in Figs. 4, 5 and Table 5. It is essential to highlight that Deep Hit provided acceptable results during the backtesting experiments (see Table 4, and Figs. 2, 3) where the data contained a stable behavior before the pandemic. However, when the training data contained several new regulations due to the pandemic, Deep Hit achieved erratic values, which risk analysis experts corroborated. On the other hand, Logistic Hazard provided forecasts more acceptable for risk analysis experts.

5   Conclusions

Nowadays, a financial institution is inconceivable without an accurate machine learning model for predicting the probability of default. Based on the predictions of this type of model and risk analysis experts, financial institutions save millions of dollars because they can deny those loans that have a high risk of write-offs. During the pandemic years, the economy has become more unstable, and jointly with the governments' moratorium regulations have increased the borrowers' delinquencies, creating much uncertainty during the KYC process and the borrower's life cycle.

Currently, there are several borrowers that, due to the pandemic, have lost their jobs or decreased their income, producing several borrowers' delinquencies, even write-offs by frequent delinquencies. Therefore, having a behavioral model for estimating the probability of default during the loan lifetime is vital for financial institutions. Hence, in this paper, we proposed the first survival analysis-based approach for predicting the behavioral probability of default. From our experimental results, by using two loan databases coming from two different countries, we conclude that Logistic Hazard provided better results than Deep Hit for predicting the behavioral probability of default. Also, Deep Hit achieved inconsistent results for forecasts greater than six months. On the other hand, Logistic Hazard is more accurate in forecasting the behavioral probability of default for a year. It is essential to highlight that Deep Hit provided acceptable results during the backtesting experiments where the data contained a stable behavior before the pandemic. However, when the training data contained several new regulations due to the pandemic, Deep Hit achieved erratic values, which risk analysis experts corroborated. On the other hand, Logistic Hazard provides forecasts more acceptable for risk analysis experts.

Like any proposal, our approach leaves room for improving it. Therefore, we plan to perform deep experimentation for finding the adequate warning threshold for write-off considering different borrowers' characteristics, such as occupation, type of payment, age; among others. Also, we plan to extract rules from our proposal to provide an explainable model [7] for risk analysis experts. Lastly, a natural iteration of this work is the usage of Recurrent Neural Networks (RNNs) as we are currently introducing new features to consider evolution through time, which is native to RNNs.

References

1. Arya, S., Eckel, C., Wichman, C.: Anatomy of the credit score. J. Econ. Behav. Organ. **95**, 175–185 (2013)
2. Gensheimer, M.F., Narasimhan, B.: A scalable discrete-time survival model for neural networks. PeerJ **7**, e6257 (2019)
3. Gerds, T.A., Schumacher, M.: Consistent estimation of the expected brier score in general survival models with right-censored event times. Biom. J. **48**(6), 1029–1040 (2006)

4. Kvamme, H., Borgan, Ø., Scheel, I.: Time-to-event prediction with neural networks and cox regression. J. Mach. Learn. Res. **20**(129), 1–30 (2019)
5. Kvamme, H., Borgan, Ø.: Continuous and discrete-time survival prediction with neural networks. Lifetime Data Anal. **27**(4), 710–736 (2021). https://doi.org/10.1007/s10985-021-09532-6
6. Lee, C., Zame, W.R., Yoon, J., van der Schaar, M.: Deephit: a deep learning approach to survival analysis with competing risks. In: Thirty-Second AAAI Conference on Artificial Intelligence, pp. 2314–2321 (2018)
7. Loyola-González, O.: Black-box vs. white-box: understanding their advantages and weaknesses from a practical point of view. IEEE Access **7**, 154096–154113 (2019)
8. Merćep, A., Mrčela, L., Birov, M., Kostanjčar, Z.: Deep neural networks for behavioral credit rating. Entropy **23**(1), 27 (2020)
9. Narain, B.: Survival analysis and the credit-granting decision. In: Thomas, L., Crook, J., Edelman, D. (eds.) Credit Scoring and Credit Control, pp. 109–122. Oxford University Press, Oxford (1992)
10. Rychnovsky, M.: Survival analysis as a tool for better probability of default prediction. Acta Oeconomica Pragensia **26**(1), 34–46 (2018)
11. Tong, E.N., Mues, C., Thomas, L.C.: Mixture cure models in credit scoring: if and when borrowers default. Eur. J. Oper. Res. **218**(1), 132–139 (2012)
12. Uno, H., Cai, T., Pencina, M.J., D'Agostino, R.B., Wei, L.J.: On the c-statistics for evaluating overall adequacy of risk prediction procedures with censored survival data. Stat. Med. **30**(10), 1105–1117 (2011)
13. Wang, Z., Jiang, C., Ding, Y., Lyu, X., Liu, Y.: A novel behavioral scoring model for estimating probability of default over time in peer-to-peer lending. Electron. Commer. Res. Appl. **27**, 74–82 (2018)
14. Yeh, I.C., hui Lien, C.: The comparisons of data mining techniques for the predictive accuracy of probability of default of credit card clients. Expert Syst. Appl. **36**(2, Part 1), 2473–2480 (2009)

Mining Mixed Data Bases Using Machine Learning Algorithms

Angel Kuri-Morales[✉]

Instituto Tecnológico Autónomo de México, Río Hondo No. 1, 01000 México D.F., Mexico
akuri@itam.mx

Abstract. We discuss numerical algorithms (based on metric spaces) to explore data bases (DB) even though such DBs may not be metric. The following issues are treated: 1. Determination of the minimum equivalent sample, 2. The encoding of categorical variables and 3. Data analysis. We illustrate the methodology with an experimental mixed DB consisting of 29,267 tuples; 15 variables of which 9 are categorical and 6 are numerical. Firstly, we show that information preservation is possible with a (possibly) much smaller sample. Secondly, we approximate the best possible encoding of the 9 categorical variables applying a statistical algorithm which extracts the code after testing an appropriate number of alternatives for each instance of the variables. To do this we solve two technical issues, namely: a) How to determine that the attributes are already normal and b) How to find the best regressive function of an encoded attribute as a function of another. Thirdly, with the transformed DB (now purely numerical) it is possible to find the regressive approximation errors of any attribute relative to another. Hence, we find those attributes which are closer to one another within a predefined threshold (85%). We argue that such variables define a cluster. Now we may use algorithms such as Multi-Layer Perceptron Networks (MLPN) and/or Kohonen maps (SOM). The classification of a target attribute "salary" is achieved with a MLPN. It is shown to yield better results than most traditional conceptual analysis algorithms. Later, by training a SOM for the inferred clusters, we disclose the characteristics of every cluster. Finally, we restore the DB original values and get visual representations of the variables in each cluster, thus ending the mining process.

Keywords: Entropy · Categorical variables · Central limit theorem · Ascent algorithm · Self-oganized maps

1 Introduction

Mixed data bases [i.e. those consisting of both numerical and non-numerical (from now on "categorical") attributes] are not prone to their manipulation with metric algorithms which are designed to handle processes where only numerical attributes are included. We are interested in applying such numerical algorithms because of their generality and inherent ruggedness. Therefore, a basic issue has to do with the need to transform mixed DBs into purely numerical ones. We argue that, to preserve the patterns underlying the categorical data, one must consider the statistical properties of the data. This implies the

O. O. Vergara-Villegas et al. (Eds.): MCPR 2022, LNCS 13264, pp. 70–80, 2022.
https://doi.org/10.1007/978-3-031-07750-0_7

statistical test of an unbounded set of numerical codes with which to replace the categorical instances. This, in turn, carries a high computational cost which can be improved
upon by selecting the most adequate minimum data sample. Once this "economic" sample has been determined, numerical encoding for pattern preservation becomes feasible.
In part 2 we explore the problem of finding the best minimum sample. Next, statistical
encoding allows us to find the codes for every one of the instances of every categorical
attribute in a mixed DB where there are M numerical attributes and N categorical ones.
The algorithm we implemented (called CESAMO [1]) ensures the preservation of the
patterns in the mixed DB. It basically relies on the fact that any distribution of means will
become Gaussian [2]. CESAMO a) Goes through the set of the N categorical variables
($i = 1, ..., N$) and replaces the instances of the i-th categorical variable by randomly
selected codes. b) It then approximates the remaining attributes ($k = 1, ..., M + N - 1$)
as a function of the (now numerical) attributes of the DB. c) The $M + N - 1$ remaining
attributes are approximated with the proposed i-th attribute encoded. The approximation error is computed. d) Thereafter the set of numerical codes is stored and indexed
as per the approximation error. Steps (a) through (d) are performed 36 times [3] and e)
The average approximation error is calculated. Once the average errors (for the attribute
being tested) distribute normally (as we know they must) CESAMO selects the code
which yields the smallest average error. The "best average approximation code" from
step (e) is the one which will take place of the categorical attributes' instances in the
originally mixed (now numerical) DB. Two technical issues arise: i) How to determine
that the average errors are already Gaussian and ii) How to calculate the approximation
errors of (c) above. In part 3 we offer a detailed discussion of the whole process. In part
4 we discuss cluster identification and membership. We set a distance threshold which
defines the number and boundaries of the clusters present in the DB. Finally, in part 5
we end by showing how to mine the resulting Kohonen's SOMS [4]. In part 6 we offer
our conclusions.

2 Best Minimum Sample

We illustrate the whole process with the DB [5] exemplified in Fig. 1 and 2.
  It consists of 29,267 tuples: 9 categorical and 6 numerical.

Age	Workclass	Fnlwgt	Education	Edunum	Marstat	Occup
39	State-gov	77516.0000000000	Bachelors	13.000000000000	Never-married	Adm-clerical
50	Self-emp-not-inc	83311.0000000000	Bachelors	13.000000000000	Married-civ-spouse	Exec-managerial
38	Private	215646.000000000	HS-grad	9.000000000000	Divorced	Handlers-cleaners
53	Private	234721.000000000	11th	7.000000000000	Married-civ-spouse	Handlers-cleaners
28	Private	338409.000000000	Bachelors	13.000000000000	Married-civ-spouse	Prof-specialty
37	Private	284582.000000000	Masters	14.000000000000	Married-civ-spouse	Exec-managerial
49	Private	160187.000000000	9th	5.000000000000	Married-spouse-absen	Other-service
52	Self-emp-not-inc	209642.000000000	HS-grad	9.000000000000	Married-civ-spouse	Exec-managerial

Fig. 1. Example of the mixed data base (part 1)

Relat	Race	Sex	Gain	Loss	Hours	Country	Salary
Not-in-family	White	Male	000000000	00000000000	40.000000000000	United-States	<=50K
Husband	White	Male	000000000	00000000000	13.000000000000	United-States	<=50K
Not-in-family	White	Male	000000000	00000000000	40.000000000000	United-States	<=50K
Husband	Black	Male	000000000	00000000000	40.000000000000	United-States	<=50K
Wife	Black	Female	000000000	00000000000	40.000000000000	Cuba	<=50K
Wife	White	Female	000000000	00000000000	40.000000000000	United-States	<=50K
Not-in-family	Black	Female	000000000	00000000000	16.000000000000	Jamaica	<=50K
Husband	White	Male	000000000	00000000000	45.000000000000	United-States	>50K

Fig. 2. Example of the mixed data base (part 2).

The first step is to map the numerical variables into [0,1), for reasons which will become apparent in what follows. This is illustrated in Fig. 3.

ORIGINAL

Age	Workclass	Fnlwgt	Education	Edunum	Marstat	Occup
39	State-gov	77516.0000000000	Bachelors	13.000000000000	Never-married	Adm-clerical
50	Self-emp-not-inc	83311.0000000000	Bachelors	13.000000000000	Married-civ-spouse	Exec-managerial
38	Private	215646.000000000	HS-grad	9.000000000000	Divorced	Handlers-cleaners
53	Private	234721.000000000	11th	7.000000000000	Married-civ-spouse	Handlers-cleaners
28	Private	338409.000000000	Bachelors	13.000000000000	Married-civ-spouse	Prof-specialty

Relat	Race	Sex	Gain	Loss	Hours	Country	Salary
Not-in-family	White	Male	2174.00000000000	0.000000000000	40.000000000000	United-States	<=50K
Husband	White	Male	0.000000000000	0.000000000000	13.000000000000	United-States	<=50K
Not-in-family	White	Male	0.000000000000	0.000000000000	40.000000000000	United-States	<=50K
Husband	Black	Male	0.000000000000	0.000000000000	40.000000000000	United-States	<=50K
Wife	Black	Female	0.000000000000	0.000000000000	40.000000000000	Cuba	<=50K

SCALED

Age	Workclass	Fnlwgt	Education	Edunum	Marstat	Occup
0.301369863014	State-gov	0.043337711498	Bachelors	0.800000000000	Never-married	Adm-clerical
0.452054794521	Self-emp-not-inc	0.047277379845	Bachelors	0.800000000000	Married-civ-spouse	Exec-managerial
0.287671232877	Private	0.137243904561	HS-grad	0.533333333333	Divorced	Handlers-cleaners
0.493150684932	Private	0.150211837905	11th	0.400000000000	Married-civ-spouse	Handlers-cleaners

Relat	Race	Sex	Gain	Loss	Hours	Country	Salary
Not-in-family	White	Male	0.021740217402	0.000000000000	0.397959183673	United-States	<=50K
Husband	White	Male	0.000000000000	0.000000000000	0.122448979592	United-States	<=50K
Not-in-family	White	Male	0.000000000000	0.000000000000	0.397959183673	United-States	<=50K
Husband	Black	Male	0.000000000000	0.000000000000	0.397959183673	United-States	<=50K

Fig. 3. Original and scaled DBs

2.1 Data Reduction as a Practical Alternative

The first thing to note is that "Data" and "Information" are not equivalent. In the computation disciplines we need a precise desription of what we mean by "information". In this regard, the defintition of "entropy" $H(X)$ or average information is

$$H(X) = \sum_{i=1}^{m} -p_i \log(p_i)$$

where "X" is the message, p_i is the probability of a symbol appearing and m is the number of symbols in the message. In, practically all cases, the information contained in a DB may be preserved without using all the data. The key idea is "Instead of working with a large amount of data, let us work with those data which preserve the equivalent amount of information". That is, let us extract the minimal sample which provides the same information as the original data. We can then advance the following hypothesis: *The information contained in a random sample S (extracted from a large data base D) of size M is approximately equal to the one in D when the entropies of D and S are similar AND the behavior of the variables in M is analogous to that of the variables in S.* To achieve this two steps are taken. Step 1: Find a reduced sample with the same amount of information. Step 2: Model the variables of the system to certify that, in both data sets (D and M) the attributes are similarly inter-related.

Step 1. Determine the sample with equivalent entropy

In Fig. 4 we show the program which calculates the entropy of S. The column on the left displays the number of samples needed to achieve entropy equivalence for every attribute. The number of samples needed to achieve the required equivalent entropy corresponds to the largest necessary sample. In this example it corresponds to variable 4 (Education).

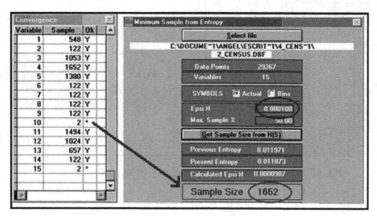

Fig. 4. Calculation of the minimum number of samples to achieve entropic equivalence for D and M.

We iteratively approximate the entropy in all attributes until the difference of consecutive values of the experimental entropy is smaller than a predefined threshold T. In the example $T = 0.0001$. When the entropy calculated in step i and the difference calculated in step $i + 1$ are less than T the entropies are equivalent.

Step 2. Equivalent behavior of the Attributes (Fig. 5 and 6)

In Fig. 5 and 6 we show the determination of the equivalent behaviour of an attribute (age) in D and M.

A uniform random sample without replacement of size 2,000 was obtained. Now we know that this sample is informationally equivalent to manipulating the whole DB D. An impressive ratio of size |S|/|DB|=2,000/29,267≈0.0683 is achieved.

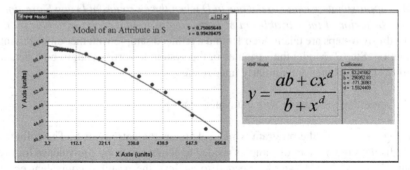

Fig. 5. Determination of the equivalent attribute behaviour in D.

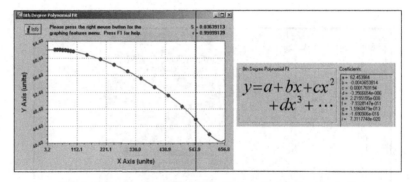

Fig. 6. Determination of the equivalent attribute behaviour in S.

3   Categorical Encoding

The basic idea is to aproxímate the best code using a statistical methodology which extracts the code after testing a set of possible values for each of the instantes of every one of the categorical variables. An example of categorical attributes and their corresponding instances is shown in Fig. 7.

In Fig. 8 we show the pseudo code of CESAMO.

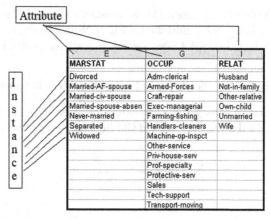

Fig. 7. Illustration of categorical attributes and their instances.

```
For i = 1 to Number of Categorical Attributes
    Select the i-th categorical attribute (Let if be "P")
    ℓ = 1
    While Distribution of the Average Approximation Error [AVG(P)] is not normal
        For j =1 to 36
            SEED(ℓ) = RGR (root of the generator of random numbers)
            Initialize RGR with SEED(ℓ)
            For k = 1 to Number of Instances in P
                    Assign a random code [0,1) to P(k)
            Endfor
            Randomly choose an attribute ≠ i (Let it be S)
            Find P(ℓ) = F(S)
            ℓ = ℓ + 1
        Endfor
        Calculate AVG(P)
    EndWhile
    Select the index (best) corresponding to the minimum fit
    error of P
    Initialize RGR with SEED(best)
    For k = 1 to Number of instances in P
        Assign  a random code [0,1) to P(k)
    Endfor
    For k = 1 to Number of instances in P
        Replace the k-th categorical instance with P(k)
    Endfor
Endfor
```

Fig. 8. CESAMO: algorithm to identify best codes for categorical variables.

When CESAMO runs for the data in [5] every instance's numerical pattern preserving code in [0,1) is identified. This is illustrated in Fig. 9. Which is why numerical data was scaled into the same [0,1) interval. Codes are thusly congruent with CESAMO's codes.

3.1 How to Determine that the Average Errors Are Already Gaussian

CESAMO keeps iterating as long as the approximation errors do not distribute normally. Normality is ascertained using the modified Chi-Squared distribution [6].

$$\pi = \sum_{i=1}^{Q} \frac{(O_i - E_i)^2}{E_i} \wedge [O_i \geq \Phi \forall i].$$

3.2 How to Calculate the Approximation Errors

We know that any function may be closely approximated by a lineal combination of a constant and a set of k monomials of odd power each of whom has a highest degree of 11 [7]. The fast ascent algorithm [8] allows us to calculate the approximation errors with a polynomial of the form $P(l) = c_0 + c_1 S + \ldots + c_9 S^9 + c_{11} S^{11}$.

MARSTAT		OCCUP		RELAT	
Divorced	0.7771	Adm-clerical	0.7771	Husband	0.7771
Married-AF-spouse	0.6621	Armed-Forces	0.6621	Not-in-family	0.6621
Married-civ-spouse	0.4321	Craft-repair	0.4321	Other-relative	0.4321
Married-spouse-absen	0.8986	Exec-managerial	0.8986	Own-child	0.8986
Never-married	0.5955	Farming-fishing	0.5955	Unmarried	0.5955
Separated	0.7078	Handlers-cleaners	0.7078	Wife	0.7078
Widowed	0.2778	Machine-op-inspct	0.2778		
		Other-service	0.1695		
		Priv-house-serv	0.4368		
		Prof-specialty	0.5233		
		Protective-serv	0.2217		
		Sales	0.1537		
		Tech-support	0.9862		
		Transport-moving	0.0133		

Fig. 9. Best codes for data in Fig. 8.

In Fig. 10 and 11 we show the DB before and after replacing the original categorical attributes with CESAMO's numerical equivalents.

Age	Workclass	Fnlwgt	Education	Edunum	Marstat
0.5479	Federal-gov	0.0053	Some-college	0.6000	Divorced
0.4384	State-gov	0.0878	HS-grad	0.5333	Married-civ-spouse
0.3836	State-gov	0.1201	Prof-school	0.9333	Divorced

Age	Workclass	Fnlwgt	Education	Edunum	Marstat
0.54795	0.77712	0.00534	0.48896	0.60000	0.77712
0.43836	0.70777	0.08776	0.15365	0.53333	0.43208
0.38356	0.70777	0.12008	0.96936	0.93333	0.77712

Fig. 10. Mixed data base.

Occup	Relat	Race	Sex	Gain	Loss	Hours	Country	Salary
Other-service	Not-in-family	White	Male	0.0000	0.0000	0.3980	United-States	<=50K
Prof-specialty	Husband	White	Male	0.0000	0.0000	0.3980	United-States	>50K
Prof-specialty	Unmarried	Black	Male	0.2524	0.0000	0.3571	United-States	>50K

Occup	Relat	Race	Sex	Gain	Loss	Hours	Country	Salary
0.16948	0.66213	0.59548	0.66213	0.00000	0.00000	0.39796	0.36541	0.77712
0.52332	0.77712	0.59548	0.66213	0.00000	0.00000	0.39796	0.36541	0.66213
0.52332	0.59548	0.43208	0.66213	0.25236	0.00000	0.35714	0.36541	0.66213

Fig. 11. All numerical (after CESAMO) data base

4   Finding the Clusters

With the mixed DB transformed in numerical DB we may calculate the relations (here whimsically denoted as *eigenvalues*) between the attributes. Values closer to "1" correspond to better approximations (Fig. 12).

	Fnlwgt	Education	Hours	Country	Salary
AGE	0.5431195953	0.5883877111	0.6746281846	0.6413954557	0.6142311786
WORKCLASS	0.3031325653	0.4228106777	0.5320134346	0.4847233134	0.7070573502
FNLWGT	1.0000000000	0.6904122436	0.8402341706	0.8625161994	0.6140451937
EDUCATION	0.3417455775	1.0000000000	0.4941881253	0.4674742695	0.5793451225
EDUNUM	0.1394468132	0.3525440594	0.3655133932	0.2975298194	0.6975442073
MARSTAT	0.2466247931	0.3927479014	0.4675299970	0.4283312732	0.7766122089
OCCUP	0.1908027729	0.3391590480	0.3505872451	0.3176121531	0.5433000255
RELAT	0.0000000000	0.1978152629	0.2612571292	0.1814401084	0.7908662087
RACE	0.1951105757	0.3618949504	0.4253824333	0.4209208544	0.7593112957
SEX	0.0424684078	0.2527857671	0.3121448926	0.2651431081	0.8198277269
GAIN	0.8686513494	0.5130232465	0.6962916031	0.7740870504	0.2191602837
LOSS	0.8725608234	0.7392127842	0.8221079903	0.8438620566	0.5489984083
HOURS	0.4325091890	0.5167543186	1.0000000000	0.5830012942	0.7080384336
COUNTRY	0.5060487005	0.5408809430	0.6900072978	1.0000000000	0.7399203281
SALARY	0.0000000000	0.1925597135	0.2460476659	0.2159727762	1.0000000000

Fig. 12. Partial table of *eigenvalues*.

Now we find the attributes which are closer to one another (whose approximation fitness are similar) for a determined closeness (85%). These determine the clusters in the data (Fig. 13).

Correlated Variables															
	Age	Workclass	Fnlwgt	Education	Edunum	Marstat	Occup	Relat	Race	Sex	Gain	Loss	Hours	Country	Salary
AGE															
WORKCLASS															
FNLWGT														X	
EDUCATION															
EDUNUM															
MARSTAT															
OCCUP															
RELAT															
RACE															
SEX															
GAIN			X												
LOSS			X							X					
HOURS															
COUNTRY							X								
SALARY															

Fig. 13. Clusters determined by attributes with similar distance.

5 Mining the Data

Once having only numerical data we may use algorithms (such as Neural Networks). For example, using a multi-layer perceptron we may model the variable "salary". In Fig. 14. we show a comparison between older algorithms and the results we achieved after treating the data as described here.

```
 |    Algorithm              Error        OBTAINED
 |   ------------------      -----        FROM THE
 |    NN                     15.75   ◄─── ENCODED
 | 1  C4.5                   15.54   ┐    VARIABLES
 | 2  C4.5-auto              14.46   │
 | 3  C4.5 rules             14.94   │
 | 4  Voted ID3 (0.6)        15.64   │
 | 5  Voted ID3 (0.8)        16.47   │    Algorithms
 | 6  T2                     16.84   │    working with
 | 7  1R                     19.54   │    original data
 | 8  NBTree                 14.10   │
 | 9  CN2                    16.00   │
 | 10 HOODG                  14.82   │
 | 11 FSS Naive Bayes        14.05   │
 | 12 IDTM (Decision table)  14.46   │
 | 13 Naive-Bayes            16.12   │
 | 14 Nearest-neighbor (1)   21.42   │
 | 15 Nearest-neighbor (3)   20.35   ┘
```

Fig. 14. Results from several algorithms

Also, a self-organizing map was trained. In Fig. 15 we show the calculated centroids for 3 clusters.

	age 口	workclass 口	fnlwgt 口	education 口	edunum 口	marstat 口	occup 口
Neuron	0.293	0.479	0.118	0.161	0.533	0.537	0.275
Neuron2	0.282	0.500	0.119	0.602	0.628	0.535	0.330
Neuron3	0.305	0.513	0.123	0.411	0.643	0.549	0.827

	relat 口	race 口	sex 口	gain 口	loss 口	hours 口	country 口	salary 口
Neuron	0.733	0.586	0.689	0.005	0.013	0.411	0.368	0.759
Neuron2	0.736	0.587	0.695	0.012	0.019	0.395	0.367	0.746
Neuron3	0.729	0.583	0.708	0.017	0.019	0.410	0.370	0.743

Fig. 15. Centroids of the 3 clusters of the Calculated SOM.

And we may de-scale the data to see the graphical representation of the clusters. A partial view of variable "Age" in the three determined clusers is shown in Fig. 16.

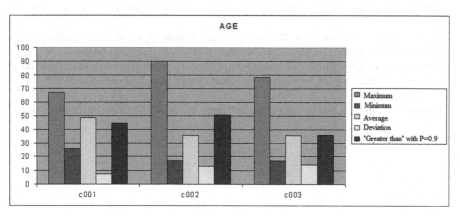

Fig. 16. "AGE" in the three clusters.

6   Conclusions

We have shown that algorithms designed to treat numerical data are accessible to categorical data if appropriate encoding is achieved. Furthermore, we also showed that adequate pre-processing allows the users to achieve objective results (where these are not conditoned by a priori considerations as is usual in the heuristics usually employed in categorical analysis). A case in point is the possible predictive analysis of a target attribute. Another clear example is the determination of the clusters expressed by the data and their quantitative characteristics.

Furthermore, the strategy employed in CESAMO does not restrict to texts. It may be employed to encode objects such as those found in musical pieces, pictorical works and son on. At present, our group is exploring the determination of authorship from a collection of paintings using CESAMO.

We expect to report on these issues in the near future.

References

1. Kuri-Morales, A.: Pattern discovery in mixed data bases. In: Martínez-Trinidad, J.F., Carrasco-Ochoa, J.A., Olvera-López, J.A., Sarkar, S. (eds.) MCPR 2018. LNCS, vol. 10880, pp. 178–188. Springer, Cham (2018). https://doi.org/10.1007/978-3-319-92198-3_18
2. Rosenblatt, M.: A central limit theorem and a strong mixing condition. Proc. Natl. Acad. Sci. U.S.A. **42**(1), 43–47 (1956). https://doi.org/10.1073/pnas.42.1.43
3. https://www.investopedia.com/terms/c/central_limit_theorem.asp. Ganti, Akhilesh, "Central Limit Theorem"
4. Kaski, S.: Self-Organizing Maps. In: Sammut, C., Webb, G.I. (eds.) Encyclopedia of Machine Learning. Springer, Boston (2011). https://doi.org/10.1007/978-0-387-30164-8_746
5. https://archive.ics.uci.edu/ml/datasets/census+income
6. Kuri-Morales, A.F., López-Peña, I.: Normality from monte carlo simulation for statistical validation of computer intensive algorithms. In: Pichardo-Lagunas, O., Miranda-Jiménez, S. (eds.) Advances in Soft Computing: 15th Mexican International Conference on Artificial Intelligence, MICAI 2016, Part II, pp. 3–14. Springer, Cham (2017). https://doi.org/10.1007/978-3-319-624 28-0_1
7. Kuri-Morales, A., Cartas-Ayala, A.: Automatic closed modeling of multiple variable systems using soft computation. In: Castro, F., Miranda-Jiménez, S., González-Mendoza, M. (eds.) Advances in Soft Computing: 16th Mexican International Conference on Artificial Intelligence, MICAI 2017, Part I, pp. 185–196. Springer, Cham (2018). https://doi.org/10.1007/978-3-030-02837-4_15
8. Cheney, E.W.: Introduction to Approximation Theory, pp. 34–45. McGraw-Hill Book Company (1966)

Neural Networks and Deep Learning

A CNN-Based Driver's Drowsiness and Distraction Detection System

Jonathan Flores-Monroy⬤, Mariko Nakano-Miyatake⁽☒⁾ ⬤, Hector Perez-Meana⬤, Enrique Escamilla-Hernandez⬤, and Gabriel Sanchez-Perez⬤

Mechanical and Electrical Engineering School, Instituto Politecnico Nacional, Coyoacan, 04440 Mexico City, Mexico
mnakano@ipn.mx

Abstract. The driver's drowsiness and distraction are the principal causes of traffic accidents in the world. To attack this problem, in this paper we propose a visual-based driver's drowsiness and distraction detection system, which is based on a face detection algorithm and a CNN-based driver state classification. To be useful the proposed system, we consider that the system must be implemented in a compact mobile device with limited memory space and computational power. The proposed system in compact mobile device can be used in any type of vehicle, avoiding accident caused by lack of driver's alert. The proposed system is evaluated using public dataset, obtaining 95.77% of global accuracy. The proposed system is compared with five finetuned off-the-shelf CNNs, in which the proposed system shows a favorable performance, providing higher operation speed and lower memory requirement compared with these five CNNs, although the detection accuracy is slightly lower compared with the best CNN. The performance of the proposed system guarantees the real-time operation in the compact mobile device.

Keywords: Convolutional Neural Networks (CNN) · Driver's drowsiness detection · Driver's distraction detection · Real-time implementation · Finetuning model

1 Introduction

According to the several statistical reports, such as [1, 2], more than 30% of traffic accidents are caused by driver's drowsiness or distraction. Several circumstances, such as lack of sleep of driver, driver's physical or mental fatigue, monotonous road condition, etc. are considered as main factors of driver's drowsiness. On the other hand, the spread of the use of cell phone during driving causes driver's distraction and then lack of alert to the situation around the driver. In Mexico, approximately 16,500 mortal accidents occur by year, whose economic burden becomes about 150 billion Mexican pesos, according to the report of the National Council for Prevention against Accidents (CONAPRA) [3].

Considering this problem, several approaches have been proposed to detect driver's drowsiness or distraction and then avoid timely a lamentable accident. Basically, these

O. O. Vergara-Villegas et al. (Eds.): MCPR 2022, LNCS 13264, pp. 83–93, 2022.
https://doi.org/10.1007/978-3-031-07750-0_8

approaches are classified into three categories, which depend on the input information used for detection process. The first category is vehicle behavior-based or driving pattern-based system, in which the data obtained from the vehicle, such as velocity, acceleration, steering angle and lane deviation are used to detect driver's abnormal condition [4, 5]. This approach is implemented as Advanced Driver Assistance Systems (ADAS) in some luxury vehicle models. However, the detection performance varies according to the road condition and driver's driving ability. The second category uses driver's physiological signals [6, 7], such as Electrooculogram (EOG), Electrocardiogram (ECG), Electromyogram (EMG) and Electroencephalogram (EEG). Although these signals can be related directly to the grade of driver's physiological condition, such as fatigue and distraction, the driver must put on the wearable sensors for the signal acquisition, which is invasive for driver and obstacle to drive.

The third category is visual-based system, in which the driver face or driver's eye image is captured by video camera, and eye blinking frequency, eyelid closure duration, yawning and nodding frequency, etc. are measured to determine the driver's drowsiness [8–10]. Because this category of systems is not invasive for drivers and does not depend on the type of vehicle and driver's driving ability, recently it has attracted the interest of many researchers. Zhao et al. proposed a visual features-based driver fatigue detection [8], in which Single-Shot Detector (SSD) is used to detect the driver's face and a pre-trained VGG16 [11] is used to detect the video frames with closed eyelids. Finally, using PERCLOS values [12], which is rate of frames with closed eyelids over the whole frames, determine if the driver is drowsy or not. The system provides an accuracy of 91.88% using NTHU-Drowsy Driver Detection (NTHU-DDD) data set [13]. In [9], Pan et al. proposed driver's drowsiness detection system applying a transfer learning technique to the MobileNet-V2 [14] and ResNet-50V2 [15]. They obtained 97% of the detection accuracy using their private data set. The principal difficulty of these systems is its real-time implementation in the mobile devices, because the pretrained off-the-shelf CNNs, such as VGG16, MobileNet-V2 and ResNet-50V2, still have a high complexity with large memory space requirement to operate in the portable mobile devices. We provide the numerical data in the Sect. 3.3. The authors of [10] proposed a driver's drowsiness detection system using a shallow CNN to reduce computational complexity. This system provided 98.95% in drowsiness detection accuracy; however, this system cannot detect driver's distraction state.

In this paper, we proposed a driver's drowsiness and distraction detection system based on the Convolutional Neural Networks (CNN), in which video frames taken by a Webcam located inside of the vehicle are used as input signal, and the system's output is one of the three driver's conditions: Alert, Distract and Drowsy. We consider two face detection algorithms with lower computational complexities, which are Viola-Jones algorithm [16] and Mediapipe Face detection algorithm [17]. The principal objective of the proposed system is portability, which means that the proposed system can be implemented in any types of vehicles using a mobile device and a low-price Webcam. To this end, the memory and computational power consumptions of the proposed system must be as low as possible. Considering these requirements, we analyze several CNN-based architectures to determine a best model. The performance of the proposed system is evaluated using the NTHU-DDD data set. The proposed system, which is trained from scratch, is compared with the off-the-shelf CNNs in the different aspects, such as detection accuracy, memory space requirements and global operation velocity. To adapt the pretrained off-the-shelf CNNs to our detection task, all of them are finetuned, re-training latter layers, including Fully Connected (FC) layers, while freezing some early layers. As the off-the-shelf CNNs, we considered MobileNet-V2 [14], VGG16 [11], ResNet-50V2 [15], InceptionV3 [18], Xception [19].

The rest of the paper is organized as follows: In Sect. 2, the proposed system together with face detection algorithms is described, and in Sect. 3, we provide the system performance and comparative results with the fine-tuned off-the-shelf CNNs. Finally, Sect. 4 concludes our work pointing out some future direction of the work.

2 Proposed System

The proposed system is depicted by Fig. 1, which composed on face detection module and drowsiness/distraction detection module. In the face detection module, we considered two algorithms: Viola-Jones algorithm [16] and Mediapipe Face detection algorithm [17], because these two algorithms provide low computational complexity compared with other face detection algorithms, such as YOLO-Face [20]. Mediapipe Face detection algorithm was developed for mobile application, which is based on the SSD, but adapted to only face detection.

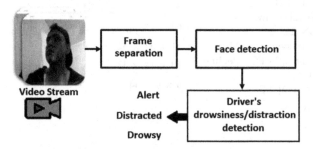

Fig. 1. Proposed driver's drowsiness and distraction detection system

To determine the most adequate CNN architecture for our objective, which can be operated in the mobile device with a limited memory space and computational power. We evaluated several CNN architectures and Table 1 shows three configurations with best performance from accuracy and memory space limitation points of view. Figure 2 shows the selected CNN architecture, which is trained by scratch using the following hyper-parameters: Adam optimizer with 0.001 learning rate, ReLU activation function is used after all 2D-Conv layers and FC layers, except final FC layer, in which Softmax activation function is used. The categorical cross-entropy is used as loss function. The input images are resized as 64×64. The Data augmentation techniques, such as scaling with range of [0.8, 1.2], horizontal and vertical shifting within 20% of the width and height of the image, sharing, rotation within angle $10°$ and horizontal flipping, are applied randomly to increase training data.

Table 1. Performance comparison among different CNN configurations

Models	Architecture	Additional settings		Model size	Trainable params.	Accuracy (%)
Selected model	Image input [64,64,3] 3x (2D Conv, BN, 2 × 2 MaxPooling) Flatten, 2x FC [128], Dp [0.2], FC [3]	2D Conv	**32** **32** **64**	3.98 MB	340,835	95.77
		Max Pooling	**6 x 6 x 64** **31 x 31 x 32** **14 x 14 x 32**			
Proposed model V2	Image input [64,64,3] 3x (2D Conv, BN, 2 × 2 MaxPooling) Flatten, 2x FC [128], FC [3]	2D Conv	**32** **32** **128**	5.42 MB	700,547	95.77
		Max Pooling	**31 x 31 x 32** **14 x 14 x 64** **6 x 6 x 128**			
Proposed model V3	Image input [64,64,1] 3x (2D Conv, BN, 2 × 2 MaxPooling) Flatten, 2x FC [128], Dp [0.2], FC [3]	2D Conv	**32** **32** **64**	3.98 MB	340,259	95.5
		Max Pooling	**31 x 31 x 32** **14 x 14 x 32** **6 x 6 x 64**			

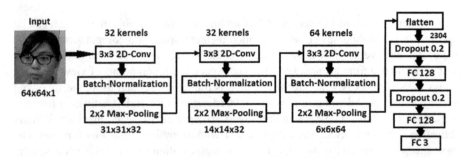

Fig. 2. Proposed CNN architecture

In the training phase, we introduced dropout with dropout rate 0.2 in the first two FC layers to avoid overfitting. As shown in Fig. 2, after each 2D-Conv layer, Batch Normalization process is performed, which improves the training and test accuracy.

3 Experimental Results

3.1 Dataset

To evaluate the proposed system, we used the NTHU-DDD dataset [13], in which 36 subjects of different ethnic participate under five different conditions, which are with and without glasses under normal illumination, use of sunglasses under normal illumination, with and without glasses under infrared illumination (IR). We used four conditions from five, excluding video frames with sunglasses, because in the proposed system, the visibility of the driver's eyes is indispensable for the drowsiness detection. The duration of each video is approximately 1.5 min, and the size of each frame is 640 × 480 pixels. From the video frames provided the NTHU-DDD, we constructed training and test datasets according to driver's state, Alert, Drowsiness and Distraction. Then we selected in total 4,800 video frames, which are composed by 1,600 frames with alert, 1,600 frames with drowsiness and 1,600 frames with distraction. Figure 3 shows some examples of the video frames used in training process, in which the frames in first, second and third row belong to "Alert", "Drowsiness" and "Distraction", respectively. And each column indicates different condition, from the first to last column: normal illumination without glasses, normal illumination with glasses, IR illumination without glasses and IR illumination with glasses. It is worth to mention that number of frames of all subsets is same, avoiding data imbalance problem.

Fig. 3. Some video frames used in training phase of the proposed system.

3.2 Performance of Proposed System

The detection accuracy of the proposed system is evaluated globally and in each one of four different conditions: without glasses under normal illumination, with glasses under normal illumination, without glasses under IR illumination and with glasses under IR illumination. Table 2 shows the performance of proposed system under four different conditions which cover almost all driving conditions.

Table 2. Performance of proposed system

Condition	Detection accuracy (%)
Without glasses under normal illumination	96.67
With glasses under normal illumination	95.83
Without glasses under IR illumination	95.91
With glasses under IR illumination	94.67
Global performance	95.77

From the Table 1, we can observe that the proposed system provides the best accuracy in the condition that the driver without glasses is driving under normal illumination, and the worst accuracy in the condition that the driver with glasses is driving in the night and his/her face video frames are taken by IR camera. However, the performance difference between the best condition and the worst condition is only 2%. The global performance of the proposed system is approximately 95.77%.

Figure 4 shows confusion matrices under four different conditions. Figures 4(a)–(d) present confusion matrices of "without glasses under normal illumination", "with glasses under normal illumination", "without glasses under IR illumination", and "with glasses under IR illumination", respectively. The more frequent confusion occurs between the state "Alert" and "Drowse".

3.3 Performance of Finetuned Off-the-Shelf CNNs

In many driver's drowsiness detection systems, some off-the-shelf CNNs, such as MobileNet, VGG16 and ResNet, with transfer learning technique are used their own private dataset [8, 9]. Therefore, to realize a fair comparison of the proposed system, we realized finetuning of five off-the-shelf CNNs to solve our problem. The finetuning is a technique that adjust the connection weights from certain layer to the last FC layer of the CNN to solve a specific problem, in our case driver's drowsiness and distraction detection. This technique is effective, when the size of dataset is relatively small and the task is an image classification, because some earlier frozen layers that dedicate to extract elemental features of images can be used without training process. Five CNNs that we

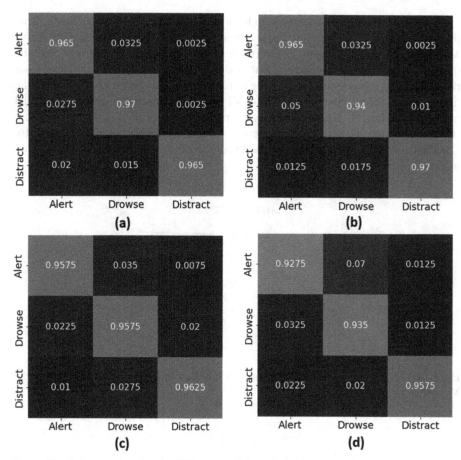

Fig. 4. Confusion matrices in four different conditions. (a) without glasses under normal illumination, (b) with glasses under normal illumination, (c) without glasses under IR illumination and (d) with glasses under IR illumination.

finetuned are MobileNet-V2 [14], VGG16 [11], ResNet-50V2 [15], InceptionV3 [18], Xception [19]. The MobileNet-V2 was designed to perform well in the mobile devices, reducing number of connection weights while keeping good performance. The VGG16 repeats module composed by two 3 × 3 Conv2D, and Pooling. The depth of this CNN is relatively small; however, number of connection weight is huge. The ResNet-50V2 is one of the ResNet classes, which was designed to avoid gradient vanishing problem in the deeper CNN, introducing residual module. The InceptionV3 is composed by several inception modules, which apply different kernel size to input data in parallel. The Xception has similar concept with that of InceptionV3, but inception module of the Xception contains larger number of CNNs.

To obtain an optimum finetuned model of each CNN, we unfreeze gradually from the last FC layer to earlier layers (layers close to the input layer). For example, in the MobileNet-V2, which contains 17 inverted residual modules, so we unfreeze from the final FC layer to earlier inverted residual modules to obtain an optimum model for our task. Figure 5 shows relationship between test accuracy and unfrozen modules. From the figure, we can observe that the MobileNet-V2 finetuned from the third inverted residual module to the last FC layer provides better performance. In the same manner, Fig. 6 shows the relationship between test accuracy and finetuned unfrozen layers of VGG16. Consecutively, other three CNNs are finetuned using the same manner to get optimum models.

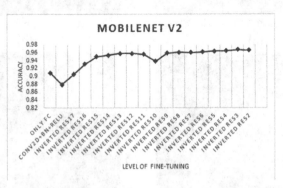

Fig. 5. Relationship between accuracy and start unfrozen inverted residual modules of the MobileNet-V2

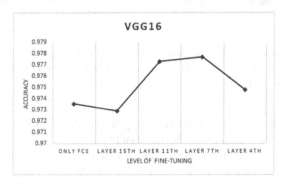

Fig. 6. Relationship between accuracy and start unfrozen layers in VGG16

Table 3 shows comparison results among the proposed system and five finetuned CNNs. We compare not only accuracy but also several important aspects for its implementation in the mobile device.

Table 3. Performance comparison

Model	Accuracy	Input Image size	Model size (MB)	Total params.	Operation speed (fps)	
					Mediapipe	V&J
Proposed	**0.9577**	**64 × 64**	**3.98**	**341,091**	**22**	**21**
MobileNetV2 [14]	0.9675	64 × 64	10.30	2,590,083	17	16
VGG16 [11]	0.9777	64 × 64	56.80	14,850,179	15	16
ResNet50V2 [15]	0.9760	64 × 64	92.50	24,116,419	14	13
InceptionV3 [18]	0.9600	75 × 75	84.50	21,938,275	13	12
Xception [19]	0.9713	64 × 64	81.90	21,390,187	16	12

From Table 3, the proposed system can operate 22 frames per second using Mediapipe face detector and 21 frames per second using Viola and Jones face detector algorithm. This fast operation speed is very important for real-time implementation, although the detection accuracy is slightly lower, for example, 0.03% lower than InceptionV3 and 2% lower than VGG16. In the required memory space to implement in the mobile device, the proposed system only requires 4 MB, which is approximately 2.6 times smaller than MobileNet-V2 and 23 times smaller than ResNet-50V2. This favorable specification of the proposed system makes possible a real-time operation in the mobile devices with limited memory space and computational power. We implemented the proposed system in two smartphones, which are Motorola Moto-One and Samsung S22 FE, operating 21 and 14 frames per second, respectively. The minimum requirements of smartphone for implementation of the proposed algorithm are operating system Android version 8 or above and the camera resolution is more than 5M pixels/inch.

4   Conclusions

In this paper, we proposed a CNN-based driver's drowsiness and distraction detection system. The principal objective of this work is that the system operates in real-time in a compact mobile device with limitation memory space and computational power. To this end, we selected two face detection algorithms with lowest computational complexity, which are Viola-Jones face detector and MediaPipe Face detector. As the CNN-based classifier, after several evaluations we selected most appropriate CNN architecture from the following points of view: detection accuracy, operation speed and required memory space. The proposed CNN-based system is evaluated using NTHU-DDD dataset, obtaining 95.77% of global accuracy. The experimental results shown that the proposed system is robust to the different illumination condition and use of glasses or not. The difference between the best accuracy (96.67%) under normal illumination without glasses, and the worst one (94.67%) under IR illumination with glasses is only 2%. The proposed system was compared with five finetuned off-the-shelf CNNs, which are MobileNet-V2, VGG16, ResNet-50V2, InceptionV3 and Xception. Although the accuracy of these CNNs is slightly better than the proposed one, this difference is not critical, because in the video operation small difference of accuracy in each frame can be absorbed in the total performance. Besides that, these CNNs require a large memory space to operate, and the operation speed decreases 23–40% compared with the proposed one. For example, the operation speed is 16 fps in Xception compared with 22 fps in the proposed system. The limitation shown by the finetuned CNNs makes difficult for their implementation in the mobile device. We implemented the proposed system in smartphones, providing frame rate with 21 frames/sec, which allows a real-time operation.

We consider the implementation of the proposed system in the wide range of the mobile devices and its performance evaluation in real driving condition as a near future work.

References

1. Facts and Stats. http://drowsydriving.org/about/facts-and-atats/. Accessed 30 Jan 2022
2. Chacon-Murguia, M., Prieto-Resendiz, C.: Detecting driver drowsiness: a survey of system designs and technology. IEEE Consum. Electron. Mag. **4**(4), 107–119 (2015)
3. Páez, M., Abarca, E.: Tools for security in movements, Predictive models of driver's drowsiness. https://imt.mx/resumen-boletines.html?IdArticulo=449&IdBoletin=168. Accessed 30 Jan 2022
4. Wang, J., Zhu, S., Gong, Y.: Driving safety monitoring using semisupervised learning on time series data. IEEE Trans. Intell. Transp. Syst. **11**(3), 728–737 (2010)
5. Wu, B., Chen, Y., Yeh, C., Li, Y.: Reasoning-based framework for driving safety monitoring using driving event recognition. IEEE Trans. Intell. Transp. Syst. **14**(3), 1231–1241 (2013)
6. Kokonogi, A., Michail, E., Chouvarda, I., Maglaveras, N.: A study of heart rate and brain system complexity and their interaction in sleep-deprived subjects. In: Proceeding on Computational Cardiology, pp. 969–971 (2008)
7. Zhang, C., Wang, H., Fu, R.: Automated detection of driver fatigue based on entropy and complexity measures. IEEE Trans. Intell. Transp. Syst. **15**(1), 168–177 (2014)
8. Zhao, G., He, Y., Yang, H., Tao, Y.: Research on fatigue detection based on visual features. IET Image Process. **16**, 1–20 (2020)
9. Phan, A., Nguyen, N., Trieu, T., Phan, T.: An efficient approach for detecting driver drowsiness based on deep learning. Appl. Sci. **11**, 8441 (2021)
10. Flores-Monroy, J., Nakano-Miyatake, M., Perez-Meana, H., Sanchez-Perez, G.: Visual-based real time driver drowsiness detection system using CNN. In: Proceedings of International Conference on Electrical Engineering, Computing Science and Automatic Control, IEEE, Mexico City, Mexico (2021)
11. Simonyan, K., Zisserman, A.: Very deep convolutional networks for large-scale image recognition. In: International Conference on Learning Representations (ICLR), San Diego (2015)
12. Flores, M., Armingo, J., De la Escalera, A., Elissa, K.: A. Real-time warning system for driver drowsiness detection using visual information. J. Intell. Rob. Syst. C. **69**(2), 103–125 (2010)
13. Weng, C., Lai, Y., Lai, S.: Driver drowsiness detection via a hierarchical temporal deep belief network. In: Proceedings of the Asian Conference on Computer Vision, pp. 117–133. IEEE, Taipei, Taiwan (2016)

14. Sandler, M., Howard, A., Zhu, M., Zhmoginov, A., Chen, L.: MobileNetV2: inverted residuals and linear bottlenecks. In: Proceedings the IEEE Conference on Computer Vision and Pattern Recognition, pp. 4510–4520. IEEE, Salt Lake City (2018)
15. He,. K., Zhang, X., Ren, S., Sun, J.: Deep residual learning for image recognition. In: Proceedings of the IEEE Computer Society Conference on Computer Vision and Pattern Recognition, pp. 770–778. IEEE, Las Vegas (2016)
16. Viola, P., Jones, M.: Robust real-time object detection. In: Proceedings of the 2nd International Workshop on Statistical and Computation Theories of Vision – Modeling, Learning, Computing and Sampling, p. 25 (2001)
17. Bazarevsky, V., Kartynnik, Y., Vakunov, A., Raveendran, K., Grundmann, M.: BlazeFace: sub-millisecond neural face detection on mobile GPUs. In: Proceedings of Computer Vision & Pattern Recognition (2019)
18. Szegedy, C., et al.: Going deeper with convolutions. In: Proceedings of the IEEE Conference on Computer Vision and Pattern Recognition, pp. 1–9, IEEE, Boston (2015)
19. Chollet, F.: Xception: deep learning with Depthwise separable convolutions. In: Proceedings of the IEEE Conference on Computer Vision and Pattern Recognition, pp. 1800–1807, IEEE, Honolulu (2017)
20. Chen, W., et al.: YOLO-face: a real-time face detector. Vis. Comput. 37(4), 805–13 (2021)

3D Convolutional Neural Network to Enhance Small-Animal Positron Emission Tomography Images in the Sinogram Domain

Leandro José Rodríguez Hernández[1]($\boxtimes$) ,
Humberto de Jesús Ochoa Domínguez[1] , Osslan Osiris Vergara Villegas[1] ,
Vianey Guadalupe Cruz Sánchez[1] , Juan Humberto Sossa Azuela[2] ,
and Javier Polanco González[1]

[1] Instituto de Ingeniería y Tecnología, Universidad Autónoma de Ciudad Juárez,
Ciudad Juárez, Mexico
al194726@alumnos.uacj.mx,
{hochoa,overgara,vianey.cruz,javier.polanco}@uacj.mx
[2] Instituto Politécnico Nacional, Centro de Investigación en Computación,
Laboratorio de Robótica y Mecatrónica, México City, Mexico

Abstract. In this work, we propose a three dimensional (3D) convolutional neural network (CNN) to enhance sinograms acquired from a small-animal positron emission tomography (PET) scanner. The network consists of three convolutional layers created with 3D filters of sizes 9, 3, and 5, respectively. We extracted 15250 3D patches from low- and high-count sinograms to build the low- and high-resolution pairs for training. After training and prediction, the enhanced sinogram is reconstructed using the ordered subset expectation maximization (OSEM) algorithm. The results revealed that the proposed network improved the spillover ratio and the uniformity of the standard NU4-2008 phantom up to 8% and 75%, respectively.

Keywords: Positron emission tomography · Convolutional neural network · Sinogram · Image enhancement

1 Introduction

Positron emission tomography (PET) is a noninvasive technique to acquire images of the metabolic activity of the body. The main fields of application are oncology [1] and neurology [2]. PET combines nuclear medicine and biochemical analysis by using a radiotracer composed of a small dose of radioactive material, injected on the patient before the scan, to interact mainly with the ill cells during a time frame. For cancer studies, the radiotracer is the fluorodeoxyglucose (F^{18}), which decays by a neutrino and a positron ($\beta+$) with a mean lifetime of about $109\,\mathrm{min}$.

O. O. Vergara-Villegas et al. (Eds.): MCPR 2022, LNCS 13264, pp. 94–104, 2022.
https://doi.org/10.1007/978-3-031-07750-0_9

The positrons emitted by the radiotracer annihilate with an electron in the body, producing two high-energy photons that travel in opposite directions. These events are counted upon reaching the scanner's detectors within a time window. The annihilation point is ideally located on a straight line, known as the line of response (LOR) connecting a pair of detectors. The detected event might not be a true event because the pair of photons inside the body do not always travel straight. Therefore, the photons could be deviated, producing scattered events. Also, two detected photons could come from different annihilation points. This produces random events, which are the main sources of degradation. Randoms introduce noise. Besides, the reduced acquisition time, the small dose of F^{18}, and the Poisson noise involved in the counting process result in degraded reconstructed images that negatively affect the medical diagnoses [3].

In this paper, we propose a three-dimensional (3D) convolutional neural network (CNN) to enhance PET sinograms, as a volume, acquired with a MicroPET Focus 120 scanner. The main contributions of the paper are the following:

1. We introduce a shallow 3D CNN capable of increasing the counts of sinogram from a small-animal scanner.
2. We show that processing the sinogram as a volume instead of independent 2D slices, improves the quality of the reconstructed image.

The paper is organized as follows: In Sect. 2, the state of the art is presented. Section 3 presents the main concepts related to the topic and the proposed method. In Sect. 4, we show the results of the experimentation. Finally, the conclusions are presented in Sect. 5.

2   State of the Art

In the past work, a number of techniques have been proposed to solve the problem of poor quality of reconstructed PET images. Conventional approaches include processing algorithms after reconstruction [4], anatomically guided [5] and magnetic resonance imaging (MRI) algorithms [6]. Although these methods try to minimize the noise, loss of spatial resolution is still observed. In other works like [7] the researches have applied different techniques, such as a term of Tikhonov or a hybrid regularization term, to regularize the solution. Although this approach improves the image quality, the results are based on multiple images and the methods are applied after reconstructing the image.

Recently, artificial intelligence algorithms have been proposed in the area of medical image reconstruction and enhancement. Most of the research focus on the reconstructed images. They propose to use trained networks with pairs of low resolution and high resolution images [8]. The high resolution images are obtained from an acquisition with a modern ultra high definition scanner and degraded to obtain the low resolution version. Other authors incorporate into the network training, anatomical information obtained from a computer tomography (CT) or MRI scanner [9], arguing that this information is helpful for estimating a more robust model and higher quality images. Another study [10] proposes to use the U-Net network with residual and concatenation connections to use a similar data set formed by PET and MRI images. Other network proposed is the deep auto-context CNN model [11], where the anatomical information is incorporated through T1-weighted MRI images. In [9], the authors used three variants of the U-Net network to reduce noise in the reconstructed images, relying on the MRI information.

Recent studies have focused on improving the sinogram instead of the reconstructed image. For example, in [12], the authors use Monte Carlo simulations and CNN to recover improved 2D sinograms from the low quality originals produced by simulated tomographs with large and small crystals. The increase of the computing power allows to address the problem of the low quality PET images in a 3D form, using deep learning systems. For example, in [13], a 3D variant of the U-Net network is proposed to reduce the noise of PET images from the brain and chest. Nevertheless, to our knowledge, no deep learning technique has been used to enhance the volume of sinograms from small animal scanners before image reconstruction.

2.1 The Importance of the Third Dimension

In CT, PET, and MRI techniques, the images are acquired in 3D space and processed as 2D slices. When using machine learning techniques, the volume is divided into 2D slices and passed to a model, trained to perform the desired task. The downside to this approach is that valuable information from the 3D context is lost. For example, if there is a lesion in a slice, there is highly likely information about a tumor in the adjacent slices because the adjacent interslice correlation is high [14]. In addition, the third dimension is not taken into account if the network is trained with a 2D slice. The main benefit of the 3D approach is that we capture contexts across the width, height, and depth simultaneously [15].

3   Materials and Methods

This section, describes the materials used and the methods related to the present work.

3.1   MicroPET Focus 120 Scanner and Nema NU4-2008 Phantom

The MicroPET Focus 120 scanner for preclinical studies is a cylindrical scanner with a diameter of 15 cm, 48 rings and an axial field of views of 7.6 cm [16]. Using the Gamos software [17], we simulated the MicroPET Focus 120 and the NEMA phantom [18], shown in Fig. 1 (a), to perform the experiments. The standard used was the NEMA NU4-2008 [18] that specifies the methodology to evaluate the performance of small-animal PET scanners. It is a cylindrical container with 50 mm in length and 15 mm in radius, divided into three regions identified as (1), (2), and (3). The uniform region (2) is 15 mm length. Region (1) contains five fillable rods of 20 mm length and 1, 2, 3, 4 and 5 mm in diameter, evenly distributed at a distance of 7 mm from the axial axis. In the last part (3), there are two cylindrical chambers, also called cold chambers, of 15 mm and 8 mm length in diameter, filled with air and water respectively, and uniformly distributed at 7.5 mm from the cylinder axis.

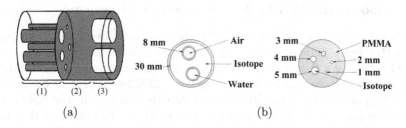

(a)   (b)

Fig. 1. Schematic views of (a) NEMA NU 4-2008 phantom, (b) dimensions in cross-sectional view

3.2   PET Sinogram

Figure 2(a) shows a scanner with the arrow pointing to the z axial axis. Figure 2(b) shows the acquisition of 2D sinograms. Figure 2(c) shows that the events detected by crystals, from different rings, are stored in a 3D matrix that represents the sinogram. This implies a substantial increase in the size and in the reconstruction time. The quality of reconstructed images is higher due to the greater amount of information available. Figure 2(d) shows a slice (2D) of a sinogram and Fig. 2(e) shows the sinogram as a volume. PET scanners acquire the data in 3D, as shown in Fig. 2(c).

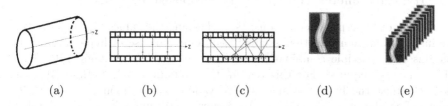

(a)   (b)   (c)   (d)   (e)

Fig. 2. Schematic representation of (a) a tomograph, (b) acquisition of 2D sinograms (one sinogram per ring detector), (c) acquisition of a sinogram (as volume), (d) 2D sinogram slice and (e) the sinogram.

3.3   Training Set

For the acquisition of sinograms, five phantoms of spheres and cylinders of diameters ranging from 0.5 mm to 5 mm were created using the scanner simulator. These objects were randomly distributed in the scanner. As a result, the low count (LC) and high count (HC) sinograms were generated with 10 million and 100 million events, respectively. The training set consisted of 15250 pairs of 3D patches of size $32 \times 32 \times 32$, selected randomly from the LC and HC sinograms, and the validation set consisted of 5000 pairs.

3.4   Proposed 3D CNN for PET Sinogram Enhancement

Figure 3 shows the proposed 3D CNN. The network has three layers. The input layer with a ReLU activation, extracts the 32-dimensional feature vectors using 32 filters of $9 \times 9 \times 9$ coefficients each. The second layer performs a nonlinear mapping to 16-dimensional feature vectors using 16 filters of $3 \times 3 \times 3$ coefficients each. We apply the ReLU ($\max(0, x)$) on the filter responses. The last layer is the transpose convolution layer (deconvolution) to recover the enhanced sinogram with linear activation and consists of one filter of $5 \times 5 \times 5$ coefficients.

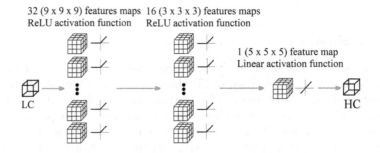

Fig. 3. Proposed 3D CNN.

3.5   Hyperparameter Tuning for the Proposed 3D CNN

The tuning of hyperparameters consists of choosing the values that achieve the maximum performance of the assigned task. Our universe of hyperparameters contains 6912 possible combinations. To test all possible variants, 27648 h of GPU time are required. For this reason, the random search method [19] was used to adjust the hyperparameters with validation loss monitored up to 50 epochs. The algorithm was allowed to perform 500 randomized trials. Table 1 shows a summary of the results of the hyperparameter tuning.

4   Experimental Results

The simulated NEMA phantom filled with F^{18} was used to acquire volumes of sinograms for testing. Following, we show the quantitative and visual results of the experiments.

Table 1. The results of hyperparameter tuning.

Parameter	Value
First convolutional layer	
Number of features maps	32
Kernel size	$9 \times 9 \times 9$
Activation function	ReLU
Second convolutional layer	
Number of features maps	16
Kernel size	$3 \times 3 \times 3$
Activation function	ReLU
Transpose convolutional layer	
Number of features maps	1
Kernel size	$5 \times 5 \times 5$
Activation function	Linear
Network training	
Loss function	Mean squared error (MSE)
Optimization algorithm	Adam
Learning rate	0.001
Batch size	32
Epochs	200

The spillover ratio (SOR) is the ratio of the average value of each cold chamber to the average of the hot uniform region. A volume of interest (VOI) of $6 \times 6 \times 15$ voxels was taken in the cold chambers. Table 2 shows the results of SOR and relative standard deviation (%STD) for the cavities filled with water and air. Figure 4 shows the maximum intentisity projections (MIPs) of the reconstructed images of the (a) LC sinogram, (b) the enhanced sinogram using the proposed method after reconstruction with OSEM [20], and (c) the profiles of the dotted lines (a) and (b). We can see that the proposed method increases the counts and preserves the edges.

Table 2. SOR and %STD measured in the cold chambers.

	Water chamber		Air chamber	
	SOR	%STD	SOR	%STD
Low count image	0.1071	150.2672	0.1764	115.64
Recovered image with the proposed method	**0.0988**	**37.9092**	**0.1693**	**28.9256**

A 15 × 15 × 15 voxels VOI was taken at the center of the uniform region to measure uniformity. The average activity concentration, the maximum and minimum values, and the percentage standard deviation are calculated and shown in Table 3. Figure 5 shows the MIPs of the (a) LC sinogram, (b) the enhanced sinogram using the proposed method after reconstruction with OSEM and (c) the profiles of the dotted lines in (a) and (b). We can see that in this region, the proposed method increases the counts, preserves the edges, and reduces the oscillation of the uniform region.

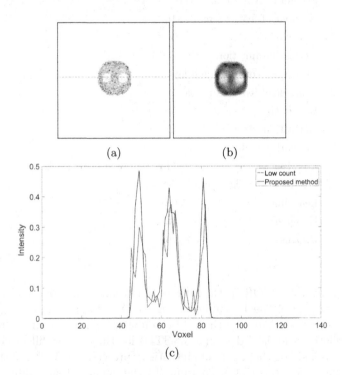

Fig. 4. MIPs of the transversal view for the chambers region in the simulated Nema phantom. (a) Original LC, (b) proposed method, (c) activity profiles of the cross-sections.

Table 3. Measures in the uniform region.

	Average	Max.	Min.	%STD
Low count image	0.0900	0.4992	0.0034	69.7008
Recovered image with the proposed method	0.2118	0.3531	0.0939	**15.6831**

Figure 6 shows the MIPs for the rods for the (a) LC sinogram and (b) the HC recovery sinogram by our method. Figure 6 (c), (d) and (e) show the profile along the 1 mm, 3 mm, and 5 mm rod in the axial direction, respectively.

The results obtained allow us to see that the proposed method applied to the 3D PET sinograms is able to improve the spillover ratio in the cold region, as shown in Table 2. In the water chamber, the SOR is improved by 8% and in the air chamber by 4%, allowing a better definition of the limits between the area of the radiotracer and the cold areas. Figures 4(a–b) visually show that when the LC sinograms are processed by our method, valuable information is recovered when compared against the standard reconstruction procedure. Figure 4(c) shows how our method increases contrast and reduces noise in the reconstructed images.

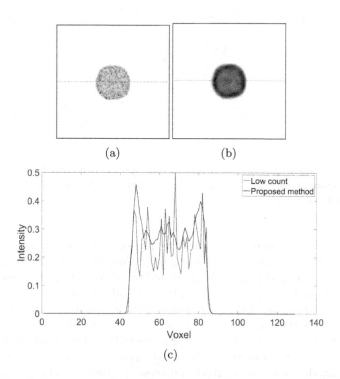

Fig. 5. MIPs of the transversal view for the uniform region in the simulated Nema phantom. (a) Original LC, (b) proposed method, (c) activity profiles of the cross-sections.

In the Nema standard, the central region of the phantom is used to measure uniformity. The greater the uniformity in the area, the better the visualization result. Uniformity is expressed as the relative standard deviation represented as a percentage (%STD). Table 3 shows that the %STD improves by 77% when sinogram is enhanced by our method. In the same way, the intensity profile of Fig. 5(c) shows how the variability is reduced with the proposed method. Uniformity measurements were also made in the cold chambers, which are reported in Table 2. Improvements in the %STD metric of approximately 75% were obtained.

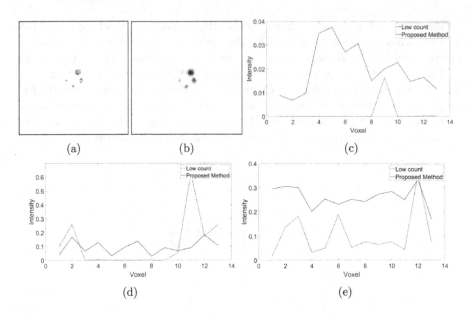

(a)   (b)   (c)

(d)   (e)

Fig. 6. MIPs of the transversal view for the rods region in the simulated Nema phantom. (a) Original LC, (b) proposed method, and axial profiles along the (c) 1-mm rod, (d) 3-mm rod and (e) 5-mm rod.

The volume containing the rods is useful for evaluating how small structures are recovered and visualized. Figures 6(a) and (b) show the reconstructed images corresponding to the LC sinogram and the result obtained by our method. Figure 6(c) shows that the network can recover and enhance the 1 mm structure compared to the original LC image. We can observe that the network recovers the 1 mm rod in the entire axial axis, while in the LC image, only one slice contains information of the 1 mm rod. Figures 6(d) and (e) show that the network recovers valuable information in the 3 mm and 5 mm rods. Figures 7(b) and (e) show that the proposed method manages to recover effective counts in the sinograms, while the LC sinograms (Figs. 7(a) and 7(d)) contain little information, after being processed by our method, useful information is recovered before reconstruction. As far as we know, there is no other similar network to process the volume of PET sinograms for small animals.

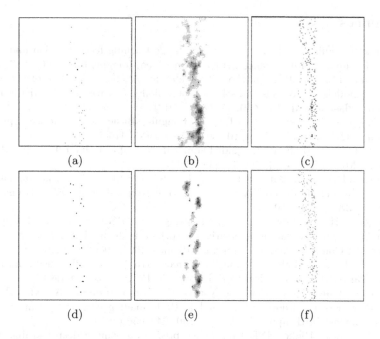

Fig. 7. Slices from the 3D sinogram. (a, d) Original LC sinograms, (b, e) corresponding enhanced sinogram with the proposed method, and (c, f) corresponding ground truth sinogram.

5   Conclusions

In this paper we propose a 3D convolutional neural network to enhance PET images in the sinogram domain. High count and their corresponding low count sinograms were generated. Patches of 32 × 32 × 32 were extracted from both pairs of sinograms to form the training sets. The images were reconstructed using the OSEM algorithm. The Nema NU4-2008 quality metrics and phantom were used to evaluate the results. In addition, an analysis of the profiles obtained from the MIPs of the reconstructed images was carried out. The results show that the proposed network increases the counts of sinograms in an orderly manner. This positively influences the quality of the reconstructed images. The increase of the SOR and %STD metrics means that more details were found and preserved in the reconstructed enhanced images. Although the proposed method is more computationally extensive than a 2D implementation, it is worth noting that a better estimation is achieved because the proposed method takes advantage of the intra-slice information. In future work, we will modify the network to increase the resolution of the recovered image and use measured data.

Acknowledgment. L. J. Rodríguez thanks the UACJ for the support provided and the CONACYT for the scholarship granted to pursue his doctoral studies.

H. Sossa thanks CONACYT and IPN for the economical support under funds: FORDECYT-PRONACES 6005 and SIP 20220226.

References

1. Kumar, A., Fulham, M., Feng, D., Kim, J.: Co-learning feature fusion maps from PET-CT images of lung cancer. IEEE Trans. Med. Imaging **39**(1), 204–217 (2020)
2. Klyuzhin, I.S., Fu, J.F., Shenkov, N., Rahmim, A., Sossi, V.: Use of generative disease models for analysis and selection of radiomic features in PET. IEEE Trans. Radiat. Plasma Med. Sci. **3**(2), 178–191 (2019)
3. Kanhaiyalal, A., Annah, S.: PET/CT Imaging, Basics and Practice. Springer, Cham (2021). https://doi.org/10.1007/978-3-030-75476-1
4. Arabi, H., Zaidi, H.: Spatially guided nonlocal mean approach for denoising of PET images. Med. Phys. **47**(4), 1656–1669 (2020)
5. Chan, C., Fulton, R., Barnett, R., Feng, D., Meikle, S.: Postreconstruction nonlocal means filtering of whole-body PET with an anatomical prior. IEEE Trans. Med. Imaging **33**(3), 636–650 (2014)
6. Zhang, J., He, X., Qing, L., Gao, F., Wang, B.: BPGAN: brain PET synthesis from MRI using generative adversarial network for multi-modal Alzheimer's disease diagnosis. Comput. Methods Programs Biomed. **217**, 106676 (2022)
7. Ren, X., Lee, S.: High-resolution image reconstruction for PET using local and non-local regularizations. Electron. Imaging **2017**(17), 174–178 (2017)
8. Chen, K., Gong, E., de Carvalho Macruz, F., Xu, J., Boumis, A., Khalighi, M.: Ultra-low-dose (18)f-florbetaben amyloid PET imaging using deep learning with multi-contrast MRI inputs. Radiology **290**, 649–656 (2019)
9. Liu, C., Qi, J.: Higher SNR PET image prediction using a deep learning model and MRI image. Phys. Med. Biol. **64**(11), 115004 (2019)
10. Xu, J., Gong, E., Pauly, J., Zaharchuk, G.: 200x low-dose PET reconstruction using deep learning. arXiv (2017). eprint arXiv:1712.04119
11. Xiang, L., et al.: Deep auto-context convolutional neural networks for standard-dose PET image estimation from low-dose PET/MRI. Neurocomputing **267**, 406–416 (2017)
12. Hong, X., Zan, Y., Weng, F., Tao, W., Peng, Q., Huang, Q.: Enhancing the image quality via transferred deep residual learning of coarse PET sinograms. IEEE Trans. Med. Imaging **37**(10), 2322–2332 (2018)
13. Lu, W., et al.: An investigation of quantitative accuracy for deep learning based denoising in oncological PET. Phys. Med. Biol. **64**(16), 5019 (2019)
14. Zhang, J., Xie, Y., Wang, Y., Xia, Y.: Inter-slice context residual learning for 3D medical image segmentation. IEEE Trans. Med. Imaging **40**(2), 661–672 (2021)
15. Bustin, A., et al.: Isotropic reconstruction of MRI images using 3D patch-based self-similarity learning. IEEE Trans. Med. Imaging **37**(8), 1932–1942 (2018)
16. Kim, J.S., et al.: Performance measurement of the microPET Focus 120 scanner. J. Nuclear Med. **48**, 1527–1535 (2007)
17. Al-Tuweity, J., et al.: GAMOS/GEANT4 simulation and comparison study of x-ray narrow-spectrum series at the national secondary standard dosimetry laboratory of morocco. Appl. Radiat. Isot. **175**, 109789 (2021)
18. National Electrical Manufacturers Association: Performance measurements of small animal positron emission tomographs. National Electrical Manufacturers Association, Rosslyn, VA (2008)
19. Bergstra, J., Bengio, Y.: Random search for hyper-parameter optimization. J. Mach. Learn. Res. **13**, 281–305 (2012)
20. Zhu, Y.M.: Ordered subset expectation maximization algorithm for positron emission tomographic image reconstruction using belief kernels. J. Med. Imaging **5**(4), 044005 (2018)

Learning Dendrite Morphological Neurons Using Linkage Trees for Pattern Classification

Samuel Omar Tovias-Alanis[1]([✉])(iD), Wilfrido Gómez-Flores[1](iD),
Gregorio Toscano-Pulido[1](iD), and Juan Humberto Sossa-Azuela[2,3](iD)

[1] Centro de Investigación y de Estudios Avanzados del IPN, Unidad Tamaulipas,
Ciudad Victoria, Tamaulipas, Mexico
samuel.tovias@cinvestav.mx, wgomez@cinvestav.mx
[2] Instituto Politécnico Nacional, Centro de Investigación en Computación,
07738 Mexico City, Mexico
[3] Tecnológico de Monterrey, Escuela de Ingeniería y Ciencias, Zapopan,
Jalisco, Mexico

Abstract. This article presents a Dendrite Morphological Neuron
model learned by Linkage Trees (LT-DMN). It is presented as an alternative to modern DMN model training approaches based on k-means
clustering that must tune the number of dendrites per class by defining
a k-value. Also, the k-means based methods have a problem of non-
reproducibility and, for each potential solution, they may present the
risk of falling into local minima. The LT-DMN algorithm selects the centroids from a deterministic hierarchical clustering, which builds a linkage
tree for each class of patterns. In addition, the simulated annealing algorithm is used to automatically fit a suitable cut-off point in the structure
of each tree that minimizes the classification error and the number of
dendrites. The proposed method is evaluated on nine synthetic data sets
and 17 real-world problems. The results reveal that the proposed method
is competitive or even better than seven DMN models from the literature. Furthermore, LT-DMN achieves low architectural complexity by
using few dendrites.

Keywords: Dendrite morphological neuron · Spherical dendrites ·
Linkage trees · Classification

1 Introduction

Dendrite Morphological Neurons (DMNs) are artificial neural models that
present two main characteristics: 1) dendrites are represented by a geometric
shape to cover the input space locally, and 2) the activation functions are defined
by the minimum (min) and maximum (max) functions [7]. Besides, a single
DMN can solve nonlinearly separable classification problems, unlike linear per-
ceptrons based on dot product, which require layered units to enable nonlinear
responses [6].

© The Author(s), under exclusive license to Springer Nature Switzerland AG 2022
O. O. Vergara-Villegas et al. (Eds.): MCPR 2022, LNCS 13264, pp. 105–115, 2022.
https://doi.org/10.1007/978-3-031-07750-0_10

DMN learning procedure distributes dendrites over the input space so that all the classes of patterns are adequately wrapped according to their distribution shape. A DMN learning algorithm is designed according to the dendrites' geometry, which can be boxes, ellipses, and spheres; all of them are defined by two parameters: location and spread [5].

The box-shaped dendrites are isooriented (i.e., their faces are parallel to Cartesian axes of the input space): the location is defined by the lowest extreme point, while the side lengths give the spread for each dimension. The divide-Hyperbox per Class (d-HpC) is a straightforward training method that splits an initial HpC solution into halves concerning all dimensions [8]. Then, the linear divide and conquer method (LDCM) performs the dHpC splittings recursively using a binary search. This method requires adjusting two hyperparameters: margin distance and tolerance error, tuned by the Differential Evolution (DE) algorithm [8].

Also, optimization-based methods have been used to train box-shaped DMNs. The Stochastic Gradient Descent (SGD) refines an initial solution defined by some heuristic like the dHpC method [10]. Another approach uses the DE algorithm to evolve the parameters of a population of DMNs using the genetic operators of crossover, mutation, and selection. The location and spread of every candidate solution in the population are codified into a real-valued vector [3].

The elliptical DMNs are trained using the k-means algorithm to distribute dendrites over the input space. The number of dendrites per class (i.e., clusters) is defined by a hill-climbing-like method until a tolerance error is reached. Therefore, a cluster centroid defines the dendrite location, whereas the corresponding covariance matrix determines its spread [2].

In the case of spherical DMNs, the k-means algorithm also defines the dendrites' location, while the spheres' radii stand for the dendrites' spread. Besides, the number of dendrites per class is automatically adjusted by the Simulated Annealing (SA) algorithm [4].

Recently, we demonstrated that DMN classification performance is improved by replacing the standard min and max functions with smoothed versions to soften the decision boundaries. Our first approach used box-shaped dendrites trained with LDCM, where DE tuned its hyperparameters and the smoothness factor [6]. Our second approach evaluated the three abovementioned geometries using smooth min and max functions. A framework called the Up-Down algorithm was used to adjust both the smoothness factor and the number of dendrites per class, where k-means defined dendrites' locations. The results revealed that spherical dendrites outperformed the other geometric shapes [5].

Notice that there is no standard algorithm to train DMN parameters; hence, there is still open the possibility to test other learning algorithms. Specially, we are interested in using Linkage Trees (LT), initially defined for hierarchical clustering, to overcome the non-reproducibility of k-means since it starts with random clusters; hence, it is prone to get trapped in local minima. Besides, DMN learning methods based on k-means require adjusting the number of dendrites per class by specifying the k-values. The tuning methods automatically search

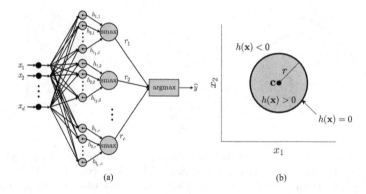

(a)   (b)

Fig. 1. (a) DMN topology based on spherical dendrites and smooth maximum function given by (1). (b) A spherical dendrite in $\mathbb{R}^2$ defined by centroid $\mathbf{c} = [c_1, c_2]$ and radius r, whose response is given by (2).

for an adequate number of dendrites, although for every potential solution, the k-means is run, risking falling into local minima. Contrarily, the algorithm for creating LT is deterministic and can be run once for each class of patterns. The number of dendrites per class can be adjusted by defining an adequate cut-off point in the hierarchy. We propose using a DMN based on spherical dendrites and the SA algorithm to adjust the LT's cut-off point per class and the smoothness factor of the smooth max function.

2 Proposed Approach

2.1 DMN Basics

Let $\mathbf{x} = [x_1, \ldots, x_d]$ be an input pattern in $\mathbb{R}^d$ associated with a class label $y \in \Omega = \{\omega_1, \ldots, \omega_c\}$, where c is the total number of classes. Moreover, a training set with n instances is denoted by $X = \{\mathbf{x}_1, \ldots, \mathbf{x}_n\}$, and the set $Y = \{y_1, \ldots, y_n\}$ contains the corresponding class labels for each training pattern in X.

Figure 1 shows the typical DMN topology with spheres representing dendrites in an $\mathbb{R}^d$ space, where each dendrite is labeled with the class of its enclosed training patterns during learning.

In addition, we use the smooth max function to soften decision boundaries. Let $\mathbf{u} = [u_1, \ldots, u_k]$ be an array with k real numbers; then, the smooth maximum is defined as [6]

$$\text{smax}(\mathbf{u}) = \sum_{i=1}^{k} \frac{\exp(\beta u_i)}{\sum_{j=1}^{k} \exp(\beta u_j)} u_i, \quad \text{with} \quad \beta > 0, \tag{1}$$

where β is the smoothness factor. If $\beta \to \infty$, then the smax function approximates to the conventional max function.

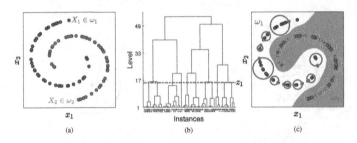

Fig. 2. (a) Nonlinearly separable data with two classes and 50 points per class. (b) Linkage tree of patterns in class ω_1. The dashed line is a cut-off level that creates a clustering. (c) Trained DMN where circles are dendrites obtained from clustering solutions obtained by cutting the linkage trees at level z_k, for $k = 1, 2$.

The classification flow of an input pattern is as follows. First, a dendrite response is triggered to determine whether $\mathbf{x}$ is inside or outside its coverage region. So, the jth dendrite response (with $j = 1, \ldots, l_k$) in the kth class (with $k = 1, \ldots, c$) is expressed as [5]

$$h_{j,k}(\mathbf{x}) = r_{j,k} - \|\mathbf{x} - \mathbf{c}_{j,k}\|, \tag{2}$$

where $\|\cdot\|$ is the Euclidean norm, $\mathbf{c}_{j,k} = [c_{1,j,k}, \ldots, c_{d,j,k}]$ is the sphere's centroid, and $r_{j,k} > 0$ is its corresponding radius. Next, the maximum function activates the response of a group of dendrites for the kth class, which is expressed as [6]

$$r_k(\mathbf{x}) = \operatorname*{smax}_{j=1,\ldots,l_k} \left(h_{j,k}(\mathbf{x}) \right). \tag{3}$$

Finally, the argmax function outputs the predicted class label $\hat{y} \in \Omega$ as [6]

$$\hat{y}(\mathbf{x}) = \operatorname*{arg\,max}_{k=1,\ldots,c} \left(r_k(\mathbf{x}) \right). \tag{4}$$

2.2 Linkage Trees

Let X_k be the set of instances in class ω_k obtained from the training set X with $k = 1, \ldots, c$ classes. The linkage tree of X_k is the hierarchical cluster tree (also known as dendrogram) of its n_k instances using an agglomerative hierarchical clustering algorithm: each instance is a cluster at the beginning, and clusters are merged in every iteration using a distance metric, commonly the Euclidean distance. The linkage tree hierarchy for class ω_k has $n_k - 1$ levels. Here, the linkage trees per class are constructed using the complete linkage algorithm, which uses the farthest distance of a pair of objects to define inter-cluster distance [9].

Figure 2(a) shows an example of nonlinearly separable data with two classes and 50 instances per class. Additionally, Fig. 2(b) shows the linkage tree of patterns in class ω_1, which has 49 levels. Notice that the cut-off point (dashed line) creates ten clusters in X_1, each one related to a dendrite (i.e., a sphere) that covers class ω_1, as shown in Fig. 2(c).

2.3   Dendrite Parameters

Let $\mathbf{C}_k = \{C_{1,k}, \ldots, C_{l_k,k}\}$ be a clustering solution formed by a cut-off point z_k on the linkage tree of X_k. Then, the centroid of the jth hypersphere in the kth class is given by the mean point in the cluster $C_{j,k}$:

$$\mathbf{c}_{j,k} = \frac{1}{n_{j,k}} \sum_{\mathbf{x}_i \in C_{j,k}} \mathbf{x}_i, \tag{5}$$

where $n_{j,k}$ is the number of patterns in the cluster. On the other hand, the radius of the hypersphere is the distance of the farthest point in cluster $C_{j,k}$ to its centroid $\mathbf{c}_{j,k}$:

$$r_{j,k} = \max_{\mathbf{x}_i \in C_{j,k}} \left(\| \mathbf{x}_i - \mathbf{c}_{j,k} \| \right). \tag{6}$$

Figure 2(c) shows the dendrites covering the class distributions in Fig. 2(a). The dendrite parameters were calculated with (5) and (6). Besides, the decision regions obtained with (4) are also shown. Notice the softened decision boundaries obtained by the smooth max function in (1).

2.4   Automatic DMN Tuning Based on SA

Simulated Annealing (SA) is a stochastic local search method for global optimization, allowing gradual convergence to a near-optimal solution [1]. Here, SA is used to automatically tune the proposed DMN architecture, as summarized in Algorithm 1 [4]. An initial solution is randomly initialized and is composed of two parts. The first one codifies c cut-off levels of integer values in the range $z_k \in [1, n_k - 1]$, where n_k is the number of patterns in the kth class. The second part codifies the smoothness factor in the range $\beta \in [0.1, 30.0]$. Hence, a potential solution is represented by the vector $\mathbf{s} = [z_1, \ldots, z_c, \beta]$. In addition, a perturbation function creates a new solution $\mathbf{s}'$ by randomly altering the entries of $\mathbf{s}$ in the ranges mentioned above with a probability of 0.5. Therefore, for each variable, a random number taken from $\mathcal{U}(0, 1)$ greater than 0.5 indicates that the corresponding entry value will increase, otherwise decrease. In this case, the cut-off levels and the smooth factor change in steps of 1 and 0.01, respectively.

The cost function is devised to minimize the classification error and the number of dendrites and is defined by the weighted sum

$$f(\mathbf{s}) = w \left(\frac{1}{n} \sum_{i=1}^{n} I\left(y_i \neq \hat{y}_i \right) \right) + (1 - w) \left(\frac{n_d - c}{n - c} \right), \tag{7}$$

where $w \in [0, 1]$ weights the importance of each term. In the first term, $I(\cdot)$ denotes the 0–1 loss function to measure the error rate, where $\hat{y}$ is given by (4). In this case, the training set was used to evaluate the cost function, and the validating set was employed to test the accepted solution and update the best DMN architecture. The second term reduces the number of dendrites n_d in the model, normalized in the range $[0, 1]$. Notice that the minimum number

---

Algorithm 1. Automatic DMN tuning based on SA.

input: Training dataset $\{X_1, \ldots, X_c\}$; Linkage trees per class $\{LT_1, \ldots, LT_c\}$
$t \leftarrow 5$ // Initial temperature
$s \leftarrow s_0 = [z_1, \ldots, z_c, \beta]$ // Generate initial solution randomly
Train DMN using $\{X_1, \ldots, X_c\}$, $\{LT_1, \ldots, LT_c\}$, and initial solution s
$s^* \leftarrow s$, $f^* \leftarrow f(s)$ // Save best solution
repeat
   for $i \leftarrow 1$ **to** 50 **do** // Iterations at temperature t
      Generate a new solution s' by perturbing s randomly
      Train DMN using $\{X_1, \ldots, X_c\}$, $\{LT_1, \ldots, LT_c\}$, and perturbed solution s'
      $\Delta f \leftarrow f(s') - f(s)$ // Compute cost difference
      if $\Delta f < 0$ **then**
         $s \leftarrow s'$, $f(s) \leftarrow f(s')$ // Accept the new solution
      else
         if $\exp(-\Delta f/t) > \mathrm{rand}(0,1)$ **then**
            $s \leftarrow s'$, $f(s) \leftarrow f(s')$ // Accept with some probability
      if $f(s) < f^*$ **then**
         $s^* \leftarrow s$, $f^* \leftarrow f(s)$ // Save best solution so far
   $t \leftarrow 0.99 \cdot t$ // Decrease temperature
until $t < 1 \times 10^{-6}$
return s^*

Table 1. Synthetic (S) and real-world (R) datasets with different classes c and dimensions d. The training and test patterns are n and n_t, respectively.

ID	Dataset name	c	d	n	n_t	ID	Dataset name	c	d	n	n_t
S_1	Concentric	3	2	1455	162	R_5	Credit Approval	2	15	587	66
S_2	Horseshoes	2	2	1350	150	R_6	Dermatology	6	34	322	36
S_3	Moons	2	2	1350	150	R_7	Echocardiogram Data	2	9	55	6
S_4	Ripley	2	2	1000	250	R_8	Heart Disease Cleveland	2	13	267	30
S_5	Three Gaussians	3	2	1440	360	R_9	Iris Data	3	4	135	15
S_6	Three Spirals	3	2	1350	150	R_{10}	Mice Protein Expression	8	80	497	55
S_7	Two Gaussians	2	2	960	240	R_{11}	Ozone Level Detection	2	72	1664	184
S_8	Two Spirals	2	2	1350	150	R_{12}	Parkinsons Dataset	2	22	175	20
S_9	XOR Problem	2	2	1260	140	R_{13}	SPECTF Heart Dataset	2	44	241	26
R_1	BCWD	2	30	512	57	R_{14}	Seeds	3	7	179	20
R_2	BCWO	2	9	614	69	R_{15}	Statlog	7	18	2079	231
R_3	Car Evaluation	4	6	1555	173	R_{16}	Vowel	11	11	891	99
R_4	Climate Model	2	18	486	54	R_{17}	Wine	3	13	160	18

of dendrites is c, that is, one dendrite per class, and the maximum number of dendrites is n, that is, one dendrite per pattern. The proposed cost function aims to improve generalization while reducing the DMN architecture complexity.

3   Experimental Setup

Nine synthetic and 17 real-world datasets were used to evaluate the LT-DMN$_w$ algorithm and the comparative methods. The real-world datasets were taken from the UCI Machine Learning Database Repository[1] and present a different number of classes $c = \{2, \ldots, 11\}$ and dimensions $d = \{4, \ldots, 80\}$.

Also, the synthetic datasets were employed to visualize the decision boundaries generated by the proposed approach and the comparative techniques.

Table 1 summarizes the characteristics of the datasets used in this study. The datasets were normalized in the range $[-1, 1]$ with the min-max method, and divided with stratification into training (90%) and test (10%) sets.

We also evaluated the impact of the weight value in the cost function given in (7). Specifically, for $w = 0.5$, where both terms have the same importance, and for $w = 1.0$, in which reducing the number of dendrites is not considered but only minimizes the classification error. So, given these considerations, the proposed approach will be identified as LT-DMN$_{0.5}$ and LT-DMN$_{1.0}$.

Moreover, seven DMN approaches in the literature were considered for comparison purposes: SA-DSN [4], DE-DMN [3], SGD-DMN, LDCM [8], DEN [2], DE-SDMN [6], and UP-DOWN [5]. All of them were compared in terms of classification accuracy (ACC) and DMN complexity given by the number of dendrites (ND).

All the algorithms were developed in MATLAB 2021b (MathWorks, Massachusetts), and the source codes are available upon the request to the authors.

4   Results

Figure 3 shows the results of the DMN methods regarding classification accuracy measured on the training and test sets and the number of selected dendrites.

Concerning the accuracy measured on the test set, LT-DMN$_{0.5}$ attained the second-highest value (ACC $= 0.96$), while the DEN algorithm reached the best result (ACC $= 0.97$). Nevertheless, DEN obtained ACC < 0.7 for three datasets, whereas LT-DMN$_{0.5}$ attained ACC > 0.7 for all the datasets, indicating more consistency than DEN. Contrarily, SGD-DMN achieved the lowest classification performance (ACC $= 0.86$). Furthermore, the remaining methods obtained the same accuracy (ACC $= 0.95$), but only LDCM got a slightly lower value (ACC $= 0.94$).

The accuracy of the training set was also measured, aiming to determine the overfitting. In general, all the DMN models results are almost similar between training and set test sets (i.e., the boxplots of both sets are similar). However, it is noticeable that LDCM is prone to overfitting because the training accuracy is much higher than test accuracy.

Additionally, the Wilcoxon rank-sum test ($\alpha = 0.05$) was performed to determine statistical differences between the proposed approach and its counterparts.

---

[1] http://archive.ics.uci.edu/ml.

Table 2 shows the p-values regarding the classification performance. Remarkably, the proposed method was statistically similar to all the DMN models, except SGD-DMN, which was outperformed by the proposed approach.

Table 2. Wilcoxon rank sum test results. The rows show the p-values regarding the classification performance. In bold, $p < 0.05$. Symbols denote: $(=)$ statistically equal, and $(-)$ statistically inferior respect to the LT-DMN$_w$ method.

	SA-DSN	DE-DMN	SGD-DMN	LDCM	DEN	DE-SDMN	UP-DOWN
LT-DMN$_{0.5}$	0.88 (=)	0.89 (=)	**0.03 (−)**	0.63 (=)	0.69 (=)	0.90 (=)	0.65 (=)
LT-DMN$_{1.0}$	0.33 (=)	0.48 (=)	0.10 (=)	0.81 (=)	0.34 (=)	0.56 (=)	0.28 (=)

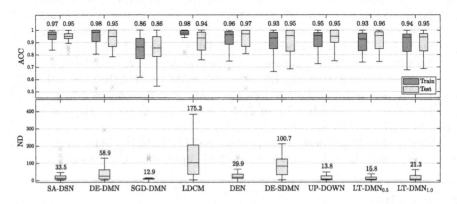

Fig. 3. Results of the DMN methods evaluated on the 26 datasets. The upper graphic shows the pairs of box plots of classification accuracy measured on the training and test sets. The lower graphic presents the number of dendrites of each DMN model. Above each box are the median (upper graphic) and the average (lower graphic) values.

Figure 4 shows the decision regions generated by the DMN methods on the synthetic datasets. Notably, the proposed LT-DMN$_{0.5}$ reached the highest classification accuracy (ACC $= 0.97$) and tied with SA-DSN, DE-DMN, DEN, DE-SDMN, and UP-DOWN. Also, LT-DMN$_{1.0}$ attained the same performance as LDCM (ACC $= 0.95$). On the other hand, SGD-DMN achieved the lowest accuracy (ACC $= 0.84$). Notice the effect of the smooth activations functions in DE-SDMN, UP-DOWN, and LT-DMN approaches, where the decision boundaries are softer than the DMN models that use conventional min and max functions.

Regarding the number of dendrites, a low architectural complexity in the DMN model is desirable to reduce the computational cost in the prediction task and build decision boundaries that enable a high generalization. In this context, SGD-DMN achieved the lowest complexity (ND $= 12.9$), followed by UP-DOWN (ND $= 13.8$). Notably, the two variants of the proposed LT-DMN$_w$ reached the third and fourth lower values (ND < 22), respectively. Also, SA-DSN and DEN

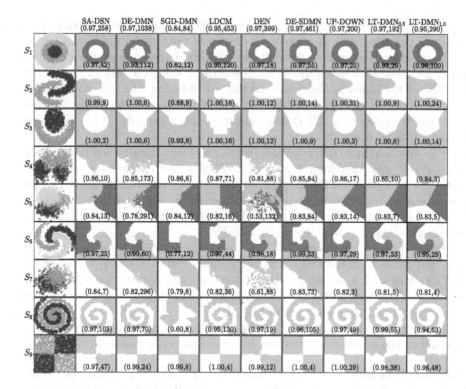

Fig. 4. Decision regions obtained by DMN methods trained on synthetic datasets. In parenthesis, the accuracy measured on the test data and the number of selected dendrites (ACC, ND). Below the name of each method, in parenthesis, the median accuracy and the total sum of dendrites (ACC, Σ).

achieved models with low complexity (ND < 34). On the contrary, LDCM got the DMN models with the largest number of dendrites (ND $= 175.3$).

In particular to synthetic datasets, SGD-DMN obtained the smallest value of selected dendrites ($\Sigma = 84$); however, for S_1, S_2, and S_8, it built decision regions with poor generalization on the test set. Contrarily, DE-DMN got the models with the highest complexity ($\Sigma = 1038$). Notably, the proposed LT-DMN$_{0.5}$ reached the second-lowest value ($\Sigma = 192$), and LT-DMN$_{1.0}$ was more complex ($\Sigma = 290$) since the cost function used a unit weight value to dismiss reducing the number of dendrites.

5   Conclusions and Future Work

This paper introduced a method for training DMN models based on linkage trees and spherical dendrites. The proposed algorithm was modeled as an optimization problem to minimize the classification error and the architectural complexity given by the number of dendrites in the model. The simulated annealing algorithm was selected to automatically adjust the cut-off levels of c linkage trees (i.e., one per class) and the smoothness factor of the smooth max function.

In this case, the number of dendrites per class is determined from a cut-off point using the LT's structure, which allows overcoming the non-reproducibility problem of the k-means algorithm and the risk of falling into local optima. This behavior can be observed in SA-DSN and DEN models, which obtained outliers with less accuracy than LT-DMN, indicating the possibility of having gotten trapped in local optimum.

The proposed approach attained a similar accuracy distribution on the training and test sets; therefore, it avoided overfitting and reached a good generalization performance. Furthermore, seven DMN methods from the literature presented similar behavior to the proposed approach except for LDCM, which got a higher accuracy in the training set than in the test data. Also, this method attained the highest architectural complexity.

Remarkably, the proposed LT-DMN$_{0.5}$ attained a slightly better classification performance on the test set than its counterpart LT-DMN$_{1.0}$ since it can find solutions with a smaller number of dendrites and better generalization performance. Therefore, increasing the complexity of the DMN models can produce overfitting problems as observed in LDCM.

Future work considers adding a softmax output layer to the LT-DMN model to evaluate the classification performance from posterior probability responses.

Acknowledgements. S. O. Tovias-Alanis thanks to CONACYT, Mexico, for the doctoral scholarship, and Cinvestav for the economic support. This work was funded in part by the CONACYT FORDECYT-PRONACES under grant 6005 and SIP 20220226.

References

1. Amine, K.: Multiobjective simulated annealing: principles and algorithm variants. J. Multivar. Anal. **143**, 1–13 (2019)
2. Arce, F., Zamora, E., Fócil-Arias, C., Sossa, H.: Dendrite ellipsoidal neurons based on k-means optimization. Evol. Syst. **10**(3), 381–396 (2018). https://doi.org/10.1007/s12530-018-9248-6
3. Arce, F., Zamora, E., Sossa, H., Barrón, R.: Differential evolution training algorithm for dendrite morphological neural networks. Appl. Soft Comput. **68**, 303–313 (2018)
4. Gómez-Flores, W., Sossa-Azuela, J.H.: Towards dendrite spherical neurons for pattern classification. In: Figueroa Mora, K.M., Anzurez Marín, J., Cerda, J., Carrasco-Ochoa, J.A., Martínez-Trinidad, J.F., Olvera-López, J.A. (eds.) MCPR 2020. LNCS, vol. 12088, pp. 14–24. Springer, Cham (2020). https://doi.org/10.1007/978-3-030-49076-8_2
5. Gómez-Flores, W., Sossa, H.: Improving the classification performance of dendrite morphological neurons. IEEE Trans. Neural Netw. Learn. Syst. 1–15 (2021)
6. Gómez-Flores, W., Sossa, H.: Smooth dendrite morphological neurons. Neural Netw. **136**, 40–53 (2021)
7. Ritter, G.X.: Introduction to Lattice Algebra: With Applications in AI, Pattern Recognition, Image Analysis, and Biomimetic Neural Networks. Chapman & Hall/CRC, Boca Raton (2021)

8. Sossa, H., Guevara, E.: Efficient training for dendrite morphological neural networks. Neurocomputing **131**, 132–142 (2014)
9. Xu, R., II, D.W.: Clustering. Wiley, Hoboken (2009)
10. Zamora, E., Sossa, H.: Dendrite morphological neurons trained by stochastic gradient descent. Neurocomputing **260**, 420–431 (2017)

Deep Variational Method with Attention for High-Definition Face Generation

Esteban Reyes-Saldana and Mariano Rivera[✉]

Centro de Investigación en Matemáticas A.C., 36120 Guanajuato, Mexico
{esteban.reyes,mrivera}@cimat.mx

Abstract. We present a method based on four different neural network architectures to generate realistic high-resolution faces. Our model consists of four modules: a convolutional Variational Auto-Encoder (VAE), a convolutional *pix2pix* network, a super-resolution transformer, and a cross-scaling module. Our work combines a variational model with an attention model based on transformers to improve the quality of generated high-definition images that looks realistic. Our method's performance is demonstrated by experiments with a High-Quality Faces dataset.

Keywords: High-definition face generation · Variational autoencoders · Texture transformers · Texture transference

1 Introduction

Super-Resolution (SR) methods estimate a high-resolution image with natural and realistic textures from a low-resolution image. There has been a notable advance in applications that improve the photos' content quality, e.g., image enhancement for digital televisions, medical imaging tasks, and remote sensing. SR methods based on Deep Neural Network are classified between two paradigms: single image SR (SISR) and reference image-based SR (RefSR). Some of the problems of traditional SISR are blurring effects; such methods achieve a kind of interpolation. For this reason, Generative Adversarial Networks (GANs) have surged as an option for introducing textures; however, it could cause hallucination of textures or unnatural textures. Recently, RefSR methods transfer high-resolution textures from a given reference (Ref) image, producing visually pleasing results. Some of the problems with state-of-the-art (SoTA) algorithms are the inaccuracy of the textures when the viewpoints change between the low-resolution image (x') and the reference image (y).

We present a model that combines different neural network architectures to generate realistic human faces. Our model architecture consists of four modules: a Variational Auto-Encoder (VAE) [6,9], a *pix2pix* network, a Texture Transformer (TT), and a cross-scaling network (CS) [16]. Our procedure consists of a sequence of stages based on deep networks. Firstly, we use a VAE to generate a base face's image with general properties (globally consistent proportions), but without details: the faces look over smoothed. Then, we impose

O. O. Vergara-Villegas et al. (Eds.): MCPR 2022, LNCS 13264, pp. 116–126, 2022.
https://doi.org/10.1007/978-3-031-07750-0_11

some texture to the base image using a convolutional pix2pix model. Although the computed image presents some texture, the convolutional model may introduce distortions that result in global inconsistencies. At this point, the textured face's symmetry and proportions may show distortions. For example, the eyes may show different colors or shapes. Then, we use a Transformer model that takes the images produced by the VAE (globally consistent without texture) and the *pix2pix* (textured with global inconsistencies) and a real face's image as reference to compute the spatial matches between the textured-inconsistent image and the real. Finally, a Cross-scaling module adds texture to the VAE's image using multiscale attention matrices computed by the Transformer [16]. We demonstrate our method's performance by experiments with the *CelebA-HQ* dataset [7]. Our work combines a variational model with an attention model based on transformers to improve the quality of generated high-definition images that looks realistic.

2 Proposed General Procedure

2.1 Estimating and Sampling Distributions

The problem of generating realistic faces is better understood if we analyze the general problem of estimating and sampling distributions. Let us assume that U is the universe set of the data of interest (in our case, all the images of faces). Then given a sample of m data $\Omega \subset U$, with $\Omega = \{x_i\}_{i=1,2,...,m}$ of dimension n $(x_i \in \mathbb{R}^n)$, one must estimate the underlying distribution of such data, $P(x)$. The estimated distribution $\tilde{P}$ must satisfy:

1. High likelihood for the real data, $x \in U$.
2. Low likelihood for those that do not belong to, $x \notin U$.
3. Allows to generate samples $\tilde{x} \sim \tilde{P}$ with high likelihood $P(\tilde{x})$.

The last condition is challenging in the case of high-dimensional data: $512 \times 512 \times 3$ faces with a range of 256 values (only the possible number of $4 \times 4 \times 3$ RGB images is larger than 10^{115}). However, it is possible to assume that the high-dimensional data of interest "live" in a much lower-dimensional subspace (manifold). Hence, the task is to find a function f that maps a reduced vector of latent variables z [with known and simple distribution $P(z)$] to the subspace of the images:

$$\tilde{z} \sim P(z). \tag{1}$$

Then, a synthetic data is computed with

$$\tilde{x} = f(\tilde{z}). \tag{2}$$

Thus, we must propose a simple distribution for the latent variables, and find the function f that maps from the latent variables to the images. In this way, each $\tilde{z}$ sampled from $P(z)$ corresponds to an image $\tilde{x}$ that falls into the manifold where the real images live. It is simpler to say than implement since we consider that small changes in $\tilde{z}$, should produce slight variations in the generated image $\tilde{x}$. Furthermore, if $\tilde{z}$ has a high likelihood value according to $P(z)$, then the generated image $\tilde{x}$ must be very realistic [high likelihood according to $P(x)$]. In this work, we propose a procedure to achieve this goal based on recent advances in neural networks.

2.2   Proposed Strategy

Among the data-generating deep networks, the variational auto-encoders are distinguished by the way they naturally allow defining the distribution of the latent variables $P(z)$. However, VAEs are known to produce over-smoothed results. On the other hand, the GAN models produced very realistic results but are generally challenging to train and tend to represent only regions of the authentic data subspace (the well-known mode collapse problem). These GAN's problems accentuate when dealing with high-dimensional data. Therefore, in this work, we start from a VAE and modify the f function that maps the latent variable to the real data space to improve the quality of the generated data but always maintain the latent space's interpretability.

Following is discussed a simplified description of our strategy: the purpose is to serve as a guide map in the rest of the article. Assuming we want to generate RBG images of dimension $H \times W$ (Height and Width). Then our approach starts by training a VAE that codifies and decodes images of size $h \times w$; said $h = H/2$ and $w = W/2$. The reason is that the VAE over smooths the generated images, and a high-definition is unnecessary at this point. The VAE model can be represented by

$$x \overset{C}{\mapsto} z \overset{D}{\mapsto} x'; \tag{3}$$

where C represents the encoder that codify the data x into a latent variable z, providing $P(z)$ would be simple, and D decodes z into the image with $x' \approx x$. In this point one can note that x' preserves essential characteristics of the datum x but lacks of details that make it look realistic.

Thus, we train a *pix2pix* model [5] to introduce texture into the VAE's generated image. This pix2pix model is again a convolutional auto-encoder (but not variational) of the kind of the UNet model. The pix2pix model can be represented by

$$x' \overset{p2p}{\mapsto} x''. \tag{4}$$

In this stage, x'' may include details of real images. However, it can present inconsistencies in the symmetry and shape of the face; *e.g.*, eyes with different colors, eyebrows with different expression, etc. We need a mechanism that sees the face as a whole and corrects such inconsistencies.

In order to correct inconsistencies we need to impose relationships between image regions: symmetry between face's sides, spatial relationship between elements of the face, etc. To achieve this goal, we compute correspondences between the current result x'' and a high-quality reference image y codified as an attention matrix [13]. The rows in the attention matrix H are associated with a region of the partial results x'' and the columns with the regions in the reference image y; for use of transformers in image analysis problems, see [1,3,8]. To describe this process, we assume that the partial results and the reference are split in K chunks, then each chunk is transformed by a feature extractor:

$$x'' \overset{T_x}{\mapsto} \{c_k\}_{k=1,2,...,K}, \text{ and } y \overset{T_y}{\mapsto} \{C_k\}_{k=1,2,...,K}. \tag{5}$$

Hence, an attention matrix H can be computed with

$$H_{ij} = \langle c_i, C_j \rangle; \tag{6}$$

where $\langle a, b \rangle$ is the cosine of the angle between the vectors a and b.

Now, we can reform the inconsistent partial results x'' using the reference image y and the attention information H. This is accomplished by a Deep network known as *Cross-scale*. This mode is again an autoencoder built upon the UNet model. The process can be expressed by

$$(x'', y, H) \overset{CS}{\mapsto} \hat{x}; \tag{7}$$

where $\hat{x}$ denotes our final generated image obtained deterministically from a sampled vector $\tilde{z} \sim P(z)$.

3 Subnet Models

In this section, we present details of the previously described models.

3.1 Variational Autoencoder

The VAE model is an encoder-decoder model but restricting the latent space to be Normal Gaussian. The VAE schema is depicted in Fig. 1. A more detailed model than (3) is

$$x \overset{C}{\mapsto} y \overset{\overbrace{f}^{S}}{\mapsto} (\mu, \sigma^2) \overset{g}{\mapsto} z \overset{D}{\mapsto} \hat{x}. \tag{8}$$

We include a new function S that given the internal representation vector y computed by the codifier C, computes the latent variable $z \sim \mathcal{N}(0, I)$. This is enforced by penalizing the Kullback–Leibler divergence $\text{KL}[\mathcal{N}(0, I)|\mathcal{N}(\mu, \sigma^2)]$ where μ is the mean vector and σ^2 is the variances vector of the entries of the latent variables $z \in \mathbb{R}^d$. We select $d = 150$ empirically. In our implementation we use the VAE loss variant that uses the L_1 norm:

$$L_{vae} = \gamma \|x - \hat{x}\|_1 + \text{KL}[\mathcal{N}(0, I)|\mathcal{N}(\mu, \sigma^2)], \tag{9}$$

because the norm L_1 showed to produce better results and $\gamma = 10,000$ can be see as an extra penalization (regularization) that enforce the VAE to produce more realistic results.

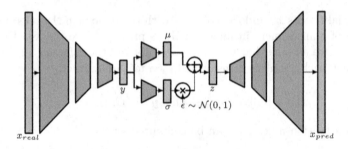

Fig. 1. Variational autoencoder.

3.2 Pix2pix

The *pix2pix* is actually a UNet model used as Generator (G) and a GAN training strategy with the aim of transforming, pixel by pixel, images from one domain $x' \in A$ to another domain $x \in B$; assuming that aligned pairs $[x', x]$ are available [5]. Using a UNet, it is predicted the transformation x'' of x'. Next, the pairs $[x', x]$ and $[x', x'']$ are composed, where the first corresponds to the perfect transformation (Real pair) and the second the transformation predicted by the Generator (Fake pair). The training is carried out through a GAN scheme, where a Discriminator (R) net aims to distinguish between real and synthetic pairs. On the other hand, the Generator seeks to deceive the Discriminator. The GAN training is accelerated by dividing into regular regions the images. Then, it is calculated a realness rating $[0, 1]$ for each patch. The final evaluation of a pair of images corresponds to the sum of the individual ratings of each patch. Hence, the generator focuses on problematic areas and does not overwork regions with adequate transformations, resulting in fast and robust training. Mathematically the process is represented by

$$x'' = G(x'; W_g), \tag{10}$$
$$f = R([x', x'']; W_d), \tag{11}$$
$$r = R([x', x]; W_d); \tag{12}$$

where W_g and W_d denote the parameters of the Generator (G) and Discriminator (R), respectively. Note that f and r are tensors where the entries can be understood as the probability that a region of the image is real. Then, the Generator loss function is given by

$$\min_{W_g} = H[\mathbf{1}, f] + \gamma_2 \|x'' - x\|_1; \tag{13}$$

where $H[p, q]$ is the cross-entropy between the probability distributions p and q. The second term, weighted by γ_2, is a global discrepancy measure between the prediction and the expected image. The Discriminator loss is given by

$$\min_{W_d} = H[\mathbf{1}, r] + H[\mathbf{0}, f]. \tag{14}$$

Such optimizations are simultaneously performed. Figure 2 depicts the training process of the pix2pix model.

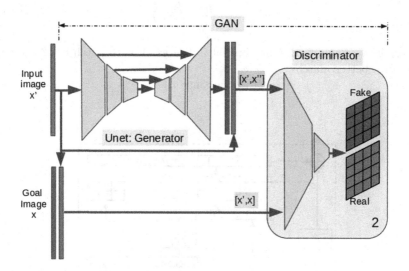

Fig. 2. Pix2pix model, see text.

4   Attention Matrix

Figure 3 shows the scheme of how attention is calculated, the model was initially proposed in a method for single image Super-resolution [16]. In our approach, we start state that x (high-quality image to be generated) is unknown and, a) x' is the base image generated by the VAE, over-smoothed. b) y is a high-quality reference image. c) x'' is our best attempt to texture x' with pix2pix. d) y'' is the result of putting y through a degradation process similar to x and then trying to restore it like the methods previously discussed. That is, it is our first approximation to the inverse problem. Mathematically this process corresponds to

$$y'' = (G \circ D \circ S \circ C)(y). \tag{15}$$

Thus, we transform the data into a new representation with more evident complex characteristics at different resolutions. For this, we use the VGG16 backbone previously trained with ImageNet:

$$s \overset{vgg}{\mapsto} S; \tag{16}$$

where $s \in \{x', y, y'', x''\}$. The datum in the new representation is denoted by the tensors $\{F, V, K, Q\}$, respectively.

Now, we infer the correlations between x' and y by computing such correlations between x'' and y''. First we split Q and K into patches $q_i : i \in$

$[1, 2, \ldots, H_{LR} \times W_{LR}]$ y $k_j : j \in [1, 2, \ldots, H_{Ref} \times W_{Ref}]$, respectively. Next, we compute the similarity scores r_{ij} for each patch pair (q_i, k_j) with

$$r_{i,j} = \left\langle \frac{q_i}{||q_i||}, \frac{k_j}{||k_j||} \right\rangle. \tag{17}$$

Following, we compute the matrix that indicates for each patch in x'' the patch in y'' with better match:

$$h_i = \arg\max_k r_{ik} \tag{18}$$

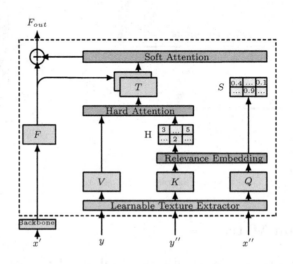

Fig. 3. Texture transformer, see text.

and build the Hard Attention matrix H with integer entries $h_i : i \in [1, 2, \ldots, H_{LR} \times W_{LR}]$. Moreover, while the hard attention matrix H stores the patch index with the best score, the soft attention matrix S stores the score value:

$$s_i = \max_k r_{ik} \tag{19}$$

for $i = 1, 2, \ldots, H_{LR} \times W_{LR}$. Then, we ensemble the tensor T where each patch $t_i : i \in [1, 2, \ldots, H_{LR} \times W_{LR}]$ corresponds to the patch in V, $v_j : j \in [1, 2, \ldots, H_{LR}$, with the most aligned texture according to H:

$$t_i = v_{h_i}. \tag{20}$$

Now, the idea is to combine the original textures F with the transplanted texture candidates T. Since F are the texture information in the base image x' and we want to correct such textures using computations of the attention mechanism, we adopt a residual scheme of the form $F_{out} = F + g(F, T, S)$ where g computes the needed changes in the textures values. Such changes are allow only at those patches where there is a high confidence that the reference image y could provide useful information. The mechanism is implemented as

$$F_{out} = F + g(\text{ccat}(F, T)) \odot S \tag{21}$$

where g is implemented as a convolutional block, ccat denotes the concatenation and $\odot$ the element–wise product.

4.1 Cross-Scale Integration

Inspired by SoTA methods for style/texture transferring [2,16,17]. We also applied the previous attention mechanism at different levels of partial outputs of the feature extractor network VGG16. So the array of reconstructed textures at different scales $\{F_{out}^{(i)}\}_{1=1,2,...}$ are integrated with a cross-scaling reconstruction network (I); this can be modeled as

$$x_{pred} = I(\{F_{out}^{(i)}\}_{1=1,2,...}) \tag{22}$$

where x_{pred} is our final generated face. Figure 4 depicts the cross-scaling model for integrating the reconstructed textures at different scales.

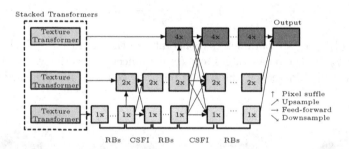

Fig. 4. Cross-scaling model, see text.

4.2 Implementation

Our method to generate realistic faces can be understood as an ensemble of functions whose particular implementation is not the relevant point of our contribution. Although we explored different architectures and our implementations to facilitate the reader could reproduce our work, the results shown in this work are based on modules (models) publicly available online. The global method can be implemented by using the Convolutional Variational Autoencoder code [11] (adapted to CelebA-HQ in [10]), the pix2pix code [12] and the TTST code [15] that implements the attention mechanism and the cross texture integration. It is important to note that the description of the method presented implies increasing the dimensions of the base image x. However, the original application of the TTSR model is to achieve super-resolution on general images and increase the dimensions of the image x' to $(2h, 2w)$. In the experiments shown, we maintain this increase in resolution, the change we make is only to generate the base image x' in reduced size (h, w), keeping the remaining ones $\{y, y''\, x''\}$ into $(H = 2h, W = 2w)$.

5   Experiments

We use two metrics to evaluate the results: Peak Signal to Noise Ratio (PSNR) and Structure Similarity Index (SSIM) [4]. The PSNR is defined as

$$PSNR(f, g) = 10\log_{10}(255/\mathrm{mse}(f, g)) \tag{23}$$

where mse is the Mean Square Error. On the other hand, SSIM emulates the perceptual distance of the human visual system when comparing two images, see Ref. [14]. The SSIM models any distortion in the image as a combination of three factors: luminance distortion, contrast distortion, and loss of correlation. It is defined as

$$SSIM(f, g) = l(f, g)c(f, g)s(f, g) \tag{24}$$

with

$$l(f, g) = \frac{2\mu_f\mu_g + k_1}{\mu_f^2 + \mu_g^2 + k_1}, \quad c(f, g) = \frac{2\sigma_f\sigma_g + k_2}{\sigma_f^2 + \sigma_g^2 + k_2} \text{ and } s(f, g) = \frac{2\sigma_{fg} + k_3}{\sigma_f\sigma_g + k_3}; \tag{25}$$

where $\{c_k\}_{k=1,2,3}$ are parameters (constants) of the metrics, the $\{\mu_z\}_{z=f,g}$ and $\{\sigma_z^2\}_{z=f,g,fg}$ are the mean values and (co)variances, respectively. The first term compares the luminescence, the second term the contrast and the third term the structure.

Fig. 5. Images by column: VAE generated image (x'), Pix2pix enhanced image (x''), final generated image (x_{pred}), and target image (x).

We conduct our numerical experiments using the CelebA-HQ dataset [7] with 30,000 face photos of celebrities, previously aligned by the eye's positions. The 80% where used for training/validation and the 20% for testing Fig. 5 shows the generated image with the VAE and the enhanced (textured), the resulted of pix2pix, the final HQ generated image, and the target image. The error metrics (testing) where 25.67 of PSNR and 0.732 of SSIM. The computational times for a full-training were: VAE, 167 min for 400 epochs; pix2pix 87.1 min for 150 epochs; and TTSR, 450.1 min for 50 epochs.

6   Conclusions

We presented a method to generate high-resolution images of faces from a variational formulation. Our formulation compresses relevant information on a face image into a vector, with dimension 150, of Gaussian-normal variables (latent space), which is simple to sample. The reconstruction function maps the latent variables to the face image is deterministically composed of the three stages. Such stages are the VAE decoder, a convolutional texture implanter (pix2pix), and, finally, a conditional spatial consistency corrector. The consistency corrector is conditional because it uses the image of another face y in high definition to make corrections. Our future work will focus on performing a deeper evaluation of our generator, extending to applications based on operations in the latent space, and developing a network that encodes the information of a set of images used to avoid explicit conditioning.

Acknowledges. Work supported by Conacyt, Mexico (Grant CB-A1-43858).

References

1. Dosovitskiy, A., et al.: An image is worth 16x16 words: transformers for image recognition at scale. CoRR (2020)
2. Gatys, L., Ecker, A., Bethge, M.: A neural algorithm of artistic style. J. Vis. **16**(12), 326–326 (2016)
3. Han, K., et al.: A survey on visual transformer. CoRR (2020)
4. Horé, A., Ziou, D.: Image quality metrics: PSNR vs. SSIM. In: ICPR, pp. 2366–2369 (2010)
5. Isola, P., Zhu, J.Y., Zhou, T., Efros, A.A.: Image-to-image translation with conditional adversarial networks. In: IEEE CVPR, pp. 1125–1134 (2017)
6. Kingma, D.P., Welling, M.: Auto-encoding variational bayes. Stat **1050**, 1 (2014)
7. Lee, C.H., Liu, Z., Wu, L., Luo, P.: Maskgan: towards diverse and interactive facial image manipulation. In: IEEE CVPR (2020)
8. Liu, Y., et al.: A survey of visual transformers. CoRR (2021)
9. Pu, Y., et al.: Variational autoencoder for deep learning of images, labels and captions. In: Lee, D., Sugiyama, M., Luxburg, U., Guyon, I., Garnett, R. (eds.) Advances NIPS, vol. 29. Curran Associates, Inc. (2016)
10. Rivera, M.: Autocodificador variacional convolucional: Conv-vae (2022). http:// personal.cimat.mx:8181/~mrivera/cursos/aprendizaje_profundo/vae_conv/vae_conv.html

11. Tutorial, T.: Convolutional variational autoencoder (2022). https://www.tensorflow.org/tutorials/generative/cvae
12. Tutorial, T.: pix2pix: image-to-image translation with a conditional GAN (2022). https://www.tensorflow.org/tutorials/generative/pix2pix
13. Vaswani, A., et al.: Attention is all you need. In: NIPS 30 (2017)
14. Wang, Z., Bovik, A.C., Sheikh, H.R., Simoncelli, E.P.: Image quality assessment: from error visibility to structural similarity. IEEE Trans. Image Process. **13**(4), 600–612 (2004)
15. Yang, F., Yang, H., Fu, J., Lu, H., Guo, B.: TTSR (2022). https://github.com/researchmm/TTSR
16. Yang, F., Yang, H., Fu, J., Lu, H., Guo, B.: Learning texture transformer network for image super-resolution. In: IEEE CVPR (2020)
17. Zeng, Y., Fu, J., Chao, H., Guo, B.: Learning pyramid-context encoder network for high-quality image inpainting. In: IEEE/CVF CVPR, pp. 1486–1494 (2019)

Indoor Air Pollution Forecasting Using Deep Neural Networks

Jorge Altamirano-Astorga$^{(\boxtimes)}$, Ita-Andehui Santiago-Castillejos$^{(\boxtimes)}$,
Luz Hernández-Martínez$^{(\boxtimes)}$, and Edgar Roman-Rangel$^{(\boxtimes)}$ (ID)

Instituto Tecnológico Autónomo de México, Mexico City, Mexico
{jaltami9,isantia2,lhern123,edgar.roman}@itam.mx
https://philwebsurfer.github.io/dlfinal/

Abstract. Atmospheric pollution components have negative effects in the health and life of people. Outdoor pollution has been extensively studied, but a large portion of people stay indoors. Our research focuses on indoor pollution forecasting using deep learning techniques coupled with the large processing capabilities of the cloud computing. This paper also shares the implementation using an open source approach of the code for modeling time-series of different sources data. We believe that further research can leverage the outcomes of our research.

Keywords: Air quality index forecast · Deep learning · Public data

1 Introduction

Monitoring the air quality and forecasting air pollution are both paramount for many daily activities [4], as air quality has direct impact on human health, agriculture, and the environment in general. Moreover, it is directly related to global warming and climate change [11].

Typically, air quality systems focus on monitoring specific components of outdoors atmospheric pollutants, including NO_2, NO_3, NO_x, O_2, CO_2, PM_{10}, $PM_{2.5}$, and IAQ index, using public monitoring stations that report their concentrations either daily, hourly, or by the minute [15]. However, some times these reports can be inaccurate, noisy, or simply not provided by the official sources during specific periods [12]. Outdoor air pollution has been demonstrated to have negative consequences in human health, specially in large metropolitan areas. Furthermore, tracking indoors air quality has been a neglected research area.

To face the potential lack of public information, as well as to contribute to the monitoring of indoors air quality, we propose the use of affordable indoors devices, that report air quality every few seconds, and that can be installed inside apartments. For the task of predicting air quality IAQ, we evaluate the predictive performance of different deep neural network-based approaches. Namely, we compare the performance of the multi-layer perceptron (MLP), convolutional

O. O. Vergara-Villegas et al. (Eds.): MCPR 2022, LNCS 13264, pp. 127–136, 2022.
https://doi.org/10.1007/978-3-031-07750-0_12

neural networks (CNN), and the long short-term memory (LSTM). Our results show that it is possible to obtain an air quality monitoring system that is affordable and reliable for domestic usage.

Concretely, our contribution consists in presenting an exploration of different deep learning models and architectures with full open code, which allows replicability of time-series forecasting using cloud techniques.

The rest of this paper is organized as follows. Section 2 comments on previous work using deep learning techniques for air quality prediction. Section 3 provides details on the data acquired with the indoors device. Section 4 explains the different architectures evaluated for the task of air quality forecast. Section 5 presents our results, and Sect. 6 our conclusions.

2 Related Work

There are some underlying reproductions that use models of neural systems from the perspective of their understanding of how neural networks work. Among other things, we find that some authors work with artificial neural nets based on MLP-based architecture [3], unlike this research which tries different architectures, mainly based on LSTM. In addition to this, we try with different time windows and other hyperparameter tuning in order to find the one that best predicts the air quality index.

Some researchers have proposed a systems to monitor individual pollution components (pollutants) through wireless networks connecting arrays of sensors. Other studies have incorporated indexes (such IAQ) or score-based systems to determine and forecast IAQ level. We adopted the latter. Additionally, we compared for data accuracy from different sources such as OpenWeatherMap [18] and Mexico City Government Air Quality Monitoring [17,19].

Based on the scope of our investigations, it is common that IAQ monitoring Artificial Neural Networks (ANNs) are used to predict or forecast the value of air quality or the value of air pollution. This project differs from previous research since we use a wide variety of architectures and expanded processing capacity with Google Vertex. The functionality of this system and the methodology of this project are explained in the next section.

No outstanding results were found in weather or pollution forecasting in the papers cited. So, it is natural to build and improve upon these weaknesses and address them.

In the paper of Abdullah [1] the authors make special emphasis on the complexity and non-linear associations between air quality, meteorological, and traffic variables. This is often a limitation of traditional machine learning methods. They also had the idea of updating ANN weights with genetic algorithms, calling it Optimized ANN (OANN). The data includes 16 h of daily information from 2014 to 2016, it came from the Ministry of Works, Malaysia, while the air pollution and meteorological datasets are collected from the Department of Environment (DOE), Malaysia. These data were used to predict the concentration of CO, NO, NO_2, and NO_x. The models included are ANN, RF, Decision

Trees, and the metrics used to measure their performance were: MAE and MSE for all four pollutants.

The objective of the work of Cakir [2], 2020 was to compare the performance of the ANN against multiple linear regression; associating the weather condition with some ambient air measures. The data corresponds to the average hourly concentrations of the particles during the years 2012–2015. The authors make predictions of PM_{10}, NO_2, and O_3. The performance was measured with MAE, RMSE and R^2. They found a correlation between in and out variables, also found that shallow ANNs seem to work better than deeper ones, but MLR seems to work better than ANN. This seems to be more competitive against their previous work (2017), where the MLR equations obtained were used to predict the concentrations for the period of 2012–2013. The same data sets used to simulate both ANN and MLR, but predictors used in ANN are not the same with the independent variables of regression equations. During the model development in the work of 2020, independent variables of the MLR equations were used as a predictor in different ANN configurations; however, the obtained performances were not better than ANN trained with predictors given in this paper.

The dataset used in the work of Singh et al. [10] came from Indira Gandhi International Airport at New Delhi, India, which includes 9 months of hourly information about meteorological factors, pollutant concentrations, and traffic information. The target variable is $PM_{2.5}$. Authors present an exploratory model using an LSTM with 75 units; however, they came with no strong conclusion, only that RMSE is lower for deeper LSTM (hence the 75 units).

The work of Saad [5] plays with information of continuous monitoring of indoor air quality among 22 days between 9.00 a.m. and 5.00 p.m. The authors try to identify source influence among 9 input variables (to known: CO_2, CO, O_3, NO_2, VOCs, O_2 and PM_{10}, temperature and humidity) and 5 conditions: ambient air, chemical presence, fragrance presence, foods and beverages presence, and human activity. Within the written work they talk about the engineering application system which is made up of three parts: sensor module cloud, base station, and service-oriented client. They used 2-layers ANN to learn to predict 5 outputs: Ambient environment, Chemical presence, Fragrance presence, Human activity, and Food and beverages. The performance measure used was the mean accuracy, which was found between 45 to 99%. With this measure they concluded that the ANN was a good tool to identify the most relevant predictors.

Bekkar et al. [6] in their research published the negative impact on air in human health triggering cardiovascular diseases related to mortality, and therefore having an impact on the domestic economy. It also hints a probable relationship of pollutants and COVID-19 propagation. Their research also highlights the complexity of modelling the $PM_{2.5}$ pollution with different traditional statistical methods and machine learning methods. Bekkar focuses on deep learning with different architectures, comparing them using performance metrics. The dataset used in this research also contained less than 4% of missing values, and the spline linear interpolation method was used to fill the gaps in the missing data. The results presented in the paper show that the combined convolutional and

LSTM network combination offered the best results. We found that this research is noteworthy in their ability to present the information and compare models; but lacks information regarding time-series preprocessing methods, such as the window sizes and fall short on explaining why the least history has the best results, which is contrasting with our own research.

Sotomayor-Olmedo et al. [7] research focused on using Support Vector Machines with Mexico City data. They explored different kernels for SVM but did not provide further details on preprocessing on how they dealt with the missing values. The research explained briefly, but clearly, the general weather and pollution conditions of Mexico City. The authors of this paper highlight the computational overhead that may impose in forecasting applications, therefore suggesting lower Support Vector Machines with high accuracy as the best option. We tried focusing on covering those areas that could improve replicability of air quality research for other researchers' work.

Ramos-Ibarra et al. [8] focused their paper research on the trends of atmospheric pollution in the greater Mexico City area using Kalman filters as an smoothing technique for several pollutants in the region. They use Mean absolute deviation, mean square error and mean absolute percentage error as their metrics for evaluation of their techniques. Their research handled the missing variables through the Kalman filters. Their research focused on the non compliance at the time of the local and global environmental regulations, and forecasting of the pollution concentration on a 7 day horizon from 2008 until 2018. The most remarkable outcome of this research is that the Kalman filters and the techniques used in the paper may be used by decision makers to tackle the air pollution problem from an integral perspective using statistical tools based on data.

Bing et al. [9] research focused on predicting ozone air pollution in Mexico City forecasting using multiple linear regressions, neural networks, support vector machines, random forests and ensemble techniques. Their research clearly show the difficulties of having a greater prediction performance than 50%. They used all these techniques to evaluate contradictory outcomes of previous research on whether the Support Vector Machines versus Multi-layer Perceptron offer better performance, but the researchers published better performance with ensemble techniques that combine neural networks and support vector machines. This research used the performance metric: RMSE and MAE; but the paper lacked information regarding if those errors were scaled, as is usual in machine learning techniques with different variables in different scales, and it didn't explained how the data preprocessing was handled. Therefore, it is very difficult to replicate their findings. Their conclusions highlighted some of the limitations found using a single station.

None the previously described research presented public code published or it lacked the required technical detail for replicability. A lack of baseline models as suggested in Keras documentation regarding time-series processing was also addressed.

3   Data

We use the sensor Bosch BME680 [15] that has a published precision of $\pm 5\%$ and a resolution of 1 IAQ. Our exploratory data analysis confirmed this. This sensor collects data every 3 s [16].

Additionally, we use two more data sources: OpenWeatherMap and Mexican Federal Government Pollution data (SINAICA), which have new observations every hour.

Preprocessing. We explored the data sets and we had 6,285,103 records of our sensors from February 2nd, 2021 until September 27th, 2021. Our average IAQ readings were 161.23 with an standard deviation of 72.85.

We resampled our sensor data every 1, 2 and 5 min. Getting the mean values for 1, 2 and 5 min windows, respectively. We created a linear interpolation for the missing data points. The 5 min resampled data was found to be a good balance between dataset size performance wise. Our data was split into training (70% of the data) and validation datasets (30%), without reshuffling, i.e. keeping the oldest records for the training dataset, and the validation dataset with the most recent data.

We had missing data on all datasets. Nonetheless, this was not a big concern on our experiments by using the above mentioned interpolation methods.

Variables. The 5 min resampled data has 62,724 observations with the following variables:

- Sensor data:
  1. Temperature: continuous variable in Celsius degrees.
  2. Pressure: continuous variable in hectopascals (hPa).
  3. Humidity: continuous variable in relative humidity percentage (% rh).
  4. IAQ: discrete variable in EPA Indoor Air Quality Index.
- SINAICA Government Pollution Data:
  1. NO: continuous variable for Nitric Oxide parts per billion (ppb).
  2. NO_2: continuous variable for Nitrogen Dioxide parts per billion (ppb).
  3. NO_x: continuous variable for Nitrogen Oxide parts per billion (ppb). This is the sum of NO and NO_2 pollutants.
  4. CO: continuous variable for Carbon Monoxide parts per million (ppm).
  5. O_3: continuous variable for Carbon Monoxide parts per million (ppm).
  6. PM_{10}: continuous variable for Particle Matter with diameters of less than 10 microns measured in micrograms per cubic meter ($\mu g/cm^3$).
  7. $PM_{2.5}$: continuous variable for Particle Matter with diameters of less than 2.5 μ measured in micrograms per cubic meter ($\mu g/cm^3$).
  8. SO_2: continuous variable for Sulfur Dioxide parts per billion (ppb).
- OpenWeatherMap Data:
  1. Outdoor Temperature: continuous variable in Celsius Degrees.

2. Outdoor Pressure: continuous variable in hectopascals (hPa).
3. Outdoor Humidity: continuous variable in relative humidity percentage (% rh).

We use the previous list of variables as independent variables to forecast IAQ. More precisely, our models are fed with a vector of length 15, and predict an scalar output.

Postprocessing. All variables described in Variables subsection are numeric but on different scales, therefore we used the `MinMaxScaler()` transformation of Scikit-Learn for training our models. This transformation is inverted for the reporting of the Mean Absolute Error, to have the error metric in an interpretable scale.

We also applied time-series processing using Keras `timeseries_dataset_from_array()` function with hyperparameter tuning to find the "sweet spot" of performance and accuracy. This function creates a tensor, i.e., a vector of arrays with the history of previous observations of certain length in a sliding window fashion. This is "learned" during the training process of the models we applied in this research.

Data Access. We are planning to publish the sensor data on the paper repository hosted on GitHub for replicability and further research purposes. SINAICA Mexican Government data will be published in this repository. Due to the rights of OpenWeatherMap, we cannot publish them, but they are easily afforded in their website [18].

4   Methods

We tested several architectures, hyperparameters, and different types of processing units to minimize the mean square error (MSE) of the AQI forecast.

Procedure and General Workflow. Our research used Google coLaboratory [20] as our interactive experiment environment using ADAM as our optimizer, though we used Stochastic Gradient Descent on some experiments. We minimized the MSE as our loss function. All our experiments were performed with Tensorflow in Python [22].

For scalability purposes we used the novel platform Google Vertex AI [21] platform, as it offered more performance and automated hyperparameter tuning successfully using a Python script. This code and the notebook experiments code will be published on GitHub.

Experimental Protocol. We compare different types of artificial neurons:

- **DNN**: Dense neural networks (Multilayer perceptron, MLP) are deep neural networks that are the foundation for artificial neural networks (ANNs) with multiple layers between input and output layers.
- **RNN**: Recurrent neural networks are the most classical architecture used for time series prediction problems.
- **CNN**: Convolutional Neural Network is very popular in image processing applying 2-D convolutions. However, it is also useful for one-dimensional data using 1-D convolutions.
- **LSTM**: "Long-Short-Term Memory" (LSTM) neural networks that are an evolution of RNNs developed to overcome the disappearing gradient problem;
- A mix of the best models, in this case, **CNN + LSTM**.

5   Results

Our best results were consistently as shown in Fig. 1:

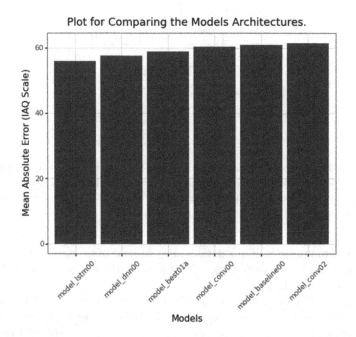

Fig. 1. We tested 10 different neural network types, including: Dense (MLP), LSTM, Convolutional, Recursive networks and combinations of them.

Performance of the Models. These architectures were tuned with different time-series hyperparameters to check for consistency of performance on our architectures with our data and to optimize our computational budget. We found

Table 1. Comparison of different architectures. Stride and for Sample Rate were handled as hyperparameters of Tensorflow time-series window generator [13,14]. W. Sz. means Window size in days.

Model	Time	Epochs	W. Sz.	Stride	Samp. Rt.	MSE	MAE	Resample
lstm00	47.62	11	30	2	2	0.0249	55.97	10 Min
dnn00	29.58	14	15	1	2	0.0309	57.58	10 Min
best01a	890.75	28	15	1	2	0.0244	59.03	05 Min
conv00	79.88	14	15	1	2	0.0301	60.34	10 Min
baseline00	24.97	14	15	1	2	0.0325	60.90	10 Min
conv02	799.29	28	15	1	2	0.0207	61.58	05 Min

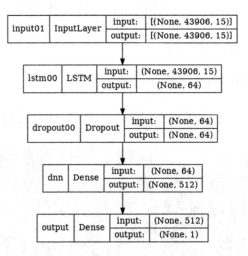

Fig. 2. lstm00 model is a 3 layer combining LSTM, dropout and dense layers in the following fashion. LSTM layer was implemented as 64 LSTM neurons, a second dropout layer with a rate of 0.5 to avoid overfitting and lastly a 512 MLP RELU activated layer. This model has a total of 576 neurons.

that the re sampling size of our dataset, i.e.: instead of processing all our sensor records every 3 s it is useful to get the means of these records every 1, 2 and 5 min (Table 1 and Fig. 2).

Our budget did not allow us to fully test the performance of the 1 min re sampling data, as it was very expensive. And the 2 and 5 min resamples are comparable performance-wise. We tested an even larger resample of 10 min with great results.

6   Conclusions

This paper faced the problem of not having accurate and up-to-date information of air quality while living in a city with known pollution problems. This lack of information led us to ask ourselves what could we contribute as Data Scientists, so we have developed some air quality prediction models based on neural network systems. We proposed a variety of methods with both the scopes of concerned: to perform multi-layer perceptron models for predicting IAQ concentration in an indoor sensor, and to compare the performances between different time-windows and a baseline model.

Data for model classification training was collected using an IAQ Bosch monitoring system. In addition to information from our sensor, we collated data with information from external sources that included particulates such as carbon dioxide, carbon monoxide, ozone, nitrogen dioxide, oxygen, volatile organic compounds, and particulates, temperature, and humidity. Based on the results of the network models, the LSTM model was the best with a MAE of 55.97, nevertheless, all our models presented a similar performance.

In general, it can be concluded that the system delivered a high classification rate based on LSTM. We attribute this success to the appropriate use of time windows and the advantage that Vertex gave us to be able to perform tests with large amounts of data.

The developed models can help environmental agencies and governments monitor air pollution levels more efficiently. Moreover, the model can help to correct missing information in order to protect the health of the citizens who are inhabiting in metropolitan areas.

With high hopes, in the future we would like to work, at least, with data from a full year, to deal with seasonality and its effects on the measurement. We will probably extend this work to a project where the effects of air quality in a pandemic environment are considered.

Acknowledgements. We thank the Asociación Mexicana de Cultura A.C., for its support. We also thank Montserrat Altamirano-Astorga for her valuable help proofreading this manuscript.

References

1. Abdullah, A., Raja, S., Thulasyammal, R., Mohsen, M., Ibrahim, A.: An optimized artificial neural network model using genetic algorithm for prediction of traffic emission concentrations. Int. J. Adv. Comput. Sci. Appl. **12** (2021). https://doi.org/10.14569/IJACSA.2021.0120693
2. Cakir, S., Moro, S.: Evaluating the performance of ANN in predicting the concentrations of ambient air pollutants in Nicosia. Atmos. Pollut. Res. **11**(12), 2327–2334 (2020). https://doi.org/10.1016/j.apr.2020.06.011
3. Ghazali, S., Lokman, H.: Air quality prediction using artificial neural network. Universiti Tun Hussein Onn Malaysia. In: The International Conference on Civil and Environmental Engineering Sustainability (2012)
4. Patni, J., Sharma, H.: Air quality prediction using artificial neural networks. In: International Conference on Automation, Computational and Technology Management (2019). https://doi.org/10.1109/icactm.2019.8776774
5. Saad, S., Andrew, A., Shakaff, A., Saad, A., Yuzof, A., Zakaria, A.: Classifying sources influencing indoor air quality (IAQ) using artificial neural network (ANN). Sensors **15**(5), 11665–11684 (2015)

6. Bekkar, A., Hssina, B., Douzi, S., Douzi, K.: Air-pollution prediction in smart city, deep learning approach. J. Big Data **8**(1), 1–21 (2021). https://doi.org/10.1186/s40537-021-00548-1
7. Sotomayor-Olmedo, A., et al.: Forecast urban air pollution in Mexico City by using support vector machines: a kernel performance approach. Int. J. Intell. Science **3**(3), 126–135 (2013)
8. Ramos-Ibarra, E., Silva, E.: Trend estimation and forecasting of atmospheric pollutants in the Mexico City Metropolitan Area through a non-parametric perspective. Atmósfera **33**(4), 401–420 (2020). https://doi.org/10.20937/ATM.52757
9. Bing, G., Ordieres-Meré, J., Cabrera, C.: Prediction models for ozone in metropolitan area of Mexico City based on artificial intelligence techniques. Int. J. Inf. Decis. Sci. **7**(2), 115–139 (2015)
10. Singh, S.K., Yang, R., Behjat, A., Rai, R., Chowdhury, S., Matei, I.: PI-LSTM: physics-infused long short-term memory network. In: 18th IEEE International Conference On Machine Learning And Applications (ICMLA), 2019, pp. 34–41 (2019)
11. Kim, Y., Knowles, S., Manley, J., Radoias, V.: Long-run health consequences of air pollution: evidence from Indonesia's forest fires of 1997. Econ. Hum. Biol. **26**, 186–198 (2017). https://doi.org/10.1016/j.ehb.2017.03.006
12. NORMA Oficial Mexicana NOM-156-SEMARNAT-2012, Establecimiento y operación de sistemas de monitoreo de la calidad del aire. §10.4.2, pp. 8, 14 (2012)
13. Timeseries forecasting for weather prediction. https://keras.io/examples/timeseries/timeseries_weather_forecasting/
14. Tensorflow: Tutorial on Time series forecasting Time series forecasting. https://www.tensorflow.org/tutorials/structured_data/time_series
15. Bosch BME680 Datasheet. https://www.bosch-sensortec.com/media/boschsensortec/downloads/datasheets/bst-bme680-ds001.pdf
16. Mancuso, D.: Indoor Air Quality Monitor — Hackster.io. https://www.hackster.io/damancuso/indoor-air-quality-monitor-b181e9. Accessed 3 Oct 2021
17. Dirección de Monitoreo Atmosférico de la Secretaría del Medio Ambiente del Gobierno de la Ciudad de México. http://www.aire.cdmx.gob.mx/
18. OpenWeatherMap: History weather bulk for Camarones (19.48,-99.18) from January 01, 1979 to September 27, 2021
19. Sistema Nacional de Información de la Calidad del Aire del Gobierno Federal México https://sinaica.inecc.gob.mx/. Accessed 3 Oct 2021
20. Google AI Blog: Doing Data Science with coLaboratory. https://ai.googleblog.com/2014/08/doing-data-science-with-colaboratory.html
21. Google Cloud launches Vertex AI, unified platform for MLOps — Google Cloud Blog. https://cloud.google.com/blog/products/ai-machine-learning/google-cloud-launches-vertex-ai-unified-platform-for-mlops
22. Abadi, M., Agarwal, A., Barham, P., et al.: TensorFlow: large-scale machine learning on heterogeneous systems (2015). https://arxiv.org/abs/1603.04467

Extreme Machine Learning Architectures Based on Correlation

Hubert Cecotti$^{(\boxtimes)}$

Department of Computer Science, California State University, Fresno, USA
hcecotti@csufresno.edu
https://csm.fresnostate.edu/csci/

Abstract. The relationships between features can guide the architecture of pattern recognition systems. It is the case with images where the spatial relationship of pixels allows to use convolutions to filter images and extract high level features. In this paper, we consider extreme learning machine (ELM) classifiers and propose to modify the selection of the inputs of a hidden unit based on correlation matrix of the input features. The proposed approach is tested on databases of handwritten digits (MNIST and Devanagari). The results show that input selection based on the correlation matrix provides better performance and leads to a sparse representation of the weights in the network.

Keywords: Extreme learning machine · Correlation · Classification

1 Introduction

Efficient pattern recognition systems often require some domain knowledge to determine the pre-processing steps and the architecture of the model. It includes the knowledge related to the type of deformations that may occur across examples of a given class. Multiple approaches have been proposed in the literature, including database augmentation with the addition of new examples in the training model. For neural networks, and in particular deep learning, it can be necessary to have some domain knowledge to select the sequence of layers and their parameters in the network architecture. We assume that there are problems in which the underlying relationships between the input features are unknown or that it requires domain knowledge that is not accessible, and it is not possible to design a specific architecture for a neural network.

In this paper, we propose to investigate the architecture of extreme learning machine (ELM) models by selecting a subset of inputs for the different units of the hidden layer. ELMs have showed that they can be applied on a large number of classification tasks with surprising high performances. It combines a very fast learning method, and it has a powerful performance for pattern recognition tasks [1,4,14]. ELMs are a class of feedforward neural networks. Single hidden layer feedforward neural networks have been studied exhaustively in the last decades. The connections between the inputs and the hidden layer are typically

O. O. Vergara-Villegas et al. (Eds.): MCPR 2022, LNCS 13264, pp. 137–146, 2022.
https://doi.org/10.1007/978-3-031-07750-0_13

set with random weights, however multiple improvements have been proposed to change the way the random weights are initialized, and the relationships between the different sets of weights [19].

The key rationale of this study is related to convolutional neural networks that are applied on computer vision tasks or signal processing tasks where there exists a high relationship between the input units or features that are connected to a unit in the upper layer. For images, the inputs in a convolution are constrained by the 2D space and the spatial proximity between the different units. The same principle applies in 1D signal where inputs represent data points within a window of the point of interest.

While we may know that we are dealing with an image and impose directly a specific architecture between two layers, i.e., different than fully connected, an interest is to determine these connections automatically based on the input data. In addition, while knowing that the inputs corresponds to images, the size of the windows for applying a convolution should be ideally determined in relation to the images. We propose to use the correlation between the input features to determine the set of inputs that should be used by the units in the next layer. We propose to test this type of connection on the state-of-the-art MNIST database, which is a database of well segmented images, hence it is possible to assess if the connections based on the correlation between pixels can provide an advantage over the traditional approach.

The remainder of the paper is organized as follows. First, the ELM classifier for a single hidden layer and multiple layers is detailed in Sect. 2. The performance of the proposed approach is presented in Sect. 3. Finally, the results are discussed in Sect. 4.

2   Methods

Extreme Learning Machine networks are a particular type of artificial feedforward neural networks that contain a single hidden layer [7,8,18]. This type of network can be used for both classification and regression [2,13,16]. It corresponds to a linear combination of non-linear representations of the input data (e.g. using a sigmoid function). The main characteristic of this system is the way in which the parameters (i.e. the weights) are assigned. The input weights and biases are set randomly and do not change over time. While this step is simple and it may seem inefficient due to the lack of training as it is data independent, ELMs have the capability of universal approximation if the dimension of the input representation is large enough [10]. The parameters of an ELM network can be obtained with linear regression methods using only matrix inversions and multiplications. It is worth noting that these operations are particularly well adapted for distributed learning [15]. Finally, ELM networks can be estimated with a least square approach for learning the weights in the last layer.

We first consider a regression problem with one-dimensional scalar outputs $y \in \mathbb{R}$. A Functional Link Artificial Neural Network (FLANN) with a single output neuron is defined as a weighted sum of B non-linear transformations of the input $\mathbf{x}$ [13]:

$$f(\mathbf{x}) = \sum_{m=1}^{B} \beta_m h_m(\mathbf{x}; \mathbf{w}_m) = \beta^T h(\mathbf{x}; \mathbf{w}_1, \ldots, \mathbf{w}_B) \tag{1}$$

where the mth transformation is obtained with the parameters $\mathbf{w}_m$, and $\mathbf{x} \in \mathbb{R}^d$. Each functional link h_m maps the input data to a real number. The non-linearity is obtained with an activation function such as the sigmoid function in the multilayer perceptron:

$$h_m(\mathbf{x}; \mathbf{w}_m; b) = \frac{1}{1 + \exp^\sigma} \tag{2}$$

where $\sigma = -\mathbf{w}^T\mathbf{x} + b$. The set of parameters $\mathbf{w}_m$, $1 \leq m \leq B$, is chosen before the learning process and without any prior assumptions about the data. Moreover, the parameters are set randomly, in relation to a predefined probability distribution [16]. After the estimation of the set of parameters, the weights β must be estimated. We consider a dataset $\mathcal{X}_{Train} = \{(\mathbf{x}_i, y_i)\}$ of N couples that contain an example $\mathbf{x}_i$ and the expected output y_i, $1 \leq i \leq N$. We denote by $\mathbf{H}$ the matrix containing the B representations of the N examples.

$$H = \begin{pmatrix} h_1(\mathbf{x}_1) & \ldots & h_B(\mathbf{x}_1) \\ \vdots & \ddots & \vdots \\ h_1(\mathbf{x}_N) & \ldots & h_B(\mathbf{x}_N) \end{pmatrix} \tag{3}$$

where each function h_m includes the corresponding set of parameters $\mathbf{w}_m$. The estimation of $\beta = [\beta_1, \ldots, \beta_B]^T$ can be obtained through a regularized least-square problem:

$$\beta = \arg\min_{\beta \in \mathbb{R}^B} \frac{1}{2} \|\mathbf{H}\beta - \mathbf{Y}\|_2^2 + \frac{\lambda}{2} \|\beta\|_2^2 \tag{4}$$

where the vector $\mathbf{Y} = [y_1, \ldots, y_N]^T$ is the ground truth of $\mathcal{X}_{Train}$. As the problem is convex, an estimation of $\hat{\beta}$ can be obtained by:

$$\hat{\beta} = \left(\mathbf{H}^T\mathbf{H} + \lambda\mathbf{I}\right)^{-1} \mathbf{H}^T\mathbf{Y} \tag{5}$$

where I is the identity matrix of size $B \times B$. For a multiclass classification problem with M classes, $M \geq 2$, the ground truth $\mathbf{Y}$ is a matrix of size $N \times M$. $\mathbf{Y}(i,j) = 1$ if $\mathbf{x}_i$ belongs to the class j, $1 \leq j \leq M$, $\mathbf{Y}(i,j) = 0$ otherwise.

2.1 Inputs Selection

We consider X_{train} of size $N_{train} \times N_f$, where N_{train} is the number of examples and N_f is the number of features. We create the correlation matrix C, $(N_f \times N_f)$, then we sort the absolute value of the different coefficient for each feature. The correlation coefficient of two features is a measure of their linear dependence.

$$\rho(A, B) = \frac{1}{N_{train} - 1} \sum_{i=1}^{N_{train}} \left(\frac{A_i - \mu_A}{\sigma_A}\right) \left(\frac{B_i - \mu_B}{\sigma_B}\right) \tag{6}$$

where μ_A and σ_A are the mean and standard deviation of A across the different examples, same for B. The correlation coefficient matrix of two random variables is the matrix of correlation:

$$C = \begin{pmatrix} 1 & \rho(f_1, f_2) & \cdots & \rho(f_1, f_N) \\ \rho(f_2, f_1) & 1 & \cdots & \rho(f_2, f_N) \\ \vdots & & \ddots & \vdots \\ \rho(f_N, f_1) & & \cdots & 1 \end{pmatrix} \tag{7}$$

where f_i denotes a feature in the inputs, $1 \leq i \leq N_f$.

The different coefficients are then normalized in relation to the sum of all the coefficients. The number of inputs corresponding to the unit i, s_i is defined by:

$$s_i = \underset{1 \leq j \leq N_f}{\arg\max} \left(\sqrt{\frac{1}{j} \sum_{k=1}^{j} \mathbf{C}_{\mathbf{sort}\,i}(k) - \mathbf{C}_{\mathbf{sort}\,i}} \right) \tag{8}$$

It computes the standard deviation across the different sorted values of the correlation matrix, and we select the size that maximizes the standard deviation.

Because each unit in the hidden layer correspond to an input feature and we can have a different number of units in the hidden layer than the number of features in the input layer, we select randomly in the hidden layer the corresponding unit of the input layer.

2.2   Multi-layer ELM

Different variations of ELM networks have been successfully used in a range of diverse but popular classification problems [9], and have been inspired by other techniques [5,6]. ELM can be extended for deep learning architectures (ML-ELM) [11,17]. The learning approach performs layer-by-layer unsupervised learning by using ELM auto-encoder (ELM-AE), which represents features based on singular values. With an ELM-AE model, the output $\mathbf{Y}$ is similar to the input $\mathbf{X} = [\mathbf{x}_1, \ldots, \mathbf{x}_N]$. The decoder represents the function mapping the input representation $h_1(x), \ldots, h_B(x)$ of the input x to itself, it corresponds to the parameters $\hat{\beta}$ that are estimated. The random weights in each layer are constrained to be orthogonal [11]. To create the coder afterward, $\hat{\beta}^T$ is used to map x to the representation that was obtained. Then, ML-ELM stacks on top of ELM-AE to create a multilayer neural network similar to other deep architectures. ML-ELM is a greedy approach; it doesn't require fine-tuning after the estimation of the weights of the last layer. In the EML with a single hidden layer, we denote by $\hat{\beta}^1$

the estimation of the weights for the first hidden layer. We denote $\hat{\beta}^l$ as the estimation of the weights for the layer l, $1 \leq l \leq L$, for ML-ELM of L hidden-layers. An ELM-AE is used for each layer l, and the extracted weights of an ELM-AE l are used to generate the inputs of the ELM-AE at layer $l+1$. A multilayer ELM with two hidden layers is depicted in Fig. 1.

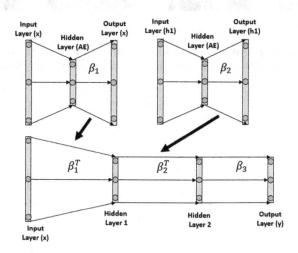

Fig. 1. A multi-layer ELM with two hidden layers.

2.3   Dataset

We consider two datasets of handwritten digits: the state-of-the-art MNIST (60,000 images for the training and 10,000 images for the test) database, and the Devanagari dataset (18794 for training, 3762 for the test) containing digits in the Devanagari script [3,12]. Each image has a size 28 × 28. The correlation between the different pixels, and the extracted number of inputs per pixel in Fig. 2. The figure suggests that the relationships between pixels and their neighborhoods are not homogeneous across the image. The sorted correlation factors are displayed in Fig. 3.

2.4   Performance Evaluation

We denote by Corr_1, Corr_2, Corr_3, and Corr_4 the approaches where 1) the number of connections per hidden unit is unique, it depends on the correlation of the corresponding unit in the input layer, 2) the number of connections is the same for all the units, it is the average number across the number of connections per unit that were estimated, 3) the number of connections is the same for all the units, it corresponds to $\sqrt{N_f}$, 27 for MNIST, 4) the number of connections is the same for all the units, it corresponds to $N_f/2$, 358 for MNIST. Based on the chosen criterion for determining the number of connections to use, the average

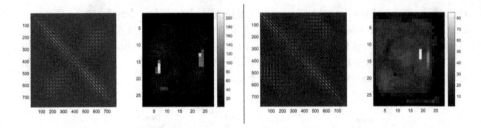

Fig. 2. Graphical representations of number of inputs per pixel (correlation between pixels, Right: number of inputs for each pixel) on MNIST (left) and Devanagari (right).

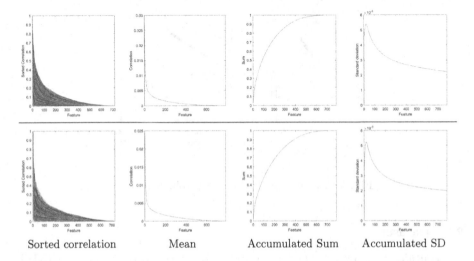

| Sorted correlation | Mean | Accumulated Sum | Accumulated SD |

Fig. 3. Representation of the correlation factors (absolute values) for the different features (top: MNIST, bottom: Devanagari).

number of connections is 21.728 ± 21.5639 for $Corr_2$. For the classification, we normalize the images by using the z-score (zero mean, standard deviation of one). We remove all the features/pixels with a standard deviation that is null, reducing the input size to 717 for MNIST.

3   Results

The classification accuracy with a single hidden layer is represented in Tables 1 and 2. Each value corresponds to the average and standard deviation accuracy across 10 runs. The standard deviation highlights the variability that can exist across training examples using the same approach. The condition "All" corresponds to the default ELM approach with the selection of all the input units, i.e., a fully connected layer. On the test database, the best accuracy is achieved with the approach using a subset of input units, $Corr_2$, with an accuracy of

94.51% for MNIST and 92.67% for Devanagari. The pattern of performance is similar between the two datasets where the correlation based architecture lead to a better performance compared to the default ELM. This result is close to $Corr_3$ because the number of connection is close 22 for $Corr_2$ vs. 27 for $Corr_3$. It is worth noting that this number is also close to 25, a square mask of size 5×5 that is often used for the size of spatial filters. When considering a low number of hidden units, e.g., 100, then it is not possible to see an improvement as the default approach provides better results despite having $Corr_4$ giving the best accuracy. The more we increase the number of hidden units, the more the accuracy increases. It is also worth noting that there is not a substantial difference between the performance on the training and test databases, suggesting a good level of generalization despite the inner limitations of the model.

Table 1. Accuracy (in %) on MNIST - 1 hidden layer.

	100	250	500	1000	1500	2000
Training						
All	80.32 ± 0.34	85.03 ± 0.11	87.17 ± 0.13	89.77 ± 0.1	91.55 ± 0.13	92.86 ± 0.1
$Corr_1$	76.94 ± 1.08	84.77 ± 0.37	88.11 ± 0.2	91.33 ± 0.17	93.37 ± 0.19	94.48 ± 0.11
$Corr_2$	79.53 ± 1.46	85.87 ± 0.36	88.69 ± 0.27	92.24 ± 0.2	93.95 ± 0.19	95.18 ± 0.08
$Corr_3$	79.45 ± 1.3	85.92 ± 0.4	89.06 ± 0.15	92.3 ± 0.21	93.98 ± 0.19	95.14 ± 0.09
$Corr_4$	81.9 ± 0.34	86.02 ± 0.19	88.51 ± 0.14	91.37 ± 0.11	93.07 ± 0.08	94.18 ± 0.1
Test						
All	81.23 ± 0.34	85.63 ± 0.13	87.41 ± 0.2	89.53 ± 0.19	90.85 ± 0.09	91.86 ± 0.18
$Corr_1$	78.21 ± 1.18	85.64 ± 0.46	88.59 ± 0.26	91.39 ± 0.24	93.15 ± 0.13	94.01 ± 0.14
$Corr_2$	80.37 ± 1.51	86.67 ± 0.36	89.03 ± 0.31	92.07 ± 0.2	93.48 ± 0.21	94.49 ± 0.2
$Corr_3$	80.61 ± 1.23	86.64 ± 0.4	89.41 ± 0.11	92.22 ± 0.18	93.53 ± 0.29	94.51 ± 0.16
$Corr_4$	82.76 ± 0.4	86.56 ± 0.26	88.76 ± 0.21	90.95 ± 0.23	92.38 ± 0.16	93.25 ± 0.15

The classification accuracy with two hidden layers are given in Tables 3 and 4. The first hidden layer has 2000 units and the second hidden layer has units defined in the column of the two tables (500, 1000, and 2000). We observe the same pattern of performance where the sparse connections based on the correlation across features provide a better performance than the fully random weights. The best performance for MNIST and Devanagari is obtained with $Corr_3$, with an accuracy of 94.55% and 93.34%, respectively.

Table 2. Accuracy (in %) on Devanagari - 1 hidden layer.

	100	250	500	1000	1500	2000
Training						
All	80.97 ± 0.39	87.01 ± 0.39	89.31 ± 0.03	91.94 ± 0.14	93.9 ± 0.03	95.23 ± 0.08
Corr$_1$	80.11 ± 1.36	87.53 ± 0.39	90.61 ± 0.32	93.58 ± 0.08	95.56 ± 0.26	96.78 ± 0.04
Corr$_2$	81.34 ± 0.78	87.93 ± 0.19	91.33 ± 0.14	94.46 ± 0.21	96.14 ± 0.09	97.24 ± 0.07
Corr$_3$	81.63 ± 0.68	87.86 ± 0.42	91.24 ± 0.19	94.51 ± 0.16	96.3 ± 0.18	97.31 ± 0.07
Corr$_4$	82.54 ± 0.38	87.71 ± 0.14	90.33 ± 0.07	93.07 ± 0.1	94.87 ± 0.11	96.03 ± 0.12
Test						
All	77.09 ± 0.43	82.59 ± 0.49	84.69 ± 0.39	86.78 ± 0.14	87.93 ± 0.17	88.9 ± 0.31
Corr$_1$	75.96 ± 1.29	83.55 ± 0.36	86.5 ± 0.26	89.15 ± 0.17	90.82 ± 0.43	92.15 ± 0.35
Corr$_2$	77.5 ± 1.2	83.88 ± 0.38	87.13 ± 0.09	89.69 ± 0.38	91.32 ± 0.27	92.67 ± 0.16
Corr$_3$	77.41 ± 0.9	83.98 ± 0.42	87.35 ± 0.38	90.23 ± 0.24	91.9 ± 0.46	92.63 ± 0.26
Corr$_4$	78.68 ± 0.75	83.86 ± 0.13	86.44 ± 0.3	88.33 ± 0.34	89.53 ± 0.21	90.27 ± 0.35

Table 3. Accuracy (in %) MNIST - 2 hidden layers.

	Training			Test		
	500	1000	2000	500	1000	2000
All	87.54 ± 0.13	90.24 ± 0.06	93.06 ± 0.11	87.69 ± 0.25	90 ± 0.2	92.05 ± 0.21
Corr$_1$	88.48 ± 0.3	91.63 ± 0.18	94.28 ± 0.11	87.75 ± 0.81	90.06 ± 1.23	92.69 ± 0.73
Corr$_2$	89.42 ± 0.21	92.3 ± 0.11	94.96 ± 0.11	89.68 ± 0.24	92.07 ± 0.29	94.23 ± 0.14
Corr$_3$	89.62 ± 0.21	92.75 ± 0.21	95.22 ± 0.12	89.89 ± 0.14	92.53 ± 0.29	94.55 ± 0.14
Corr$_4$	88.93 ± 0.08	91.68 ± 0.07	94.26 ± 0.09	89.08 ± 0.2	91.31 ± 0.22	93.35 ± 0.16

Table 4. Accuracy (in %) Devanagari - 2 hidden layers.

	Training			Test		
All	89.35 ± 0.12	92.33 ± 0.13	95.6 ± 0.09	84.77 ± 0.17	86.84 ± 0.28	89.01 ± 0.32
Corr$_1$	91.15 ± 0.22	94.21 ± 0.14	96.79 ± 0.1	86.12 ± 0.75	89.12 ± 0.68	91.98 ± 0.47
Corr$_2$	91.99 ± 0.22	95.14 ± 0.15	97.76 ± 0.13	88.07 ± 0.43	90.84 ± 0.37	93.34 ± 0.33
Corr$_3$	92.04 ± 0.15	95.14 ± 0.1	97.74 ± 0.1	88.24 ± 0.24	90.92 ± 0.3	93.34 ± 0.26
Corr$_4$	90.41 ± 0.11	93.36 ± 0.13	96.38 ± 0.12	86 ± 0.25	88.36 ± 0.28	90.77 ± 0.36

4   Discussion and Conclusion

When using images as inputs, it has become natural to use convolutional layers in the first hidden layers of the processing stage. We have proposed to go in the opposite direction and investigate if it is possible to retrieve meaningful connections between units without knowing that the input is an image. In that sense, the approach can be generalized to any type of inputs, structured or not, as the links can be automatically created without prior knowledge of the input sets. The performance is inferior to state of the art approaches but it uses a minimum amount of knowledge from the problem: no information about the fact the inputs are images and no training, as we use random projections.

In this paper, we have proposed the selection of input connections based on the correlation between input features applied to ELM models. ELM based classifiers have random weights in the hidden layers until the last hidden layer. The ELM approach allows to focus on the architecture and separate learning from the architecture. The approach can be implemented in ELM with a single hidden layer or with multiple hidden layers, using the multilayer ELM principles. While the accuracy is lower than state of the art approaches that aim to get the best accuracy, this study aimed at proposing an alternative to the fully random weights. The evaluation shows that the proposed approach gives better results and would allow an increase of speed due to the sparse representation of the matrix containing the weights.

An advantage of the approach is that it does not require to have the input data with fixed dimensions. In the present work, we have removed all the features that have a null standard deviation, hence reducing the input feature with MNIST from 784 to 717. Such a reduction also breaks the 2D aspect of the image. Yet, it is still possible to recapture relationships between data points through the correlation coefficients. While these coefficients provide relevant information, a problem is to determine the number of inputs to select. The rationale of our approach using the standard deviation was to include high values as well as some small values within the input set. As the distance or relationship between two pixels increases, the number of pixels increases as well. Hence, the standard deviation seems to be a good choice, as verified in the evaluation. Other approaches could be used to determine the number of inputs and set the weights to improve the performance. When the number of inputs is unique for each hidden unit, then it is not possible to change the weights using an orthonormal base as it can be performed with the regular.

The approach for the selection of the inputs can be extended to other types of classifiers beyond the ELM models. It could be used with a convolutional neural network, where the convolutions can be replaced by the correlation based connections. Contrary to the use of convolutional layers in neural networks in which the same set of weights is used across all the pixels of the image, the proposed approach gives different sets of weights for each unit of the hidden layer.

References

1. Akusok, A., Björk, K.M., Miche, Y., Lendasse, A.: High-performance extreme learning machines: a complete toolbox for big data applications. IEEE Access **3**, 1011–1025 (2015). https://doi.org/10.1109/ACCESS.2015.2450498
2. Alhamdoosh, M., Wang, D.: Fast decorrelated neural network ensembles with random weights. Inf. Sci. **264**, 104–117 (2014)
3. Bhattacharya, U., Chaudhuri, B.: Databases for research on recognition of handwritten characters of indian scripts. In: Proceedings of the 8th International Conference on Document Analysis and Recognition (ICDAR 2005), pp. 789–793 (2005)

4. Cecotti, H.: Deep random vector functional link network for handwritten character recognition. In: Proceedings of the International Joint Conference on Neural Networks, pp. 1–6 (2016)
5. Chen, C.L.P.: A rapid supervised learning neural network for function interpolation and approximation. IEEE Trans. Neural Networks **7**(5), 1220–1230 (1996)
6. Chen, C.L.P., Wan, J.Z.: A rapid learning and dynamic stepwise updating algorithm for flat neural networks and the application to time-series prediction. IEEE Trans. Syst. Man Cybern. Part B **29**(1), 62–72 (1999)
7. Huang, G.B., Saratchandran, P., Sundararajan, N.: A generalized growing and pruning RBF (GGAP-RBF) neural network for function approximation. IEEE Trans. Neural Networks **16**(1), 57–67 (2005)
8. Huang, G.B., Siew, C.K.: Extreme learning machine with randomly assigned RBF kernels. Int. J Inf. Technol. **11**(1), 16–24 (2005)
9. Huang, G.B., Zhu, Q.Y., Siew, C.K.: Extreme learning machine: a new learning scheme of feedforward neural networks. In: Proceedings of IEEE International Joint Conference on Neural Networks, vol. 2, pp. 985–990 (2004)
10. Igelnik, B., Pao, Y.H.: Stochastic choice of basis functions in adaptive function approximation and the functional-link net. IEEE Trans. Neural Networks **6**(6), 1320–1329 (1995)
11. Kasun, L.L.C., Zhou, H., Huang, G.B., M., V.C.: Representational learning with extreme learning machine for big data. IEEE Intell. Syst. **28**(6), 31–34 (2013)
12. Pal, U., Chaudhuri, B.B.: Indian script character recognition: a survey. Pattern Recogn. **37**(9), 1887–1899 (2004)
13. Pao, Y.H., Takefuji, Y.: Functional-link net computing: theory, system architecture, and functionalities. Computer **25**(5), 76–79 (1992)
14. Savojardo, C., Fariselli, P., Casadio, R.: BETAWARE: a machine-learning tool to detect and predict transmembrane beta-barrel proteins in prokaryotes. Bioinformatics **29**(4), 504–505 (2013)
15. Scardapane, S., Wang, D., Panella, M., Uncini, A.: Distributed learning for random vector functional-link networks. Inf. Sci. **301**, 271–284 (2015)
16. Schmidt, W.F., Kraaijveld, M.A., Duin, R.P.W.: Feedforward neural networks with random weights. In: Proceedings of 11th IAPR International Conference on Pattern Recognition, Conference B: Pattern Recognition Methodology and Systems, vol. 2, pp. 1–4 (1992)
17. Tang, J., Deng, C., Huang, G.B.: Extreme learning machine for multilayer perceptron. IEEE Trans. Neural Networks Learn. Syst. **27**(4), 809–21 (2016)
18. Wang, L.P., Wan, C.R.: Comments on the extreme learning machine. IEEE Trans. Neural Networks **19**(8), 1494–1495 (2008)
19. Zhu, W., Miao, J., Qing, L.: Constrained extreme learning machines: a study on classification cases. arXiv preprint arXiv:1501.06115 (2015)

Image and Signal Processing and Analysis

Evaluating New Set of Acoustical Features for Cry Signal Classification

Sergio Daniel Cano-Ortiz$^{(\boxtimes)}$ (iD), Yadisbel Martinez-Canete (iD), and Liette Veranes-Vicet (iD)

Universidad de Oriente, 90900 Santiago de Cuba, Cuba
{scano,ymartinez,liette}@uo.edu.cu

Abstract. Searching for new features that contribute to the improvement of the performance of classification algorithms within the scientific area of infant crying classification for diagnostic purposes is a priority. Although several studies have suggested that some acoustic features present in the spectrogram of the signal of infant crying: stridor, melody, and shifts, could be interesting to reflect the pathological status of the newborn independently, a deeper study is still missing. This paper aims to demonstrate the potential of those attributes not sufficiently addressed in the state of the art of cry analysis when they're properly combined. For this purpose, the Random Forest and k-Nearest Neighbor classification algorithms are used. The set of input vectors to the classifier also incorporates other well-known cry features that have proven to be effective in cry classification such as the Mel Frequency Cepstral Coefficients (MFCCs), fundamental frequency (F_0), and the energy (E). The 10-fold cross-validation method was also used to evaluate the classifier performance as well as some standard metrics were used to evaluate the classifier results. Finally, a binary classifier for Central Nervous System (CNS) disorders with a Hypoxia background is proposed. The used experimental corpus comprises 616 samples of 1-s duration (253 pathological and 363 normal), corresponding to 54 children in age ranging from 0 to 3 months. The experimental results support the validity of the proposed feature set (stridor, melody, and shifts) for a child crying classification task as diagnostic method.

Keywords: Cry classification · MFCC · Qualitative crying features

1 Introduction

Feature extraction is used to get representative features which can characterize different patterns of cry utterances. In that sense, relevant characteristics from the cry signal are extracted and irrelevant information (i.e. the channel distortion and background noise) is eliminated. Many research works have been emphasized that feature extraction plays an important role in the field of automatic infant cry analysis.

Analyzing within infant cry signal a great variety of acoustic and prosodic information at different levels are found. The feature extraction procedure could be done in time or frequency domain. The frequency domain features have a strong ability to model

© The Author(s), under exclusive license to Springer Nature Switzerland AG 2022
O. O. Vergara-Villegas et al. (Eds.): MCPR 2022, LNCS 13264, pp. 149–158, 2022.
https://doi.org/10.1007/978-3-031-07750-0_14

the characteristics within infant cry signals despite time domain features which are not robust enough to represent the variations within infant cry signals and the features are sensitive to background noises. The high-level information, such as prosodic features, are important to improve the discriminative ability within signals. To manage physical and physiological information in cry signal a combination of prosodic domain features together with time or frequency domain features usually is needed. Another feature to consider is the spectrogram, it is an image that is a time-frequency representation of an infant cry utterance. The last one has a strong ability to represent the cry signal and include both acoustic and prosodic information.

In recent years, simple feature extraction techniques have been used. In this section, we review three feature extraction approaches in the latest research work.

A. Prosodic domain features

In neonate cry classification, many researchers used pitch based features which provided and have good results. In 2004, Varallyay et al. [1] proposed three different methods for the detection of the fundamental frequency. Moreover, Varallyay [2] reported a work based on time-domain analysis mainly from the duration of the signal. In his study, pitch, formant, and other features such as segment density, specific segment length, average pause length, and average segment length are analyzed and compared between normal babies and infants with hearing disorders whereas the classification part is not conducted. Dror Lederman in 2010 [3] considered the estimation of fundamental frequency for four different types of cries (Normal, Cri-du-Chat, Hydrocephalus, and Cleft Palate) using simple inverse filtering tracking method (SIFT) which is capable of overcoming the underestimation and over-estimation of the cry fundamental frequency.

Finding variability rates in features such as intensity, fundamental frequency (F_0), formants (F_i), and duration are typical acoustic cues that carry prosodic information about infant cry and speech [4]. Other researchers have also found that F_0 is critical in identifying infant cry signals [5]. Authors in [6] used F_0 to calculate unvoiced segments ratio, a relevant characteristic for analysis of infant cry. To set differences between full-term and preterm infant cry other features like mean, median, standard deviation, and minimum and maximum of F_0 and F_i were considered by Orlandi et al. [7].

B. Mel-Frequency Cepstrum Coefficients (MFCCs) and Linear Prediction Coefficients (LPC)

Mel frequency cepstral coefficients are one of the common, successful, and well-known acoustic features which have been explored by researchers in infant cry classification analysis [8–10]. MFCCs are used to encode speech signals that contain irrelevant information with large amounts of storage space into compressed and useful features. The main idea of Linear Prediction Cepstral Coefficients (LPCC) is to remove the redundancy from a signal and try to predict next values by linearly combining the previously known coefficients. It is used in [9] for cry detection problems. Moreover, Linear Predictive Coding (LPC) serves as a time-domain measure of how close two different waveforms are and it is used for infant cry classification [11].

C. Image domain features

The spectrogram is an image that is a time-frequency representation of an utterance. It has a strong ability to represent the acoustic signal (utterance) and include both acoustic and prosodic information. Using spectrograms as input into classifiers is a way to solve the problem of different cry signals having different durations. Thus in order to avoid the zero-padding to achieve same length of feature vectors, a normalization procedure is applied in the process of spectrogram generation, which produces the same size images without changing the original signal. Besides feeding the spectrogram into CNN [12–14], researchers also consider using the spectrogram image to retrieve extra features such as Local Binary Pattern (LBP), Local Phase Quantization (LPQ), and Robust Local Binary Pattern (RLBP) [15] to help improve the classification performance.

Picking Up Clues Lost in the Past

From the above state-of-the-art, we noticed that feature selection techniques to determine which of these features best performs in the cry classification system, have been hardly studied. Although the MFCCs and LPCs, as well as the spectral characteristics, have been the most commonly used attributes in cry classification, there are still niches not sufficiently studied in the area of parameter extraction (parameters or features with diagnostic potential). In 1980 Michelsson described the behavior of certain acoustic attributes in the spectrogram of a child crying signal in the presence of certain CNS pathologies [16]. Michelsson concluded that some of these acoustic phenomena such as stridors (turbulences), shifts of the fundamental frequency and the melody could be clues for the diagnosis but unfortunately they had not been objecting to a deep investigation. The author also commented in his article that in the case of stridor the Scandinavian Group worked on its objective measurement, but not on the link between the number of stridors present in a crying frame with F_0 and the type of melody in the shift segment. The approach to this aspect is not reported in the later state of the art. Although several authors consider the presence of shifts in healthy crying cases, their correlation with the presence of other acoustic phenomena such as stridor, energy and melody patterns is not addressed. These circumstances led the authors in [17] to consider this aspect in their hybrid classifier proposal. Although they limited themselves to visualizing this perspective and not demonstrating this condition experimentally. In 2018 Reyes-Garcia et al. took up 2 forgotten qualitative parameters such as shifts and glide and combined them with melody patterns to study the crying of indigenous children in Mexico [18]. They concluded that the malnutrition factor in these communities indeed affects the performance of these acoustic characteristics, as well as that the combination of this set of acoustic parameters served as clues to differentiate healthy from pathological crying, evidencing its diagnostic potential. It was shown that even the analysis of qualitative characteristics of crying aimed at diagnosing newborns is an open topic.

This paper focuses on the analysis of a new set of qualitative features such as shifting, stridor and melody pattern to investigate their potentials for diagnostic when combined with state-of-the-art features like MFCCs.

2   Materials and Methods

2.1   The Need for Clinical Cry Analysis

Previous studies have shown that preterm infants and infants with neurological conditions have different cry characteristics such as fundamental frequency (F_0), when compared to healthy full-term infants. Research has been carried on to study possible differences between full-term and preterm infants in their neuro-physiological maturity and the possible risk to the brain for the premature infant caused by prolonged deoxygenation due to crying [19–22]. The results from those studies show major discriminative differences between healthy infants and infants who suffered from diseases of the central nervous system.

2.2 The Hand-Craft Features

MFCC: The MFCC's have been used with high efficiency in a lot of works related to crying classification. The Mel scale filter bank is a series of L triangular bandpass filtering believed to occur in the auditory system (corresponding to a series of bandpass filters with constant bandwidth and spacing on a Mel frequency scale). The MFCC's can be computed by generating small segments from the signal, calculating the Discrete Fourie Transform (DFT) for each segment, the spectrum is then converted into a logarithmic scale, the scale is transformed into a soft Mel spectrum, and finally the discrete cosine transform DCT is calculated.

Energy: For a real discrete-time signal x(n) such as the cry signal, the energy is defined as

$$E = \sum_{n=-\infty}^{\infty} x^2(n) \tag{(1)}$$

However, since we are interested in a time-varying indication of energy, we use a time-varying calculation:

$$E(n) = \sum_{m=0}^{N-1} [w(m)x(n-m)]^2 \tag{(2)}$$

where $w()$ is the window function which determines the nature of the short time energy representation.

Fundamental Frequency or Pitch: Infant cry comprises the rhythmic alteration of cry sounds, utterances and inspirations. Crying is part of the expiratory phase of respiration with sound or phonation produced by the larynx, which contains the vocal cords or folds and glottis. When air is forced through adducted vocal cords, the increased airspeed due to passage through a constricted tube, results in a drop in air pressure, causing the vocal cords to open and close rapidly (approx. 250 to 450 Hz or cycles per second in a normal healthy newborn). This vibration is the fundamental frequency and is heard as the pitch of the cry. There are a lot of methods for F_0 estimation, in this paper we use the SIFT method.

2.3 New Set of Acoustical Features (Manually Estimated) to Be Validated

Shift: The shift is a sudden large change in pitch (fundamental frequency) caused by the vocal cords crashing into "overdrive" thereby instantly increasing the fundamental frequency to a much higher value (a sudden upward change of the fundamental frequency between 100 and 600 Hz in less than 10 msg). For our study, we use an alternative technique used by Escobedo et al. in [23] in which a rising shift (RS) is defined as the pitch frequency change increasing approximately by four octaves in 2 or 3 window segments of 62.5 ms (ms). These audible octaves ranging from A0 = 27.5 Hz to A4 = 440 Hz, i.e. from key 1 to 49 of 88 notes from the standard piano. These RS, among others, are appreciable melody or intonation changes in a relatively short time, which shows the relationship of the fundamental frequency with larynx control stability.

Diagnostic cue: 5 or more occurrences is abnormal in 12 s-cry recordings.

Estimation mode: visual by experienced specialists (rising shifts in the F_0 contour).

Melody Pattern: The melody is a newborn cry feature (time-domain F_0 contour) widely used for research purpose. Schönweiler et al. in [5] used four categories of melody: falling, rising, rising-falling, flat.

Diagnostic cue: Only the occurrence of a rising melody type will be used in the classification (presence or not). This is considered a valid strategy since, in earlier works, it was concluded that the occurrence of the rising melody type was allegedly greater in disorder cases.

Estimation mode: The melody pattern has been estimated visually by experienced specialists (when they visually inspect one cry unit in the spectrogram, coupled with aural inspection of the sound, they can determine which melody type applies to the cry utterance).

Stridor: Stridor is another form of vocal cord hyperfunction. In this case, a rapid increase in air pressure causes the vocal cords to enter a turbulent state resulting in the sudden loss of pitch. This creates a short noise (voiceless) within the harmonic frame.

Diagnostic cue: two or more occurrences is abnormal.

Estimation mode: Stridor have been estimated visually by experienced specialists (turbulence noise concentrations within spectrogram).

Summary of the Acoustical Indicators. Hereafter we summarize the acoustical indicators of disorder: (a)instant changes in the fundamental frequency of four or more octaves (shift) occur significantly more often in abnormal cases; (b) the melody type in test cases is, more often than in normal cases, of the rising type, (c) the number of turbulent noises (stridor) is increased in abnormal cases. In general, the number of shifts and stridor tends to be higher in abnormal cases.

2.4 Datasets and Experiments

For experiments two classes will be handled: normal babies (normal transpelvian delivery and cesarean dysthocic) and pathological babies (asphyxia, retarded intra-uterine growth, asphyxia with another risk and hyperbilirrubin)[1]. We used our own BDLLanto crying dataset with 54 cry samples (31 normal cases and 23 pathologic cases). The dataset has

---

[1] Two classes derived from six clinical control groups just for medical purpose.

been recorded at the Eastern Maternity Hospital of Santiago de Cuba. The crying was induced by a standardized stimulus, and 12 s of crying were recorded for each child with a SONY CFS-210 device. The used experimental corpus comprises 616 samples of 1-s duration (253 pathological and 363 normal), corresponding to 54 children in age ranging from 0 to 3 months. Then these cries were digitized by the PCVOX speech acquisition system. The original files are coded to 16 bits and sampled at 8000 Hz. In this paper, according to the needs, several soft-tools are used: MATLAB toolboxes, ANAVOZv3.0, and WEKA.

2.5   Cry Segmentation for Feature Extraction

Pre-processing. Each cry utterance is segmented in 1 s and each one represents one sample. Thus every 1 s, labelled with a previously established code, is segmented in 50 ms frames (instances). At the end a classifier will process the following data structure (Table 1):

Table 1. The data structure

	Newborn samples	Number of 1-s segments	Number of instances
Normal group	31	363	6897
Pathological group	23	253	4807
Total of newborns	54	616	11704

Feature Extraction. The samples are processed one by one extracting their MFCC acoustic features, this process is done with the Praat freeware program. The acoustic features are extracted as follows: for each segment, we extract 16 coefficients for every 50 ms, F_0, and Energy. The new features as stridor, melody pattern, and shift are manually extracted and coded by experienced researchers.

2.6   Cry Classification Methods

All experiments were conducted using the state-of-the-art classifiers the k-Nearest Neighbor algorithm (k-NN) and Random Forest algorithm (RF).

The k-NN) algorithm is a non-parametric method used for classification. The input consists of the k closest training examples in the feature space. In k-NN classification, the output is a class membership. An object is classified by a plurality vote of its neighbors, with the object being assigned to the class most common among its k nearest neighbors.

Random forests are built by combining the predictions of several decision trees, each of which is trained in isolation, and then the predictions of the trees are combined through averaging. The individual trees are constructed using a simple algorithm that represents a top-down decision tree induction algorithm in which the decision tree is not pruned and at each node, the inducer randomly samples N of the attributes and chooses the best split from among those variables. The classification of an unlabeled instance is performed using the majority vote. One important advantage of the random forest method is its ability to handle a very large number of input attributes. Another important feature of the random forest is that it is fast.

3 Discussion of Results

Two sets of experiments are implemented in this paper: a set 1 for input data vector without new features (only MFFCs, F_0 and Energy) and a set 2 for input data vector with full features (MFFCs, F_0, Energy + Stridor, Melody pattern and Shifts). We used RF and k-NN (k = 1, 3, 5) classifiers supported by WEKA platform, for the classification. For the evaluation of classifiers, the 10-fold cross-validation was used. Moreover, several metrics are also considered to evaluate the results: TP rate, FP rate, and ROC area. Results obtained for each experimental set are shown in Table 2 and Table 3.

Table 2. Results of classification for set 1 (only 16 MFCC, Energy and F_0)

Classifier	TP Rate	FP Rate	ROC Area
Random Forest	0.792	0.220	0.863
k-NN k=1	0.838	0.169	0.836
k-NN k=3	0.825	0.185	0.883
k-NN k=5	0.813	0.201	0.884

Table 3. Results of classification for set 2 (16 MFCC, Energy and F_0 + F_0, Stridor and Shift)

Classifier	TP Rate	FP Rate	ROC Area
Random Forest	0.914	0.091	0.969
k-NN k=1	0.936	0.066	0.937
k-NN k=3	0.926	0.075	0.969
k-NN k=5	0.917	0.085	0.972

As can be seen, it is evident that for each classifier, the presence of the three new parameters (stridor, melody, and shifts) substantially improves the classification results as they expel the values of the metrics used. The improvement in TP rates and the decrease in the FP rates suggests the diagnostic potential of these parameters in clinical applications. Another element to be highlighted is the improvement in the predictive performance of the classifiers in the presence of these attributes as expressed by the ROC values (it increases by approximately 10% reaching values above 0.95).

As can be seen in Figs. 1 and 2, the area under the ROC curve is greater for the k-NN method, which means a better performance of the method. In turn, it is observed in Fig. 2 that both trajectories ascend to the upper edge so that the area under the ROC curve in both trajectories increases (due to the presence of the new attributes), this

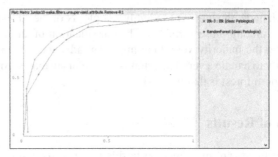

Fig. 1. ROC area for RF and IBk (k = 3) classifiers for set 1 (only 16 MFCC, Energy, and F_0).

Fig. 2. ROC area for RF and k-NN (k = 3) classifiers for set 2 (16 MFCC, Energy and F_0 + Melody pattern, Stridor, and Shift).

corroborates the idea of Michelsson and Wasz-Höckert about the diagnostic potential of those attributes. In turn, it is confirmed that for these attributes their diagnostic potential increases as they are associated with other parameters. Although the idea was outlined in hybrid classifiers [17], its contribution has been validated from state-of-the-art classifiers and a higher number of samples than that used in [17].

Regarding the performance of the classifiers used, it is observed that the k-NN with a value of k = 3, with the complete set of parameters (including stridor, melody, and shift), was the best performance for classification, with a ROC area above 0.95 and with better TP Rate and FP Rate values (substantially decisive in medical applications) than those shown by the RF algorithm.

4 Conclusions and Recommendations

The present paper addresses the potentiality of a set of three qualitative attributes of cry signals which have not been sufficiently studied in the specialized literature, namely, Stridor, Melody pattern and Shift. Supported by two state-of-art classification algorithms, two experimental sets are implemented and their performances properly compared, displaying an improvement in the classification when the new feature set (stridor, melody, shift) was considered. It is recommended in future work to perform a cross-correlation analysis to study the contribution of each of the new attributes as well as the effect of their combination on the performance of these classifiers.

Acknowledgments. This work has been fully supported by the Belgian Development Cooperation through VLIR-UOS (Flemish Interuniversity Council-University Cooperation for Development) in the context of the Institutional University Cooperation programme with Universidad de Oriente.

References

1. Varallyay, G., Benyo, Z., Illenyi, A., Farkas, Z., Kovacs, L.: Acoustic analysis of the infant cry: classical and new methods. In: 26th Annual International Conference of the IEEE EM BS, pp. 313–316. San Francisco, CA, USA (2004)
2. Varallyay, G.: Future prospects of the infant cry in the medicine. Periodica Polytechnica Ser. El. Eng. **50**(1–2), 47–62 (2006)
3. Lederman, D.: Estimation of infant's cry fundamental frequency using a modified SIFT algorithm. arXiv:1009.2796v1 [cs. SD] 14 Sep, pp. 1–5 (2010)
4. Osmani, A., Hamidi, M., Chibani, A.: Machine learning approach for infant cry interpretation. In: Proceedings – International Conference on Tools with Artificial Intelligence, ICTAI. (2018). https://doi.org/10.1109/ICTAI.2017.00038
5. Huckvale, M.: Neural network architecture that combines temporal and summative features for infant cry classification. In: Proceedings of the Annual Conference of the International Speech Communication Association, INTERSPEECH in the Interspeech 2018 Computational Paralinguistic Challenge, pp. 137–141 (2018). https://doi.org/10.21437/Interspeech. 2018-1959
6. Chittora, A., Patil, H.A.: Significance of unvoiced segments and fundamental frequency in infant cry analysis. In: Král, P., Matoušek, V. (eds.) TSD 2015. LNCS (LNAI), vol. 9302, pp. 273–281. Springer, Cham (2015). https://doi.org/10.1007/978-3-319-24033-6_31
7. Orlandi, S., Reyes Garcia, C.A., Bandini, A., Donzelli, G., Manfredi, C.: Application of pattern recognition techniques to the classification of full-term and preterm infant cry. J. Voice. **30**(6), 656–663 (2016). https://doi.org/10.1016/j.jvoice.2015.08.007
8. Zabidi, A., Khuan, L. Y., Mansor, W., Yassin, I. M., Sahak, R.: Detection of infant hypothyroidism with mel frequency cepstrum analysis and multi-layer perceptron classification. In: Proceedings -CSPA 2010: 2010 6th International Colloquium on Signal Processing and Its Applications, pp. 140–144 (2010). https://doi.org/10.1109/CSPA.2010.5545331
9. Gu, G., Shen, X., Xu, P.: A set of DSP system to detect baby crying. In: Proceedings of 2018 2nd IEEE Advanced Information Management, Communicates, Electronic and Automation Control Conference, IMCEC 2018, pp. 411–415 (2018). https://doi.org/10.1109/IMCEC. 2018.8469246
10. Galaviz, O.F.R., García, C.A.R.: Infant cry classification to identify hypo acoustics and asphyxia comparing an evolutionary-neural system with a neural network system. In: Gelbukh, A., de Albornoz, Á., Terashima-Marín, H. (eds.) MICAI 2005. LNCS (LNAI), vol. 3789, pp. 949–958. Springer, Heidelberg (2005). https://doi.org/10.1007/11579427_97
11. Liu, L., Li, W., Wu, X., Zhou, B.X.: Infant cry language analysis and recognition: an experimental approach. IEEE/CAA J. Autom. Sin. **6**(3), 778–788 (2019). https://doi.org/10.1109/ JAS.2019.1911435
12. Franti, E., Ispas, I., Dascalu, M.: Testing the Universal Baby Language hypothesis - automatic infant speech recognition with CNNs. In: 2018 41st International Conference on Telecommunications and Signal Processing, TSP 2018, pp. 1–4 (2018). https://doi.org/10.1109/TSP. 2018.8441412

13. Le, L., Kabir, A.N.M.H., Ji, C., Basodi, S., Pan, Y.: Using transfer learning, SVM, and ensemble classification to classify baby cries based on their spectrogram images. In: Proceedings - 2019 IEEE 16th International Conference on Mobile Ad Hoc and Smart Systems Workshops, MASSW 2019. (2019). https://doi.org/10.1109/MASSW.2019.00028
14. Chang, C.-Y., Tsai, L.-Y.: A CNN-based method for infant cry detection and recognition. In: Barolli, L., Takizawa, M., Xhafa, F., Enokido, T. (eds.) WAINA 2019. AISC, vol. 927, pp. 786–792. Springer, Cham (2019). https://doi.org/10.1007/978-3-030-15035-8_76
15. Felipe, G.Z., et al.: Identification of infants' cry motivation using spectrograms. In: 2019 International Conference on Systems, Signals and Image Processing (IWSSIP), pp. 181–186 (2019). https://doi.org/10.1109/IWSSIP.2019.8787318
16. Michelsson, K.: Cry characteristics in sound spectrographic cry analysis. In: Murry, T., Murry, J. (eds.) Infant Communication: Cry and Early Speech, pp. 85–105. College-Hill Press, Houston (1980)
17. Cano, S., Suaste, I., Escobedo, D., Reyes-García, C.A., Ekkel, T.: A combined classifier of cry units with new acoustic attributes. In: Martínez-Trinidad, J Francisco, Carrasco Ochoa, J.A., Kittler, J. (eds.) CIARP 2006. LNCS, vol. 4225, pp. 416–425. Springer, Heidelberg (2006). https://doi.org/10.1007/11892755_43
18. Reyes-García, C.A., Torres-García, A.A., RuizDiaz, M.A.: Extracción de Características Cualitativas del Llanto de Bebé y su Clasificación para la Identificación de Patologías Utilizando Modelos Neuro-Difusos. In: Memorias del Congreso Nacional de Ingeniería Biomédica, vol. 5, no. 1, pp. 106–109 (2018)
19. Wasz-Höckert, O., Koivisto, M., Vuorenkoski, V., Partanen, T., Lind, J.: Spectrographic analysis of pain cry in hyperbilirubinemia. Biol. Neonate. 17, 260–271 (1971)
20. Michelsson, K., Sirviö, P., Wasz-Höckert, O.: Pain cry in full-term asphyxiated newborninfants correlated with late findings. Acta Paediatr. Scand. 66(5), 611–616 (1977)
21. Michelsson, K., Sirviö, P., Wasz- Höckert, O.: Sound spectrographic cry analysis of infants with bacterial meningitis. Dev Med Child Neurol. 19(3), 309–315 (1977). https://doi.org/10.1111/j.1469-8749.1977.tb08366.x. PMID: 18378
22. Hariharan, M., Yaacob, S., Awang, S.A.: Pathological infant cry analysis using wavelet packet transform and probabilistic neural network. Expert Syst. Appl. 38(12), 15377–15382 (2011). https://doi.org/10.1016/j.eswa.2011.06.025
23. Escobedo, D., Cano, S., Coello, E., Regueiferos, L., Capdevila, L.: Rising shift of pitch frequency in the infant cry of some pathologic cases. In: 2nd International Conference, MAVEBA 2001, Firenze, Italy (2001)

Motor Imagery Classification Using Riemannian Geometry in Multiple Frequency Bands with a Weighted Nearest Neighbors Approach

Girish Tiwale[ID] and Hubert Cecotti[(✉)][ID]

Department of Computer Science, California State University, Fresno, USA
hcecotti@csufresno.edu
https://csm.fresnostate.edu/csci/

Abstract. Brain-Computer Interface (BCI) provides a direct communication from a brain to a computer through the analysis of brain evoked responses. The detection of motor imagery (MI) is one of the main paradigm used in BCI. We investigate the classification of MI using Riemannian geometry, a density based approach for discriminating brain evoked responses in multiple frequency bands. We compare classifiers based on the minimum distance to the mean (MDM) and k-nearest neighbors (KNN) approaches, with decisions weighted in relation to the kappa value of each frequency band. For the multi-class classification, the best performance was achieved with the weighted KNN with an average kappa value of 51.9%.

Keywords: Motor imagery · Riemannian geometry · Classification · K-nearest neighbor · Brain-machine interface

1 Introduction

A Brain-Computer Interface (BCI) is a system that provides a direct and non-muscular pathway of communication for the individuals with motor disabilities namely, spinal chord injury and Locked-In syndrome to communicate with electronic peripheral without needing physical contact [14]. BCI automatically translates the recorded brain responses into commands, which can be used to move a cursor on a screen or toggle switches. The primary aim of BCI is to detect and classify the signals by identifying well defined patterns in EEG activities [11]. It can have many applications where neuroprosthetic device can be controlled by the brain evoked responses. An individual is required to perform an imagination of a movement (e.g. right hand, left hand, foot and tongue) and the brain activity is recorded using non-invasive electroencephalography (EEG) with the electrodes placed at the surface of the scalp. Motor imagery (MI) is a popular example for BCI communication [15]. MI is the mental execution of a movement without any overt movement or without any peripheral (muscle) activation. The MI activates the

O. O. Vergara-Villegas et al. (Eds.): MCPR 2022, LNCS 13264, pp. 159–168, 2022.
https://doi.org/10.1007/978-3-031-07750-0_15

same brain areas as the actual movement [13]. Several attempts have been made to understand the dynamics of EEG signals by exploring different frequency bands, such as μ (8–13 Hz) and β (13–25 Hz) rhythms [6].

The goal of this paper is to classify brain evoked responses using EEG signals during MI activities. The brain evoked responses are specific to individuals and highly variable. Different ways are possible to tackle this problem: 1) It is possible to use a discriminant approach by using classifiers, e.g., linear classifiers combined with spatial filtering, convolutional neural networks that will take as an input a segment of signal and return the extent to which it belongs to a given class (for example left hand or right hand). In this approach, the model tries to find the differences between the types of evoked responses; 2) It is possible to use a density-based approach where we extract high-level features from the brain evoked responses, and we compare the test signals with other known signals using distances. In this approach, we compare signals we get during the test phase with labeled signals we have in a training database.

In this paper, we focus on the second approach by using distances. An efficient distance that is present in the literature is based on Riemannian geometry. Riemannian geometry is an efficient way to deal with the drawbacks of the Euclidean space for comparing the features based on covariance matrices. The distance used for this classification task is Riemannian distance using covariance matrices as input. The Riemannian mean calculation requires a large number of computations [1]. The size of the covariance matrix can become large when considering multiple frequency bands and a large number of sensors. We propose to investigate the minimum distance to the mean (MDM) and the k-nearest neighbors (KNN) approaches, combined with multiple frequency bands, and determine their performance when combined with the Riemannian Geometry for the classification of the MI responses in a publicly available EEG database that contains MI tasks [3]. We propose to weigh the contributions of the each frequency band by their discriminant power based on the Cohen kappa value. For KNN, the decisions are weighted twice: 1) based on the Cohen kappa value at the level of the frequency bands, 2) based on the distance of the closest examples to the test example.

2   Related Works

Studies have been performed that concentrate on KNN classifier on EEG data. The KNN classifier had received the best results when used with Minkowski distance with 70.08% accuracy when compared to the one with Manhattan, Euclidean Chebychev, and Hamming distance [8]. The distance metric that is considered has a key impact on the classifier's accuracy. For the classification task, the most widely used methods are Artificial Neural Networks (ANN), KNN, LDA and SVM. The KNN classifiers are easy to implement and deploy, and by definition they do not forget previously seen examples. However, the KNN classifier is highly sensitive to irrelevant and redundant features [7]. The KNN classifier with the help of cosine distance has also been tested over EEG signals and has performed quite well [4].

However, the classifiers performance depends on the dataset, e.g., the amount of trials and the variability across these trials. Thus, the selection of the best classifier depends on the characteristics of the dataset. The most widely used density-based approach is the Riemannian geometry. In the case of EEG data with input data corresponding to matrices (space × time), a covariance matrix is formed (space × space). Covariance matrices lie in the Symmetric Positive Definite Matrices (SPD) and hence in the Riemannian geometry domain [1]. The classification in the Riemannian tangent space provides better results than the minimum distance to the Riemannian Mean (MDRM) [2]. Currently various MI classification approaches such as deep learning and graph based approaches used in Riemannian geometry domain provide state-of-the-art performance [9]. There had been studies to solve the problem of subject specific frequency selection by using multiple Riemannian graph fusion that optimizes the subject specific frequency band [16].

3   Riemannian Geometry

The Riemannian manifold Z is a differentiable manifold where at each point, the tangent space is a finite-dimensional Euclidean space [12]. It contains the Symmetric and Positive Definite (SPD) matrix $Q(N_c)$. The vector space T_Q over the manifold Z contains the tangent space for the derivatives of a covariance matrix Q. The dimension of the tangent space and the manifold is provided by: $d_{ts} = (N_c(N_c + 1))/2$. We consider 2 data points, Q_1 and Q_2 corresponding to 2 covariance matrices. The geodesic distance on the manifold is the minimum length curve joining Q_1 and Q_2. It is defined by:

$$\delta_R(Q_1, Q_2) = \left\|log(Q_1^{-1}Q_2)\right\|_F = \left[\sum_{i=1}^{N_c} log^2\lambda_i\right]^{1/2} \qquad (1)$$

where λ_i, $i = 1,\ldots,N_c$ are the real eigenvalues of $Q_1^{-1}Q_2$ and N_c is the number of channels. Each tangent vector P_i is seen as the derivative at $t = 0$ of the geodesic $D_i(t)$ between exponential mapping $Q_i = Exp_Q(P_i)$ and Q, Q defined as:

$$Exp_Q(P_i) = Q_i = Q^{1/2}exp(Q^{-1/2}P_iQ^{-1/2})Q^{1/2} \qquad (2)$$

The logarithmic mapping gives the inverse mapping which is defined as,

$$Log_Q(Q_i) = P_i = Q^{1/2}log(Q^{-1/2}Q_iQ^{-1/2})Q^{1/2} \qquad (3)$$

More details about the geometrical procedure can be found in [2]. The Riemannian mean of $J \times 1$ SPD matrices in terms of geodesic distance is given by:

$$G(Q_1,\ldots,Q_J) = \underset{Q\in Q(N_c)}{\arg\min} \sum_{i=1}^{J} \delta_R^2(Q, Q_i) \qquad (4)$$

At a specific time instant j, $x_j \in \mathbb{R}^{N_c}$ denotes the EEG signal vector, where N_c is the number of channels.

The spatial covariance matrix is defined by:

$$Cov = E\left\{(x_j - E\{x_j\})(x_j - E\{x_j\})^T\right\} \tag{5}$$

where the functions $E\{.\}$ and superscript T represent the expected value and matrix transpose operation.

A time segment of EEG signal (X) corresponding to a given trial, where the segment is selected after N_{shift} time points after the start of the trial, and with a length $(N_t = D \cdot f_s$ where D is the duration of the trial and f_s is the sampling rate of the signal using N_c channels. $X_i \in \mathbb{R}^{N_c \times N_t}$ is the segment containing the EEG signal for the ith trial. The spatial covariance matrix (SCM) for the ith trial is denoted by Q_i, $Q_i \in \mathbb{R}^{N_c \times N_c}$. Q_i is estimated by:

$$Q_i = \frac{1}{N_t - 1} X_i X_i^T \tag{6}$$

Let X_{train} and X_{test}, the training and test databases containing N_{train} and N_{test} covariance matrices. We have $X_{train} \in \mathbb{R}^{N_c \times N_c \times N_{train}}$ and $X_{test} \in \mathbb{R}^{N_c \times N_c \times N_{test}}$.

4   Dataset

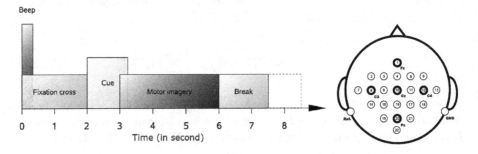

Fig. 1. Timing scheme of the paradigm

We used the four class MI dataset 2a of the BCI Competition IV [3]. The experimental paradigm is depicted in Fig. 1. This dataset has the EEG data from 9 different subjects; it consists of four different MI tasks ($N_{class} = 4$). The classes correspond to the imagination of left hand movement (class 1), right hand movement (class 2), both feet movement (class 3) and tongue (class 4). The dataset contains the data of two different sessions for each subject recorded on two different days. Each session contains 6 runs and each run consists of 48 trials (12 for each class), totalling 288 trials per session. Twenty two EEG channels were used and three EOG channels were used, with a sampling rate 250 Hz. The signal was band-pass filtered between 0.5–100 Hz, with a notch filter 50 Hz [3]. In the subsequent sections, we consider only a subset of 17 electrodes (FC3, FC1, FCz, FC2, FC4, C5, C3, C1, Cz, C2, C4, C6, CP3, CP1, CPz, CP2 and CP4) covering the central area. We consider a time segment of duration 3 s, after 3 s post-trial onset. Therefore, we have $N_c = 17$ and $N_t = 3 \cdot f_s = 750$.

5   Methods

5.1   Feature Extraction

The EEG signal was first filtered in 5 frequency bands ($N_f = 5$) ([8 12]; [12 16]; [16 20]; [20 24]; [8 24]) using a Butterworth bandpass filter of order 4. The band [8 12] corresponds to the μ band, the three next bands are in the β band, while the last band includes both the μ and β bands. Considering the number of sensors selected from the channels, number of frequency bands, number of trials each run has and the total number of runs, the covariance matrix of the dimensions ($N_{sensors} \times N_{filters}, N_{sensors} \times N_{filters}, N_{trials} \times N_{runs}$) is maintained for the features extracted from the signal.

5.2   Classification

For the classification, we have considered the minimum distance to the mean (MDM) and the k-nearest neighbors (KNN) classifiers. We use a Riemannian distance algorithm to compute the distance between class-wise covariance matrix $Q_G^{(c)}$ and an unknown test trial. The main drawback of calculating distance is that the noise can be present in the information contained by the distance between two covariance matrices. In that case, some important information related to the class might get overshadowed by the noise. Therefore, an improved approach includes the Fisher Geodesic Discriminant Analysis (FGDA) in [1]. It searches for the geodesics that contain the information about the class. The covariance matrices are filtered using these FGDA filters in Riemann space to discard irrelevant information. This approach is inspired by the Principal Geodesic Analysis [5].

Apart from the 'Distance to the mean' [2], we have investigated 'Weighted KNN' [8, 10] classifiers to classify the MI data. We have considered all 5 frequency bands in the Mu and Beta bands for band pass filters to investigate the classification of MI data. It is worth noting that using multiple filters together increases the size of the covariance matrix, and the FGDA requires a substantially larger amount of memory to be tested. Instead of having a covariance matrix of size $N_{sensors}N_{filters} \times N_{sensors}N_{filters}$, we consider only $N_{filters}$ covariance matrices of size $N_{sensors} \times N_{sensors}$.

Minimum Distance to Mean (MDM). From the training dataset, the means of each classes are computed in the training phase. Then, the distances from these means are calculated for the entire test data. For each frequency band, the confidence value is calculated for the entire test dataset with respect to each class. We calculate the confidence value based on the distance between the test trial and the mean of each class. The class C_j corresponding to the trial i is given by:

$$j_{out} = \underset{1 \leq j \leq N_{class}}{\arg\min} \sum_{f=1}^{N_f} \left(\frac{1/\delta_R(Q_i^f, C_j^f)}{\sum_{l=1}^{N_{class}} 1/\delta_R(Q_i^f, C_l^f)} \right) \tag{7}$$

where C_j^f is the mean of the covariance matrices corresponding to the jth class for the frequency band f using the Riemannian geometry to find the barycenter of the trials belonging to this class, and Q_i^f is the covariance matrix for the trial i in the fth frequency band.

Kappa Weighted Minimum Distance to Mean (KW-MDM). For the kappa weighted minimum distance to mean algorithm, we use the kappa value for each frequency band to weigh the decisions. We use the kappa value obtained from each frequency band in the training dataset to weigh the contribution of each individual frequency band during the test phase. If a frequency band provides a high kappa value, then this frequency band has a high contribution in the classification.

First we run the MDM classifier on the training dataset and calculate the kappa value for each frequency band. Then, the confidence value (p_i) to classify the trial i as belonging to the class C_j, $1 \leq j \leq N_{class}$ is given by:

$$j_{out} = \underset{1 \leq j \leq N_{class}}{\arg\min} \sum_{f=1}^{N_f} \left(\frac{\kappa(f) \cdot 1/\delta_R(Q_i^f, C_j^f)}{\sum_{l=1}^{N_{class}} 1/\delta_R(Q_i^f, C_l^f)} \right) \tag{8}$$

where, K_f is the Cohen's Kappa coefficient corresponding to the frequency band f obtained with the training dataset. C_j is the mean of the covariance matrices corresponding to the jth class using the Riemanian geometry to find the barycenter of the trials belonging to this class, and Q_i^f is the covariance matrix for the fth frequency band. Cohen's kappa is the agreement between two experts that classify N items into N_{class} mutually exclusive categories: $\kappa = (p_o - p_e)/(1 - p_e)$ where p_o is the relative observed agreement among experts, and p_e is the probability of chance agreement ($p_e = 1/N_{class}$).

Weighted KNN. In this approach, during the training phase after the geodesic filtering, the Riemannian distance between each example in the test dataset and training dataset is calculated. Then, for each example in the test dataset, the k closest examples with the minimum distances from the training dataset are selected. For each of these k examples, the weight of the corresponding label is updated w.r.t. the distance between the test example and the example from that class. Finally, the class belonging to the unknown test trial i is given by:

$$
j_{out} = \arg\max_{1 \leq j \leq N_{class}} \left(\frac{\sum\limits_{l=1}^{k} \omega(s(l), j) \cdot 1/\sqrt{\sum\limits_{f=1}^{N_f} \delta_R(Q_i^f, Q_{s(l)}^f)}}{\sum\limits_{l=1}^{k} 1/\sqrt{\sum\limits_{f=1}^{N_f} \delta_R(Q_i^f, Q_{s(l)}^f)}} \right) \tag{9}
$$

where $\omega(l, j)$ is a function that returns 1 if the trial l belongs to the class $\mathcal{C}_j$ and 0 otherwise. Q_i^f and Q_j^f are the covariance matrices of the test example and $s(l)^{th}$ example respectively for the fth frequency band. $s(l)$ is the index of the trial at position l after being sorted by the distances.

Kappa-Weighted KNN. Similar to the KW-MDM classifier, we use the kappa value calculated in the training phase for each frequency band to weigh each frequency band's contribution when classifying the trial. We use the weighted KNN approach for the training phase and calculate the kappa value for each frequency band. Then, we use this kappa value in the test phase while classifying the unknown test trial i. The belonging class $\mathcal{C}_j$ for the given trial i is given by:

$$
j_{out} = \arg\max_{1 \leq j \leq N_{class}} \sum\limits_{f=1}^{N_f} \left(\frac{\kappa(f) \cdot \sum\limits_{l=1}^{k} \omega(s(l), j) \cdot 1/\delta_R(Q_i^f, Q_{s(l)}^f)}{\sum\limits_{l=1}^{k} 1/\delta_R(Q_i^f, Q_{s(l)}^f)} \right) \tag{10}
$$

where $\omega(l, j)$ is a function that returns 1 if the trial l belongs to the class $\mathcal{C}_j$ and 0 otherwise. Q_i^f and $Q_{s(l)}^f$ are the covariance matrices of the test example and the $s(l)^{th}$ example respectively. $s(l)$ is the index of the trial at position l after being sorted by the distances. $\kappa(f)$ is the Cohen's Kappa coefficient corresponding to the frequency band f obtained with the training dataset, and Q_i^f is the covariance matrix for the fth frequency band. For the performance evaluation, we have considered a subject dependent evaluation i.e., training on the 'A0_T' dataset, and test on the 'A0_E' dataset.

6   Results and Discussion

The classification model has been trained with all the training trials from A0_T and for the evaluation, all four methods of classification have been tested on A0_E.

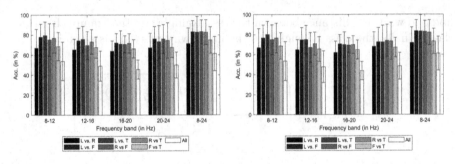

Fig. 2. Accuracy for each frequency band with the MDM (left) & KNN (right) classifiers

Figure 2 presents the accuracy for each frequency band. It shows that there is no significant difference between the accuracy while considering one classifier over the other (MDM vs Weighted KNN). Furthermore, it suggests that each frequency band has a specific discriminant power in the MI classification task.

Table 1. Kappa (in %) with all the classifiers and classification tasks, using all the frequency bands. Mean and standard deviation (SD) across subjects.

Classifier	Mean/S.D.	LvsR	LvsF	LvsT	RvsF	RvsT	FvsT	All
MDM	Mean	45.52	69.91	64.66	65.43	67.28	50.31	49.95
	SD	32.08	21.4	25.33	23.1	22.75	24.06	20.55
KW-MDM	Mean	46.3	71.61	65.74	66.67	67.59	50.62	51.34
	SD	32.94	21.51	24.91	23.27	23.18	24.94	20.4
KNN	Mean	46.45	69.29	68.52	70.06	67.44	56.17	51.9
	SD	34.32	23.52	25.09	23.03	23.89	19.96	20.77
KW-KNN	Mean	46.14	65.28	58.8	63.89	55.71	51.85	39.61
	SD	34.32	21.33	33.68	27.77	28.53	20.15	27.38

Furthermore, the weight of the kappa value for each the frequency band computed in the training phase is used in the test phase. The mean and standard deviation across subjects of the kappa value, for all the classifiers, are presented in Table 1. The best performance is achieved with the Weighted KNN classifier for LvsR ($\kappa = 46.45\%$), LvsT ($\kappa = 68.52\%$), RvsF ($\kappa = 70.06\%$), FvsT ($\kappa = 56.17\%$) and also the multi-class classification which has a kappa value of 51.9%. The KW-MDM classifier provides the best performance for LvsF ($\kappa = 71.61\%$) and RvsT ($\kappa = 67.59\%$).

A Wilcoxon signed rank test was used to assess the difference of performance between the different conditions. The results indicate that there is difference between MDM and KW-MDM for the multi-class classification ($p < 0.05$). There was no significant difference of performance ($p > 0.05$) between conditions for

LvsR, LvsF, LvsT, RvsT. We found a difference for RvsF for MDM and Weighted KNN, with Weighted KNN providing better kappa at 0.7006 ($p < 0.05$). The test reveals a difference for FvsT classification between MDM and KW-MDM, MDM and Weighted KNN, with the best kappa obtained with Weighted KNN, with a value of 0.567 ($p < 0.05$). We show that the contribution provided by the weight of the kappa value allows an improvement of the performance of the multi-class classifier for MI.

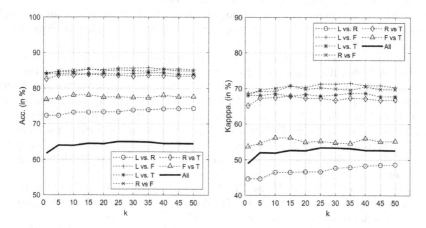

Fig. 3. Accuracy and Kappa for KNN in relation to K for the classification tasks.

Overall, the best performance is achieved by the Weighted KNN classifier ($\kappa = 51.9$). Furthermore, the KNN classifier was tested with a different values of k; Fig. 3 depicts the accuracy and the kappa values for different values of k. $k = 25$ provides the best accuracy (65.05%) and the best kappa value (53.40%) for the multi-class classifier. However, the time complexity of the KNN algorithm is directly connected to the value of k. Therefore, an optimum value for k is important to balance the accuracy and time complexity.

7   Conclusion

We have assessed the performance of 4-class MI classification using EEG signals. We have considered a multi-band approach with signals filtered in five frequency bands. Similar performance was achieved when the different frequency bands were used without considering each band's contribution. Introducing the kappa value computed in the training stage and using it to weigh each band's contribution in the classification task provided a significant improvement in the classifier's performance. When considering different pairwise and one multi-class (4 classes) classification tasks, Weighted KNN performs better than the other chosen approaches when considering 5 of the 7 tasks, while KW-MDM performs the best in the other two tasks.

Acknowledgment. This study was supported by the NIH-R15 NS118581 project.

References

1. Barachant, A., Bonnet, S., Congedo, M., Jutten, C.: Riemannian geometry applied to BCI classification. In: Vigneron, V., Zarzoso, V., Moreau, E., Gribonval, R., Vincent, E. (eds.) LVA/ICA 2010. LNCS, vol. 6365, pp. 629–636. Springer, Heidelberg (2010). https://doi.org/10.1007/978-3-642-15995-4_78
2. Barachant, A., Bonnet, S., Congedo, M., Jutten, C.: Multiclass brain-computer interface classification by riemannian geometry. IEEE Trans. Biomed. Eng. **59**(4), 920–928 (2011)
3. Brunner, C., Leeb, R., Müller-Putz, G., Schlögl, A., Pfurtscheller, G.: BCI competition 2008-GRAZ data set a. Institute for Knowledge Discovery (Laboratory of Brain-Computer Interfaces), vol. 16, pp. 1–6. Graz University of Technology (2008)
4. Chatterjee, R., Sanyal, D.K.: Study of different filter bank approaches in motor-imagery EEG. Smart Healthcare Analyt. IoT Enabled Environ. **178**, 173 (2020)
5. Fletcher, P.T., Joshi, S.: Principal geodesic analysis on symmetric spaces: statistics of diffusion tensors. In: Sonka, M., Kakadiaris, I.A., Kybic, J. (eds.) CVAMIA/MMBIA -2004. LNCS, vol. 3117, pp. 87–98. Springer, Heidelberg (2004). https://doi.org/10.1007/978-3-540-27816-0_8
6. Gaur, P., Pachori, R.B., Wang, H., Prasad, G.: A multi-class EEG-based BCI classification using multivariate empirical mode decomposition based filtering and riemannian geometry. Expert Syst. Appl. **95**, 201–211 (2018)
7. Ilyas, M.Z., Saad, P., Ahmad, M.I.: A survey of analysis and classification of EEG signals for brain-computer interfaces. In: 2015 2nd International Conference on Biomedical Engineering (ICoBE), pp. 1–6. IEEE (2015)
8. Isa, N.E.M., Amir, A., Ilyas, M.Z., Razalli, M.S.: The performance analysis of k-nearest neighbors (k-nn) algorithm for motor imagery classification based on EEG signal. In: MATEC web of conferences. vol. 140, p. 01024. EDP Sciences (2017)
9. Ju, C., Guan, C.: Tensor-cspnet: A novel geometric deep learning framework for motor imagery classification. arXiv preprint arXiv:2202.02472 (2022)
10. Khasnobish, A., Bhattacharyya, S., Konar, A., Tibarewala, D.: K-nearest neighbor classification of left-right limb movement using EEG data. In: Oral Presentation in International Conference on Biomedical Engineering and Assistive Technologies. NIT Jalandhar (2010)
11. Lebedev, M.A., Nicolelis, M.A.: Brain-machine interfaces: past, present and future. Trends Neurosci. **29**(9), 536–546 (2006)
12. Moakher, M.: A differential geometric approach to the geometric mean of symmetric positive-definite matrices. SIAM J. Matrix Anal. Appl. **26**(3), 735–747 (2005)
13. Mulder, T.: Motor imagery and action observation: cognitive tools for rehabilitation. J. Neural Transm. **114**(10), 1265–1278 (2007)
14. Nicolas-Alonso, L.F., Gomez-Gil, J.: Brain computer interfaces, a review. sensors **12**(2), 1211–1279 (2012)
15. Pfurtscheller, G., Brunner, C., Schlögl, A., Da Silva, F.L.: Mu rhythm (de) synchronization and EEG single-trial classification of different motor imagery tasks. Neuroimage **31**(1), 153–159 (2006)
16. Xie, X., Zou, X., Yu, T., Tang, R., Hou, Y., Qi, F.: Multiple graph fusion based on riemannian geometry for motor imagery classification. Appl. Intell. pp. 1–13 (2022)

Virtualizing 3D Real Environments Using 2D Pictures Based on Photogrammetry

Rafael Mercado Herrera[1]([⊠]) , Vianney Muñoz Jiménez[1] ,
Marco Antonio Ramos Corchado[1] , Félix Francisco Ramos Corchado[2] ,
and José Raymundo Marcial Romero[1]

[1] Computer Science Department, Universidad Autónoma del Estado de México,
Toluca de Lerdo, Mexico
rmercadoh098@alumno.uaemex.mx, {vmunozj,jrmarcialr}@uaemex.mx
[2] Computer Science Department, Cinvestav-IPN Unidad Guadalajara,
Zapopan, Mexico
felix.ramos@cinvestav.mx

Abstract. Virtual creatures are situated agents capable of interacting with the virtual environment where they inhabit. Experiments with virtual creatures require an environment where they can develop. Depending on the task, a scene from the real world may be the best candidate; it is possible to generate a virtual representation according to the specific case study. Usually, this is known as 3D reconstruction. This paper focuses on this possibility. It presents a quick rundown of the more common approaches to 3D reconstruction, along with some of their strengths and weaknesses. With this background information, a proposal is made and tested for a workflow for reconstruction using a photogrammetry approach. The workflow's capabilities are tested in the indoor and outdoor settings regarding the approach's ability to generate a usable environment for virtual creature experimentation. The results presented are based on using a database for the community and generating a personal database to test the proposed workflow. The result shows that the reconstruction 3D environment using photogrammetry is possible, and it is feasible to obtain a virtual environment of the real world.

Keywords: Virtual environment · 3D reconstruction ·
Photogrammetry

1 Introduction

Currently, several areas use virtual environments for different activities, ranging from learning to training. These environments are no longer based on the designer's imagination but are recreated from real environments, for example, the reconstruction or assembly of an aircraft engine. For this reason, it is necessary

Supported by CONACYT.

to have a reconstruction mechanism that allows environments of real situations to be efficiently reconstructed as closely as possible to reality. In this work, it is proposed to use photogrammetry based on taking 2D panoramic images. The difficulty consists in reconstructing the 3D environment from the 2D images, where the user can be immersed or virtual creatures use it to carry out or show some task or objective.

Throughout these experiments, an underlying requirement is an appropriate virtual environment (a field of study in itself [16]). The importance of the type of environment for virtual creature experiments was apparent since the inception of virtual creatures for biological research [17,19]. The environment gained importance with the introduction of physical simulation environments [22].

In broad terms, it is costly to prepare a virtual environment until used for different experimentations because it is generated through procedural means (e.g., [18]) or generates a virtual representation of a real-world scene.

The field of 3D scene reconstruction relies on multiple sources of information, along with different approaches to generate virtual environments. It is worth noting that each source of information and consequent approach has its benefits and drawbacks. The following list of sources presents the more common ones found in academia and the market:

Photographs. RGB or grayscale photographs. Information usually comes from batches of images of a scene through photogrammetry, which translates measures in the images into measures in a 3D space. Thanks to the ready availability of cameras in smartphones, this approach is the most accessible and has long been used even with community input [8]. It has, however, the drawback that additional processes are required to extract 3D information [9].

RGB-D images. Similar to conventional photographs with an additional channel representing the depth or distance from the camera of each pixel. Since the hardware handles the depth acquisition, processing requirements are lower than fully photogrammetric approaches and happen in real-time [23]. This approach's restrictions lie in hardware availability and affordability, but this will become less important as the offer of consumer products improves [26].

Floorplans. The visual representation, in 2D, of a building's rooms; extruding its walls forms a 3D model. Recent buildings may have machine-readable floorplans as *Computer Assisted Design* (CAD) files; older buildings, on the other hand, may only have physical drawings, and the task becomes turning an image into a floor plan [14]. Current approaches focus on adding textures and semantic labels to the rooms with the help of photographs of the scenes [24].

Inertial information. Use of odometry to identify positions and movement over time. In conjunction with photographs, this information helps position the photographs in a 3D space to use them for reconstruction.

Section 1.1 presents a short introduction to the photogrammetric approach in 3D reconstruction. This work uses photographs as the only source of information because of the ease of access to a camera and the ready availability of dataset of photographs of indoor and outdoor scenes. Section 2 presents a work-flow proposed using tools and approaches found in the state-of-the-art and the results of its application to multiple scenes, both indoors and outdoors. Section 3 displays the reconstructions resulting from applying the described approaches. The reconstructions are discussed according to their resulting geometry and the workflow's characteristics and setbacks when applied to real-world scenes.

1.1 Photogrammetric Approach

Photogrammetry is the science of extracting reliable, measurable, and inter-pretable information from photographs. The information extracted is related to surfaces and objects present in the photographs [21]. Measurements performed on the image can be transformed into measurements of the environment itself, and 2D points can be projected into a 3D space.

This transformation is possible thanks to a camera model. A model maps the projection of points in the environment to points in the image. The most common is the pinhole camera model (see Fig. 1) for ordinary cameras. This model uses projective geometry to map points in 3D space to points in a plane passing through a single point known as the camera center [9].

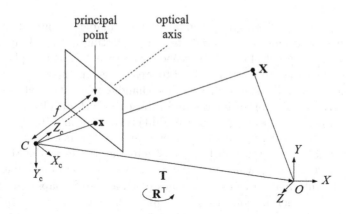

Fig. 1. Visualization of the pinhole camera model found in [20].

Multiple algorithms exist to reconstruct scenes displayed in pictures. The most common algorithm used when large sets of pictures are available is *Structure from Motion* (SfM).

SfM commonly behaves as an incremental process with a preprocessing phase known as incremental SfM [1]. Distinguishable points are found in each image and matched to ones found in other images to form image pairs. This process constitutes the preprocessing phase.

The algorithm adds each image to the scene's 3D model. Its camera model (which dictates the image's position and orientation in coordinates (x, y, z))

projects beams from its camera center through the points identified in the image. These beams intersect with beams projected by their paired images. The intersection of two or more beams represents the 3D position of the point identified in the images.

With each addition, optimization occurs to minimize misalignments of images. These errors indicate that paired images project beams to matched points that fail to intersect. This process continues until all images form part of the reconstruction; the process follows the schematic in Fig. 2.

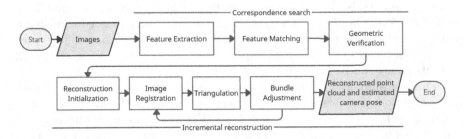

Fig. 2. Identification of each phase of incremental SfM as described by [1].

This incremental approach is standard and available in multiple tools and environments. This can be an initial step in generating a virtual environment since its result is a point cloud of the scene's structure. SfM can apply a surface reconstruction process to the point cloud to create a geometry usable as an environment for virtual creatures. Other methods handle different situations, such as the progressive acquisition of images and robustness lack of initial information [15] or robustness to repeating patterns in different locations [10].

In order to extract the scene's geometry and generate its surface, further processing is necessary. Since SfM also positions the images in the 3D space, it can apply approaches known as Multi-View Stereo. These approaches extract additional 3D information from the images (such as depth maps) and fuse this information into a denser point cloud or a 3D surface [6].

2   Environment Generation

Figure 3 shows the workflow used to carry out the experiment and treatment of photographs to reconstruct 3D virtual environments, using photogrammetry as a method.

An SfM approach processes a set of images and produces an initial model consisting of a sparse point cloud and the configuration (position and orientation) in 3D of the image set.

A *Multi-View Stereo* (MVS) approach further processes the model to generate a representation of the scene's geometry. The representation of the geometry can have different modalities depending on the approach, ranging from a dense point cloud to a set of depth maps.

Finally, a surface reconstruction approach converts the geometric representation into a 3D surface. Depending on the approach used, surfaces with different characteristics will result.

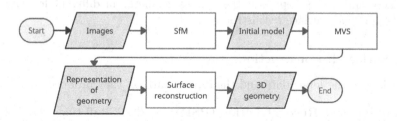

Fig. 3. Diagram of the workflow used for 3D virtual environment construction.

The following subsections explain each step of the workflow diagram for the 3D reconstruction.

2.1 Structure from Motion

This work utilizes SfM and MVE to reconstruct the 3D environment explained in the following paragraph.

Visual SfM [25]. SfM focuses on optimization requiring only $O(n)$ time on many significant steps. It has a good balance between speed and accuracy. One of its drawbacks is a greater dependence on a good initial image pair from the set. A lousy image pair can cause the approach to produce multiple partial models.

Multi-View Environment (MVE). MVE is a reconstruction environment using SfM proposed by Fuhrmann et al. [3], who improved their performance by removing the natural distortion caused by the camera lens during reconstruction.

SfM and MVE approaches have a high optimization degree to the point that an ordinary desktop computer can reconstruct building-level scenes with processing power and memory availability.

2.2 Multi-View Stereo

The following two approaches are part of the experiment due to their interoperability with the SfM approaches and the requirement of surface reconstruction approaches:

CMVS/PMVS [5,7]. MVS approach divides the scene into more manageable clusters for parallel processing. This approach uses image analysis to identify regions with consistent texture in the image as surfaces and populate their respective 3D position with patches of points. The resulting model is a dense point cloud.

These approaches represent the scene's geometry in different formats that are the input for surface reconstruction.

2.3 Surface Reconstruction

According to the input data and the type of surface, they produce:

Poisson Surface Reconstruction (PSR) [11,12]. PSR distinguishes between the interior and exterior of the solid using the orientation of the points and converts a point cloud into an impermeable surface. It uses an implicit indicator function that indicates whether a point is within it, where the point cloud is a sample of this function. The points generate a vector field and a scalar function to extract the surface. PSR allows you to interpolate and fill in any gaps in the point cloud to generate an impervious surface.

Floating Scale Surface Reconstruction (FSSR) [2]. FSSR considers that each sample point represents a finite surface of the scene and not a single point. Its main idea is that the sample points have a scale; this makes the approach robust against redundancy and noise, as high-resolution information subsumes low-resolution samples. This approach does not perform interpolation, leaving the regions empty compared to the PSR operation.

Both approaches offer different reconstruction options based on the point cloud and handle these to obtain a full reconstructed 3D model. The following Sect. 3 shows the experimentation of the presented approaches based on photographs and videos obtained from public sources of the Pyramid of the Sun located in Teohihucán, Mexico.

3   Results

The following paragraphs show the results obtained by applying the aforementioned methods to reconstruct 3D virtual environments outdoors and indoors.

3.1   Outdoor Environments

Figure 4 shows the reconstruction of a 3D object using SfM, CMVS/PMVS, and PSR. The images used came from a public data source acquired by drones corresponding to the Temple of the Sun in Teotihuacán, Mexico. Images needed to be preprocessed for use in the proposed workflow. In this first experiment, it was observed that the point cloud treatment was viable to obtain the total reconstruction of the virtual environment taken images of the real world.

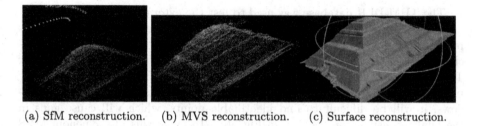

(a) SfM reconstruction.   (b) MVS reconstruction.   (c) Surface reconstruction.

Fig. 4. 3D reconstruction of the Pyramid of the Sun in Mexico.

It is necessary to specify that the images were taken from a video that captured part of the flat surface of the terrain, which caused this surface to be reconstituted as part of the main object through the SfM and MVS processes. Removing those points outside the object or environment from the point cloud was necessary to optimize the object's reconstruction cost. Figure 4c shows the final result of the 3D reconstruction where it was observed that there were no holes in the surface, and an original representation of the real world was obtained.

The following experiment used a dataset known as TUM-DLR [13]. The reconstruction results are shown in Fig. 5.

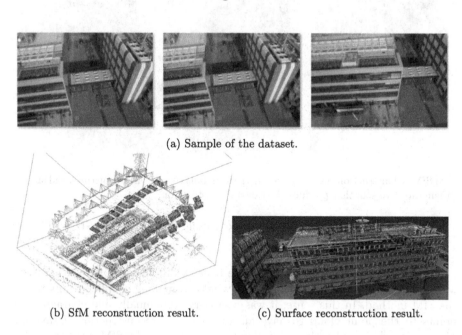

(a) Sample of the dataset.

(b) SfM reconstruction result.   (c) Surface reconstruction result.

Fig. 5. Reconstruction of the outdoor scene in the dataset TUM-DLR [13].

The TUM-DLR database was used to test the exterior reconstruction workflow, which provided a dataset for multiple remote sensing modalities. This reconstruction used only the photographs taken from an Unmanned Aerial Vehicle of the facade of the *Institute of Remote Sensing Technology* (IMF) building. The approaches used for this reconstruction were MVE, MVS for community photo collections, and FSSR. In images that show objects with mirrors and windows, it will be difficult to find identifiable points, which will cause gaps in the final reconstruction, as seen in Fig. 5(c). To avoid this phenomenon, MVS combined with SfM and PMVS was used, which minimized this type of inconvenience.

3.2   Indoor Environments

Figure 6 shows the interior reconstruction using the IMF interior corridor from the TUM-DLR dataset.

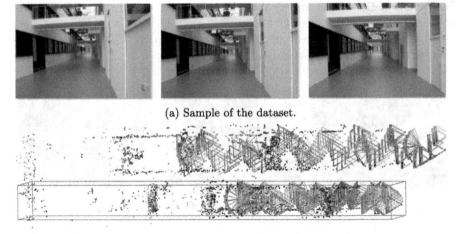

(a) Sample of the dataset.

(b) SfM reconstruction result; the reconstruction fails to align all the pictures and splits them into two sets that produce their own reconstruction.

Fig. 6. Reconstruction of the indoor scene using the dataset TUM-DLR [13].

The difficulty in reconstruction arose because the images presented smooth walls and uniform colors as well as glass windows, making it difficult only to use the SfM method. In this sense, it was necessary to manually add characteristic points to the point cloud to have an adequate 3D reconstruction. Using the MVE method (Fig. 6b), the point cloud was similar to the SfM method, and it was necessary to manually add characteristic points that allowed the adequate reconstruction of the 3D model.

Figure 7 shows the reconstruction of interiors based solely on a point cloud of a single room using the SfM and CMVS/PMVS methods.

(a) Sample of the dataset.   (b) SfM reconstruction result.

Fig. 7. Reconstruction of a room in the dataset [4].

The [4] database used ambient lighting and artwork placed on the walls. In this reconstruction, problems with light management were observed since the methods discriminated significant points for the reconstruction or obtained clusters of points due to the occlusion in corners and edges. The unwanted effects caused by ambient lighting generated solid structures instead of discriminating. These were added in the reconstruction, which affected its coherence. The center of Fig. 7b shows one of these solid structures that interfered with a correct reconstruction.

Figure 8 used personal work center images using SfM, MVS, and FSSR methods. The database comprised images with different information such as furniture, windows, doors, and objects belonging to the staff that works in this space. The interest in using this database was because the objects within the space produced variations in textures and colors and the occlusion of walls, making a correct virtual reconstruction of the environment difficult. At first glance, a similar result was observed in reconstructing a room. However, with a preprocessing of the images, the accumulation of point clouds that could affect the adequate reconstruction of the environment could be omitted. Therefore, the methods used properly allowed the reconstruction of virtual environments in 3D.

4   Discussion

The methods used to reconstruct 3D virtual environments offer advantages and disadvantages that we will discuss in the following paragraphs. One of the main advantages of the exposed methods is the possibility of reconstructing scenarios based on reality. These can be used in different areas, such as simulations of crowds or virtual creatures. The need to make an adequate preprocessing of the images that will be used to reconstruct the virtual environment is observed,

Fig. 8. Reconstruction of a cluttered room. The walls are occluded by the clutter and have a uniform texture.

avoiding high processing costs. One of the drawbacks of these methods is the manual manipulation of the cloud points. These drawbacks can be avoided by acquiring images with photographic equipment superior to conventional ones. However, it is noteworthy that the images obtained were obtained employing a camera from a cell phone.

5   Conclusions

The reconstructions carried out during this research work showed that the reconstruction of 3D virtual environments through photogrammetry can generate geometries applicable to virtual environments using only 2D photographs as a source.

The methods studied yield better results for the reconstruction of exteriors. However, it is necessary to reconstruct interiors to manipulate the point cloud by adding additional features that allow a correct virtual environment generation.

When the used images have information saturation, obtaining the point cloud is somewhat complex to be treated due to the difficulty of identifying the structures of interest at the time of reconstruction.

However, it is possible to use photogrammetry-based methods to generate virtual environments quickly if they do not require them to be minutely detailed.

Acknowledgments. This research was possible thanks to the National Council for Science and Technology (CONACYT)'s National Scholarship Program.

References

1. Bianco, S., Ciocca, G., Marelli, D.: Evaluating the performance of structure from motion pipelines. J. Imaging **4**(8) (2018). https://doi.org/10.3390/jimaging4080098
2. Fuhrmann, S., Goesele, M.: Floating scale surface reconstruction. ACM Trans. Graph. **33**(4), 46 (2014). https://doi.org/10.1145/2601097.2601163
3. Fuhrmann, S., Langguth, F., Goesele, M.: MVE - a multi-view reconstruction environment. In: Klein, R., Santos, P. (eds.) Eurographics Workshop on Graphics and Cultural Heritage. The Eurographics Association (2014). https://doi.org/10.2312/gch.20141299
4. Furukawa, Y., Curless, B., Seitz, S.M., Szeliski, R.: Reconstructing building interiors from images. In: 2009 IEEE 12th International Conference on Computer Vision, pp. 80–87 (2009). https://doi.org/10.1109/ICCV.2009.5459145
5. Furukawa, Y., Curless, B., Seitz, S.M., Szeliski, R.: Towards internet-scale multiview stereo. In: 2010 IEEE Conference on Computer Vision and Pattern Recognition (CVPR), pp. 1434–1441. IEEE (2010). https://doi.org/10.1109/cvpr.2010.5539802
6. Furukawa, Y., Hernández, C.: Multi-view stereo: a tutorial. Found. Trends Comput. Graph. Vis. **9**, 1–148 (2015). https://doi.org/10.1561/0600000052
7. Furukawa, Y., Ponce, J.: Accurate, dense, and robust multiview stereopsis. IEEE Trans. Pattern Anal. Mach. Intell. **32**(8), 1362–1376 (2010). https://doi.org/10.1109/tpami.2009.161
8. Goesele, M., Snavely, N., Curless, B., Hoppe, H., Seitz, S.M.: Multi-view stereo for community photo collections. In: 2007 IEEE 11th International Conference on Computer Vision, pp. 1–8. IEEE (2007). https://doi.org/10.1109/iccv.2007.4408933
9. Hartley, R., Zisserman, A.: Multiple View Geometry in Computer Vision, 2 edn. Cambridge University Press (2003). https://doi.org/10.1017/CBO9780511811685
10. Kataria, R., DeGol, J., Hoiem, D.: Improving structure from motion with reliable resectioning. In: 2020 International Conference on 3D Vision (3DV), pp. 41–50 (2020). https://doi.org/10.1109/3DV50981.2020.00014
11. Kazhdan, M., Bolitho, M., Hoppe, H.: Poisson surface reconstruction. In: Sheffer, A., Polthier, K. (eds.) Symposium on Geometry Processing. The Eurographics Association (2006). https://doi.org/10.2312/SGP/SGP06/061-070
12. Kazhdan, M., Hoppe, H.: Screened poisson surface reconstruction. ACM Trans. Graph. **32**(3), 29 (2013). https://doi.org/10.1145/2487228.2487237
13. Koch, T., d'Angelo, P., Kurz, F., Fraundorfer, F., Reinartz, P., Korner, M.: The TUM-DLR multimodal earth observation evaluation benchmark. In: Proceedings of the IEEE Conference on Computer Vision and Pattern Recognition Workshops, pp. 19–26 (2016). https://doi.org/10.1109/cvprw.2016.92
14. Liu, C., Wu, J., Kohli, P., Furukawa, Y.: Raster-to-Vector: revisiting floorplan transformation. In: Proceedings of the IEEE Conference on Computer Vision and Pattern Recognition, pp. 2195–2203 (2017). https://doi.org/10.1109/iccv.2017.241
15. Locher, A., Havlena, M., Van Gool, L.: Progressive structure from motion. In: Ferrari, V., Hebert, M., Sminchisescu, C., Weiss, Y. (eds.) ECCV 2018. LNCS,

vol. 11208, pp. 22–38. Springer, Cham (2018). https://doi.org/10.1007/978-3-030-01225-0_2

16. Miras, K., Eiben, A.: Effects of environmental conditions on evolved robot morphologies and behavior. In: Proceedings of the Genetic and Evolutionary Computation Conference, pp. 125–132 (2019). https://doi.org/10.1145/3321707.3321811

17. Ofria, C., Bryson, D.M., Wilke, C.O.: Avida: a software platform for research in computational evolutionary biology. Artificial Life Models in Software, pp. 3–35 (2009). https://doi.org/10.1007/978-1-84882-285-6_1

18. Raies, Y., von Mammen, S.: A swarm grammar-based approach to virtual world generation. In: Romero, J., Martins, T., Rodríguez-Fernández, N. (eds.) EvoMUSART 2021. LNCS, vol. 12693, pp. 459–474. Springer, Cham (2021). https://doi.org/10.1007/978-3-030-72914-1_30

19. Ray, T.S.: An evolutionary approach to synthetic biology: zen and the art of creating life. Artif. Life 1(1_2), 179–209 (1993). https://doi.org/10.1162/artl.1993.1.1_2.179

20. Robertson, D.P., Cipolla, R.: Practical Image Processing and Computer Vision, chap. Structure from Motion, p. 49. John Wiley, Hoboken, NJ, USA (2009)

21. Schenk, T.: Introduction to Photogrammetry, gS400.02 Department of Civil and Environmental Engineering and Geodetic Science The Ohio State University (2005)

22. Sims, K.: Evolving virtual creatures. In: Proceedings of the 21st Annual Conference on Computer Graphics and Interactive Techniques, pp. 15–22 (1994). https://doi.org/10.1145/192161.192167

23. Sun, J., Xie, Y., Chen, L., Zhou, X., Bao, H.: Neuralrecon: Real-time coherent 3D reconstruction from monocular video. In: Proceedings of the IEEE/CVF Conference on Computer Vision and Pattern Recognition (CVPR), pp. 15598–15607 (2021). https://doi.org/10.1109/cvpr46437.2021.01534

24. Vidanapathirana, M., Wu, Q., Furukawa, Y., Chang, A.X., Savva, M.: Plan2scene: converting floorplans to 3D scenes. In: Proceedings of the IEEE/CVF Conference on Computer Vision and Pattern Recognition, pp. 10733–10742 (2021). https://doi.org/10.1109/cvpr46437.2021.01059

25. Wu, C.: Towards linear-time incremental structure from motion. In: 2013 International Conference on 3D Vision-3DV 2013, pp. 127–134. IEEE (2013). https://doi.org/10.1109/3dv.2013.25

26. Yuan, Z., Li, Y., Tang, S., Li, M., Guo, R., Wang, W.: A survey on indoor 3D modeling and applications via RGB-d devices. Front. Inf. Technol. Electron. Eng. 22(6), 815–826 (2021). https://doi.org/10.1631/fitee.2000097

Factorized U-net for Retinal Vessel Segmentation

Javier Gurrola-Ramos[1]([✉])[ID], Oscar Dalmau[1][ID], and Teresa Alarcón[2][ID]

[1] Mathematics Research Center, 36023 Guanajuato, GTO, Mexico
{francisco.gurrola,dalmau}@cimat.mx
[2] Centro Universitario de los Valles, 46600 Ameca, JAL, Mexico
teresa.alarcon@academicos.udg.mx

Abstract. Automatic retinal vessel segmentation in fundus images plays an important role in diagnosing several diseases such as diabetic retinopathy and hypertension. In this paper, we propose a convolutional neural network based on the U-net architecture with factorized convolutions called FCU-Net for retinal vessel segmentation. Inspired by the Inception-v2 model blocks, we propose a factorized convolutional block to replace the typical convolution operation used in the U-net. This block is intended to decrease the number of trainable parameters and the computational cost of the model without compromising its performance. Additionally, we substitute the max-pool operations by convolutions as a downsampling method in order to reduce the loss of information between levels in the encoding section of the model. We evaluate the performance of the proposed model in several publicly available datasets and compare our proposal to other recent methods. The experimental results show the potential generalization and the competitive performance of the proposed model.

Keywords: Retinal vessel segmentation · Convolutional neural networks · U-net · Factorized convolution

1 Introduction

Retinal vessel segmentation and delineation of morphological structures in color fundus images have been widely used for detecting and diagnosing diverse ophthalmologic diseases such as diabetic retinopathy, glaucoma, and hypertension [4]. Therefore, morphological changes in blood vessels have a principal diagnostic value. Throughout retinal vessel segmentation, the relevant morphological information of the retinal vascular tree can be obtained, which can also be used for biometric recognition [14].

Automatic blood vessel segmentation methods can be divided into two main categories: unsupervised and supervised methods. The unsupervised methods can segment the blood vessels without using any labeled annotation. On the other hand, supervised methods require a manually annotated set of labels of

O. O. Vergara-Villegas et al. (Eds.): MCPR 2022, LNCS 13264, pp. 181–190, 2022.
https://doi.org/10.1007/978-3-031-07750-0_17

the training images for classifying each pixel either as vessel or non-vessel in previously unseen images.

Matched filtering for detecting the blood vessels involves a convolution of a 2D kernel with the retinal image. The kernel is designed to model a feature, and the matched filter response indicates the presence of the feature. Chaudhuri et al. [2] proposed a two-dimensional linear kernel with a Gaussian profile to match a blood vessel. Dalmau and Alarcon [3] extended the idea of the matched filter combined with cellular automata to improve the segmentation generated by the matched filter and a thresholding process.

Mathematical morphology is a tool based on the set theory concept, mainly used for extracting complex image structures that provide a good representation of region shapes. These methods are well known for their speed and noise resistance. Fraz et al. [5] proposed an approach for identifying both vessel centerline and segmentation of vascular tree using the first-order derivative of a Gaussian filter followed by a morphological top-hat transform to segment the vessels.

Model based approaches apply explicit vessels models to extract the retinal vessels. Zhang et al. [24] proposed a methodology based on nonlinear projections where the green channel image is projected onto a closed convex set consisting of the oscillating functions with zero mean. The nonlinear projection can be used to capture the texture structures in images.

In recent years, convolutional neural networks (CNNs) have obtained outstanding results in different computer vision tasks such as classification, segmentation, and biomedical image processing. The U-net model [15] for biomedical image segmentation is one of the most widely used architectures nowadays. Several models have been proposed for retinal vessel segmentation based on the U-Net architecture. Wu et al. [23] proposed the Vessel-Net, an inception-residual convolutional block, and the use of multi-scale outputs. Jin et al. [10] proposed the DUNet, a model with deformable convolutions which exploits the retinal vessels' local features. Wang et al. [21] proposed the hard attention network (HAnet), which automatically focuses the network's attention on regions that are difficult to segment. Alvarado-Carrillo et al. [1] proposed a method that incorporates Distorted Gaussian Matched Filters (D-GMFs) with adaptive parameters as part of a deep convolutional model named D-GaussianNet. Although the results of the deep learning-based models have been encouraging for retinal vessel segmentation, their design and complexity can be high, and typically they are fitted to handle one fundus image dataset at a time.

In this paper, we propose a CNN based on the U-net architecture for retinal vessel segmentation in color fundus images. The proposed model, named FCU-Net, uses factorized convolutional blocks [22] to reduce the number of trainable parameters and the computation required to estimate the retinal vessel segmentation. We evaluated the FCU-Net against several U-net-based models on three different fundus image datasets: DRIVE [18], STARE [8], and CHASE_DB1 [6]. Our results show that the proposed FCU-Net model achieves the area under the ROC curve (AUC) of 0.9834, 0.9913, and 0.9873 on DRIVE, STARE, and CHASE_DB1 datasets respectively. The rest of this paper is organized as follows:

In Sect. 2, we present and describe the proposed model. In Sect. 3, we show the experimental results of the proposed model and the comparison with state-of-the-art models. Finally, Sect. 4 provides the conclusions of this paper.

2   Proposed Method

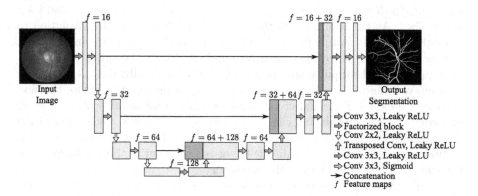

Fig. 1. Architecture of the FCU-Net model.

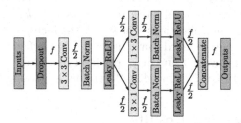

Fig. 2. Factorized convolutional block.

The architecture of the proposed FCU-Net is shown in Fig. 1. The main structure of the FCU-Net is based on the U-like encoder-decoder architecture, with three encoding and decoding levels and a bottleneck section. In every level of both encoding and decoding sections, we use a factorized convolutional block (see Fig. 2) instead of the typical pair of 3 × 3 convolutions of the U-net. In the encoding section, we use 2 × 2 strode convolution [17] instead of the standard max-pooling operation to reduce the spatial dimension and double the number of feature maps. On the other hand, in the decoding section, we use 2 × 2 transposed convolution to upsample the images. The model generates images with 16, 32, 64, and 128 feature maps (denoted as f in Fig. 1) at the first, second, and third levels and the bottleneck, respectively. The model uses Leaky ReLU [13] with parameter $\alpha = 0.01$ as activation function in every convolution, except in the output convolution, where we use the sigmoid activation function. The proposed model was designed to handle images whose spatial dimension is multiple of 8; in another case,the appropriate padding is applied to the image.

2.1 Factorized Convolutional Block

The proposed block is shown in Fig. 2. Based on the Inception-v2 block [19], we substitute the 3×3 convolution by two parallel convolutions with 3×1 and 1×3 kernel sizes. At the beginning of the block, we perform a 3×3 convolution to halve the number of feature maps (f) and summarize the input image information. Afterward, a pair of convolutions with 3×1 and 1×3 kernel sizes are applied in parallel, processing the input image along different axes. Finally, the outputs of the previous convolutions are concatenated and serve as the input image for the next stage of the model. This kind of factorization reduces the number of parameters and computation by reducing the kernel size asymmetrically, and summarizing the result with a 1×1 convolution. At the end of the block, we use Batch Normalization [9] and Dropout [7] within the factorized convolutional block to speed up the training process and reduce the overfitting.

To illustrate the reduction of trainable parameters and computational cost of the factorized convolutional block, consider an image of size $N_1 \times N_2$ with f feature maps and a $k \times k$ convolution with f input/output feature maps that preserves the spatial dimension of the image. This convolution requires $k^2 f^2$ trainable parameters and performs $k^2 f^2 N_1 N_2$ multiplications. On the other hand, the factorized convolution block requires $(k + 1)(k f^2)/2$ parameters and $(k + 1)(k f^2 N_1 N_2)/2$ multiplications. For $k = 3$, the factorized convolution block is 33% cheaper than the standard convolution. Using the factorized convolutional block and generating fewer feature maps per level compared to the original U-net model, the proposed FCU-Net has 439.31k trainable parameters.

3 Experiments and Results

3.1 Datasets

We test the proposed FCU-Net on different datasets: the digital retinal images for vessel extraction (DRIVE) [18], the structured analysis of the retina (STARE) [8], and the child heart and health study (CHASE_DB1) [6]. The DRIVE dataset consists of 40 565×584 fundus images with a 45° field of view (FOV). This dataset is divided into 20 training images and 20 testing images. Two trained human observers labeled the vessel segmentation ground truth images; in this work, we used the labels from the first observer as ground truth. This dataset also provides a binary FOV region mask for every image. The STARE dataset consists of 20 700×605 color images with a 35° FOV, with half of the images with ocular pathology. We used the first ten images as a training dataset in the experiments and the rest images to test the model. The CHASE_DB1 dataset was acquired from 14 ten years old children, yielding a total of 28 999×960 images.

This dataset presents more illumination variations compared to DRIVE and STARE datasets. In our experiments, we used the first 20 images for training and the rest images for testing. Additionally, we generate the binary FOV mask for both CHASE_DB1 and STARE datasets to evaluate the model. As a validation dataset, we randomly take one image from each training dataset partition.

We used the Contrast Limited Adaptive Histogram Equalization (CLAHE) [16] algorithm with a clipping limit of 2 and a kernel size of 17×17 to preprocess the images to highlight the vessel. Additionally, we normalize the fundus images to keep their values in the range $[0, 1]$.

3.2 Training

In order to train the model, we divided the training and validation images into patches of size 48×48. There is an overlapping between adjacent training patches of size 16 pixel for the DRIVE dataset and 24 pixels for the STARE and CHASE_DB1. We kept with the training and validation patches that contained information only, i.e., we omit patches where all the values in the binary FOV mask are 0. Additionally, we applied flips and $90°$ rotations when the training patches were generated and color jitter during the training process. According to the generation of training patches previously described, we generate 161152, 46016, and 196216 patches from the DRIVE, STARE and CHASE_DB1 datasets, respectively. To estimate the parameters of the proposed model, we solve the following optimization problem:

$$\Theta^* = \arg\min_{\Theta} \frac{1}{N} \sum_{i=1}^{N} \mathcal{L}\left(\mathcal{F}(\boldsymbol{x}_i; \Theta), \boldsymbol{y}_i\right) + \frac{\lambda}{2} \Omega(\Theta) \tag{1}$$

where Θ are the parameters of the model, $\mathcal{L}(\cdot; \cdot)$ is the loss function, $\mathcal{F}(\cdot; \Theta)$ is the model, $\Omega(\cdot)$ is the regularization term, $\lambda > 0$ is a hyperparameter to control the influence of the regularization term, and $\{(\boldsymbol{x}_i, \boldsymbol{y}_i)\}_{i=1}^{N}$ are the pairs of fundus images and vessel segmentation labels. In this work, we adopt binary cross-entropy as loss function and norm ℓ_2 as the regularization term.

To evaluate the performance and the generalization capability of the FCU-Net, we trained a single model to segment all the considered datasets and one model for segmenting each dataset independently. We use all the training datasets to fit the model for the first case. We trained one model specifically for every dataset in the second case, denoted as FCU-Net+. Although the models were trained using patches, we estimate the vessel segmentation of the whole image directly. First, we apply vertical and horizontal flips, and $90°$ rotation transforms to generate eight versions of the same fundus image. Then, the model estimates every image independently, and the inverse transforms are applied to recover the original image orientation. Finally, the average of all the estimations is used to generate the binary segmentation.

We trained the proposed model with a batch size of 64 for 60 epochs. We use the AdamW [12] optimization algorithm with parameters $\beta_1 = 0.9$, $\beta_2 = 0.999$, $\epsilon = 10^{-8}$, and the regularization parameter $\lambda = 0.02$. The initial learning rate is

$\alpha_0 = 0.001$, with an exponential decay at the end of every epoch with parameter 0.975. The dropout rate was set to 0.25 for all the dropout layers. Our model was implemented in Python 3.6 using the PyTorch framework using an Nvidia RTX Titan GPU. The source code, pre-trained models, and dataset splits are available at GitHub (https://github.com/JavierGurrola/FCU-Net).

3.3   Results

Figure 3 shows one example of the test images. We can see that using the CLAHE algorithm in the green channel enhances the retinal vessels for simplifying their detection by visual inspection and intuitively makes segmentation methods have better results. In the third row, we can see that the FCU-Net estimates the main vessel structures on image with high probability. Comparing the fourth and fifth rows in Fig. 3, we can see that the binary estimation preserves most of the main structure but leaves some thin vessels disconnected from it. Notice the high similarity between the probabilities estimations and the ground truth images, which suggests that using some post-processing method could improve the results obtained by the FCU-Net instead of direct thresholding.

To evaluate and compare the proposed model, we consider the Sensitivity (TPR), Specificity (TNR), Accuracy (ACC), and F1-Score (F1). These metrics are defined by the following expressions:

$$TPR = \frac{TP}{TP + FN} \tag{2}$$

$$TNR = \frac{TN}{TN + FP} \tag{3}$$

$$ACC = \frac{TP + TN}{TP + FP + TN + FN} \tag{4}$$

$$F1 = \frac{2TP}{2TP + FP + FN} \tag{5}$$

where TP, TN, FP, and FN are the true positive, true negative, false positive, and false negative pixels, respectively. The area under the ROC curve (AUC) is also reported. We compare the proposed FCU-Net model with other U-net-based models: Vessel-Net [23], DUNet [10], HAnet [21], RCED-Net [11], CSU-Net [20], and D-GaussianNet [1] models.

Table 1 summarizes the results of the compared models. We can see that the FCU-Net obtains the highest AUC values, with 0.9834, 0.9913, and 0.9873 for DRIVE, STARE, and CHASE DB1 datasets, respectively. In particular, for the case of the DRIVE dataset, the highest AUC value is achieved by the FCU-Net trained on the three datasets. On the other hand, the FCU-Net+ obtains the best F1 values for the DRIVE and CHASE DB1 datasets with 0.8322 and 0.8197, respectively, and the FCU-Net achieves the best F1 value for the STARE dataset. Notice that the gap between the FCU-Net and FCU-Net+ is low for some metrics, particularly for the CHASE DB1 dataset. This fact points out

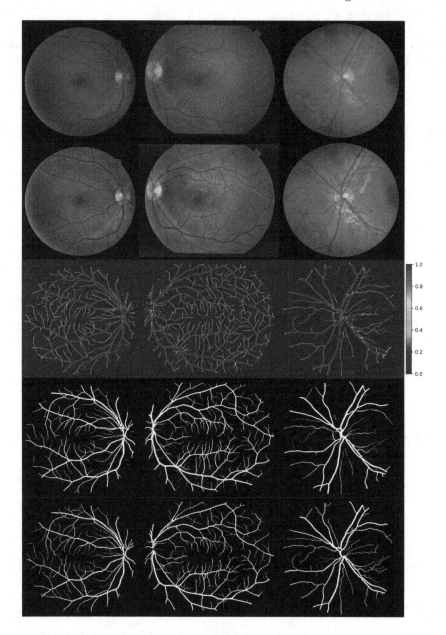

Fig. 3. Examples of test images from DRIVE (first column), STARE (second column), and CHASE_DB1 (third column). The first row shows the retinal images, the second row shows the preprocessed images, the third row shows the probability estimation, the fourth row shows the binary segmentation, and the fifth row represents the ground truth.

a good generalization capacity of FCU-Net model, where a single model can achieve competitive performance. Additionally, it can be seen that the results of the FCU-Net on the STARE dataset are better by the presence of the other datasets during the training. In contrast, the results on the DRIVE dataset are slightly affected by the same factor.

Table 1. Performance of different vessel segmentation models. The best and second best results are shown are shown in **bold** and *italic* respectively.

Dataset	Method	Year	TPR	TNR	AUC	ACC	F1
DRIVE	Vessel-Net [23]	2019	0.8038	0.9802	0.9821	*0.9578*	–
	DUNet [10]	2019	0.7963	0.9800	0.9802	0.9566	0.8237
	HAnet [21]	2020	0.7991	*0.9813*	*0.9823*	0.9581	*0.8293*
	RCED-Net [11]	2020	*0.8252*	0.9787	0.9780	**0.9649**	–
	CSU-Net [20]	2021	0.8071	0.9782	0.9801	0.9565	0.8251
	D-GaussianNet [1]	2021	0.7960	0.9799	0.9772	0.9565	0.8233
	FCU-Net	2022	0.7836	**0.9828**	0.9822	0.9571	0.8220
	FCU-Net+	2022	**0.8273**	0.9771	**0.9834**	*0.9578*	**0.8322**
STARE	DUNet [10]	2019	0.7595	**0.9878**	0.9832	0.9641	0.8143
	HAnet [21]	2020	0.8186	0.9844	0.9881	0.9673	*0.8379*
	RCED-Net [11]	2020	0.8397	0.9792	0.9810	0.9659	–
	CSU-Net [20]	2021	*0.8432*	0.9845	0.9825	**0.9702**	*0.8516*
	D-GaussianNet [1]	2021	0.7904	0.9843	0.9837	0.9647	0.8141
	FCU-Net	2022	**0.8658**	0.9819	**0.9913**	*0.9700*	**0.8546**
	FCU-Net+	2022	0.8394	*0.9851*	*0.9909*	0.9698	0.8499
CHASE_DB1	Vessel-Net [23]	2019	0.8132	0.9814	0.9860	0.9661	–
	DUNet [10]	2019	0.8155	0.9752	0.9804	0.9610	0.7883
	HAnet [21]	2020	0.8239	0.9813	*0.9871*	0.9670	0.8191
	RCED-Net [11]	2020	0.8440	0.9810	0.9830	**0.9722**	–
	CSU-Net [20]	2021	0.8427	*0.9836*	0.9824	*0.9706*	0.8105
	D-GaussianNet [1]	2021	0.7530	**0.9863**	0.9798	0.9609	0.8077
	FCU-Net	2022	*0.8490*	0.9776	**0.9873**	0.9657	*0.8195*
	FCU-Net+	2022	**0.8579**	0.9764	**0.9873**	0.9655	**0.8197**

4   Conclusion

In this paper, we proposed the FCU-Net, a U-net-based convolutional neural network for automatic retinal vessel segmentation in color fundus images. The proposed factorized convolutional block reduces the number of trainable parameters and computational cost compared to the traditional convolution operation. The experiments carried out on different retinal fundus image datasets and the comparisons using distinct evaluation metrics showed that both the global FCU-Net and the specific one for each data set, the FCU-Net+, obtain competitive results with state-of-the-art methods and show the generalization capability of the proposed model.

Acknowledgements. This work was supported by CONACYT (Mexico) under Grant 258033 and the project "Laboratorio de Supercómputo del Bajío (No. 300832)"

References

1. Alvarado-Carrillo, D.E., Ovalle-Magallanes, E., Dalmau-Cedeño, O.S.: D-GaussianNet: adaptive distorted gaussian matched filter with convolutional neural network for retinal vessel segmentation. In: Nguyen, M., Yan, W.Q., Ho, H. (eds.) ISGV 2021. CCIS, vol. 1386, pp. 378–392. Springer, Cham (2021). https://doi.org/10.1007/978-3-030-72073-5_29
2. Chaudhuri, S., Chatterjee, S., Katz, N., Nelson, M., Goldbaum, M.: Detection of blood vessels in retinal images using two-dimensional matched filters. IEEE Trans. Med. Imaging **8**(3), 263–269 (1989). https://doi.org/10.1109/42.34715
3. Dalmau, O., Alarcon, T.: MFCA: matched filters with cellular automata for retinal vessel detection. In: Batyrshin, I., Sidorov, G. (eds.) MICAI 2011. LNCS (LNAI), vol. 7094, pp. 504–514. Springer, Heidelberg (2011). https://doi.org/10.1007/978-3-642-25324-9_43
4. Fraz, M., Remagnino, P., Hoppe, A., Uyyanonvara, B., Rudnicka, A., Owen, C., Barman, S.: Blood vessel segmentation methodologies in retinal images - a survey. Comput. Methods Programs Biomed. **108**(1), 407–433 (2012). https://doi.org/10.1016/j.cmpb.2012.03.009
5. Fraz, M.M., Basit, A., Barman, S.: Application of morphological bit planes in retinal blood vessel extraction. J. Digit. Imaging **26**(2), 274–286 (2013). https://doi.org/10.1007/s10278-012-9513-3
6. Fraz, M.M., Remagnino, P., Hoppe, A., Uyyanonvara, B., Rudnicka, A.R., Owen, C.G., Barman, S.A.: An ensemble classification-based approach applied to retinal blood vessel segmentation. IEEE Trans. Biomed. Eng. **59**(9), 2538–2548 (2012). https://doi.org/10.1109/TBME.2012.2205687
7. Hinton, G.E., Srivastava, N., Krizhevsky, A., Sutskever, I., Salakhutdinov, R.R.: Improving neural networks by preventing co-adaptation of feature detectors (2012)
8. Hoover, A., Kouznetsova, V., Goldbaum, M.: Locating blood vessels in retinal images by piecewise threshold probing of a matched filter response. IEEE Trans. Med. Imaging **19**(3), 203–210 (2000). https://doi.org/10.1109/42.845178
9. Ioffe, S., Szegedy, C.: Batch normalization: accelerating deep network training by reducing internal covariate shift. In: Proceedings of the 32nd International Conference on Machine Learning. Proceedings of Machine Learning Research, vol. 37, pp. 448–456. PMLR (2015)
10. Jin, Q., Meng, Z., Pham, T.D., Chen, Q., Wei, L., Su, R.: DUNet: a deformable network for retinal vessel segmentation. Knowl.-Based Syst. **178**, 149–162 (2019). https://doi.org/10.1016/j.knosys.2019.04.025
11. Khan, T.M., Alhussein, M., Aurangzeb, K., Arsalan, M., Naqvi, S.S., Nawaz, S.J.: Residual connection-based encoder decoder network (RCED-Net) for retinal vessel segmentation. IEEE Access **8**, 131257–131272 (2020). https://doi.org/10.1109/ACCESS.2020.3008899

12. Loshchilov, I., Hutter, F.: Decoupled weight decay regularization. In: 7th International Conference on Learning Representations, ICLR 2019, 6–9 May 2019. OpenReview.net, New Orleans, LA, USA (2019). https://openreview.net/forum?id=Bkg6RiCqY7
13. Maas, A.L., Hannun, A.Y., Ng, A.Y.: Rectifier nonlinearities improve neural network acoustic models. In: In ICML Workshop on Deep Learning for Audio, Speech and Language Processing (2013)
14. Mariño, C., Penedo, M.G., Penas, M., Carreira, M.J., Gonzalez, F.: Personal authentication using digital retinal images. Pattern Anal. Appl. 9(1), 21–33 (2006)
15. Ronneberger, O., Fischer, P., Brox, T.: U-Net: convolutional networks for biomedical image segmentation. In: Navab, N., Hornegger, J., Wells, WM., Frangi, A.F. (eds.) MICCAI 2015. LNCS, vol. 9351, pp. 234–241. Springer, Cham (2015). https://doi.org/10.1007/978-3-319-24574-4_28
16. Setiawan, A.W., Mengko, T.R., Santoso, O.S., Suksmono, A.B.: Color retinal image enhancement using CLAHE. In: International Conference on ICT for Smart Society, pp. 1–3 (2013). https://doi.org/10.1109/ICTSS.2013.6588092
17. Springenberg, J.T., Dosovitskiy, A., Brox, T., Riedmiller, M.: Striving for simplicity: the all convolutional net. arXiv preprint arXiv:1412.6806 (2014)
18. Staal, J., Abramoff, M., Niemeijer, M., Viergever, M., van Ginneken, B.: Ridge-based vessel segmentation in color images of the retina. IEEE Trans. Med. Imaging 23(4), 501–509 (2004). https://doi.org/10.1109/TMI.2004.825627
19. Szegedy, C., Vanhoucke, V., Ioffe, S., Shlens, J., Wojna, Z.: Rethinking the inception architecture for computer vision. In: 2016 IEEE Conference on Computer Vision and Pattern Recognition (CVPR), pp. 2818–2826 (2016). https://doi.org/10.1109/CVPR.2016.308
20. Wang, B., Wang, S., Qiu, S., Wei, W., Wang, H., He, H.: CSU-Net: a context spatial u-net for accurate blood vessel segmentation in fundus images. IEEE J. Biomed. Health Inform. 25(4), 1128–1138 (2021). https://doi.org/10.1109/JBHI.2020.3011178
21. Wang, D., Haytham, A., Pottenburgh, J., Saeedi, O., Tao, Y.: Hard attention net for automatic retinal vessel segmentation. IEEE J. Biomed. Health Inform. 24(12), 3384–3396 (2020). https://doi.org/10.1109/JBHI.2020.3002985
22. Wang, M., Liu, B., Foroosh, H.: Factorized convolutional neural networks. In: Proceedings of the IEEE International Conference on Computer Vision Workshops, pp. 545–553 (2017)
23. Wu, Y., et al.: Vessel-Net: retinal vessel segmentation under multi-path supervision. In: Shen, D., et al. (eds.) MICCAI 2019. LNCS, vol. 11764, pp. 264–272. Springer, Cham (2019). https://doi.org/10.1007/978-3-030-32239-7_30
24. Zhang, Y., Hsu, W., Lee, M.L.: Detection of retinal blood vessels based on nonlinear projections. J. Signal Process. Syst. 55(1), 103–112 (2009). https://doi.org/10.1007/s11265-008-0179-5

Multi-view Learning for EEG Signal Classification of Imagined Speech

Sandra Eugenia Barajas Montiel$^{(\boxtimes)}$, Eduardo F. Morales ,
and Hugo Jair Escalante

Computer Science Department, Instituto Nacional de Astrofísica,
Óptica y Electrónica, Luis Enrique Erro No. 1, Sta. María Tonantzintla,
72840 Puebla, Mexico
{sandybarajas,emorales,hugojair}@inaoep.mx

Abstract. Multi-view Learning (MVL) has the objective of combining
the information that describes an object from different groups of features.
This machine learning paradigm has proven useful to improve generalization performance of classifiers by taking advantage of the complementary
information from different views of the same object. This work explores
the use of three Co-training-based methods and three Co-regularization
techniques to perform supervised learning to classify electroencephalography signals (EEG) of imagined speech. Two different views were used
to characterize these signals, extracting Hjorth parameters and the average power of the signal. The results of six different approaches of MVL
applied to classify the imagined speech of five different words are reported,
showing an improvement up to 14.27% in accuracy average of classification compared with single view classification.

Keywords: Multi-view learning · Co-training · Co-regularization ·
EEG · Imagined speech

1 Introduction

The perception of the objects that surround us, their recognition and classification are subject to different stimuli. For example, to recognize people, we observe
the features of their faces, the color of their hair, and we use information such
as voice timbre to identify whether we know them and who they are. Multi-view
Learning (MVL) is a machine learning approach based on the combination of
characteristics of the same object from different representations. Each of these
representations is called a view. The intuition behind MVL is to take advantage
of the complementariness of information that can be obtained from different
views to better characterize an object and to create classification models that
better generalize the representation of these objects. This is possible considering
that the views must be compatible and independent to each other [1].

MVL has been used in different fields [2–4] like recognition of various patterns
in Electroencephalography signals (EEG) [5,6], among many others. This paper

O. O. Vergara-Villegas et al. (Eds.): MCPR 2022, LNCS 13264, pp. 191–200, 2022.
https://doi.org/10.1007/978-3-031-07750-0_18

explores MVL applied to EEG signal classification of imagined speech, which consists of the categorization of brain waves captured during the imagination of the pronunciation of a word without making gestures, movements or sounds. Imagined speech have been studied using different machine learning approaches [7,8], but according to research carried out in this work, Multi-view Learning is a technique that has not been reported as a strategy to classify imagined speech. We compare three Co-training style algorithms: Basic Co-training algorithm based on [9] and we propose two simple variations of it, Simple Co-training and Majority Vote Co-training. Also we compare three Co-regularization style algorithms: Concatenation, MULDA [10] and SVM-2K [11].

This work aims to explore the use of MVL to build more robust classifiers when complementary information that describes a set of objects is available. Specifically, EEG signals can be represented and analyzed in different domains, such as time and frequency. Two approaches of Multi-view Learning are studied in this paper: Co-training and Co-regularization. The main idea of Co-training is to create separate classifiers for each representation and then combine their results. Co-regularization first combines the different views of the objects to be classified to obtain a single set of characteristics that is used to create a Multi-view classifier. This paper presents the implementation of six different methods of MVL to classify imagined speech, an approach that according to the research carried out during this work, has been little explored. The results show that the use of two views improves the accuracy in the classification of imagined speech compared to the classification of a single view. For the views and features extracted in this work, a Co-training method showed the best results in classification, reaching an average accuracy of 74.38%.

The remainder of this paper is organized as follows: In Sect. 2, basic concepts on MVL and the two approaches adopted, as well as the implemented algorithms are presented. Section 3 provides a brief description of the imagined speech problem. In Sect. 4, the characteristics extracted to obtain two different views of EEG are described. The performed experiments and the results obtained using Co-training and Co-regularization are presented and compared in Sect. 5. Finally, conclusions and future research directions can be found in Sect. 6.

2   Multi-view Learning

Multi-view Learning (MVL) is a machine learning variant that has its foundation in the work of Blum and Mitchell [1] in which they propose the use of two different views to classify web pages. Since then, MVL has grown in multiple directions of machine learning. There have been different categorizations for MVL algorithms [12,13], this work is based in the categories given in [14] focusing on Co-training and Co-regularization.

2.1   Co-training

Co-training was originally proposed to combine labeled and unlabeled data from different views of an object. This technique has shown that even when there are no naturally different views to describe an object, generating these views and combining them by Co-training can improve the results of other classifiers not using different views [15]. According to [1] there are two principal considerations in Co-training: (i) Each set of features is sufficient for classification, and (ii) the two feature sets of each instance are conditionally independent given the class. Research on Multi-view supervised learning is comparatively less studied than Multi-view semi-supervised learning.

It is possible to adapt Co-training semi-supervised learning for supervised learning, for example, Chen and Sun [16] proposed the Multi-view Fisher discriminant analysis, where each view gives a predicted label and the final predicted label of an input is determined by the view that has the maximum confidence. Taking this into account, three different Co-training style algorithms to perform supervised learning were explored to classify EEG signals: Basic Co-training, Simple Co-training, and Majority Vote Co-training, as described below. In all cases we use Random Forest (RF) as base classifier.

Basic Co-training (BCT). This approach is based on the Agreement Co-training strategy presented in [9]. We train separate RF for each view, we consider the most confident model and used it to label a new example, then this new labeled example is added to the training set of individual models and iterate until there are no more unlabeled (test) objects. To establish which is the most confident model we use the misclassification probability of each tree in the ensemble (RF). We select the tree with the minimum misclassification probability to label test samples of each view (Fig. 1).

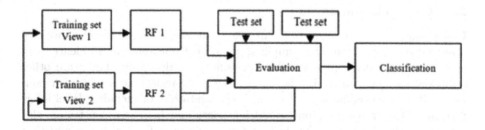

Fig. 1. Basic co-training algorithm.

Simple Co-training (SCT). We propose a slight variation of the basic Co-training algorithm. Again, we worked with two views, and we modeled a different Random Forest for each. We observed the resulting models and the more confident model was used to classify the whole test data set. As in the previous approach, we select the most confident model according to misclassification probability, but in this case, there are not incremental construction of the models. Each model is trained just once with the corresponding training set, then for each test object the most confident model is used to label it (Fig. 2).

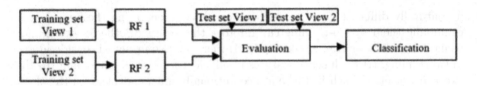

Fig. 2. Simple co-training algorithm.

Majority Vote Co-training (MVCT). We propose this approach that has an initial stage as the previous variation presented. Two different RFs are modeled, one for each view, then each model classifies the complete test set. This process in repeated through a ten-fold cross validation schema, meanwhile the label assigned to each sample is stored. Finally stored labels are used to emit a vote, and test samples are classified according to the most voted class (Fig. 3).

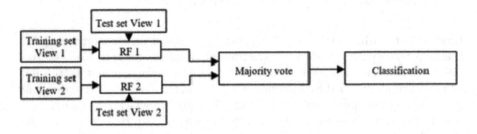

Fig. 3. Majority vote co-training (MVCT).

2.2 Co-regularization

Co-regularization style algorithms are based on integrating different views into a unified representation. One simple approach is Concatenating the features of each view and then run a standard classification algorithm. There are other strategies summarized in [14] like constructing a transformation, linear or nonlinear, from the original views to a new representation, or including label information to the transformation to add intraclass and interclass constrains, also combining the data and label information using classifiers with the aim that the results obtained from different views be as consistent as possible. In this work three methods were applied: Concatenation of characteristics from different views, MULDA [10] that extracts uncorrelated features in each view and computes transformations of each view to project data into a common subspace, and SVM-2K [11] that combines into a single optimization kernel Canonical Correlation Analysis and Support Vector Machine.

Concatenation (CC). Given X_i and X_j, two views of EEG signals, we concatenated them into a single set $X_{ij} = [X_i, X_j]$. This set is divided into training, validation, and testing subsets to model a RF for classification of EEG signals (Fig. 4).

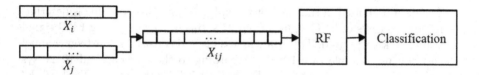

Fig. 4. Concatenation strategy.

MULDA. The purpose of this method, introduced in [10], is to take advantage of Canonical Correlation Analysis (CCA) and Uncorrelated Linear Discriminant Analysis (ULDA), so that useful features can be exploited for Multi-view applications. Through optimizing the corresponding objective, discrimination in each view and correlation between two views can be maximized simultaneously. We apply the method developed in [10], given X_i and X_j, two views of imagined speech EEG signals, the characteristics are combined in correlation matrices, then features containing minimum redundancy are extracted. The resulting sets of features are divided into training, validation and testing subsets to model a RF for classification of EEG signals.

SVM-2K. In [11], the authors trained a Support Vector Machine (SVM) from each individual view and then regularized the consistencies across different views. This study takes advantage of kernel Canonical Correlation Analysis (kCCA) to represent the common relevant information from two different correlated views using this as a preprocessing stage to improve performance of a SVM combining them into a single optimization SVM-2K. We apply the method developed in [11], given X_i and X_j, two views of imagined speech EEG signals.

3   Imagined Speech

Imagined speech, also known as unspoken speech, is the internal pronunciation or imagined pronunciation of words without making sounds or gestures. The present work uses Electroencephalography (EEG) signals to recognize the imagined pronunciation of words from a reduced vocabulary made up of five words in Spanish language: *arriba* (up), *abajo* (down), *izquierda* (left), *derecha* (right), and *seleccionar* (select).

The electroencephalogram (EEG) is the recording of brain electrical potentials measured from electrodes on the human scalp. EEG involves placing electrodes over the scalp in a noninvasive way. These electrodes capture voltage differences generated due to ion movement along the brain neurons. These measurements are obtained over a time period to form an EEG signal [17]. Classifying EEG signals from imagined speech is a problem that presents several challenges. EEG signals are biosignals that by nature are considered extremely non-linear, non-stationary, and prone to artifacts. These signals contain data from numerous electrodes. Many training trials are required to generate a suitable model of the target user and an unacceptably long calibration period for a realistic model.

The data base used in this project to explore Multi-view learning is described in [18] and consists of EEG signals from 27 subjects. For acquiring EEG signals an EMOTIV kit was used. This is a wireless kit and consists of fourteen channels which frequency sample rate 128 Hz. According to the international 10–20 system, channels are named: AF3, F7, F3, FC5, T7, P7, O1, O2, P8, T8, FC6, F4, F8, AF4. Each subject imagined 5 words: *arriba* (up), *abajo* (down), *izquierda* (left), *derecha* (right), and *seleccionar* (select). Samples collected included 33 repetitions (epochs) of each word.

4   Extracting Views from Imagined Speech Signals

Two representative feature extraction methods were used to generate two different views of the original EEG signals: Average band power and Hjorth parameters. The objective was to analyze the signals in both frequency and time domains. Each imagined speech sample consist of 14 columns, corresponding to 14 channels of the EEG, for each view 14 features were extracted from each of the signals.

A common way to analyze EEG data is to decompose the signal into functionally distinct frequency bands. To move the EEG signal from time domain to frequency domain we used the Fast Fourier Transform (FFT). Once in frequency domain, average band power (AVP) was computed, which consists of computing a single number that summarizes the contribution of the given frequency band to the overall power of the signal [19]. Present work identifies this view as view 1 (V1-AVP).

The Hjorth parameters described in [20] are three characteristics extracted from a signal. They were designed to obtain important information from EEG signals in time domain. These characteristics are Activity, Mobility, and Complexity. Activity represents the variance of the time function giving a measure of the squared standard deviation of the amplitude of the signal. The Mobility parameter is defined as the square root of the ratio of the variance of the first derivative of the signal and that of the signal. The Complexity parameter indicates how the shape of a signal is similar to a pure sine wave. The value of Complexity converges to 1 as the shape of signal gets more similar to a pure sine wave. After several experiments, the Hjorth Parameter selected to perform the classification was Activity (ACT), which is used to represent view 2 (V2-ACT).

5   Experiments and Results

To build a data corpus for the experiments, we took EEG signals from 27 healthy individuals (S1–S27), two of them are left-handed and the rest are right-handed. The corpus has 33 samples for each of the words: *arriba* (up), *abajo* (down), *izquierda* (left), *derecha* (right), and *seleccionar* (select), imagined by each individual.

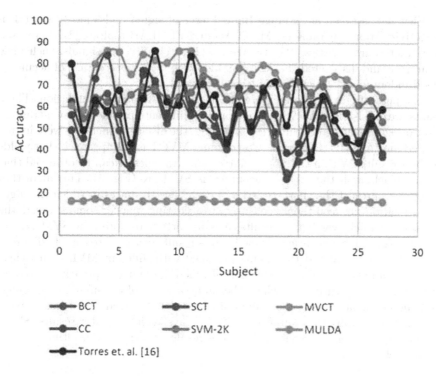

Fig. 5. Accuracy reached by multi-view learning approaches explored and Torres et al. [18]

The first experiment seeks to evaluate different classifiers to select one of them to apply Multi-view Learning. For this, the recorded EEG epochs go through a feature extraction process, each imagined word is described by a vector consisting of 14 characteristics plus its class value, for each view.

Table 1. Results and comparison with related work. Accuracy percentage of classification of the first 5 subjects as well as average accuracy of all 27 subjects using a single view and MVL methods.

Subject	V1-AVP	V2-ACT	BCT	SCT	MVCT	CC	SVM-2K	MULDA	Torres et al. [18]
1	33.5	62.5	49.09	62.42	60.61	56.13	74.33	16	79.96
2	31.88	43.63	34.12	49.09	58.18	45.38	54.49	16	49.08
3	54.38	73.13	57.51	61.45	80	73.13	64.2	17	63.09
4	61.75	74.75	66.11	57.58	86.06	84	62.31	16	57.87
5	34.5	55.63	48.98	36.97	85.45	56.5	59.35	16	67.68
Average	38.25	56.83	49.08	51.95	**74.38**	58.19	**64.86**	16.11	**60.11**

View 1 was taken as Average Band Power of signal and View 2 was taken as Activity Hjorth parameter. MATLAB and EEGLAB toolbox [21] were used to extract characteristics. We use Weka [22] to classify the signals, each view separately, and discovered that the classifier with higher percentage of accuracy, was Random Forest (RF) with 50 trees.

The percentages of accuracy are obtained by 10-fold cross validation. These results are consistent with [18]. To explore the different approaches of Co-training and Co-regularization of Multi-view Learning, the discussed methods were implemented in MATLAB. Regarding Co-training, MVCT is the approach that yields the best results. Within the Co-regularization strategies, it can be observed that the approach with the greatest accuracy is SVM-2K (Fig. 5). This algorithm manages to project the characteristics of each view to spaces in which the highest correlation between them is ensured. Considering that for some subjects the CC approach achieves better results, it is important to note that SVM-2K, on average, has a higher accuracy. Table 1 shows results using RF to classify different views independently and the results obtained with different MVL approaches. Also, we can see the comparison of Multi-view Learning approaches explored with results reported in [18], where the same problem of classifying EEG imagined speech signals, using the same data base, is addressed but using a single view. For practically each subject, MVCT always achieves better results. SVM-2K has higher average precision than the results shown in [18], although they are very close.

6   Conclusions and Future Work

Multi-view Learning is an interesting strategy that has shown to be effective in improving generalization performance of traditional classifiers [14]. This work presents experiments with six Multi-view methods. The results shown here help to conclude that it is possible to improve classification accuracy of imagined speech by combining the information from different views. Over all the experiments with MVL, Majority Vote Co-training is the approach that reaches the highest average accuracy (74.38%), followed by SVM-2K (64.86%).

It is important to highlight that the feature extraction process was made over raw EEG signals, without any extra preprocessing since the main objective of this work was to study Multi-view Learning performance. Results obtained are competitive when compared with the results reported in [18] where the same database is used to classify imagined speech. Other works like [23] have shown improvement in classification accuracy through an important preprocessing and a thorough extraction and selection of characteristics of EEG signals from the same database.

Recent studies have applied Multi-view Learning [24] in motor imagery classifications task or Multimodal approaches [8] to enhance imagined speech EEG recognition performance. According to the research carried out, Multi-view Learning is a less explored area for the imagined speech classification task. This paper explores the application of Multi-view Learning, comparing six different algorithms, through the use of only two views and simple classifiers such as

Random Forest, showing improvement in the classification results of EEG signals compared to previous studies carried out with the same analyzed database.

As future work we propose to explore different feature extraction methods to have different views capable of distinguishing characteristics that could help us to maximize intra-class distance and minimize inter-class distance. Also, pre-processing of signals, exploring new configurations, including more views, trying different kernel functions, and different classifiers could lead to more powerful models to classify motor imaginary EEG signals.

Acknowledgement. This work was supported by CONACyT under grant 49245.

References

1. Blum, A., Mitchell, T.: Combining labeled and unlabeled data with co-training. Proc. Eleventh Ann. COLT **1998**, 92–100 (1998). https://doi.org/10.1145/279943. 279962
2. Calero Espinosa, J.C.: Multi-view learning for hierarchical topic detection on corpus of documents. Doctoral dissertation. Universidad Nacional de Colombia (2021)
3. Han, Z., Zhang, C., Fu, H., Zhou, J.T.: Trusted multi-view classification. In: 9th International Conference on Learning Representations, ICLR 2021, 3–7 May. Virtual Event, Austria (2021)
4. Hsueh, Y.L., Lie, W.N. and Guo, G.Y.: Human behavior recognition from multi-view videos. Inf. Scie. **517**, 275–296 (2020) https://doi.org/10.1016/j.ins.2020.01. 002
5. Yuan, Y., Xun, G., Jia, K., Zhang, A.: A multi-view deep learning framework for EEG seizure detection. IEEE J. Biomed. Health Inform. **3**(1), 83–94 (2018). https://doi.org/10.1109/JBHI.2018.2871678
6. Jiang, Y., et al.: Recognition of epileptic EEG signals using a novel multiview TSK fuzzy system. IEEE Trans. Fuzzy Syst. **25**(1), 3–20 (2016). https://doi.org/ 10.1109/TFUZZ.2016.2637405
7. Antonio, T.G.A., Reyes, C.A., Villasenor-Pineda, L., Mendoza-Montoya, O.: Chapter 12 - A survey on EEG-based imagined speech classification. In: Biosignal Processing and Classification using Computational Learning and Intelligence: Principles, Algorithms, and Applications. Essay. Academic Press (2021)
8. Rini A.S., Murthy, H.A.: Correlation based Multi-phasal models for improved imagined speech EEG recognition. arXiv preprint arXiv:2011.02195 (2020)
9. Güz, Ü., Cuendet, S., Hakkani-Tür, D. and Tür, G.: Co-training using prosodic and lexical information for sentence segmentation. In: Interspeech, pp. 2597–2600 (2007)
10. Sun, S., Xie, X., Yang, M.: Multiview uncorrelated discriminant analysis. IEEE Trans. Cybern. **46**(12), 272–3284 (2015). https://doi.org/10.1109/TCYB.2015. 2502248
11. Farquhar, J.D., Hardoon, D.R., Meng, H., Shawe-Taylor, J., Szedmák, S.: Two view learning: SVM-2K, Theory and Practice. In: NIPS (2005)
12. Sun, S.: A survey of multi-view machine learning. Neural Comput. Appl. **23**(7), 2031–2038 (2013). https://doi.org/10.1007/s00521-013-1362-6
13. Xu, C., Tao, D., Xu, C.: A survey on multi-view learning. arXiv preprint arXiv:1304.5634 (2013)

14. Zhao, J., Xie, X., Xu, X. and Sun, S. Multi-view learning overview: recent progress and new challenges. Inf. Fus. **38**, 43–54 (2017). https://doi.org/10.1016/j.inffus. 2017.02.007
15. Nigam, K., Ghani, R.: Analyzing the effectiveness and applicability of co-training. In: Proceedings of the Ninth International Conference on Information and Knowledge Management, pp. 86–93 (2000). https://doi.org/10.1145/354756.354805
16. Chen, Q., Sun, S.: Hierarchical multi-view fisher discriminant analysis. In: Leung, C.S., Lee, M., Chan, J.H. (eds.) ICONIP 2009. LNCS, vol. 5864, pp. 289–298. Springer, Heidelberg (2009). https://doi.org/10.1007/978-3-642-10684-2_32
17. Singh, A., Gumaste, A.: Decoding imagined speech and computer control using brain waves. J. Neurosci. Methods **358**, 109196 (2021). https://doi.org/10.1016/j. jneumeth.2021.109196
18. Torres-García, A.A., Reyes-García, C.A., Villaseñor-Pineda, L., Ramírez-Cortés, J.M.: Análisis de senales electroencefalográficas para la clasificación de habla imaginada. Revista mexicana de ingeniería biomédica **34**(1), 23–39 (2013)
19. Compute the average bandpower of an EEG signal. https://raphaelvallat.com/ bandpower.html. Accessed 21 Sept 2019
20. Hjorth, B.: EEG analysis based on time domain properties. Electroencephalogr. Clin. Neurophysiol. **29**(3), 306–310 (1970). https://doi.org/10.1016/ 0013-4694(70)90143-4
21. Delorme, A., Makeig, S.: EEGLAB: an open source toolbox for analysis of single-trial EEG dynamics including independent component analysis. J. Neurosci. Methods **134**(1), 9–21 (2004). https://doi.org/10.1016/j.jneumeth.2003.10.009
22. Azuaje, F., Witten, I.H., Frank, E.: Data Mining: Practical Machine Learning Tools and Techniques, 2nd ed. BioMedical Engineering OnLine, vol. 5, issue 1. (2006). https://doi.org/10.1186/1475-925x-5-51
23. Torres-García, A.A. Análisis y clasificación de electroencefalogramas (EEG) registrados durante el habla imaginada. Doctoral dissertation, Instituto Nacional de Astrofísica, Óptica y Electrónica, México (2016)
24. Jiao, Y., Zhou, T., Yao, L., Zhou, G., Wang, X., Zhang, Y.: Multi-view multi-scale optimization of feature representation for EEG classification improvement. IEEE Trans. Neural Syst. Rehabil. Eng. **28**(12), 2589–2597 (2020). https://doi.org/10. 1109/tnsre.2020.3040984

Emotion Recognition Using Time-Frequency Distribution and GLCM Features from EEG Signals

Oscar Almanza-Conejo[ID], Dora-Luz Almanza-Ojeda[ID],
Jose-Luis Contreras-Hernandez[ID], and Mario-Alberto Ibarra-Manzano[✉][ID]

Laboratorio de Procesamiento Digital de Señales, Departamento de Ingeniería
Electrónica, DICIS, Universidad de Guanajuato, Carr. Salamanca-Valle de Santiago
Km. 3.5 + 1.8 Km., 36885 Salamanca, GTO, Mexico
{o.almanzaconejo,dora.almanza,jose.contreras,ibarram}@ugto.mx

Abstract. Deep learning techniques are commonly used for emotion recognition from Electroencephalography (EEG) signals. However, some disadvantages of employing these classifiers are the high memory requirements and the low number of available EEG samples in datasets. This work proposes a novel approach for increasing the number of extracted features based on the Gray Level Co-occurrence Matrices (GLCMs) technique using reassigned spectrogram images. EEG signals are transformed using spectral analysis to construct the reassigned spectrogram images. Different feature sets are employed to train multiple classification models based on the leave-one-out method. K-Nearest Neighbor technique achieves the highest accuracy results, 77.40% and 77.30% for valence and arousal primitive emotion classification. Comparative results show that the proposed approach is competitive to those existing in the state-of-the-art.

Keywords: EEG · Primitive emotion recognition · GLCM · KNN

1 Introduction

The importance of human emotion recognition based on artificial intelligence techniques has recently increased. Emotion recognition provides a better understanding of human behavior characterization, communication, and decision-making [24]. Emotion classification is categorized into physiological and non-physiological signals. Non-physiological signals are characterized by measuring or collecting information from the superficial behavior of subjects; such signals are usually based on facial expressions from images [4,5,12] and speech recognition [7,14]. On the other hand, physiological signals respond to electrical potential differences in organs or biological tissues. An example of physiological signals is heart rate (ECG) [17], electrical muscle stimulation (EMG) [6], and electrical

University of Guanajuato & Consejo Nacional de Ciencia y Tecnologia.

brain activity (EEG). Emotion recognition commonly employs artificial intelligence models for characterizing and classifying EEG signals. Frequently, EEG signals are acquired using non-invasive tools to offer subjects a comfortable and safe tests environment. The most common non-invasive sensor is an electrode headband to measure electrical activity on the cortical surface generated by brain structures [19].

Artificial intelligence models focused on primitive emotion classification, like valence and arousal. In [22] valence is defined as a range of emotions with values from negative to positive, where sadness and happiness are mutually related extremes of emotional valence. Similarly, arousal is the range of stimuli produced for an emotion. Integrating non-stationary signals, such as EEG, has shown a high complexity in emotion classification tasks. One of the main problems is characterizing EEG signals in the time domain. Therefore, several research suggests a time-frequency, by the use of Fourier Transform (FT), [1,18,23] or time-scale domain, using Wavelet Transform (WT), [9,20,26]. Applying spectral analysis, it is possible to obtain a graphical distribution of the energy given a discrete signal and use it as a database for feature extraction employing image processing techniques. One of the most popular techniques in pattern recognition is the use of gray-level co-occurrence matrix (GLCM) used to quantify features in images of forms and textures [15]. In our approach, we propose a novel study to classify the valence and arousal primitive emotions performing a signal processing to electroencephalographical signals from the Database for Emotion Analysis using Physiological Signals (DEAP) dataset [8]. The methodology in this work focuses on FT to process EEG signals, obtain energy distribution images, and perform a feature extraction algorithm based on GLCM. In addition, the application of hyperparametric classification algorithms using ML techniques is explored by obtaining a classification model for each primitive emotion.

This paper is divided into six sections. Section 2 presents the existing works related to primitive emotion recognition in the literature. Section 3 describes the methodology applied to this work. Section 4 presents the results obtained from the methodology and evaluation metrics per trained model, and Sect. 5 presents the conclusions of this work.

2   Background

Several studies in the emotion recognition area have been applied to the classification of primitive emotions, where most of the proposed methodologies use Deep Learning (DL) based algorithms. It is remarkable the contribution of DL based strategies, for instance, in [3], authors determine statistical features, to classify four primitive emotions, valence, arousal, dominance, and linking, applying an LSTM architecture network. The accuracy values achieved are in the range of 80.72–84.37%. Based on DL classification, other techniques like [16] presented a high accuracy. In this work, a classification fusion model is proposed, whereby exploiting EEG signals in a two-dimensional array and images of facial expressions, a 3D Convolutional Neural Network (3D-CNN) is created. This model achieved an accuracy of 93.13% for value and 96.79% for arousal.

ML-based methodologies have also been developed for primitive emotion classification from time-frequency feature extraction using 32 electrodes channels from the DEAP dataset. An example of these approaches is proposed in [11] where a k-Nearest Neighbors algorithm yielded an accuracy of 69.97% for value and 71.23% accuracy for arousal. Similarly, in [10], based on a Random Forest algorithm, very close results to the one proposed by [11] were achieved. In addition, by combining statistical and time-frequency feature extraction on Continuous Wavelet Decomposition (CWD) images, in [1], using a Support Vector Machine (SVM) algorithm, an accuracy of 85.8% is achieved in the valence classification model and 86.6% in arousal. In [25], classification of EEG signals from the DEAP dataset is performed. This work implements two approaches based on the time-frequency feature extraction from Intrinsic Mode Functions (IMF). The first model uses eight electrode channels, achieving an accuracy of 69.10% in valence and 71.99% in arousal. The second model yielded 70.41% and 72.10% on primitive emotions using 32 electrode channels.

A GLCM feature extraction on pseudo-Wigner-Ville distribution (SPWVD) images of EEG signals, in [13], is used to classify three states of the depth of anesthesia (DoA). In this work, 15 electrodes channels are used for the classification task using homogeneity, correlation, energy, and contrast features, an average accuracy between 87.95% and 94.87% was achieved over the number of gray levels $(2^x; x \in [2-6])$ in six different test subjects. Similarly, transforming EEG signals using the Short-Time Fourier Transform (STFM), in [2] a feature extraction is performed using a GLCM algorithm to three different datasets, one for EEG signals in epileptic stage and another two datasets for sleep stage classification. The results achieved from an ML-based classifier yielded an accuracy of 76.20%, 81.23%, and 75.46% for each dataset. It is important to note that the two works above employ a combination of time-frequency distribution images and GLCM features with an ML-based algorithm. Using the described methodologies above as motivation, this paper proposes a classification method based on ML algorithms by performing feature extraction applied to images in a time-frequency distribution. In addition, k-Nearest Neighbors hyperparametric algorithms are explored to improve the classification of valence and arousal primitive emotions based on EEG signals. The following section presents the methodology used in this work.

3   Proposal Method

This approach used pattern recognition based on image processing for valence and arousal emotion classification from an EEG signal dataset. By computing the FT with EEG signals to obtain images of energy distribution in the time-frequency domain, namely spectrogram reassigned, an algorithm based on feature extraction from the GLCM is applied to spectrogram images to extract a set of features. To obtain the most significant features, multiple pieces of training are performed to 21 features, splitting features into three clusters and performing a set of seven training models for each cluster, following the leave one out methodology. Figure 1 shows the method described above.

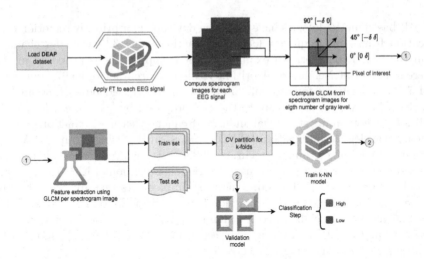

Fig. 1. General diagram of proposed methodology

3.1 Signal Description and Time-Frequency Domain Change

The DEAP dataset contained the electrical difference potential information of 32 subjects stimulated with 40 music videos. The electroencephalographic activity was acquired using an electrode headband fitted with 32 electrodes. Each subject is stimulated for 60 s, where each signal period is sampled at 128 Hz. Figure 2a shown the EEG distribution data. We use only the electrodes corresponding to the frontal lobe, where emotional stimuli are mainly presented.

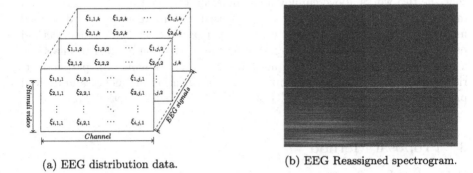

(a) EEG distribution data.

(b) **EEG Reassigned spectrogram.**

Fig. 2. EGG data storage and frequency domain for DEAP dataset.

From the $x(t)$ data vector is possible to obtain the energy associated with a signal by performing a transformation to the time-frequency domain. In [2], a reassigned spectrogram is described as the energy-aligned representation of a time-frequency distribution adjacent to the real frequency components in the signal. Furthermore, a spectrogram is defined by using the Short-Time Fourier

Transform (STFT) as in (1) , where $f(t + T)$ is the function displaced on time, $h(-t)$ the displacement per window along the function $f(T)$ and $e^{-i\omega t}$ the kernel transform. By the compute of the reassigned spectrogram, the time-frequency distribution of an EEG signal is shown graphically in Fig. 2b, to subsequently rescale the image at a size of $[224 \times 224]$.

$$STFT_h(\omega, T) = \int_{-\infty}^{+\infty} f(t + T) h(-t) e^{-i\omega t} dt \tag{1}$$

3.2   GLCM Feature Extraction

In order to obtain relevant information related to the time-frequency distribution in the EEG signals, the GLCM algorithm was used to compute a gray level matrix at eight gray levels. The co-occurrence matrix in each of the directions of the pixels neighboring to the pixel of interest, as in Fig. 1, where for this approach $\delta = [1, 2]$. The two δ elements indicate that the gray-level matrix computation is performed at one and two nearest neighbors to the pixel of interest. Obtaining the GLCMs, texture, and object feature extraction is performed using the algorithm in [21], wherefrom a set of 21 features, three different clusters are performed using a leave one out classification methodology to obtain a set of most relevant features. The extracted features using the GLCMs are namely as follows: Autocorrelation (AU), contrast (CN), correlation (CR), cluster prominence (CP), cluster shape (CS), dissimilarity (DS), energy (ENE), entropy (ENT), homogeneity (HOM), maximum probability (MP), the sum of squares variance (SQV), sum average (SA), sum variance (SV), sum entropy (SE), difference variance (DV), difference entropy (DE), information measure of correlation 1 (IMC1), information measure of correlation 2 (IMC2), the inverse difference (ID), inverse difference normalized (IDN), and inverse difference moment normalized (IDMN). The clustered feature matrix is shown in (2), (3), and (4), where each cluster has seven different features.

$$\mathbb{C}_1 = \begin{bmatrix} AU_1 & CN_1 & CR_1 & CP_1 & CS_1 & DS_1 & ENE_1 \\ AU_2 & CN_2 & CR_2 & CP_2 & CS_2 & DS_2 & ENE_2 \\ \vdots & \vdots & \vdots & \vdots & \vdots & \vdots & \vdots \\ AU_n & CN_n & CR_n & CP_n & CS_n & DS_n & ENE_n \end{bmatrix} \tag{2}$$

$$\mathbb{C}_2 = \begin{bmatrix} ENT_1 & HOM_1 & MP_1 & SQV_1 & SA_1 & SV_1 & SE_1 \\ ENT_2 & HOM_2 & MP_2 & SQV_2 & SA_2 & SV_2 & SE_2 \\ \vdots & \vdots & \vdots & \vdots & \vdots & \vdots & \vdots \\ ENT_n & HOM_n & MP_n & SQV_n & SA_n & SV_n & SE_n \end{bmatrix} \tag{3}$$

$$\mathbb{C}_3 = \begin{bmatrix} DV_1 & DE_1 & IMC1_1 & IMC2_1 & ID_1 & IND_1 & IDMN_1 \\ DV_2 & DE_2 & IMC1_2 & IMC2_2 & ID_2 & IND_2 & IDMN_2 \\ \vdots & \vdots & \vdots & \vdots & \vdots & \vdots & \vdots \\ DV_n & DE_n & IMC1_n & IMC2_n & ID_n & IND_n & IDMN_n \end{bmatrix} \tag{4}$$

3.3   ML-Based Classification Algortihm

Having computed the feature clusters in (2), (3), and (4), the training and testing process to calculate an accuracy matrix $A = [m \times j]$ is performed for each trained model per cluster. Figure 3 illustrates the training approach for each feature set, yielding the accuracy matrix in A.

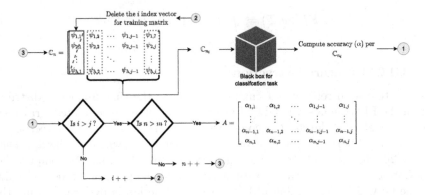

Fig. 3. Training process for compute the A matrix applying leave-one-out.

A is the general matrix accuracy, α the accuracy per cluster and leave one out method, h the number of samples, i the index vector to delate in $\mathbb{C}_n$, j the number of features per cluster, n the index for cluster matrix, and m the number of cluster matrices. Based on the A matrix, the maximum accuracy index per row vector is obtained to apply for a new leave-one-out method replacing the maximum accuracy index vector with a single feature vector from the rest of the feature clusters. This method aims to find a new set of features to replace the maximum accuracy yielded per cluster. Finally, a matrix $\mathbb{A} = [3 \times 14]$ is computed to obtain the index according to the best accuracy that contains the most relevant set of features. Figure 4 shows the procedure described above.

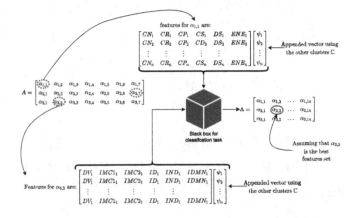

Fig. 4. Final leave one out classification task.

4   Results

Three representative cluster features are used for training a k-NN algorithm for valence and arousal primitive emotions classification. Using clusters of features, a leave one out methodology was performed to determine the most relevant set of features and to compute the accuracy matrix in $\mathbb{A}$. The matrix in (5) is mapped to the features set in $\alpha_{1,8}$ from $\mathbb{A}$ using a binary classification.

4.1   Valence and Arousal Classification Model

Two emotion recognition classification models for the primitive emotions of valence and arousal are trained using the matrix obtained from the feature set in (5). Using a data partition to 10 classification folders applied to the training feature set, a non-optimized k-NN algorithm is trained and tested for the valence primitive emotion. The total number of samples is 30145, where a random 10% is used for the testing stage, and 90% is for training. Table 1 shows the confusion matrix corresponding to the test set and achieving 77.7% for valence accuracy. In order to increase the accuracy achieved in the classification model above, the algorithm is optimized using automatic tuning performed by the software to determine the best classification algorithm based on the input data. After an optimizing process (see Fig. 5a), the model achieves an accuracy of 79.4% corresponding to the confusion matrix of Table 1.

$$
\mathbb{A}_{\alpha_{1,8}} = \begin{bmatrix} AU_1 & CR_1 & CP_1 & CS_1 & DS_1 & ENE_1 & DV_1 \\ AU_2 & CR_2 & CP_2 & CS_2 & DS_1 & ENE_2 & DV_2 \\ \vdots & \vdots & \vdots & \vdots & \vdots & \vdots & \vdots \\ AU_n & CR_n & CP_n & CS_n & DS_n & ENE_n & DV_n \end{bmatrix}
\tag{5}
$$

Table 1. General confusion matrices for valence and arousal classification.

	CM Valence non opt.		CM Valence opt.		CM Arousal non opt.		CM Arousal opt.	
	Low	High	Low	High	Low	High	Low	High
Low	**0.84**	0.16	**0.86**	0.14	**0.84**	0.16	**0.86**	0.14
High	0.28	**0.72**	0.27	**0.73**	0.29	**0.71**	0.27	**0.73**

According to the classification methodology used for the valence model, a new model for non-optimized arousal achieves an accuracy of 77.6% for the testing set and a classification performance shown in Table 1. Applying the optimization method, the accuracy improves 1.7% compared to the non-optimized model. Figure 5b shows the training process of the optimized model and Table 1 the confusion matrix according to the optimized arousal model.

4.2   Discussion

By analyzing the difference between the confusion matrices in Table 1, the accuracy improves by 1.7% with respect to the non-optimized models, using the testing set. Figure 5a and Fig. 5b illustrate that the two hyperparametric models change only the distance weight parameter. For the valence optimized model, the parameter is set as $1/d$, and $1/d^2$ in the arousal model, where d represents the distance. The cosine distance is given for both models, commonly used to compute the symmetry between two vectors. Both hyperparametric methods also present the analysis in a single next neighbor. In Fig. 5a, the estimated error is considerably different from the observed error at the third and fourth iterations. After the fifth iteration, both errors converge to the same value. After the third iteration, in Fig. 5b the estimated error is different from the observed error. The estimated error is based on a confidence interval higher than the observed error at each iteration. To summarize, the error is an estimation. Meanwhile, the observed error is the actual error per iteration. Table 2 shows an overview of the results achieved for different methodologies and classifiers applied to recognize primitive emotions using ML-based models.

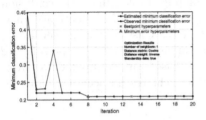   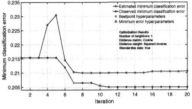

(a) Optimized k-NN for valence model   (b) Optimized k-NN for arousal model

Fig. 5. k-NN optimized training per iteration for valence and arousal.

Table 2. State-of-the-art performances in primitive emotion recognition works.

Author and Year	Feature extraction technique	Classification algorithm	Accuracy (%)	
			Valence	Arousal
Liu et al. [11] (2016)	Time-frequency features	k-NN	69.97	71.23
Zhuang et al. [25] (2017)	IMF time-frequency	SVM	70.41	72.10
Liu et al. [10] (2018)	Time-frequency features	Random forest	77.20	74.30
Alazrai et al. [1] (2018)	Statistical & time-frequency features	SVM	85.80	86.60
Our approach	GLMC features	k-NN (non-Opt)	77.70	77.60
		k-NN (Opt)	79.40	79.30

5 Conclusions

Based on a feature set extracted by the GLCM algorithm and applied to reassigned spectrogram images, this paper describes the results to classify primitive emotions using an optimized and a non-optimized k-NN algorithm. The results achieved from the classification shown competitive results compared to the existing state-of-the-art. To the best of our knowledge, the feature extraction method applied to spectrogram images for emotion recognition classification has not been reported before. Furthermore, it is noteworthy that the models presented in this work are ML-based algorithms, having the advantage of achieving results using low computational resources compared to Deep Learning-based architectures.

Future work focuses on defining different hyperparameterization parameters and exploring the use of others Machine Learning based classifiers. In addition, the application of a different number of gray levels will be examined by replacing the analysis from 8 to 64 gray levels. Due to the increase in gray levels, the set of representative features must also be increased.

References

1. Alazrai, R., Homoud, R., Alwanni, H., Daoud, M.: EEG-based emotion recognition using quadratic time-frequency distribution. Sensors **18**(8), 2739 (2018). https://doi.org/10.3390/s18082739
2. Ömer F. Alçin, Siuly, S., Bajaj, V., Guo, Y., Sengür, A., Zhang, Y.: Multi-category EEG signal classification developing time-frequency texture features based fisher vector encoding method. Neurocomputing **218**, 251–258 (2016). https://doi.org/10.1016/j.neucom.2016.08.050
3. Garg, A., Kapoor, A., Bedi, A.K., Sunkaria, R.K.: Merged LSTM model for emotion classification using EEG signals. In: 2019 International Conference on Data Science and Engineering (ICDSE). IEEE (2019). https://doi.org/10.1109/icdse47409.2019.8971484
4. Hu, M., Wang, H., Wang, X., Yang, J., Wang, R.: Video facial emotion recognition based on local enhanced motion history image and CNN-CTSLSTM networks. J. Visual Commun. Image Represent. **59**, 176–185 (2019). https://doi.org/10.1016/j.jvcir.2018.12.039
5. Jain, D.K., Shamsolmoali, P., Sehdev, P.: Extended deep neural network for facial emotion recognition. Patt. Recogn. Lett. **120**, 69–74 (2019). https://doi.org/10.1016/j.patrec.2019.01.008
6. Kehri, V., Ingle, R., Patil, S., Awale, R.N.: Analysis of facial EMG signal for emotion recognition using wavelet packet transform and SVM. In: Tanveer, M., Pachori, R.B. (eds.) Machine Intelligence and Signal Analysis. AISC, vol. 748, pp. 247–257. Springer, Singapore (2019). https://doi.org/10.1007/978-981-13-0923-6_21
7. Khalil, R.A., Jones, E., Babar, M.I., Jan, T., Zafar, M.H., Alhussain, T.: Speech emotion recognition using deep learning techniques: a review. IEEE Access **7**, 117327–117345 (2019). https://doi.org/10.1109/access.2019.2936124
8. Koelstra, S., et al.: DEAP: a database for emotion analysis; using physiological signals. IEEE Trans. Affect. Comput. **3**(1), 18–31 (2012). https://doi.org/10.1109/T-AFFC.2011.15

9. Krishna, A.H., Sri, A.B., Priyanka, K.Y.V.S., Taran, S., Bajaj, V.: Emotion classification using EEG signals based on tunable- q wavelet transform. IET Sci. Measure. Technol. **13**(3), 375–380 (2019). https://doi.org/10.1049/iet-smt.2018.5237

10. Liu, J., Meng, H., Li, M., Zhang, F., Qin, R., Nandi, A.K.: Emotion detection from EEG recordings based on supervised and unsupervised dimension reduction. Concurr. Comput. Pract. Exper. **30**(23), e4446 (2018). https://doi.org/10.1002/cpe.4446

11. Liu, J., Meng, H., Nandi, A., Li, M.: Emotion detection from EEG recordings. In: 2016 12th International Conference on Natural Computation, Fuzzy Systems and Knowledge Discovery (ICNC-FSKD). IEEE (2016). https://doi.org/10.1109/fskd.2016.7603437

12. Mehendale, N.: Facial emotion recognition using convolutional neural networks (FERC). SN Appl. Sci. **2**(3), 1–8 (2020). https://doi.org/10.1007/s42452-020-2234-1

13. Mousavi, S.M., Asgharzadeh-Bonab, A., Ranjbarzadeh, R.: Time-frequency analysis of EEG signals and GLCM features for depth of anesthesia monitoring. Comput. Intell. Neurosci. **2021**, 1–14 (2021). https://doi.org/10.1155/2021/8430565

14. Mustaqeem, Kwon, S.: A CNN-assisted enhanced audio signal processing for speech emotion recognition. Sensors **20**(1), 183 (2019). https://doi.org/10.3390/s20010183

15. Park, Y., Guldmann, J.M.: Measuring continuous landscape patterns with gray-level co-occurrence matrix (GLCM) indices: an alternative to patch metrics? Ecol. Indicat. **109**, 105802 (2020). https://doi.org/10.1016/j.ecolind.2019.105802

16. Salama, E.S., El-Khoribi, R.A., Shoman, M.E., Shalaby, M.A.W.: A 3D-convolutional neural network framework with ensemble learning techniques for multi-modal emotion recognition. Egyptian Inf. J. **22**(2), 167–176 (2021). https://doi.org/10.1016/j.eij.2020.07.005

17. Sarkar, P., Etemad, A.: Self-supervised ECG representation learning for emotion recognition. IEEE Trans. Affect. Comput. 1–1 (2021). https://doi.org/10.1109/taffc.2020.3014842

18. Taran, S., Bajaj, V.: Emotion recognition from single-channel EEG signals using a two-stage correlation and instantaneous frequency-based filtering method. Comput. Methods Programs Biomed. **173**, 157–165 (2019). https://doi.org/10.1016/j.cmpb.2019.03.015

19. Teplan, M., et al.: Fundamentals of EEG measurement. Measure. Sci. Rev. **2**(2), 1–11 (2002)

20. Ömer Türk, Özerdem, M.S.: Epilepsy detection by using scalogram based convolutional neural network from EEG signals. Brain Sci. **9**(5) (2019). https://doi.org/10.3390/brainsci9050115

21. Uppuluri, A.: GLCM texture features (2008). https://www.mathworks.com/matlabcentral/fileexchange/22187-glcm-texture-features

22. Verma, G.K., Tiwary, U.S.: Affect representation and recognition in 3D continuous valence–arousal–dominance space. Multimedia Tools Appl. **76**(2), 2159–2183 (2016). https://doi.org/10.1007/s11042-015-3119-y

23. Wang, X.-W., Nie, D., Lu, B.-L.: EEG-based emotion recognition using frequency domain features and support vector machines. In: Lu, B.-L., Zhang, L., Kwok, J. (eds.) ICONIP 2011. LNCS, vol. 7062, pp. 734–743. Springer, Heidelberg (2011). https://doi.org/10.1007/978-3-642-24955-6_87

24. Zheng, X., Liu, X., Zhang, Y., Cui, L., Yu, X.: A portable HCI system-oriented EEG feature extraction and channel selection for emotion recognition. Int. J. Intell. Syst. **36**(1), 152–176 (2020). https://doi.org/10.1002/int.22295

25. Zhuang, N., Zeng, Y., Tong, L., Zhang, C., Zhang, H., Yan, B.: Emotion recognition from EEG signals using multidimensional information in EMD domain. Biomed. Res. Int. **2017**, 1–9 (2017). https://doi.org/10.1155/2017/8317357
26. Zubair, M., Yoon, C.: EEG based classification of human emotions using discrete wavelet transform. In: Kim, K.J., Kim, H., Baek, N. (eds.) ICITS 2017. LNEE, vol. 450, pp. 21–28. Springer, Singapore (2018). https://doi.org/10.1007/978-981-10-6454-8_3

Natural Language Processing and Recognition

Leveraging Multiple Characterizations of Social Media Users for Depression Detection Using Data Fusion

Karla María Valencia-Segura$^{(\boxtimes)}$ ⓘ, Hugo Jair Escalante ⓘ,
and Luis Villaseñor-Pineda ⓘ

Language Technologies Lab, Department of Computer Science,
Instituto Nacional de Astrofísica, Óptica y Electrónica, Puebla 72840, Mexico
{valencia.karla,hugojair,villasen}@inaoep.mx

Abstract. Depression is one of the principal mental disorders worldwide, yet very few people receive the appropriate care needed due to the difficulty involved in diagnosing it correctly. Social networks have opened the opportunity to detect those users who suffer from this disease through the analysis of their posts. In this work, we propose using three types of characterizations (demographic, emotion, and text vectorization) extracted from the users' text and a fusion method for the detection of depressive users in the social network Reddit. Considering the diversity of each of the extracted characterizations, we adopted a Gated Multimodal Unit (GMU) as a fusion method. We compare this method against traditional data fusion methods and other methods that have used the same dataset. We found the proposed method improves F1-score for the depressive class by 4% when combining these three characterizations. Showing the usefulness of characterizing user content and behavior for detecting depression and highlighting the impact that data fusion methods can have in this very relevant task.

Keywords: Depression detection · Information fusion · Social media

1 Introduction

According to the World Health Organization (WHO), depression affects around 280 million people worldwide and is one of the major causes of suicide. Nonetheless, only a tiny fraction of those who suffer from this condition receive adequate treatment [1]. One of the main challenges of depression is the difficulty of diagnosing it. This stigmatized illness prevents that people with this condition to look for medical help [2]. For this reason, we continue to search for strategies that allow their appropriate detection.

Nowadays, there is a trend on research for developing improved traditional depression diagnostic methods, as those based on interviews. Such methods rely on the use of machine learning techniques for analysing user's data. Among these, there are methods based on the observation of the depression indicators that

ⓒ The Author(s), under exclusive license to Springer Nature Switzerland AG 2022
O. O. Vergara-Villegas et al. (Eds.): MCPR 2022, LNCS 13264, pp. 215–224, 2022.
https://doi.org/10.1007/978-3-031-07750-0_20

the people could show through written communication [3,4]. This approach has gained popularity among the language processing and machine learning fields, as it has shown that it is possible to detect depression to some extent with these type of techniques [5–7].

The adoption of methods based on the analysis of textual information for detecting depression can have a huge impact now more than ever. This mainly due to the establishment of social networks as the leading communication channel of people with the world [8]. However, the difficulty of finding useful indicators of this condition from text is not trivial. Mainly because there are many factors involved that should be taken into account when dealing with users. These include, age and gender [2], personality traits [9] and even users' interests and social context [10].

In this work, we analyze different approaches to characterize users in social media with the aim objective of identifying the different depression indicators that could be captured with these characterizations. Subsequently, these features must be fused through an adequate fusion method in which we expect to capture their redundancies and/or complementarities. Our goal is to obtain a deep understanding of the contribution of each feature type and the impact of using a sophisticated data fusion method for combining information. Specifically, we explore different fusion methods, achieving better results using a multimodal fusion method (*Gated Multimodal Unit* [11]). We experimentally evaluate in a widely used dataset for depression recognition[1]. Experimental results show the effectiveness of the adopted approach, that outperforms state-of-the-art on the same dataset. Additionally, we found that the features related to emotions have a relevant impact on the recognition of depression in social media users; also, different groups of people like gender manifest their depression differently.

2   Related Work

To detect signs of depression in social networks, we seek to characterize a user based on his or her history. Works in the area have explored different characterizations to detect signs of depression. Chen et al. [5] considered an emotion-based characterization to detect depression users on Twitter; concluding that the analysis of emotions is an essential factor in detecting depression. On other hand, Preoţiuc-Pietro et al. [6] focused on estimating demographic information (age and gender) through the analysis of posts on Twitter. Obtaining a high performance to identify users with depression.

Although there are different ways of characterizing users in social networks, there is enormous diversity among them, resulting in models that ignore the existing complementarity among characterizations. Therefore there have been some efforts to adopt information fusion to this problem. Peng et al. [12] used a model based on SVM Multi-Kernel to select the optimal kernels and combat the heterogeneity of three characterizations (text from microblogs, information on the user profile, and the behavior of the user); to identify depression users

---

[1] https://early.irlab.org/2018/index.html.

on Sina Weibo. On the other hand, Meng et al. [13] used different modalities (facial expressions and audio) to predict depression, applying the *linear opinion pool* method as a fusion technique. Although good results were obtained, the performance could be improved if the naturalistic vocal expressions in the audio modality is improved.

Other works have been proposed to analyze textual information using the same dataset we used herein. Some of these implement fusion techniques, as in [14] where use multiple features such as linguistic metadata at the user level, bag of words, neural word embeddings, and Convolutional Neural Networks (CNN); and an ensemble was implemented as a fusion method for the final prediction. In [15] used various classification techniques (Ada Boost, Random Forest, and Recurrent Neural Network (RNN)), using a bag of words and metamaps features; obtaining the best F1-score using Random Forest. Finally, in [16] two models were built, one for the extraction of 58 features, where 18 were chosen because the combination of these provided the best results, extracted from the user's text. The second model corresponds to vectorization using doc2vec, and a voting ensemble determines if the user is depressed or not.

The previous review shows that there are many methods out there trying to detect depression from social media posts. However, these works use complex models with various features and sophisticated approaches to text representations. Instead, this work proposes a simple model that analyses and evaluates different representations (emotions, demographics, and thematic information) extracted from the user. Please note that even when fusion methods have been used to approach this problem, they usually use different modalities to represent the user, but in this work, all characterizations associated with the user were extracted from the same modality. With this in mind, we aim to show that the relevance of each feature and the use of an adequate fusion method lead to a model that improves the prediction of depressed users on Reddit.

3   Fusion of Multiple Characterizations of Users

The aim of this study is to evaluate the usefulness of a depression detection model that leverages on characterizations of social media users. On the other hand, motivated by the tentative thematic and style differences in the use of language between genders, a demographic attribute characterization was used. Finally, text vectorization is another characterization that captures thematic content. A working hypothesis of this work is that the combination of different characterizations would result in better recognition performance. In doing so, we propose the usage of *Gated Multimodal Units* (GMU) based network. The remainder of this section elaborates on the characterizations and the fusion method that was adopted.

3.1   Feature Extraction

Pre-processing: From the data collection, the pre-processing process involved removing unnecessary information, such as special characters, numbers, URLs, and punctuation marks. Once the user's text was pre-processed, four features were chosen to represent the users, which are described below:

1. **Sentiment Analysis:** This characterization was carried out using two different approaches. The first, with the help of an *NRC Emotion Lexicon* (EmoLex)[2], which is a list of English words and their associations with eight basic emotions (anger, fear, anticipation, trust, surprise, joy, and disgust). The second approach identifies four emotions (sadness, fear, anger, and joy) using a CNN[3].
2. **Gender:** For this characterization, a lexical resource was used that is available in the *World Well-Being Project* (WWBP)[4]. The prediction, as well as the other characterizations, is made at the post level. So that they accumulate the weights of each one and the final sum of each post represents the result of the prediction in the user's history, the gender is indicated with the sign obtained from the sum, a positive result indicates a female user and a negative result indicates a male user.
3. **Thematic:** Finally, a vectorization of the users' histories was made using a weighted TF-IDF, which assigns weights to the words to discriminate between classes (depressive and non-depressive).

The emotion features were include based on the results from Chen et al. [5], who show that emotion-based features have a positive impact on the detection of depression. On the other hand, profile information such as demographic attributes has related to depressive indicators. Therefore, it was considered to include gender. Finally, a thematic analysis provides a structured, systematic approach to understanding sentiment makes it possible to spot patterns.

3.2   Information Fusion with Gated Multimodal Units

The information obtained by the different characterizations should be feed to a predictive model that will learn to discriminate depressive from non-depressive users. Since the considered characterizations capture different aspects from the user, a model that exploits the complementariness and redundancy of characterizations is expected to result in better performance. While there are many methods to fuse information from multiple modalities for classification purposes, there is not yet an established method of proven performance, apart from the late fusion and early fusion methods. After an extensive literature search, we found a promising model that could be used for this purpose: a GMU based network. This model has the advantage of finding the best representation between late

---

[2] https://saifmohammad.com/WebPages/NRC-Emotion-Lexicon.htm.
[3] https://github.com/lukasgarbas/nlp-text-emotion.
[4] https://wwbp.org/lexica.html.

and early fusion by combining attributes of different modalities and determining the relevance of each modality in the model to the predictive phase.

The neural architecture to integrate a GMU started with the various features of the text were extracted. From this, these characterizations were normalized and they were passed through the GMU module (Arevalo et al. [11]) describe this module with more detail. Once the GMU module is obtained, it goes through a fully connected hidden layer, a dropout of 0.2, and finally an output layer, with sigmoid activation, to carry out the classification of the depression. The hyperparameters established for this network were optimized using the Kerashypetune library[5] in the training data set.

4 Experiments

This section details the evaluation of this model and other data fusion methods base line for the depression detection task and also, result from a comparison of various methods is conducted to find out which performed the best.

4.1 Data Collection

For the evaluation of the proposed method we used the data set provided by the CLEF 2018 forum (eRisk2018), Table 1 reports the statistics of the data set. This data set is made up of the users' publication history and published time. For this work, only the text was considered.

Table 1. Statistics of the train and test dataset.

	Train		Test	
	Depressed	No-depressed	Depressed	No-depressed
Subjects	135	752	79	741
Number of post	49557	481837	40655	504523

4.2 Data Fusion Baselines

We considered traditional data fusion and neural networks methods as baselines: 1) *Concatenation*: Different works have concluded that a simple concatenation of representation could be good [11]. In this case, we concatenate the four characterizations to train a simple SVM with linear Kernel, 2) *Features-Union* [17]: This method concatenates results of multiple objects to create a single representation; the principal difference with concatenation is that this method assign the same weight to each modality and it is useful to combine several feature extraction mechanisms into a single. 3) *Multi-kernel:* has shown a high performance between heterogeneous data. We performed experiments with two types of Multi Kernel

---

[5] https://github.com/cerlymarco/keras-hypetune.

Learning with SVM: 3.1) *MLK (Average)* [18]– It's a simple wrapper defining the combination as the average base kernels– and 3.2) *MKL (GRAM)* [19]– Gradient-based RAdius-Margin optimization, this method focuses on finding the combination of the kernel that simultaneously maximizes the margin between classes while minimizing the resulting kernel's radius. Finally 4) *EmbraceNet:* This method guarantees compatibility with any learning model and deals properly with cross-modal information [20]. Moreover, this model has already been compared with several neural network fusion techniques (Late, Early, Intermediate, Compact multi-linear pooling, and Multimodal autoencoders) obtaining better performance.

4.3   Performance Metrics and Results

Different measurement criteria are shown here to evaluate how well our model performed, Precision, Recall, and F1-score of the depressive class. It's important to note that in this work, we are focused on improving the F1-score of the depressive class. Various experiments were performed to evaluate the proposed method. The first evaluates the performance of each feature individually, the second evaluates the complementarity and diversity of the combination of the features, the third experiment has the objective of compare the proposed method against three data fusion methods baseline, and the last one has the intention of evaluating the proposed method against the works present in the erisk2018 forum.

As we mention before, we explored the individual performance of each of the previously described features using a Support Vector Machine as a classification method. Table 2 shows the evaluation metrics on the depressive class of the 4 characterizations extracted from the users' posts on Reddit.

Table 2. Performance in the depressive class for each characterization.

Characterizations	Number of attributes	Precision	Recall	F1-score
Gender	1	0.32	**0.62**	0.42
Thematic	5233	**0.76**	0.43	0.55
Emo-Lex	8	0.60	0.58	**0.59**
CNN-Emotions	4	0.26	0.56	0.35

Once these results were obtained, we calculated the Coincident Failure Diversity (CFD) value [21], to evaluate the diversity and complementarity between each fusion of the four characterizations. This measure is used to determine the chance that members of the same system make mistakes coincidentally.

When $CFD = 0$, it indicates that the faults are the same for all the characteristics; therefore, there is no diversity. On the contrary, a $CFD = 1$, indicates that all the faults are unique. As can be seen in Table 3, combining these four characteristics, the highest CFD is obtained, which is equal to 0.87. This result indicates that, by choosing a good fusion method, a model with better performance can be calculated.

Table 3. Coincident Failure Diversity analysis of each of the combinations of the 4 characterizations.

Characterization	CFD	Characterization	CFD
Emo-Lex, Thematic	**0.65**	CNN-Emotions, Emo-Lex, Gender	0.36
Emo-Lex, CNN-Emotions	0.49	CNN-Emotions, Emo-Lex, Thematic	**0.83**
CNN-Emotions, Thematic	0.54	CNN-Emotions, Thematic, Gender	0.82
Emo-Lex, Gender	0.15	Thematic, Emo-Lex, Gender	0.61
CNN-Emotions, Gender	0.21		
Thematic, Gender	0.48	All Characterizations	**0.87**

To properly evaluate the GMU module, we consider using four traditional data fusion methods and a neural network fusion model described above. All the methods presented here were trained and tested with the same erisk2018 dataset. For this experiment, we expected to confirm the hypothesis presented in this work, and also we expect to determine the effectiveness of the use of GMU over the traditional fusion methods.

Table 4. Comparison of the various fusion methods and GMU.

Fusion method	Precision	Recall	F1-score
SVM (Concatenation)	0.93	0.48	0.63
SVM Features-Union	0.61	0.58	0.59
MKL-Average	**1.0**	0.46	0.63
MKL-Gram	**1.0**	0.42	0.59
EmbraceNet	0.59	0.72	0.66
GMU	0.58	**0.87**	**0.70**

As shown in Table 4, the GMU module achieves the best F1-score of 0.70 in depressive class, indicating that it learns more efficiently diversity between the four characterizations compared to the other fusion methods. Additionally, we compared the results obtained in this work against the works presented in the eRisk2018 evaluation forum. The results can be observed in Table 5.

Table 5. Results of the depressive class vs. the top three places in eRisk 2018.

Model	Precision	Recall	F1-score
FHDO-BCSGB [14]	**0.64**	0.65	0.64
Random Forest [15]	0.63	0.64	0.63
LIIRB [16]	0.38	0.67	0.48
GMU Model	0.58	**0.87**	**0.70**

The following can be highlighted from the results obtained: (i) Implementing a GMU in a simple neural architecture outperform traditional fusion techniques, which indicates that fusion of the multiple features at a deeper level is relevant for detecting depression; (ii) The approach outperformed the top ranked methods from eRisk 2018. It is essential to note that the participants tested different complex models with a wide range of characteristics with traditional fusion methods such as late and early fusion. At the same time, the one presented here was only based on four characterizations and a GMU module as a fusion method.

5 Analysis of the Proposed Model

Figure 1 illustrates how GMU weighted the relevance of each feature according to each observation, showing the standard deviation. We inspected the z_i gates of the GMU module, averaging the activations of each class (depressive and non-depressive) in the entire test set.

In Fig. 1a we can observe the standard deviation of depressive class where thematic characterization has the higher standard deviation of 0.087; this indicates that with this characterization, we have higher variability in the activation's relevance. Conversely, Emo-Lex has a lower standard deviation of 0.025, which means that the relevance activation in this characterization remained more uniform than the rest. On the other hand, for the non-Depressive class, Fig. 1b shows a higher standard derivation in CNN-Emotions with 0.101 and the lower in for Gender with 0.024, however we have atypical data for gender. In this case, the mean value makes it appear that the data values are higher than they really are.

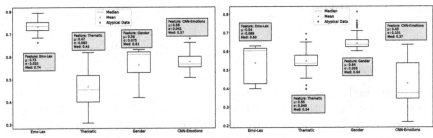

(a) Gates Activation's of Depressive Class (b) Gates Activation's of Non-Depressive Class

Fig. 1. Standard deviation, median, and mean of GMU unit activations for each class across the entire test set.

In general, Emo-lex and Gender for depressive and non-depressive classes, respectively, were the most relevant characteristics according to the GMU module. This result is expected because depressed users tend to make more emotional posts than non-depressed users, and several studies confirm a difference in depression signs between women and men.

GMU Error Analysis: Based on the results obtained, we evaluated and determined why some users were misclassified. In the case of the depressive class, ten users were misclassified, and in the case of the non-depressive class, fifty users were misclassified. The main reasons for these errors in both classes was due to the amount of information. Either because of very short history of posts (45.9 posts per history average in misclassified depressive users; 373.4 post in misclassified non-depressive users) or very large histories (with averages of 2407 for misclassified depressive users and, 14150 for misclassified non-depressive users). In the latter case, having records that span a long time is ineffective because the users could have received some treatment. Hence, the signs of depression are not so clear for the model.

6 Conclusions

With the development of the Internet, social networks provide a new approach to identifying those users who present indicators of depression. To do this, we propose a GMU-based depression recognition model. First, we analyzed and extracted characteristics with greater diversity and complementarity to represent users in social networks. Then we integrated a GMU module to fuse these characterizations to improve the identification of depressed users. We compared the performance of GMU with other fusion methods such as SVM, MLK (Average), MKL (GRAM), Features-Union and EmbraceNet, to classify the detection of depressive users, where GMU showed a better performance compared to this fusion methods. In addition, we compared the results obtained in this work against the works presented in the eRisk2018 evaluation forum, showing that our model exceeded the F1-score brought by the first place in the forum. It should be noted that the simplicity and capacity of this model contrast with the first places obtained in the evaluation forum of erisk 2018. Finally, as far as we know, the work presented in this study is the first work to recognize depression that uses a GMU, and we obtained an F1-score of 70%. We expect to replicate this work in another depression collection data; we also intend to extract and integrate other relevant features such as personality as future work.

Acknowledgments. This work was supported by CONACyT/México (scholarship 782579 and grant CB-2015-01-257383). Authors thank CONACYT for the computational resources provided by the Deep Learning Platform for Language Technologies.

References

1. Skaik, R., Inkpen, D.: Using social media for mental health surveillance: A review. ACM Comput. Surv. **53**(6), 1–31 (2020)
2. "Depressión". World Health Organization (2020). https://www.who.int/es/newsroom/fact-sheets/detail/depression
3. Zimmermann, J., Brockmeyer, T., Hunn, M., Schauenburg, H., Wolf, M.: First-person pronoun use in spoken language as a predictor of future depressive symptoms: preliminary evidence from a clinical sample of depressed patients. Clin. Psychol. Psychotherapy **24**(2), 384–391 (2017)

4. Bucci, W., Freedman, N.: The language of depression. Bull. Menninger Clin. **45**(4), 334 (1981)
5. Chen, X., Sykora, M., Jackson, T., Elayan, S., Munir, F.: Tweeting your mental health: an exploration of different classifiers and features with emotional signals in identifying mental health conditions. In: Proceedings of 51st HICSS Conference (2018)
6. Preoţiuc-Pietro, D., et al..: The role of personality, age, and gender in tweeting about mental illness. In: Proceedings of the 2nd workshop on CLPsych, pp. 21–30 (2015)
7. Aragón, M.E., López-Monroy, A.P., González-Gurrola, L.C., Montes, M.: Detecting depression in social media using fine-grained emotions. Proc. NAACL-HLT **1**, 1481–1486 (2019)
8. Baruah, T.D., Kanta, K., State, H.: Effectiveness of social media as a tool of communication and its potential for technology enabled connections: a micro-level study. Int. J. Sci. Res. Publ. **2**(5) (2012)
9. Kendler, K.S., Gatz, M., Gardner, C.O., Pedersen, N.L.: Personality and major depression: a swedish longitudinal, population-based twin study. Arch. Gen. Psychiatry **63**(10), 1113–1120 (2006)
10. Jackson, P.B., Williams, D.R.: Culture, race/ethnicity, and depression. In: Women and Depression: A Handbook for the Social, Behavioral, and Biomedical Sciences, pp. 328–59. Cambridge University Press, New York (2006)
11. Arevalo, J., Solorio, T., Montes-y-Gómez, M., González, F.A.: Gated multimodal networks. Neural Comput. Appl. **32**(14), 10209–10228 (2019). https://doi.org/10.1007/s00521-019-04559-1
12. Peng, Z., Hu, Q., Dang, J.: Multi-kernel SVM based depression recognition using social media data. Int. J. Mach. Learn. Cyb. **10**(1), 43–57 (2019)
13. Meng, H., Huang, D., Wang, H., Yang, H., Ai-Shuraifi, M., Wang, Y.: Depression recognition based on dynamic facial and vocal expression features using partial least square regression. In: Proceedings of the 3rd ACM International Workshop on Audio/Visual Emotion Challenge (2013)
14. Trotzek, M., Koitka, S., Friedrich, C.M.: Word embeddings and linguistic metadata at the CLEF 2018 tasks for early detection of depression and anorexia. In: Proceedings of the 9th CLEF Association Conference (2018)
15. Paul, S., Jandhyala, S.K., Basu, T.: Early detection of signs of anorexia and depression over social media using effective machine learning frameworks. In: Proceedings of the 9th CLEF Association Conference (2018)
16. Ramiandrisoa, F., Mothe, J., Benamara, F., Moriceau, V.: Irit at e-risk 2018. In: Proceedings of the 9th CLEF Association Conference (2018)
17. Pedregosa, F., et al.: Scikit-learn: machine learning in python. J. Mach. Lea. Res. **12**, 2825–2830 (2011)
18. Lauriola, I., Aiolli, F.: Mklpy: a python-based framework for multiple kernel learning. CoRR, vol. abs/2007.09982 (2020)
19. Lauriola, I., Polato, M., Aiolli, F.: Radius-margin ratio optimization for dot-product boolean kernel learning. In: Lintas, A., Rovetta, S., Verschure, P.F.M.J., Villa, A.E.P. (eds.) ICANN 2017. LNCS, vol. 10614, pp. 183–191. Springer, Cham (2017). https://doi.org/10.1007/978-3-319-68612-7_21
20. Choi, J.-H., Lee, J.-S.: Embracenet: a robust deep learning architecture for multimodal classification. Inf. Fus. **51**, 259–270 (2019)
21. Wang, W.: Some fundamental issues in ensemble methods. In: International Joint Conference on Neural Networks, pp. 2243–2250, IEEE (2008)

A Wide & Deep Learning Approach for Covid-19 Tweet Classification

Alberto Valdés-Chávez[1](✉), J. Roberto López-Santillán[1](✉),
L. Carlos Gonzalez-Gurrola[1](✉), Graciela Ramírez-Alonso[1](✉),
and Manuel Montes-y-Gómez[2](✉)

[1] Facultad de Ingeniería, Universidad Autónoma de Chihuahua,
Circuito Universitario Campus II, Chihuahua, 31125 Chihuahua, Mexico
{p345336,jrlopez,lcgonzalez,galonso}@uach.mx
[2] Coordinación de Ciencias Computacionales, Instituto Nacional de Astrofísica,
Óptica y Electrónica (INAOE), Luis Enrique Erro No. 1, Sta. Ma. Tonantzintla,
72840 Puebla, Mexico
mmontesg@inaoep.mx

Abstract. Public health surveillance via social media can be a useful tool to identify and track potential cases of a disease. The aim of this research was to design a method for identifying tweets describing potential Covid-19 cases. The proposed method uses a Wide & Deep (W&D) architecture, which combines two learning branches fed from different features to improve classification effectiveness. The deep branch uses a BERT-type model, while the wide branch considers two different lexical-based features. It was evaluated on the data from Task 5 of the Social Media Mining For Health (#SMM4H) 2021 competition. Results show that the proposed W&D method performed better than the wide-only and deep-only models, achieving an F1-score of 0.79 which matches the results of the 1st place ensemble-model.

Keywords: Social media · Data mining · Natural language processing · Text classification · Wide & Deep · Covid-19

1 Introduction

As of 2022, there has been over 364 million confirmed Covid-19 cases and approximately 5.6 million deaths worldwide according to the World Health Organization Covid-19 Dashboard [1]. Even though the number of reported cases is very large, it is believed that the actual number of cases is much higher. Since the beginning of the pandemic, there have been concerns about the accuracy of the number of reported cases [2], which may be due to the shortage of testing kits, overburdened medical services or mild cases that were never reported. Having access to more accurate information is crucial in making decisions to stop the disease from spreading.

A systematic review paper compiled several studies that sought to retrieve relevant information of diseases such as Influenza, Zika or Ebola by classifying social media posts. The results showed that disease surveillance through social networks is feasible [3]. In an attempt to address the lack of information regarding the current pandemic, some researchers have tried to promote the development of classification methods to identify relevant information about the spread of Covid-19. One such venue was the Workshop on Noisy User-generated Text (W-NUT) 2020 [4]. They proposed the shared task of identifying informative Covid-19 English tweets. Among the top 10 ranked submissions, 7 of them employed ensemble techniques with BERT based models. Another venue was the Social Media Mining for Health (#SMM4H) 2021 [5]. Here two of the proposed shared tasks included identifying potential cases of Covid-19 (Task 5) and classifying tweets containing Covid-19 symptoms (Task 6). Again, the highest ranked systems were either fine-tuned BERT-based models or ensembles of them [6,7].

Our objective was to design an innovative model that improves performance compared to fine-tuned BERT models and ensembles in Covid-19 related tweet classification tasks. Accordingly, in this work we propose a new Wide & Deep (W&D) method, inspired by [8] but specially suited for the task at hand. This method has two branches that are jointly trained and fed with different types of features. Each branch is able to learn different types of patterns and thus take advantage of a more comprehensive learning process. The deep branch utilizes the CT-BERT model[1], which has proved to achieve state-of-the-art (SoA) results in Covid-19 tweet related applications [9]. This model is used to calculate a contextualized embedding of a whole tweet, based on the words contained in it. In contrast, the wide branch only seeks to recognize simple lexical patterns, in other words, to identify terms commonly used in tweets where the user talks about him/herself or someone close who may have Covid-19. To achieve this, we calculate the Inverse Document Frequency (IDF) and the EXPEI [10] weights for the vocabulary terms. The former is a measure of how relevant a term is to a tweet in the context of a given collection, whereas the latter is a measure of how related each term is to the usage of first person pronouns in the set of tweets. With this method, we expect that the branches complement each other to make a more accurate prediction than deep-only models or ensembles of them.

In this paper, we first present and discuss several approaches related to the classification of medical tweets and the usage of diverse feature types to show the innovation in our approach. Next, we describe the data and methodology used to train and design our W&D method. Then, we evaluate and analyze the results. Lastly, we provide a final discussion about our contribution and future work.

2   Related Work

The identification of medical tweets is a task that has been mainly addressed from two approaches. The first one involves the use of features represented as a Bag-of-Words (BOW), such as the IDF weights, and used in conjunction with

---

[1] A model based on BERT_Large pre-trained on a large collection of Covid-19 tweets.

traditional Machine Learning (ML) algorithms. Among the most commonly used algorithms are Support Vector Machine, Logistic Regression, Dense Neural Networks and Random Forests [11]. The second approach is centered on the use of Deep Learning (DL) models such as BERT, that are based on Attention Mechanisms. They are able to generate their own contextualized features, be pre-trained on domain specific data and take advantage of transfer learning [12].

Attention-based models have been widely used in recent years as they have achieved SoA results in medical related tasks, surpassing the traditional ML methods [13]. In an attempt to further boost the performance of these models, some have used ensemble techniques with variations of BERT models [7,14]. Although ensembles show improved results, they may not always be a viable approach. One of the downsides that popular attention-based models have is that they can be very resource-consuming [15]. This is further escalated when using an ensemble, since each of the models needs to be trained individually, requiring both a great deal of time and processing power.

Other attempts to improve the results of attention models have tried to combine the capabilities of traditional ML approaches with attention-based models. In sarcasm detection and medical entities recognition, one attempt has been to merge the outputs of BERT-like models with other types of lexical features, where the resulting features are then used to train a ML classifier [16,17]. One disadvantage of this approach is that the learning capabilities of the attention models are not fully exploited, since they are only used as independent feature-extractors and not trained on the task at hand.

In order to exploit both the capabilities of traditional and attention-based approaches, another way is to design a method that incorporates the benefits of both. Inspired by the Wide & Deep architecture in [8], we can merge both methods into a single model. Following this idea, we propose a model with two branches, a deep branch containing a BERT-like model that generates its own semantic features, and a wide branch that provides lexical features. These branches are then merged and fed into a fully-connected network to be trained jointly. The union of both approaches are expected to obtain better results than when used individually.

The Wide & Deep method has already been successfully used in other text-classification tasks, such as author profiling and crisis-related social media content [18,19], but not in Covid-19 tweet categorization. In our work, we employ a BERT model as the deep part that has never been used in this way, and a set of wide features specifically adjusted to our task.

3 Our W&D Architecture for Covid-19 Tweet Classification

Figure 1 shows our proposed method for Covid-19 tweet classification. It is composed of two main branches, the deep branch and the wide branch. The deep branch contains a CT-BERT module [9], which generates a contextualized representation of the whole tweet. We chose to use the CT-BERT model, as it has proved to achieve SoA results in Covid-19 tweet classification tasks [9]. The wide branch computes the IDF and EXPEI (term personal value) weights to obtain a BOW-like representation, with the intention of capturing superficial lexical patterns. Once the features from both branches are extracted, they are concatenated and fed to a dense classification layer for prediction. This means that both branches are trained jointly, the CT-BERT module and the parameters corresponding to the wide features.

3.1 Deep Branch

The deep branch receives a tweet for deep-specific preprocessing (see Sect. 4), and it is then fed to the CT-BERT module. The output of the start token [CLS] is used as the deep representation, being considered as the contextualized embedding of the whole tweet. The [CLS] embedding has 1024 dimensions, so the final representation of a tweet d_i is a vector of the form $d_i = \langle w_1, w_2, ..., w_{1024} \rangle$.

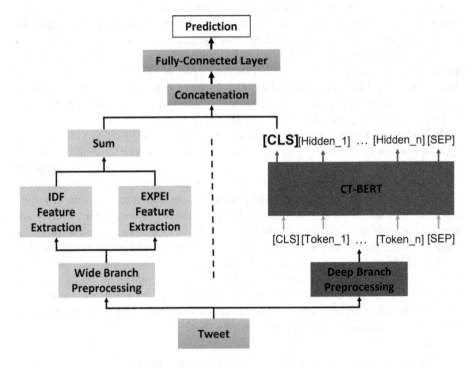

Fig. 1. Proposed Wide & Deep architecture.

3.2 Wide Branch

For the wide branch the tweets are first preprocessed following the procedure detailed in Sect. 4. From the preprocessed tweets, a vocabulary $V = \langle t_1, ..., t_N \rangle$, with N terms is extracted. With these terms, a BOW representation of each tweet is build. Each tweet or document is represented as $d_i = \langle w_{i1}, ..., w_{iN} \rangle$, where w_{ij} indicates the relevance of the term t_j in document d_i. We employed the following two approaches to calculate the term weights.

IDF Features. The IDF weighting scheme is very common in Natural Language Processing applications. This weight was chosen because it considers the discriminative property of the terms. Equation 1 computes the IDF weight for each term t_j in document (tweet) d_i, where n indicates the total number of tweets in the entire collection and $\#(d_i, t_j)$ the number of tweets that contain the term t_j.

$$w_{ij} = IDF(t_j) = 1 + log \frac{1+n}{1 + \#(d_i, t_j)} \tag{1}$$

EXPEI Features. It is commonly assumed that when a person writes using first person pronouns, he/she is referring to him/herself or someone close. In the context of detecting potential Covid-19 cases, when a symptom is mentioned, it is important to know who suffers from it. In order to capture this, we propose adapting a new weighting scheme recently introduced with the goal of measuring how personal each term is [10,18].

Using this new weighting scheme, values closer to one indicate a term that is more commonly used in personal tweets, and vice versa. Considering a tweet as personal if it contains any of the following terms: *i, i'd, i'll, i'v, i've, i'm, we, me, us, my, mine, our, ours, myself, ourselves*, the EXPEI weight for a term t_j in a tweet d_i is defined as follows.

$$w_{ij} = EXPEI(d_i, t_j) = \sqrt{\frac{\#(t_j, d_i)}{\#(d_i)}}^{1 - F(t_j)} \tag{2}$$

where $\#(t_j, d_i)$ indicates the number of occurrences of t_j in d_i and $\#(d_i)$ indicates the number of words in d_i i.e., the length of d_i. $F(t_j)$ is calculated as:

$$F(t_j) = 2\frac{\rho(t_j) \cdot \tau(t_j)}{\rho(t_j) + \tau(t_j)} \tag{3}$$

$$\rho(t_j) = \frac{\#(t_j, P)}{\#(t_j)} \tag{4}$$

$$\tau(t_j) = \frac{\#(t_j, P)}{\#(P)} \tag{5}$$

$\rho(t_j)$ is defined as the percentage of personal tweets in the subset of tweets containing the term (indicated by P), and $\tau(t_j)$ is the portion of the personal tweets covered by the term.

As indicated in Fig. 1, we can also combine both IDF and EXPEI features into a single one, by adding the term weights obtained by each approach. This incorporates both the "personal" importance for each term as well as its general frequency information. This new weight is called Term Specificity-Exponential Personal Reward (TS-XPR) and is defined as:

$$w_{ij} = TS\text{-}XPR(d_i, t_j) = IDF(t_j) + EXPEI(d_i, t_j) \tag{6}$$

4   Experimental Setup

Data. We evaluated our method using the dataset from the #SMM4H 2021 Shared Task 5 [5]. Task 5 seeks to distinguish tweets in English reporting potential Covid-19 cases (labeled as "1") from other Covid-19 related tweets (labeled as "0"). A potential case refers to the author or someone in their household being ill or suffering from a symptom, having been denied testing for the disease, or having been exposed to a contagious risk situation. The training set is composed of 1026 "Potential Case" tweets and 5439 "other" tweets. The validation set contains 122 and 594 respectively, whereas the test set contains 10,000 tweets with withheld labels. Below, we show two example tweets.

Potential Case: *I think I have the coronavirus I've been coughing nonstop all day and I feel really warm.*
Other: *Low key scared that if I cough on the bus, people will think I have coronavirus.*

Preprocessing. Both branches share the following cleanup steps: @usernames and URL's are replaced with a "user" and "url" tokens, respectively, emojis are standardized and text is lowercased. For the deep branch we replace multiple occurrences of "user" and "url" to the form "n user/url", where n is the number of occurrences of the words. Tweets are then tokenized and truncated to a maximum of 120 tokens. Tweets with less than 120 tokens are padded to the right with 0's. For the wide branch, the tweets are only tokenized and lemmatized.

Deep Branch. The CT-BERT model hyperparameters were chosen according to [6], where this same model was fine-tuned and applied to #SMM4H 2021 Task 6. Particularly, we used a batch size of 32, a learning rate of 3.154e–5 and a weight decay of 0.1328 during 3 training epochs.

Wide Branch. To calculate the IDF values we used the *TfidfVectorizer* function from the *Scikit Learn* library, with the following parameters: *Analyzer = 'word', Use_idf = True and Smooth_idf = True*. Then we scale the values using the *StandardScaler* from the same library. Then, using either the IDF, EXPEI or TS-XPR weights, we represent each tweet as a BOW, using only the 5000 most frequent words in the dataset in order to reduce dimensionality.

Fully-Connected Layer. The hyperparameters for the dense classification neural network were the following: *Dropout* = 0.1 and 6024 input units, which comes from the concatenation of the 1024 features from the deep branch and the 5000 from the wide branch. Both branches share the same loss function, *categorical-crossentropy*. Finally, we usd a *softmax* activation function for label prediction.

5   Results and Qualitative Analysis

Table 2 shows the results obtained in Task 5 of #SMM4H 2021. For comparison, we show the results from the deep-only and wide-only branches. Wide features were evaluated using a Logistic Regression model. We also show the average score of the 14 participating systems and the best score at the #SMM4H 2021 competition.

Table 1. Results for Task 5 at #SMM4H 2021.

Model	Features/Description	F1	P	R
CT-BERT	Deep-only	0.77	0.77	0.77
Logistic Regression	IDF	0.52	0.47	0.59
Logistic Regression	EXPEI	0.48	0.42	0.57
Logistic Regression	TS-XPR	0.52	0.47	0.58
Wide & Deep	CT-BERT, IDF	**0.79**	**0.81**	0.77
Wide & Deep	CT-BERT, EXPEI	0.78	0.77	**0.79**
Wide & Deep	CT-BERT, TS-XPR	0.78	0.77	**0.79**
Average at #SMM4H 2021	Average of 14 systems	0.74	0.73	0.74
Best at #SMM4H 2021	Ensemble of 5 BERT-based models	0.79	0.78	0.79

The merge of both branches show that it can achieve better results than each branch individually, which confirms that they complement each other. Our Wide & Deep method scored well above the average results reported in the Task, that correspond to several ML and DL approaches. It is also equal to the best in Task 5, showing that our method is able to compete with SoA approaches.

The best-performing system trained a total of 14 BERT-based models during a search of hyperparameters. Then, they performed an exhaustive search for every possible combination to find the ensemble with the highest validation score using the previous 14 trained models. The best ensemble was composed of 5 models [7]. While this approach achieved the best score, it greatly increased the number of trainable parameters and the computational power needed to make a prediction. In contrast, our W&D model has about one-fifth as many trainable parameters, making it much less expensive and requiring only a single training session. This means that it is a much more efficient method that achieved the same results. Also, the wide branch adds interpretability to the results, and to better understand them, qualitative analyses of the wide features are shown below.

5.1   Wide Branch Features

The wide features (IDF & EXPEI weights) were computed for each of the 5000 most frequent words found in the training set, which are shown in Fig. 2. These words appear to be highly related to the context of a potential Covid-19 case, such as "I", "sick", "symptom", "cough", etc. It could be thought that when a certain combination of these words is present, the tweet is more likely to belong to the "Potential Case" class. The wide features are able to capture these superficial lexical patterns. Taking the above into account, we believe that this is the reason why the wide features are able to enhance the performance of the deep branch.

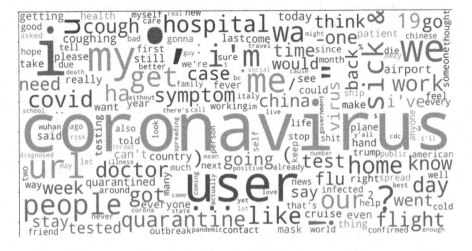

Fig. 2. Most frequent words in the dataset.

In Table 2 three "Potential Case" tweets are shown with the predicted labels obtained from the deep-only and wide-only models, as well as the W&D method. The deep-only model corresponds to CT-BERT, the wide-only to logistic regression with TS-XPR features and the W&D to CT-BERT+IDF features, each one of them achieved the best scores of their respective group. While the individual models classified the tweets incorrectly, the W&D method was able to correct the mistake. As can be noticed, these tweets contain first person pronouns highlighted by the EXPEI weights, as well as discriminative terms from the previous word cloud.

Table 2. Models predictions comparison.

Potential Case ("1") Tweets	Deep	Wide	W&D
*I got a runny nose today and started crying because **I'm** nervous about getting the coronavirus*	"0"	"1"	"1"
*I have all the symptoms of the Coronavirus so does that mean **I** have it???*	"1"	"0"	"1"
*@user **We** need more testing. Please. **I** may have coronavirus without showing symptoms. **I** live with **my** parents whom are at risk*	"0"	"0"	"1"

6 Conclusions and Future Work

In this work, we proposed a Wide & Deep method for Covid-19 tweet classification, which combines two learning branches. The deep branch used a CT-BERT model, while the wide branch used lexical-based features with two different weights, IDF and EXPEI. Results obtained from Task 5 of the #SMM4H 2021 show that proposed W&D method performed better than deep-only models. Our W&D method even achieved competitive results with respect to SoA models, which use complex combinations of several deep models.

The good performance of the W&D model depends heavily on the feature engineering for the wide branch. Each task requires finding the features that provide the most useful information. In this direction, as future work, we plan to implement different word-weighing techniques that could better fit this or other particular classification task.

References

1. WHO Coronavirus (COVID-19) Dashboard. https://covid19.who.int/. Accessed 30 Jan 2022
2. Oliver, D.: Mistruths and misunderstandings about covid-19 death numbers. In: BMJ 2021, vol. 372, pp. 352. the bmj. https://doi.org/10.1136/bmj.n352
3. Al-Garadi, M.A., Khan, M.S., Varathan, K.D., Mujtaba, G., Al-kabsi, A.M.: Using online social networks to track a pandemic: a systematic review. J. Biomed. Inform. **62**, 1–11 (2016)
4. Xu, W., Ritter, A., Baldwin, T., Rahimi, A.: Proceedings of the Sixth Workshop on Noisy User-generated Text (W-NUT 2020). Association for Computational Linguistics (2020). https://aclanthology.org/2020.wnut-1.0
5. Klein, A., et al.: Proceedings of the Sixth Social Media Mining for Health (#SMM4H) Workshop and Shared Task. Association for Computational Linguistics, Mexico City, Mexico (2021). https://aclanthology.org/2021.smm4h-1.0
6. Valdes, A., Lopez, J., Montes, M.: UACH-INAOE at SMM4H: a BERT based approach for classification of COVID-19 Twitter posts. In: Proceedings of the Sixth Social Media Mining for Health #SMM4H Workshop and Shared Task, pp. 65–68. Association for Computational Linguistics, Mexico City, Mexico (2021). https://doi.org/10.18653/v1/2021.smm4h-1.10

7. Aji, A., Nityasya, M., Wibowo, H., Prasojo, R., Fatyanosa, T.: BERT Goes BRRR: a venture towards the lesser error in classifying medical self-reporters on Twitter. In: Proceedings of the Sixth Social Media Mining for Health #SMM4H Workshop and Shared Task, pp. 58–64. Association for Computational Linguistics, Mexico City, Mexico (2021). https://doi.org/10.18653/v1/2021.smm4h-1.9
8. Cheng, H., et al.: Wide & Deep Learning for Recommender Systems (2016)
9. Müller, M., Salathé, M, Kummervold, P.: COVID-Twitter-BERT: A Natural Language Processing Model to Analyse COVID-19 Content on Twitter (2020)
10. Ortega, R., Franco, A., Montes, M.: Identificación del perfil de autores en redes sociales usando nuevos esquemas de pesado que enfatizan información de tipo personal. Computación y Sistemas 23(2), 501–510 (2019) https://doi.org/10.13053/cvs-23-2-3005
11. Banik, S., Gosh, A., Banik, S.: Classification of COVID19 Tweets based on sentimental analysis. In: 2021 International Conference on Computer Communication and Informatics (ICCCI), pp. 1–7 (2021) https://doi.org/10.1109/ICCCI50826.2021.9402540
12. Devlin, J., Chang, M., Lee, K., Toutanova, K.: BERT: Pre-training of Deep Bidirectional Transformers for Language Understanding (2019)
13. Magge, A., Pimpalkhute, V., Rallapalli, D, Siguenza, D., Gonzalez, G.: UPennHLP at WNUT-2020 task 2 : transformer models for classification of COVID19 posts on Twitter. In: Proceedings of the Sixth Workshop on Noisy User-generated Text (W-NUT 2020), pp. 378–382. Association for Computational Linguistics (2020)
14. Bai, Y., Zhou, X.: Automatic detecting for health-related Twitter Data with BioBERT. In: Proceedings of the Fifth Social Media Mining for Health Applications Workshop and Shared Task 2020, pp. 63–69. Association for Computational Linguistics, Barcelona, Spain (2020)
15. Vaswani, A., et al.: Attention Is All You Need (2017)
16. Roitero, K., Bozzato, C., Della-Mea, V., Mizzaro, S., Serra, G.: Twitter goes to the doctor: detecting medical Tweets using machine learning and BERT. In: Proceedings of the Workshop on Semantic Indexing and Information Retrieval for Health from Heterogeneous Content Types and Languages Co-located with 42nd European Conference on Information Retrieval, pp. 63–69. CEUR-WS.org, Lisbon, Portugal (2020)
17. Ifeanyi, C., Azah, N., Liyana, S.: Context-based feature technique for sarcasm identification in benchmark datasets using deep learning and BERT model. IEEE Access 9, 48501–48518 (2021)
18. López-Santillán, R., González, L., Montes-y-Gómez, M., López-Monroy, P., López-Santillán, M.: A Transformer-based Wide & Deep Neural Network for Author Profiling. In Revision (2022)
19. Burel, G., Saif, H., Alani, H.: Semantic wide and deep learning for detecting crisis-information categories on social media. In: International Semantic Web Conference, pp. 138–155 (2017)

Does This Tweet Report an Adverse Drug Reaction? An Enhanced BERT-Based Method to Identify Drugs Side Effects in Twitter

José Alberto Fuentes-Carbajal[(✉)], Manuel Montes-y-Gómez,
and Luis Villaseñor-Pineda

Instituto Nacional de Astrofísica Óptica y Electrónica (INAOE), Puebla, Mexico
{alberto.fuentes,mmontesg,villasen}@inaoep.mx

Abstract. Adverse drug reactions (ADRs) are a major cause of patients' morbidity and mortality, and a source of financial burden for health systems. In this context, pharmacovigilance plays a key role, which has led to its application on social media texts, where users often report various personal health issues, including adverse drug reactions and problems with medical treatments. This new opportunity also presents new challenges, on the one hand, posts reporting ADRs are very scarce in relation to the rest of the messages, and, on the other hand, they employ colloquial language, different from the medical terminology. In this paper, we present an enhanced BERT-based method to identify tweets reporting ADRs. This method addresses the task as one of sentence-pair classification by considering some auxiliary sentences derived from the input tweets as extra contextual information. The results obtained in data from the SMM4H-2021 shared task outperformed the best results previously reported, and also show that the use of the auxiliary sentences improved the BERT results by up to 18.5%.

1 Introduction

An adverse drug reaction (ADR) is defined as an appreciably harmful or unpleasant reaction, resulting from an intervention related to the use of a medicinal product, which predicts hazard from future administration and warrants prevention or specific treatment, or alteration of the dosage regimen, or withdrawal of the product [1]. ADRs represent a significant public health problem as they are a major cause of morbidity and mortality as well as a source of financial burden for health systems [2]. ADRs are generally caused by limited clinical trials that failed to detect all possible adverse reactions, due to factors such as the small number of samples used, the duration of testing, and the lack of diversity among study patients [3]. Under this scenario, post-marketing surveillance, also known as *pharmacovigilance*, plays a fundamental role in identifying and preventing risks associated with the use of drugs, especially those recently marketed [4].

O. O. Vergara-Villegas et al. (Eds.): MCPR 2022, LNCS 13264, pp. 235–244, 2022.
https://doi.org/10.1007/978-3-031-07750-0_22

The traditional way in which post-launch adverse drug reactions are identified is through the analysis of patients' clinical records. However, due to their scarcity in electronic format, alternative sources of information have been considered to help in the identification of new ADRs. Accordingly, and taking advantage of the common usage of social networks to share personal health information, recent works have proposed their use for this task [5], as well as for others related to public health monitoring, such as the identification of mental disorders [6], drug abuse [7], and COVID-19 symptoms [8].

Among the social networks the most used in pharmacovigilance is Twitter, this due to its ease of access and real-time nature [9–11]. However, it also presents important risks for healthcare monitoring, such as high rates of misinformation and large volumes of information that make difficult to filter relevant tweets. In addition, tweets are very short texts, which lack context, and use colloquial language, abbreviations, and show a high number of spelling and grammatical errors. Take, for example, the following tweet reporting an ADR: *"@user I've had Cipro before. Luckily for me, the only side fx I tend to get from AB is gastic upset. But I RARELY use AB."*.

This paper addresses the identification of adverse drug reactions as a text classification problem, whose objective is to distinguish between tweets that report an adverse reaction (labeled as ADR) and those that do not (labeled as NoADR). Based on previous works that show that transformers have shown the best performance in this task [12–14], we propose a BERT-based method to identify tweets reporting ADRs. In contrast to all them, which use the traditional architecture for single-text classification tasks, we propose handling it as a sentence-pair classification problem, by considering some auxiliary sentences derived from the input tweets as extra contextual information, and by using the transformer architectures especially suited for tasks such as question answering, semantic text similarity and textual entailment. It is important to point out that this idea is not entirely new, since few recent works have used BERT's second entry as a mechanism to guide the model in the classification of texts [15–18], however, it has never been tested and studied in the identification of tweets that report ADRs; this is the first contribution of our work. In addition, as a second contribution, we propose three ways to generate the auxiliary sentences from the input tweets, taking as motivation the applications for which the two-input architecture was proposed.

The rest of the paper is structured as follows. Section 2 presents a brief description of previous work in the identification of tweets reporting ADRs. Section 3 introduces the method proposed. Section 4 describes the experimental settings, and Sect. 5 shows and discusses the results obtained. Finally, Sect. 6 presents our main conclusions and future work directions.

2   Related Work

Different methods have been proposed for the identification of ADRs in Twitter. These methods can be broadly classified into three groups. The first group considers a traditional machine learning pipeline; it mainly employs hand-crafted features, mainly based on a bag of words representation, extended with part-of-speech tags in some cases, and uses a Support Vector Machine (SVM) classifier [19–21]. The second group considers word embeddings and uses neural network (NN) approaches such as Convolutional Neural Networks (CNNs) and Recurrent Neural Networks (RNNs) to learn the representation of tweets. Then, the obtained representations are fed to a NN or SVM classifier [22–24]. This second approach in particular has been little used for ADR classification, in part because of its inadequacy to deal with collections with few data and high imbalance, as well as with the use of colloquial language, abbreviations, and spelling and grammatical errors, which strongly harms the use of pre-trained word embeddings. Finally, the third group focuses on the use of pretrained transformers. Having been trained on large amounts of data, these models have shown significant improvements for a wide range of NLP-related tasks, including the identification of ADRs in tweets. For this particular task, the SMM4H[1] evaluation forum is a must reference [25]; in its 2021 edition, the best results were achieved by methods based on the RoBERTa model with sampling techniques [12,13,26], even surpassing the results from other BERT-based models [27–29].

3   Enhanced BERT-Based Model for ADR Identification

This section presents our enhanced BERT-based method to identify tweets reporting ADRs. As explained before, it addresses the task as one of sentence-pair classification by considering auxiliary sentences derived from the input tweets as extra contextual information. Figure 1 shows the general architecture of this method, which considers a module that generates the auxiliary sentences for each input tweet, a BERT model as the central module, which receives the tweet and its auxiliary sentence at the input, and a final classification module fed with the representation obtained from the transformer.

The goal of using an auxiliary sentence as extra input is to help contextualize the tweets and guide the network to better adjust its weights. Particularly, we explore three different ways to generate these sentences, two of them are adaptations of previous methods [15,18], and the third one is a new approach based on the use of the most frequent words in the positive class of the training set. The following paragraphs detail the three approaches, and Table 1 shows two example tweets with their respective three auxiliary sentences.

1. **Question.** Motivated by the outstanding results of BERT in the QA task, [15] proposed to use a question as the auxiliary sentence. Following this idea, for every tweet we use the question *"Does it report an adverse drug reaction?"* as the auxiliary sentence.
2. **Similar tweet.** Based on the application of BERT in semantic textual similarity tasks, [18] proposed to use a text similar to the entry as the auxiliary sentence. Following this idea, we propose to identify –in entire training set– the most similar tweet to the input one, regardless of whether or not it

---

[1] https://healthlanguageprocessing.org/.

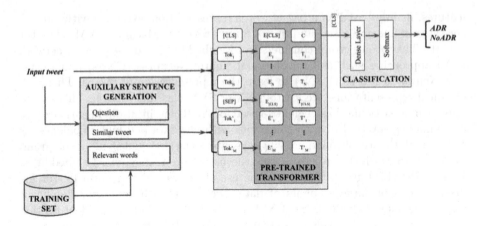

Fig. 1. General architecture of the proposed ADR classification method.

mentions an adverse drug reaction, and to use it as the auxiliary sentence. For the implementation of this idea we used a BoW representation with TF-IDF weights and the cosine distance.

3. **Relevant words.** The idea of this new approach is to provide the network with a set of words highly related to the description of ADRs, so that it can better evaluate the relationship of the input tweet with the target category. For this purpose, we consider the N most frequent words in the positive class of the training set, after removing the stopwords. In the experiments we considered $N = 10$.

Table 1. Two examples of tweets with their corresponding auxiliary sentences.

	Positive example	*Negative example*
Input tweet	My seroquel this morning got me lethargic	Does anyone have a lozenge?
Question	Does it report an adverse drug reaction?	Does it report an adverse drug reaction?
Similar tweet	This seroquel got me sleepy	I need a lozenge. Does anyone have a lozenge ?
Relevant words	Go day ill one sleep feet use makes cause have	Go day ill one sleep feet use makes cause have

4   Experimental Settings

4.1   Data Set

The data set used to evaluate our method was provided by the Social Media Mining for Health (SMM4H) evaluation forum, and corresponds to its 2021 edition[2]. Table 2 shows the overall distribution of this collection, from which the high imbalance between the ADR and NoADR categories becomes evident. Only 7% the training and validation tweets correspond to the positive class, respectively. On the other hand, no information is available on the distribution of the test set. To evaluate the methods, the predictions have to be sent through the codalab platform[3]. At the moment, 7 results are reported on this platform, which will be used for comparison purposes in the next section.

Table 2. Distribution of the SMM4H2021 dataset for classification of Adverse Drug Reactions in English tweets

Partition	ADR	NoADR	All
Training	1,258	16,449	17,707
Validation	65	884	913
Test	–	–	10,909

4.2   Model Implementation

The central module of our architecture corresponds to a BERT-based model. Supported on the previous results reported for the task, we decided to use the RoBERTa$_{LARGE}$ model, pretrained with 160 GB of data from BookCorpus, CC-News, OpenWebText, and Stories [30]. The model was trained considering a batch size of 32 and a maximum token size of 120, for a total of 15 epochs, with a learning rate of $1e^{-5}$, using the Adam optimizer, and a dropout of 0.1.

5   Results

Table 3 shows the general evaluation results of the proposed method. It compares the performance obtained with the RoBERTa model with and without the auxiliary sentences. For each implementation of the method, it shows two groups of results, the first one corresponds to the use of the original training set, whereas the second group corresponds to an augmented set, for which we applied a random oversampling strategy (with ratio equal to 0.5) in order to get the minority (ADR) class with half as many tweets as the majority (NoADR) class.

---

[2] https://healthlanguageprocessing.org/.
[3] https://competitions.codalab.org/.

Table 3. Results of the proposed method in the SMM4H-2021 data set. Evaluation measures are the F1-score (F1), precision (P), and recall (R) over the the ADR category.

Model	F1	P	R	F1	P	R
	Original data set			Augmented data set		
RoBERTa (only tweet)	0.51	0.55	0.49	0.54	0.49	0.61
RoBERTa (tweet+question)	**0.60**	0.58	**0.63**	**0.64**	0.59	**0.69**
RoBERTa (tweet+similar tweet)	0.53	0.59	0.49	0.58	0.55	0.62
RoBERTa (tweet+relevant words)	0.58	**0.60**	0.56	0.62	**0.62**	0.61

The results in Table 3 clearly show the following: first, that the use of an auxiliary sentence, regardless of how it was generated, has a positive impact on RoBERTa's performance. Nonetheless, it is important to highlight that the approach of using a *question* as the auxiliary sentence showed the best results, which could be explained by the previous successful application of this architecture in question answering tasks. Second, the use of the augmented data set in the training phase improved the results of all method configurations, highlighting the need for more resources to tackle the task at hand.

In order to put the results obtained in perspective, Table 4 compares the results from our best configuration (*RoBERTa fed with tweets and queries*) against the three best results reported so far in the SMM4H-2021 data set. As can be noticed, the proposed method is the one showing the best compromise between precision and recall, and with it a 4.9% improvement in F1 score.

Table 4. Comparison with the best three results in the SMM4H-2021 dataset. Evaluation measures are the F1-score (F1), precision (P), and recall (R) over the ADR category.

Model	F1	P	R
RoBERTa with under and oversampling [12]	0.61	0.52	**0.75**
RoBERTa + ChemBERTa [13]	0.61	0.55	0.68
BERT ensemble with oversampling [14]	0.54	**0.60**	0.49
RoBERTa (tweet+question) with oversampling	**0.64**	0.59	0.69

5.1 Error Analysis

The tweets misclassified by the different configurations of our method, both false positives and negatives, are very diverse in content and style. However, after a careful manual analysis, we distinguished the following three frequent causes:

- Tweets that report an ADR using a humorous or sarcastic style. For example, the tweet "*Cool, the Humira commercial just made me lose my appetite*".

- Tweets that report an ADR using colloquial language, and even profanity. For example, the tweet *"crap. forgot to take my doubled dose of fluoxetine and now i'm busy wanting to die a hell of a lot"*.
- Tweets that narrate an entire situation, and do not directly mention the adverse reaction, for example, *"fell asleep and woke back up again. trying a quarter of a seroquel instead of half this time. i'd like to get out of bed tomorrow"*.
- Tweets that contain several grammatical errors, abbreviations or medical terms, for example, *"@user I've had Cipro before. Luckily for me, the only side fx I tend to get from AB is gastic upset. But I RARELY use AB"*.

5.2   Handling Data Scarcity: Are Sampling Techniques a Solution?

As previously mentioned, data for this task are scarce, present high imbalance, and also correspond to short and usually poorly written texts. In consequence, the best results reported to date, including those presented here, consider the application of statistical sampling techniques.

With the intention of assessing the relevance of this kind of techniques in the task at hand, Table 5 shows the comparison of the performance obtained when using random oversampling and undersampling strategies. For both cases, we applied various ratios of increase and decrease of data. For the case of oversampling, the ratio indicates how much the minority class was made to grow with respect to the majority class (for example, 0.5 indicates that ADR instances were repeated until the minority class reached 50% of the size of the majority class). On the other hand, for undersampling, this ratio indicates the percentage of instances that were kept from the majority class, thus 0.25 indicates that only 25% of the instances of the majority class were kept. As it could be observed in the table, the application of neither of these two techniques had a significant impact on the performance of the method, which we attribute to the fact that they did not add lexical and syntactic variability to the training set. Thus, these results clearly show the need for more training data that cover the wide variety of drugs, effects and situations that can arise from their use.

Table 5. Comparison of results using random oversampling and undersampling.

Model	F1	P	R	F1	P	R
	Oversampling			Undersampling		
RoBERTa (tweet + question) 0%	0.60	0.58	0.59	–	–	–
RoBERTa (tweet + question) 25%	0.61	0.51	**0.73**	0.56	0.46	**0.71**
RoBERTa (tweet + question) 50%	**0.64**	**0.59**	0.69	0.53	0.58	0.48
RoBERTa (tweet + question) 75%	0.61	**0.59**	0.63	0.58	**0.59**	0.56
RoBERTa (tweet + question) 100%	0.62	0.58	0.67	**0.60**	0.58	0.59

6   Conclusions

The identification of tweets reporting adverse drug reactions (ADRs) is a complex task due to multiple factors, such as their colloquial language and small size, as well as the high imbalance in the current available data sets. In this paper, we introduced an enhanced BERT-based method for this task, which addresses it as one of sentence-pair classification by considering some auxiliary sentences derived from the input tweets as extra contextual information. Accordingly, we also proposed three ways to generate the auxiliary sentences from the input tweets, taking as motivation the applications for which the two-input transformer architecture was designed, such as question answering and semantic textual similarity.

Experiments in the SMM4H-2021 dataset showed that the use of the auxiliary sentences help improving the performance of a RoBERTa based classifier. In particular, the use of a *simple question* as the auxiliary sentence achieved the best results among the three proposed approaches. In addition, the experiments confirmed the relevance of applying an *oversampling* strategy to deal with the lack of data and its imbalance.

As future work we plan to explore other ways to generate the auxiliary sentences, and also to propose a method to extract and normalize the mentions of adverse drug reactions in the tweets in order to build a support tool for the pharmacovigilance process.

Acknowledgments. Work supported by CONACyT-Mexico: scholarship 1080699, grant CB-2015-01-257383 and the Deep Learning Platform for Language Technologies.

References

1. Edwards, I.R., Aronson, J.K.: Adverse drug reactions: definitions, diagnosis, and management. Lancet **356**(9237), 1255–1259 (2000)
2. Pirmohamed, M., James, S., Meakin, S., Green, C., Scott, A.K., Walley, T.J., Farrar, K., Park, B.K., Breckenridge, A.M.: Adverse drug reactions as cause of admission to hospital: prospective analysis of 18 820 patients. BMJ **329**(7456), 15–19 (2004)
3. Sultana, J., Cutroneo, P., Trifirò, G.: Clinical and economic burden of adverse drug reactions. J. Pharmacol. Pharmacotherapeut. **4**(Suppl1), S73 (2013)
4. Coloma, P.M., Trifirò, G., Patadia, V., Sturkenboom, M.: Postmarketing safety surveillance. Drug Saf. **36**(3), 183–197 (2013)
5. Nikfarjam, A., Sarker, A., O'connor, K., Ginn, R., Gonzalez, G.: Pharmacovigilance from social media: mining adverse drug reaction mentions using sequence labeling with word embedding cluster features. J. Am. Med. Inform. Assoc. **22**(3), 671–681 (2015)
6. Coppersmith, G., Dredze, M., Harman, C.: Quantifying mental health signals in Twitter. In: Proceedings of the Workshop on Computational Linguistics and Clinical Psychology: From Linguistic Signal to Clinical Reality, pp. 51–60, Association for Computational Linguistics, Baltimore, Maryland, USA (2014)

7. Hu, H., Phan, N., Chun, S.A., Geller, J., Vo, H., Ye, X., Jin, R., Ding, K., Kenne, D., Dou, D.: An insight analysis and detection of drug-abuse risk behavior on twitter with self-taught deep learning. Comput. Soc. Networks **6**(1), 1–19 (2019)

8. Lian, A.T., Du, J., Tang, L.: Using a machine learning approach to monitor Covid-19 vaccine adverse events (VAE) from twitter data. Vaccines **10**(1), 103 (2022)

9. Edo-Osagie, O., De La Iglesia, B., Lake, I., Edeghere, O.: A scoping review of the use of twitter for public health research. Comput. Biol. Med. **122**, 103770 (2020)

10. Ginn, R., et al.: Mining twitter for adverse drug reaction mentions: a corpus and classification benchmark. In: Proceedings of the Fourth Workshop on Building and Evaluating Resources for Health and Biomedical Text Processing, pp. 1–8. Citeseer (2014)

11. O'Connor, K., Pimpalkhute, P., Nikfarjam, A., Ginn, R., Smith, K.L., Gonzalez, G.: Pharmacovigilance on twitter? mining tweets for adverse drug reactions. In: AMIA Annual Symposium Proceedings, vol. 2014, p. 924. American Medical Informatics Association (2014)

12. Ramesh, S., et al.: Bert based transformers lead the way in extraction of health information from social media. In: Proceedings of the Sixth Social Media Mining for Health (# SMM4H) Workshop and Shared Task, pp. 33–38 (2021)

13. Sakhovskiy, A., Miftahutdinov, Z., Tutubalina, E.: KFU NLP team at SMM4H 2021 tasks: cross-lingual and cross-modal bert-based models for adverse drug effects. In: Proceedings of the Sixth Social Media Mining for Health (# SMM4H) Workshop and Shared Task, pp. 39–43 (2021)

14. Aji, A.F., Nityasya, M.N., Wibowo, H.A., Prasojo, R.E., Fatyanosa, T.: Bert goes BRRR: A venture towards the lesser error in classifying medical self-reporters on twitter. In: Proceedings of the Sixth Social Media Mining for Health (# SMM4H) Workshop and Shared Task, pp. 58–64 (2021)

15. Sun, C., Huang, L., Qiu, X.: Utilizing BERT for aspect-based sentiment analysis via constructing auxiliary sentence. Computing Research Repository (CoRR) - arXiv:abs/1903.09588 (2019)

16. Yu, S., Su, J., Luo, D.: Improving bert-based text classification with auxiliary sentence and domain knowledge. IEEE Access **7**, 176600–176612 (2019)

17. Ma, J., Xie, S., Jin, M., Lianxin, J., Yang, M., Shen, J.: Xsysigma at semeval-2020 task 7: Method for predicting headlines' humor based on auxiliary sentences with ei-bert. In: Proceedings of the Fourteenth Workshop on Semantic Evaluation, pp. 1077–1084 (2020)

18. Sánchez-Vega, F., López-Monroy, A.P.: Bert's auxiliary sentence focused on word's information for offensiveness detection, vol. 2943, pp. 259–269 (2021)

19. Ruchay, A., Kober, V.: Impulsive noise removal from color images with morphological filtering. In: van der Aalst, W.M.P., et al. (eds.) AIST 2017. LNCS, vol. 10716, pp. 280–291. Springer, Cham (2018). https://doi.org/10.1007/978-3-319-73013-4_26

20. Sarker, A., Ginn, R., Nikfarjam, A., O'Connor, K., Smith, K., Jayaraman, S., Upadhaya, T., Gonzalez, G.: Utilizing social media data for pharmacovigilance: a review. J. Biomed. Inform. **54**, 202–212 (2015)

21. Liza, F.F.: Sentence classification with imbalanced data for health applications. In: Proceedings of the Fifth Social Media Mining for Health Applications Workshop and Shared Task, pp. 138–145 (2020)

22. Aduragba, O.T., Yu, J., Senthilnathan, G., Crsitea, A.: Sentence contextual encoder with BERT and BiLSTM for automatic classification with imbalanced medication tweets. In: Proceedings of the Fifth Social Media Mining for Health Applications Workshop and Shared Task, pp. 165–167, Association for Computational Linguistics, Barcelona, Spain (2020)

23. Wu, C., Wu, F., Yuan, Z., Liu, J., Huang, Y., Xie, X.: MSA: Jointly detecting drug name and adverse drug reaction mentioning tweets with multi-head self-attention. In: Proceedings of the Twelfth ACM International Conference on Web Search and Data Mining, WSDM 2019, p. 33–41, Association for Computing Machinery, New York, NY, USA (2019)

24. Miranda, D.S.: Automated detection of adverse drug reactions in the biomedical literature using convolutional neural networks and biomedical word embeddings. arXiv preprint arXiv:1804.09148 (2018)

25. Magge, A., et al.: Overview of the sixth social media mining for health applications (#SMM4H) shared tasks at NAACL 2021. In: Proceedings of the Sixth Social Media Mining for Health (#SMM4H) Workshop and Shared Task, pp. 21–32, Association for Computational Linguistics, Mexico City, Mexico (2021)

26. Pimpalkhute, V., Nakhate, P., Diwan, T.: IIITN NLP at SMM4H 2021 tasks: transformer models for classification on health-related imbalanced Twitter datasets. In: Proceedings of the Sixth Social Media Mining for Health (#SMM4H) Workshop and Shared Task, pp. 118–122, Association for Computational Linguistics, Mexico City, Mexico (2021)

27. Aji, A.F., Nityasya, M.N., Wibowo, H.A., Prasojo, R.E., Fatyanosa, T.: BERT goes BRRR: a venture towards the lesser error in classifying medical self-reporters on Twitter. In: Proceedings of the Sixth Social Media Mining for Health (#SMM4H) Workshop and Shared Task, pp. 58–64, Association for Computational Linguistics, Mexico City, Mexico (2021)

28. Zhou, T., et al.: Classification, extraction, and normalization: CASIA_Unisound team at the social media mining for health 2021 shared tasks. In: Proceedings of the Sixth Social Media Mining for Health (#SMM4H) Workshop and Shared Task, pp. 77–82, Association for Computational Linguistics, Mexico City, Mexico (2021)

29. Dima, G.-A., Cercel, D.-C., Dascalu, M.: Transformer-based multi-task learning for adverse effect mention analysis in tweets. In: Proceedings of the Sixth Social Media Mining for Health (#SMM4H) Workshop and Shared Task, pp. 44–51, Association for Computational Linguistics, Mexico City, Mexico (2021)

30. Liu, Y., et al.: Roberta: a robustly optimized BERT pretraining approach. Computing Research Repository (CoRR) - arXiv:abs/1907.11692 (2019)

We Will Know Them by Their Style: Fake News Detection Based on Masked N-Grams

Jennifer Pérez-Santiago$^{(\boxtimes)}$, Luis Villaseñor-Pineda,
and Manuel Montes-y-Gómez

Laboratorio de Tecnologías del Lenguaje, INAOE, Puebla, Mexico
{jpsantiago,villasen,mmontesg}@inaoep.mx

Abstract. Thanks to the availability of digital media, users receive daily news reports, opinions and information on a wide variety of topics. These same media allow people to easily share and transmit their own opinions, thus enriching the debate and reflection on topics of public interest. Unfortunately, these circumstances have led to the emergence of fake news to misinform. This phenomenon has reached huge proportions, becoming a serious problem. Different approaches have been proposed to automatically detect fake news, based on analyzing their content, source or dispersion. The objective of the present work is to explore whether the written style of news can be used for this task. The proposed method uses a simple strategy based on keeping the most frequent words while masking the rest. The experiments in four collections, in two languages and different topics, have led to the conclusion that there are common lexical stylistic elements among fake news.

Keywords: Fake news · Text classification · Written style

1 Introduction

Nowadays, people are getting more of the news from digital media than from traditional sources, due to their immediacy and because they are free. However, online news are not necessarily checked for authenticity [25], facilitating the dissemination of fake news, and thus causing serious negative impacts on people and society; for example, they can upset the balance of authenticity in the news ecosystem, intentionally persuade consumers to accept biased or false beliefs, and are often manipulated by propagandists to convey political or influence messages [21].

The term *fake news* has been used in different ways, in this paper we consider the following definition, proposed in [1,28]: "fake news are news published by a media outlet, which includes: claims, statements, speeches, publications, among other types of information and its authenticity is not verifiable (false)".

Since fake news distort the way people interpret and respond to true news, it is very important to help mitigate the negative effects they cause by identifying discriminatory and relevant characteristics that facilitate their automatic

O. O. Vergara-Villegas et al. (Eds.): MCPR 2022, LNCS 13264, pp. 245–254, 2022.
https://doi.org/10.1007/978-3-031-07750-0_23

detection. In this direction, various approaches have been explored aimed at the analysis of their content [28], i.e., the verification of facts and style; their source [12, 26], which include information related to the news and the social context, such as users, broadcasters, etc.; or their propagation [11], that is, on the news spread.

Many of the above approaches identify fake news after they have been disseminated, and most are limited to English news articles and to a single (often political) domain. Understanding the writing style of fake news articles could facilitate the task of early detection, i.e., when they are published in a media outlet but have not yet spread on social networks, hence the importance of developing approaches that can detect fake news by focusing on the writing style of news stories. Accordingly, our proposal is oriented towards a model based solely on the writing style, which allow us for a general analysis of fake news in different domains and languages.

Under this approach, several works have explored the use of linguistic features aiming to capture lexical, syntactic and readability information. Despite their promising results, these linguistic features are technically very demanding to be extracted, analyzed, understood and interpreted [21]. On the other hand, another challenge is the feature compatibility, that is, to determine features that can capture the generality of deceptive language across domains and languages. Motivated by the fact that the style of fake news appeals to the emotions and beliefs of the reader and not necessarily to an objective argument, in this paper we explore the difference in written style between fake and true news based on the use of non-topic related terms.

Most of the works focused on the analysis of style for the detection of fake news consider discursive and syntactic information, relying on complex linguistic resources and analyses. In contrast to them, our approach does not rely on any computationally expensive resource; it is an easy and simple method focused on capturing lexical style patterns in fake news. In particular, it considers a strategy based on masking content-related terms while keeping function words and other style-based symbols. This type of strategy has been previously applied in authorship analysis tasks [9, 19, 20, 23], but to our knowledge it has never been explored in the fake news detection task. Consequently, the objective of this work is to study the relevance of these lexical style patterns for a difficult task such as fake news detection, and to verify their generality for different languages and domains.

2 Related Work

As previously mentioned, different kinds of information and attributes have already been considered for the detection of fake news, for example: content-related [27], propagation on the network [11], credibility in the networks according to the source [12, 24], users and spreaders [26], among others. On the other hand, the use of deep neural networks have become a trend in the task [24], highlighting among these the use of advanced pre-trained language models such as BERT, ELECTRA and ELMo [3, 10].

There are also several works that, like ours, have focused on analyzing the style of the notes. A style-based model helps in the early detection of false news, when it has not yet been spread on the network. There are works in the literature that represent news content by capturing its writing style at the lexical, syntactic, semantic, and discourse levels. At the lexical level, [2,14] used a BOW-like representation, considering unigrams and bigrams of words, through an exhaustive analysis in the identification of lexical characteristics in the news content. In [15], style is captured with attributes at different levels, for example, POS Tags are used as markers at the syntactic level, and the Rhetorical Structures Theory (RST) was employed to extract features at the discursive level. At the semantic level, [5,17,27] proposed using LIWC-based features. In [22], for example, word count, authenticity, influence, tone, and analytics extracted from LIWC were used to detect fake news. Finally, [8] describes a combination of some of these features; it used a wide collection of linguistic cues grouped into three broad categories: complexity, psychology (LIWC), and lexical features.

The aforementioned approaches to style-based fake news detection yield interesting results, but their implementation is complicated by the fact that they rely on language- and domain-related resources. Our method seeks to achieve greater independence from these resources, without being domain or language oriented. To this end, we propose following a simple masking approach, hiding from the textual information everything related to the news content (i.e. semantic information), leaving only the lexical style patterns –including some punctuation marks– which allows us to obtain a model capable of detecting fake news independently of domain and language.

The use of text masking techniques has been addressed in other research areas such as authorship attribution [20,23], author profiling [9], hoax detection [7], hyperpartisanship detection in news [18], and the detection of stereotypes about immigrants [19]. In these tasks, text distortion techniques have proven to be useful. The effectiveness of this strategy suggests that authors (without consciously using it) fall into a particular style. For the case of fake news, authors appeal to readers' emotions and beliefs, and not necessarily to an objective argument. Between real and fake news, punctuation marks (e.g., parentheses, quotation marks, etc.) are used to emphasize or include personal opinions in order to bias the reader. Another difference is the frequency in the use of numbers, dates or percentages to give validity to the information presented. These observations motivated us to design a fine-grained masking strategy, differentiating the masks used for certain punctuation marks as well as for quantities. The following section describes our proposed method.

3   Style-Based Method for Fake News Detection

Our research seeks to mask all thematic elements of content and leave only style-related terms, in order to observe if style information alone is enough to distinguish between false and real notes. Figure 1 shows the general outline of the proposed method. Its first step is the identification of all the tokens that will not be masked. Basically, this set is made up of terms associated with style (e.g., the most frequently used terms). Later, any term outside this set is replaced by a predetermined symbol, being careful to preserve the sequence of the original text. From these masked texts, the n-grams of words are extracted and with them a BoW-like representation of the documents is built, which is used to feed the classifier. In general, the scheme followed is the standard process in text classification except for the masking step that is explained in the following two subsections.

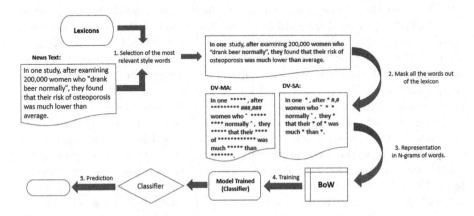

Fig. 1. General scheme of the proposed method

3.1 Selection of the Lexicons

The first step of our method is the selection of reference lexicon, formed by k highly frequent words, which are then used in the masking process to determine those terms that will not be masked. Within these words, there are several associated with the style of a text, for example: *stopwords* (prepositions, conjunctions, articles, some adverbs), auxiliary verbs, pronominal forms, etc. In our experiments, we used two different lexicons:

Lexicon 1: Most frequent words of the language. To determine this set of words, we used representative corpora of the Spanish and English languages. The most frequent words of the Spanish language were obtained from: "Current Spanish Reference Corpus" (CREA)[1], whereas the most frequent words of the language English were obtained from: *"British National Corpus"* (BNC)[2].

Lexicon 2: Most frequent words in the corpus. This second approach is limited to the corpus own vocabulary. Particularly, we selected the words showing the highest frequencies of occurrence.

---

[1] https://www.rae.es/banco-de-datos/crea.
[2] https://www.english-corpora.org/bnc/.

3.2   Text Masking

The proposed method modifies the appearance of the original texts to a different (abstract) form, hiding some words and signs by replacing them with other characters or symbols. The general idea is to mask information related to the news content while keeping the writing style elements. That is, considering a reference lexicon, formed by the k most frequent words in the given language or corpus, we mask the occurrences of the rest of the words in the news text, leaving intact only those corresponding to the lexicon. In this way, all occurrences (in both the training and test corpus) of specific (less frequent) terms are replaced by default symbols.

Two different methods were used to mask the texts: Distorted View Multiple Asterisks (DV-MA), and Distorted View Single Asterisk (DV-SA); both based on the approaches proposed in [23].

***Distorted View with Multiple Asterisks* (DV-MA):** Each word w, out of the reference lexicon, is masked by replacing each character with an asterisk ($*$); and each digit in the text is replaced with a ($\#$) symbol.

***Distorted View with Single Asterisks* (DV-SA):** Each word w, out of the reference lexicon, is masked by replacing each occurrence of the word with a single asterisk ($*$); and each sequence of digits in the text is replaced by a ($\#$) symbol.

In addition to these general rules, we propose some extra ones to perform a finer analysis, which allow to capture certain elements used by the authors of fake and true news. For both algorithms, punctuation marks are kept, particularly, period(.), comma(,), semicolon(;) and colon(:). Single quotes(''), double quotes(""), and smart quotes are replaced by the ^ symbol. Parentheses, braces, and brackets are all masked by open and closed parentheses. The exclamation (!) and question marks (?) are replaced by μ. Finally, mathematical signs such as weight($\$$), percent($\%$), sum($+$), and equals($=$) are replaced by the symbol π.

4   Experiments

4.1   Datasets

For the evaluation of the proposed method, we considered four collections of news items used in different state-of-the-art works: two in Spanish (MEX-A3T [16] and RAW-CovidES [4]), and two in English (LIAR [10] and CoAID [6]). All these collections correspond to binary classification tasks (false vs. true news), but have very different characteristics, not only their language but also their domains and distributions (refer to Table 1).

4.2   Experimental Setup

Preprocessing: We converted all words to lowercase letters and did not remove any character (e.g., symbol, punctuation mark, number or delimiter).

Table 1. Statistics of the datasets. Information on the domain, language and distribution of the classes.

Datasets	Domain	Language	Fake	True	Total
MEX-A3T	Multiple	Spanish	480	491	971
RAW-Covid	Health		95	105	200
LIAR	Politics	English	6889	8470	15359
CoAID	Health		185	3167	3352

Used parameters: The proposed method uses two parameters: the parameter k indicates the number of words extracted from the lexicon that will not be masked, and n is the order (length) of the n-grams of words used to represent the masked texts. We used $k = \{0, 100, 200, ..., 1000\}$, and $n = \{1, 2, 3\}$.

Text representation: After the masking step, we represented the transformed texts without removing any features from the calculated n-grams, and used a TF-IDF weighting scheme.

Classifier: As classifier we used a Support Vector Machine (SVM) with linear kernel. Implementation taken from Scikit-Learn library[3].

Training and Evaluation: We followed the guidelines established by the authors of each data set in order to obtain a fair comparison with the state of the art. The LIAR dataset already has three partitions: training, validation, and test. In the RAW-Covid and CoAID data sets, a CFV was performed with 5-folds. For the MEX-A3T, that has a test partition, we took 20% of the training partition for validation. The best configuration obtained in the validation set was evaluated in the test partition. We used as evaluation measure the macro F1 score.

Baseline: Our baseline method is based on the same classifier and text representation, but without applying any masking technique.

State of the art: The results obtained were compared with the best results already reported for each of the four collections.

4.3 Results and Discussion

Following our style-based model (see Fig. 1), we used two lexicons, one considering the the most frequent words of the language and other the most frequent words of the given corpus. For both kinds of lexicons, we generated several instances, using values from $k = 0$, to mask everything, to $k = 1000$, to mask the 1000 most frequent words. We then fed these lexicons to the masking algorithms DV-MA and DV-SA. Table 2 shows the best obtained results. It is important to highlight that for all collections the DV-MA method was more effective than DV-SA, hence, we only show results from the former.

The results in Table 2 show that the method works well despite the differences between data sets in terms of language and domain (i.e., multiple domains like in MEX-A3T, or single domain like in the rest of the corpora). As mentioned

---

[3] https://scikit-learn.org/stable/modules/generated/sklearn.svm.SVC.html.

Table 2. Results corresponding to the best configuration of the proposed model for each collection; all use DV-MA with the most frequent words in the given corpus. For comparison purposes, we include our baseline results and the best reported state of the art (SoA) result for each dataset.

Datasets	Model	F1-macro		
		Baseline	Result	SoA
MEX-A3T	Bigrams, $k = 500$	0.77	0.80	**0.85** [3]
RAW-Covid	Unigrams, $k = 900$	0.57	**0.89**	0.74 [4]
LIAR	Trigrams, $k = 900$	0.54	0.56	**0.62** [10]
CoAID	Unigrams, $k = 900$	0.64	**0.67**	0.58 [6]

above, masking with multiple asterisks (DV-MA) showed better performance that using simple asterisks (DV-SA), which indicates that preserving the length of words gives the classifier information to discriminate between false and true news.

Another aspect to analyze is the parameter k. Our best results were obtained when $k >= 500$, which means that we are selecting a range of frequent words that not only includes those that are very general (i.e., stopwords), but also incorporate other terms, even terms with semantic content, although not specific to a domain (for example, auxiliary verb forms, pronominal forms, etc.). On the other hand, the value of k is variable depending on the dataset, and there is no criterion for determining an adequate value, other than empirical evaluation.

Table 2 shows a comparison not only of our method with the baseline used, but also with the best result reported for each data set in the state of the art. It is important to highlight here that all of these studies have reported results with the use of neural networks. In contrast, our approach uses only textual information and style patterns to classify fake news with traditional learning algorithms. Our approach achieves interesting results, outperforming the state of the art in detecting fake news in two of the four datasets in different languages and domains.

4.4   Discriminative Style Patterns

By calculating the information gain of the representation n-grams, we were able to identify the most discriminating attributes. Analyzing these attributes, we obtained several observations. One of these observations was the length of the words, since several sequences of * appeared among the most relevant attributes, both in English and in Spanish. In Spanish, it is particularly noteworthy that very long sequences of * had high GI values, for example, words of size 8, 10 and 11. In the texts, especially in the false notes, these are associated with the excessive use of adverbs with the ending *'mente'* (*finalmente, totalmente, detenidamente, terriblemente, precariamente, retóricamente*). The opposite of this could be seen in English, here particularly very short strings ** and *** are highlighted, which when observing the texts we can associate with the very frequent use of predominant abbreviations in the false class ('gov' instead of 'government', 'rep' instead of 'republican', as well as the months of the year in abbreviation, for example 'dec' instead of 'december').

Other important aspects that we observe with the information gain analysis were the use of numerical data. What happens is that the deceitful writer intends to create the sensation of a real news item by locating himself correctly in time and space, however, he avoids giving statistical data [13], either due to ignorance or because these can be verifiable and/or comparable. For this reason, in the false notes, the numerical data have a greater frequency when we refer to: dates and ages mainly. In the true news, dates and ages are also present, but much more percentages, monetary amounts and statistical data. The writer of a true note supports his/her veracity and is not afraid to give all the mathematical details that allow validating the information as correct.

Punctuation marks were also relevant according to their information gain. We believe that their relevance in these cases had a lot to do with the difference in length of the news by class. According to the average length of words and sentences by classes, true news stories are predominantly longer for all the data sets studied, so in these cases their use becomes much more frequent. Quotation marks also a discriminative feature. They are used in our daily writing to frame textual quotes, delimit titles, and highlight words that are used in an ironic tone. For both classes, quotation marks are present, however, the main difference lies in the use of these to frame irony [13] and, above all, their use is much more common in false notes.

5   Conclusions and Future Work

This paper is a contribution to the fake news detection task following an style-based approach. The masking method is used for the first time in the area of fake news detection. The proposed model was evaluated on different datasets under very diverse conditions (different languages, single domain, and multiple domains). Concluding that the method can be easily applied to different languages, since it is independent of them, however, the nature and characteristics of each corpus influence the selection of the parameters used. Compared to traditional masking algorithms that only masked words and numbers, our method uses more detailed masks associated with the style of news reports such as punctuation and other symbols such as parentheses, quotation marks, exclamation and question marks.

As future work, we would like to test this text representation in a cross-domain scenario. To do this, the proposed method would have to be accompanied by some instance selection method in the source domain in order to successfully carry out the adaptation between domains. Another interesting experiment, given the independence of the method with respect to the language, would be the evaluation of the method in a cross-lingual scenario.

Acknowledgments. The present work was supported by CONACYT/México (scholarship 1017548 and grant CB-2015-01-257383). In addition, the authors thank CONACYT for the computational resources provided by the Deep Learning Platform for Language Technologies.

References

1. Abonizio, H.Q., de Morais, J.I., Tavares, G.M., Junior, S.B.: Language-independent fake news detection: English, Portuguese, and Spanish mutual features. Future Internet **12**(5), 87 (2020)
2. Ahmed, H., Traore, I., Saad, S.: Detection of online fake news using N-Gram analysis and machine learning techniques. In: Traore, I., Woungang, I., Awad, A. (eds.) ISDDC 2017. LNCS, vol. 10618, pp. 127–138. Springer, Cham (2017). https://doi.org/10.1007/978-3-319-69155-8_9
3. Aragón, M.E., et al.: Overview of mex-a3t at iberlef 2020: fake news and aggressiveness analysis in Mexican Spanish. In: CEUR Workshop Proceedings. vol. 2664, pp. 222–235 (2020)
4. Bonet-Jover, A., Piad-Morffis, A., Saquete, E., Martínez-Barco, P., García-Cumbreras, M.Á.: Exploiting discourse structure of traditional digital media to enhance automatic fake news detection. Expert Syst. Appl. **169**, 114340 (2020)
5. Castelo, S., et al.: A topic-agnostic approach for identifying fake news pages. In: 2019 World Wide Web Conference, WWW 2019, pp. 975–980. Association for Computing Machinery, Inc (2019)
6. Cui, L., Lee, D.: Coaid: Covid-19 healthcare misinformation dataset. arXiv preprint arXiv:2006.00885 (2020)
7. Ghanem, B., Montes-Y-Gómez, M., Rangel, F., Rosso, P.: UPV-INAOE-autoritas-check that: Preliminary approach for checking worthiness of claims. In: CEUR Workshop Proceedings 2125 (2018)
8. Horne, B.D., Adali, S.: This Just. Fake News Packs a Lot in Title, Uses Simpler, Repetitive Content in Text Body, More Similar to Satire than Real News. In: Eleventh International AAAI Conference on Web and Social Media (2017)
9. Jimenez-Villar, V., Sánchez-Junquera, J., Montes-Y-Gómez, M., Villaseñor-Pineda, L., Ponzetto, S.P.: Bots and gender profiling using masking techniques notebook for PAN at CLEF 2019. In: CEUR Workshop Proceedings 2380 (2019)
10. Khan, J.Y., Khondaker, M.T.I., Afroz, S., Uddin, G., Iqbal, A.: A benchmark study of machine learning models for online fake news detection. Mach. Learn. Appl. **4**, 100032 (2021)
11. Koumouridis, G.: Improving Fake News Detection with Linguistic Cues (2020)
12. Ma, J., Gao, W., Wong, K.F.: Rumor detection on twitter with tree-structured recursive neural networks. In: ACL 2018–56th Annual Meeting of the Association for Computational Linguistics, Proceedings of the Conference (Long Papers). vol. 1, pp. 1980–1989. Association for Computational Linguistics (2018)
13. Molina, M.D., Sundar, S.S., Le, T., Lee, D.: "Fake news" is not simply false information: a concept explication and taxonomy of online content. Am. Behav. Sci. **65**(2), 180–212 (2021)
14. Pérez-Rosas, V., Kleinberg, B., Lefevre, A., Mihalcea, R.: Automatic detection of fake news. In: Proceedings of the 27th International Conference on Computational Linguistics, pp. 3391–3401. Association for Computational Linguistics (2018)

15. Pisarevskaya, D.: Deception detection in news reports in the Russian language: lexics and discourse. In: Proceedings of the 2017 EMNLP Workshop: Natural Language Processing meets Journalism, pp. 74–79 (2017)
16. Posadas-Durán, J.P., Gomez-Adorno, H., Sidorov, G., Escobar, J.J.M.: Detection of fake news in a new corpus for the Spanish language. J. Intell. Fuzzy Syst. **36**(5), 4869–4876, 100032 (2019)
17. Reis, J.C., Correia, A., Murai, F., Veloso, A., Benevenuto, F.: Supervised learning for fake news detection. IEEE Intell. Syst. **34**(2), 76–81 (2019)
18. Sánchez-Junquera, J., Rosso, P., Montes-y Gómez, M., Ponzetto, S.P.: Unmasking Bias in News. arXiv preprint arXiv:1906.04836 (2019)
19. Sánchez-Junquera, J., Rosso, P., Montes, M., Chulvi, B., et al.: Masking and bert-based models for stereotype identication. Procesamiento del Lenguaje Natural **67**, 83–94 (2021)
20. Sánchez-Junquera, J., Villaseñor-Pineda, L., Montes-y Gómez, M., Rosso, P., Stamatatos, E.: Masking domain-specific information for cross-domain deception detection. Pattern Recogn. Lett. **135**, 122–130 (2020)
21. Shu, K., Sliva, A., Wang, S., Tang, J., Liu, H.: Fake news detection on social media: a data mining perspective. ACM SIGKDD Explor. Newsl. **19**(1), 22–36, 100032 (2017)
22. Singh, V., Dasgupta, R., Sonagra, D., Raman, K., Ghosh, I.: Automated fake news detection using linguistic analysis and machine learning. In: International Conference on Social Computing, Behavioral-Cultural Modeling, and Prediction and Behavior Representation in Modeling and Simulation (SBP-BRiMS), pp. 1–3 (2017)
23. Stamatatos, E.: Authorship attribution using text distortion. In: 15th Conference of the European Chapter of the Association for Computational Linguistics, EACL 2017 - Proceedings of Conference. vol. 1, pp. 1138–1149 (2017)
24. Trueman, T.E., Kumar, A., Narayanasamy, P., Vidya, J.: Attention-based C-BiLSTM for fake news detection. Appl. Soft Comput. **110**, 107600 (2021)
25. Vishwakarma, D.K., Jain, C.: Recent state-of-the-art of fake news detection: a review. In: 2020 International Conference for Emerging Technology (INCET), pp. 1–6. IEEE (2020)
26. Zhang, J., Dong, B., Yu, P.S.: FakeDetector: effective fake news detection with deep diffusive neural network. In: Proceedings - International Conference on Data Engineering. vol. 2020-April, pp. 1826–1829. IEEE (2020)
27. Zhou, X., Jain, A., Phoha, V.V., Zafarani, R.: Fake news early detection: an interdisciplinary study. arXiv preprint arXiv:1904.11679 (2019)
28. Zhou, X., Zafarani, R.: A survey of fake news: fundamental theories, detection methods, and opportunities. ACM Comput. Surv. **53**(5), 1–40, 100032 (2020)

Multi-document Text Summarization Based on Genetic Algorithm and the Relevance of Sentence Features

Verónica Neri-Mendoza[(✉)], Yulia Ledeneva[(✉)] [ID],
René Arnulfo García-Hernández[ID], and Ángel Hernández-Castañeda[ID]

Autonomous University of the State of Mexico, Instituto Literario No. 100, 50000 Toluca, Mexico
vnerim001@alumno.uaemex.mx,
{ynledeneva,reagarciah,anhernandezc}@uaemex.mx

Abstract. Document Text Summarization aims to create a short and condensed version from the original document, which transmits the main idea of the document in a few words. We formulated extractive multi-document text summarization as a combinatorial optimization problem. In which we used sentence features to select the most important content. We conduct experiments on Document Understanding Conference (DUC01) dataset using the ROUGE toolkit. Our experiments demonstrate that the proposed method contributes significant improvements over the state-of-the-art methods and heuristics.

Keywords: Multi-document · Text · Summarization · Genetic algorithm · Sentence features · Optimization

1 Introduction

The growth of the Internet involves that documents spread swiftly. Thus, the users get engulfed in many documents, wondering where to access them. In this context, Document Text Summarization (DTS) appears as a viable solution because it aims to generate a condensed version of documents and convey relevant information to the reader. Therefore, users can save time through summaries instead of reading the whole set document to capture the main idea [1, 2]. Due to this situation, researchers in Natural Language Processing are focused on the text summarization task [1]. Optimization-based approaches have been gaining importance because of the excellent performance obtained due to these being effective to get an optimal solution for huge and varied spaces [3–5]. These helps recognize the appropriate sentences to include in a summary in the DTS context.

A domain that has been the object of study in state-of-the-art is news. The different news sources that report on a particular event contain common components that construct the main facts. Thus, DTS from multiple news articles is a valuable field of study since the number of online publications is overgrowing. This is essential to satisfy the information need of various users. For this reason, multiple datasets have been developed, such as

© The Author(s), under exclusive license to Springer Nature Switzerland AG 2022
O. O. Vergara-Villegas et al. (Eds.): MCPR 2022, LNCS 13264, pp. 255–265, 2022.
https://doi.org/10.1007/978-3-031-07750-0_24

DUC [6], TAC (Text Analysis Conference) [7], Multi-News [8], CNN [9], among others, to evaluate the effectiveness of state-of-the-art methods.

There are three approaches to generating text summaries in the literature: extractive, abstractive, and hybrid.

Extractive Text Summarization. Proposed systems based on this approach create summaries by assigning weights to sentences according to linguistic and statistical features, then selecting the sentences with better weight by combining them. These methods generally contain two significant components: ranking and selection of sentences. In addition, extractive summarization methods ensure the generated summaries are semantically similar to the original documents [3, 10].

Abstractive Text Summarization. This approach allows the proposed methods to create summaries using new corpus words and sentences. The processing of abstractive summarization is like the human generation of summaries. However, it requires sophisticated natural language understanding and generation techniques, such as paraphrasing and sentence fusion [10, 11].

Hybrid Text Summarization. This approach combines the advantages of extractive and abstractive methods to process the input texts. The hybrid approach processes data in two steps: The first step is to reduce the input length of documents to create a selective summary. Afterward, the selective summary is used by an abstractive method to construct a final summary [3].

Depending on the number of documents, summarization can be classified into two tasks: Single-Document Text Summarization, which composes a summary from one document, and Multi-Document Text Summarization (MDTS), which produces a summary from a collection of documents about a particular topic [1, 3, 12].

We formulated MDTS as a combinatorial optimization problem, which we address through a Genetic Algorithm (GA). The GA does not require external resources, working in an unsupervised way. Moreover, we hypothesize is that both sentence position and coverage provide essential information to distinguish relevant sentences from documents to create news summaries. Additionally, we have tested the proposed method by generating summaries of 50, 100, and 200 words on the DUC01 dataset.

The rest of the paper is organized as follows: Sect. 2 presents the related work. Then, Sect. 3 describes the proposed summarization method. In Sect. 4, we show experimental results. Finally, the conclusions of this paper are drawn in Sect. 5.

2 Related Works

In the literature, the DTS has been tackled through many techniques, such as supervised-based methods convert the summarization task into supervised classification problem. Generally, these methods learn by training to classify sentences, indicating whether a sentence is included in the summary. State-of-the-art approaches usually use word embeddings for representing the contextual meaning of sentences. Nevertheless, proposed methods require a corpus manually staggered [3, 8]. On the other hand, unsupervised-based methods generally assign a score to each sentence of each document, describing the relevance of sentences in the text. Therefore, sentences with the highest values will be part of the extractive summary. [3, 5, 13]. In this approach, four steps have been identified to generate a summary: Term selection, term weighting, sentence weighting, and sentence selection [13]. For the last step, various textual features have been developed [13]. Some of them are presented in Table 1:

Table 1. Unsupervised features.

Feature	Description
Similarity with the title	This feature assigns the most important to the sentences that include words in the title [13, 14]
Similarity with other sentences	Given a sentence called the central sentence, a score is given to the other sentences of the document which contain overlapping words [3]
Sentence length	It assumes that the length of a sentence can indicate whether it is relevant to the final summary. Shorter sentences are usually not included [13, 14]
Redundancy reduction	Redundant or duplicate information in the generated summary is expected to be minimized [3]
Sentence position	The idea is that the first sentences indicate a relevant sentence [3, 14]
Coverage	This feature is based on the idea that information provided in the original documents should be included in the generated summary [3, 13]

3   Proposed Method

In MDTS, the search space is more extensive than in Single DTS, making it more challenging to select the most important sentences. In this context, MDTS can be determined as an optimization problem. The documents from the collection are considered a set of sentences, and the aim is to choose an optimal subset from sentences under a length constraint. Previous works [15, 16] have proposed the GA as an alternative for the MDTS to select an optimal combinatorial subset of sentences, obtaining competitive results compared to other state-of-the-art alternatives. However, we intend to improve its performance. Therefore, we have sought to enhance the GA exploration by increasing the size of the population. The population size is one of the essential factors that affect performance [4, 17]. In general, small population sizes might lead to premature convergence and yield substandard solutions [18].

3.1 Pre-processing

In this step, the documents of each collection were ordered chronologically. Then, the sentences of documents were hierarchically ordered according to appearance in the text to create a meta-document, which contains all collection sentences. Afterward, the text of the meta-document was separated into sentences. Finally, a lexical analysis was applied to separate sentences into words [5].

3.2 Text Modeling

After preprocessing the text, it is necessary to model it. This stage aims to predict the probability of natural word sequences. The simplest and most successful form for text modeling is the n-gram, which is a text representation model that constructs contiguous subsequences of consecutive words from a given text [5].

3.3 Weighting and Selection of Sentences

Sentence weighting and selection of sentences usually worked together [13].While the first one assigns a degree of relevance for each sentence, the second one chooses the most appropriate sentences to generate extractive summaries. However, it involves a vast search space that requires to be addressed by optimization. In view of this, we propose the following GA to select the most important sentences:

Encoding: *The binary encoding* was used, where each sentence of the meta-document represents a gene. The values 1 and 0 define if a sentence will be selected in the final summary [5, 13, 16].

Generation of Population: The initial population was randomly generated. On the other hand, the population of the next generations is generated from the selection stage. The search process concludes when a termination criterion is met. Otherwise, a new generation will be produced, and the search process will continue [5, 13].

Size of the Initial Population: The size of the population was determined according to the number of sentences from the meta-document [4, 5, 13].

Selection Operator: The selection of individuals is performed through the *roulette operator*, which selects individuals of a population according to their fitness to choose individuals with a higher value. Each individual is assigned to a proportional part of the roulette according to its fitness in this operator. Finally, the selection of parents is performed, which are needed to create the next generation, and each selected individual is copied into the parent population [5].

Crossover Operator: Crossover is a genetic operator that combines two parents to produce one or two descendants. The idea underlying crossover is that the new individual can be better than its parents if it takes the best characteristics of each parent. *Crosses with priority over common genes:* This crossover operator was designed to generate summaries, where each individual represents a selection of sentences. Of the selected parents, only one gene is randomly selected (with value 1) that will belong to the descendant to fulfill the number of words [4, 5].

Mutation Operator: We used the *flipping operator*, which consist of changing the value of each gene, inverting from 1 to 0 or vice versa [5, 13]. First, the mutation is performed considering the genes with a value of 1 and later considering the genes with a value of 0. Afterward, it is verified that the established number of words is fulfilled. If it is not fulfilled, another gene with a value of 0 will be inverted, and this process will continue until the specified minimum number of words is satisfied.

The Fitness Function: It was calculated by employing the concept of the slope of the line [4, 5, 16]. The slope defines the importance of sentences. The main idea is to consider the first sentence with the importance X_n, the second with the significance of $X_n - 1$. In a text with n sentences, if the sentence i is selected for the summary, its relevance is defined as $t(i - x) + x$, where $x = 1 + (n - 1)/2$ and t is the slope to be discovered. The formula to calculate the importance of the sentence position is in Eq. 1:

$$Sentence\ importance = \frac{\sum_{|c_i|}^{n} = 1^{t(i-x)+x}}{\sum_{j=1}^{k} t(j-x) + 1}, x = 1 + \frac{(n-1)}{2} \tag{1}$$

where k is the number of selected sentences. On the other hand, the content coverage to retrieve all aspects from meta-document was calculated by the summation of the frequencies of the n-grams that the summary weighs. (*Precision_Recall*) was calculated via the sum of the frequencies of the n-grams considered in the original text divided by sum of the frequencies of the different n-grams of summary (see Eq. 2).

$$Presicion\_Recall = \frac{\sum Original\ text\ frequency}{\sum Frequency\ Summary} \tag{2}$$

Finally, to obtain the value of the fitness function, the following formula was applied, which is multiplied by 1000 (see Eq. 3).

$$FA = Presicion\_Recall * Sentence\ Importance * 1000 \tag{3}$$

Stop Condition: For this operator, we have used the *number of generations* as a stop condition.

4   Experimental and Results

4.1   Dataset

To empirically evaluate the results of the proposed method, we use the DUC01 dataset, is an open benchmark for generic automatic summarization evaluation, which is in the English language; it is composed of 309 documents split into 30 collections, which we tested with the lengths of 50, 100, and 200 words. We choose this dataset because the gold standards summaries provided in it were typed like an abstractive approach. It allowed us to measure how competitive the proposed extractive unsupervised method can be about summaries made using paraphrases, words, and sentences that do not belong to source documents.

4.2 Evaluation Measures

ROUGE (Recall-Oriented Understudy for Gisting Evaluation). It involves measures to automatically establish the quality of a summary created by a proposed method by contrasting it to other ideal summaries created by humans, called gold standard summaries [20]. These measures count the number of overlapping units such as n-gram, word sequences, and word pairs between the computer-generated summary to be evaluated and the ideal summaries created by humans [21].

4.3 Parameter Selection

We perform tests with different parameters such as tournament and roulette selection operator, HUX crossover operator, crossover with priority on common genes, double inversion mutation, with different crossover and mutation probabilities, respectively. Also conducted our tests with varying population sizes; we multiplied the number of sentences of the meta-document from 2 and 15 to determine the best possible population size to improve the GA exploration. Per our empirical results, we conclude that good traits spread through the population for the different summaries lengths (50, 100, and 200 words) by multiplying the number of sentences from the meta-document by 9 and throughout 150 generations. Favoring the selection as parents of individuals with greater fitness value by roulette operator. Moreover, we tested n-grams of sizes from 1 to 5. According to our results, grams size 2 produces better sentence selection. In general, the parameters that produced the best results are shown in Table 2.

Table 2. Parameters used in the tests with better results.

Feature	Parameter
Selection operator	Roulette
Crossover operator	Crosses with priority on common genes 100%
Mutation operator	Double inversion mutation 0.019%
Elitism	50 and 200 words 0.02%, 100 words: 0.03%
Number of generations	150
Number of individuals	*Number of sentences by 9*

In [5] was realized an analysis of slope in, concluding when the slope value is negative the first sentences are more important. Contrariwise, if the slope value is 0, all sentences have the same importance. Due to this reason, in our experimentation, we have used tests with slope values from −0.1 to −1. To determine which slope value was best for each length, the best results are presented in Table 3.

As can be seen from the results obtained, when the summaries are created at a short length, the value of the slope that produced the best results is −0.1. According to [5, 16], this means that all the sentences of the meta-document have the same importance. While the size of the summary increases, the sentences that are considered important are found close to the beginning of the text. From the results obtained for the length of 100 words, the value of the slope was −0.6. While for summaries of 200 words, the value of the slope was −0.8. It means that the most important content is in the first sentences.

Table 3. Results with several values of slope.

Values of slope	50 words		100 words		200 words	
	Rouge-1	Rouge-2	Rouge-1	Rouge-2	Rouge-1	Rouge-2
−0.1	28.023	6.861	32.762	7.185	39.243	9.608
−0.2	27.774	6.544	32.577	7.318	39.892	9.986
−0.3	26.853	6.117	33.100	7.473	39.939	9.957
−0.4	26.430	6.039	33.249	7.475	39.761	9.959
−0.5	26.931	5.888	33.459	7.638	39.088	9.988
−0.6	26.726	6.132	34.451	8.023	39.789	10.131
−0.7	27.033	5.584	32.937	7.391	40.039	10.087
−0.8	27.337	6.429	32.499	6.817	41.008	10.607
−0.9	26.974	5.632	32.765	7.298	40.370	10.521
−1.0	27.259	5.907	32.980	7.233	39.826	10.136

4.4 Description and Comparison of the State-of-the-Art Methods and Heuristics

To examine the performance of the proposed method was compared with state-of-the-art methods and heuristics. Supervised methods were not considered in the following analysis because the proposed method generates summaries from the information given in source documents, so it does not require external resources such as corpora, dictionaries, thesaurus, and lexicons. That is, it works in an unsupervised way.

CBA: In [22] was proposed a clustering-based method for MDTS. K-means were used in clustering. To define the sentences that should be selected for the final summary. Moreover, the sequence in which it will appear. The clustering was ranked via a cosine similarity measure.

NeATS: Lin and Hovy [23] proposed an Extractive MDTS system. The textual features such as term frequency, sentence position, stigma words, and a simplified version of Maximum Marginal Relevance were applied to choose filter content.

LexPageRank: In this method, the importance of sentences was computed based on the idea of centrality in a graph representation of sentences. In this, the connectivity matrix is based on cosine similarity [24].

GA-1: This method model MDTS like an optimization problem through GA[15].

Topline: The authors calculated the upper bounds in this work, which is possible to achieve by state-of-the-art methods [10, 25].

Baseline-First: It takes the first sentence from the document collection in chronological sequence until the target summary size is fulfilled [15].

Baseline-Random: This randomly selects sentences to incorporate them as an extractive summary until the length is required [10, 15].

Baseline-First Document: It includes the first 50, 100, and 200 words from the first document of a set of them until the target summary size is fulfilled [15].

Lead Baseline: This takes the first 50, 100, and 200 words from the last document in the set, where documents are supposed to be chronologically prepared [15].

We have compared the obtained results of the proposed method to other state-of-the-art methods and heuristics. In the comparison, the values Rouge-1 and Rouge-2 are exposed. Also, there is a comparison of the level of advance between the state-of-the-art methods and heuristics. To compute the performance, we use the formula (see Eq. 4), based on the assumption that the performance of the Topline heuristic is 100% and Baseline-random is 0% [25].

$$\%Advanced = \frac{(Rouge1_{Method} - Rouge1_{Baseline-Random}) * 100}{Rouge1_{Topline} - Rouge1_{Baseline-Random}} \qquad (4)$$

Tables 4, 5, and 6 show this comparison using different summary lengths.

In the task where the summary length is 50 words (see Table 4), with the proposed method, the preceding results were improved by 12.7%, and the previous best result was the baseline-first document.

Table 4. Comparison of the state-of-the-art methods and heuristics, 50 words.

Method	Rouge-1	Rouge-2	Advanced (%)
Topline [25]	40.395	15.648	100.00%
Proposed	**28.023**	**6.861**	**39.25%**
Baseline-first document	25.435	4.301	26.55%
Baseline-first	25.194	4.596	25.36%
CBA [22]	22.679	2.859	13.02%
Lead Baseline	22.620	4.341	12.73%
NeATS [23]	22.594	2.963	12.60%
Baseline-random	20.027	1.929	00.00%

On the other hand, where the summary length is 100 words (see Table 5), the improvement is 6.08% with respect to what was considered the best result, which was Lex-PageRank method. As can be seen, in this length of summaries, there is a method whose performance, according to Eq. 4, is below the Baseline-random heuristic considered as the worst selection of sentences.

For the summary length is 200 words (see Table 6), the improvement was 4.01% more than the best method reported, which was GA-1. At this length, the heuristics have a better performance than in the 100 words task due to outperforming Baseline-Random, except Lead-Baseline, whose performance is even a negative value.

Table 5. Comparison of the state-of-the-art methods and heuristics, 100 words.

Method	Rouge-1	Rouge-2	Advanced (%)
Topline [25]	47.256	18.994	100.00%
Proposed	**34.451**	**8.023**	**36.80%**
LexPageRank [24]	33.220	5.760	30.72%
Baseline-first	31.716	6.962	23.30%
Baseline-first document	30.462	5.962	17.11%
NeATS [23]	28.195	4.037	05.92%
Lead Baseline	28.195	4.109	05.92%
Baseline-random	26.994	3.277	00.00%
CBA [22]	26.741	3.510	−01.24%

Table 6. Comparison the state-of-the-art methods and heuristics, 200 words.

Method	Rouge-1	Rouge-2	Advanced (%)
Topline [25]	53.630	22.703	100.00%
Proposed	**41.008**	**10.607**	**35.51%**
GA-1 [15]	40.224	10.306	31.50%
Baseline-first	39.280	9.339	26.68%
NeATS [23]	37.883	7.674	19.54%
Baseline-first document [15]	35.472	7.225	7.22%
CBA [22]	34.108	5.525	0.26%
Baseline-random [15]	34.057	5.240	0.00%
Lead Baseline [15]	34.009	6.195	−0.24%

5   Conclusions

In this paper, we formalized the summarization of a set of documents as a combinatorial optimization problem. In particular, GA was introduced to satisfy the extraction of the most relevant content from a collection of documents by using textual features, such as coverage and sentence position. Moreover, we improve the performance by incrementing the population size to explore an optimal solution better. Finally, we perform different experiments on the available benchmark dataset DUC01 in the English language for the lengths of 50, 100, and 200 words. The results show that the method is competitive with state-of-the-art previously reported results. Also, the summaries produced by the proposed method have achieved high evaluation scores compared with abstract gold standard summaries without needing external data.

References

1. Gao, S., Chen, X., Ren, Z., Zhao, D., Yan, R.: From Standard Summarization to New Tasks and Beyond: Summarization with Manifold Information (2020)
2. Roul, R.K., Mehrotra, S., Pungaliya, Y., Sahoo, J.K.: A new automatic multi-document text summarization using topic modeling. In: Fahrnberger, G., Gopinathan, S., Parida, L. (eds.) ICDCIT 2019. LNCS, vol. 11319, pp. 212–221. Springer, Cham (2019). https://doi.org/10. 1007/978-3-030-05366-6_17
3. El-Kassas, W.S., Salama, C.R., Rafea, A.A., Mohamed, H.K.: Automatic text summarization: a comprehensive survey (2021). https://doi.org/10.1016/j.eswa.2020.113679
4. García-Hernández, R.A., Ledeneva, Y.: Single extractive text summarization based on a genetic algorithm. In: Carrasco-Ochoa, J.A., Martínez-Trinidad, J.F., Rodríguez, J.S., di Baja, G.S. (eds.) MCPR 2013. LNCS, vol. 7914, pp. 374–383. Springer, Heidelberg (2013). https://doi.org/10.1007/978-3-642-38989-4_38
5. Mendoza, G.A.M., Ledeneva, Y., García-Hernández, R.A.: Determining the importance of sentence position for automatic text summarization. J. Intell. Fuzzy Syst. 39, 2421–2431 (2020). https://doi.org/10.3233/JIFS-179902
6. Over, P., Dang, H.: DUC in context. Inf. Process. Manag. 43, 1506–1520 (2007). https://doi.org/10.1016/J.IPM.2007.01.019
7. NIST (National Institute of Standars and Technology: TAC 2008 Summarization Track. https://tac.nist.gov/2008/summarization/. Accessed 20 July 2020
8. Fabbri, A.R., Li, I., She, T., Li, S., Radev, D.R.: Multi-News: a Large-Scale Multi-Document Summarization Dataset and Abstractive Hierarchical Model (2019)
9. Lins, R.D., et al.: The CNN-Corpus: A large textual corpus for single-document extractive summarization. In: Proceedings of the ACM Symposium on Document Engineering, DocEng 2019, pp. 1–10. Association for Computing Machinery, Inc, New York, New York, USA (2019). https://doi.org/10.1145/3342558.3345388
10. Matias, G., Ledeneva, Y., García, R.: Detección de ideas principales y composición de resúmenes en inglés, español, portugués y ruso. 60 años de investigación. Alfaomega Grupo Editor, S.A. de C.V (2020)
11. Ma, C., Zhang, W.E., Guo, M., Wang, H., Sheng, Q.Z.: Multi-document Summarization via Deep Learning Techniques: A Survey (2020). https://doi.org/10.1145/nnnnnnn.nnnnnnn
12. Hou, S.-L., et al.: A survey of text summarization approaches based on deep learning. J. Comput. Sci. Technol. 36(3), 633–663 (2021). https://doi.org/10.1007/s11390-020-0207-x
13. Ledeneva, Y., García-Hernández, R.A.: Generación automática de resúmenes Retos, propuestas y experimentos. Universidad Autónoma del Estado de México (2017)
14. Vázquez, E., García-Hernández, R.A., Ledeneva, Y.: Sentence features relevance for extractive text summarization using genetic algorithms. J. Intell. Fuzzy Syst. 35, 353–365 (2018). https://doi.org/10.3233/JIFS-169594
15. Neri-Mendoza, V., Ledeneva, Y., García-Hernández, R.A.: Unsupervised extractive multi-document text summarization using a genetic algorithm. J. Intell. Fuzzy Syst. 39, 2397–2408 (2020). https://doi.org/10.3233/JIFS-179900
16. Neri Mendoza, V., Ledeneva, Y., García-Hernández, R.A.: Abstractive multi-document text summarization using a genetic algorithm. In: Carrasco-Ochoa, J.A., Martínez-Trinidad, J.F., Olvera-López, J.A., Salas, J. (eds.) MCPR 2019. LNCS, vol. 11524, pp. 422–432. Springer, Cham (2019). https://doi.org/10.1007/978-3-030-21077-9_39
17. Sastry, K., Goldberg, D., Kendall, G.: Chapter 4 Genetic Algorithms. (2005)
18. Du, K.L., Swamy, M.N.S.: Search and optimization by metaheuristics: techniques and algorithms inspired by nature (2016). https://doi.org/10.1007/978-3-319-41192-7
19. Borges, J.L.: La doctrina de los ciclos (2013)

20. Rojas-Simón, J., Ledeneva, Y., García-Hernández, R.A.: Evaluation of text summaries without human references based on the linear optimization of content metrics using a genetic algorithm. Expert Syst. Appl. **167**, 113827 (2021). https://doi.org/10.1016/J.ESWA.2020.113827
21. Lin, C.-Y.: ROUGE: A Package for Automatic Evaluation of Summaries (2004)
22. Boros, E., Kantor, P.B., Neu, D.J.: A Clustering Based Approach to Creating Multi-Document Summaries (2001)
23. Lin, C.-Y., Hovy, E.: From single to multi-document summarization. In: Proceedings of the 40th Annual Meeting on Association for Computational Linguistics - ACL 2002, p. 457 (2002). https://doi.org/10.3115/1073083.1073160
24. Wang, D., Zhu, S., Li, T., Gong, Y.: Multi-document summarization using sentence-based topic models. In: ACL and AFNLP, p. 297 (2010). https://doi.org/10.3115/1667583.1667675
25. Rojas Simón, J., Ledeneva, Y., García Hernández, R.A.: Calculating the Upper Bounds for Multi-Document Summarization using Genetic Algorithms. Comput. y Sist. 22 (2018) https://doi.org/10.13053/cys-22-1-2903

Robotics and Remote Sensing
Applications of Pattern Recognition

On Labelling Pointclouds
with the Nearest Facet of Triangulated
Building Models

J. L. Silván-Cárdenas[(✉)] [ID]

Centro de Investigación en Ciencias de Información Geoespacial,
A.C. Contoy 137, Lomas de Padierna, Tlalpan, 14240 Mexico, Mexico
jsilvan@centrogeo.edu.mx
https://www.centrogeo.org.mx/areas-profile/jsilvan

Abstract. Labelling pointclouds with the nearest facet of triangular
meshes is a required step for a number of operations involving pointclouds and meshes, such as pointcloud registration, model parameters
optimization, error estimation and pointcloud selection, among others.
In this paper, we describe a simple method for labelling pointclouds
with nearest facet that is based on an objective function that resolves
the ambiguity around shared edges and vertices. We provide explicit
formulas for computing the barycentric coordinates of projected points
on selected facets, which are efficiently used to evaluate the point-facet
distance. The method was tested with simulated and real pointclouds
generated through standard photogrammetric procedures.

Keywords: Nearest facet · Pointcloud · Barycentric coordinates ·
Model registration

1 Introduction

Dense pointclouds of the land surface have become easily accessible thanks
to advances in computer vision of multi-view imagery and to the advent of
unmanned aerial vehicles (UAVs) for acquiring high resolution aerial photographs. For them to serve as an effective vehicle for connecting the real world to
a virtual world, efficient processing methods are needed that relate pointclouds
to geometric models [14].

A number of approaches to transform pointclouds into meaningful objects
have been developed ranging from those that are based exclusively on data
with a minimum number of restrictions or assumptions (data-driven), to those
that try to recognize predefined shapes on the data (model-driven), with hybrid
approaches being in the middle [11]. In particular, model-driven approaches are
attractive when shapes can have limited forms, such as building roofs. Unfortunately, reconstructing complex buildings often leads to producing approximate

Supported by organization CONACyT.

O. O. Vergara-Villegas et al. (Eds.): MCPR 2022, LNCS 13264, pp. 269–279, 2022.
https://doi.org/10.1007/978-3-031-07750-0_25

model parameters that may require further optimization. Such an optimization demands making the geometry explicit, in the form of triangular meshes, that must be registered back to the pointcloud.

Shape registration is a classic problem in pointcloud processing for which several methods exists [2,3,6,8,12,15], being the iterative closest point (ICP) and its variants [2,8,9] the most widely used methods. The ICP algorithm progressively matches the target shape to a reference shape by iteratively estimating a global rotation, translation and/or scaling. Recently, a deep closest point (DCP) was developed that takes advantage on recent techniques in computer vision and natural language processing for learning the underlying transformation between target and reference pointclouds [13]. In principle, these methods can be directly applied for point-point, point-mesh and mesh-mesh registration problems, by considering vertices and discarding the topology of meshes. However, in point-mesh comparisons, the registration algorithms can take advantage of topological relations between neighbour facets to increase the performance of nearest projection [8,15]. For that matter, the identification of the nearest facet for each point is critical because incorrect facet selection can lead to false local minimal of the ICP. Furthermore, correct labelling of pointclouds with the nearest label can be further used to exploit the full semantics information of the model in model-specific registration strategies. In sum, a correct nearest facet labelling of pointclouds enable the transfer of model information back to a pointcloud, such as normals, baricentric coordinates, texture information, semantics, and so on. It is within this context that the pointclouds labelling problem is addressed in this paper.

The rest of the paper is organized as follows. Section 2 formally describes the problem. Then the proposed solution is described in Sect. 3 and the results of an experimental assessment is provided in Sect. 4. Finally, major conclusions drawn are discussed in Sect. 5.

2   Problem Statement

Let $P \subset \mathbb{R}^3$ denote a pointcloud with n points and $T = (V, F)$ a triangulated surface composed by a set of m vertices $V \in \mathbb{R}^3$ and a set of l facets $F \subset V^3$. If $D(p, f)$ denotes the Euclidean distance between a point $p \in P$ and facet $f \in F$. The nearest facet problem is stated as:

$$f^*(p) = \arg\min_{f \in F} D(p, f) \tag{1}$$

for every $p \in P$.

A brute force method to solve this problem would require $O(nm)$ operations[1], which is impractical for photogrammetric pointclouds, for which n can be in the order on several million points. Space partition strategies can reduce time complexity to the order of $O(m \log(n))$. In fact, the known solutions to this problem relay on the nearest point search algorithm [5,7], assuming the nearest

---

[1] Here we consider that the number of facets is proportional to the number of vertices in the triangulated surface.

facet, or some of its neighbours up to a given order, will contain the nearest vertex to the query point. Unfortunately, the nearest vertex cannot warrant finding a correct nearest facet when there are triangles of very different sizes and there are several disconnected objects, as is the case of building models. In such cases, the closest facet may not even be connected to the closest vertex [15].

The nearest facet problem of Eq. (1) can be alternatively formulated as a pointcloud labelling with the nearest facet identifier. We define the pointcloud labelling as a function $L : P \longrightarrow [1, \ldots, l]$, such that $L(p) = k$ if the nearest point q to the query point p lies on the facet f_k. We recall that a point q on a facet $f \in F$ with vertices (v_1, v_2, v_3) can be expressed as:

$$q = \alpha_1 v_1 + \alpha_2 v_2 + \alpha_3 v_3 \qquad (2)$$

where $(\alpha_1, \alpha_2, \alpha_3) \in [0, 1]^3$ are called the the barycentric coordinates of q on f, so that $\alpha_1 + \alpha_2 + \alpha_3 = 1$. Hence, the barycentric coordinates that minimizes $D(p, q)$ define the nearest point. Such a nearest point may be shared by two or three facets and deciding which facet must be selected requires modification of the objective function in Eq. (1).

Figure 1 shows an example in which points p_3 and p_4 are equidistant to facets f_1 and f_2. In this case, we would like L to take the value of 1 for points located to the left side of the bisector from normal vectors at shared edges (p_1, p_2 and p_3), and the value of 2 for the points located to the right side of it (p_4, p_5 and p_6). Of course, points laying right on the bisector will still have the problem of two possible solutions, but these can be labelled using either facet index.

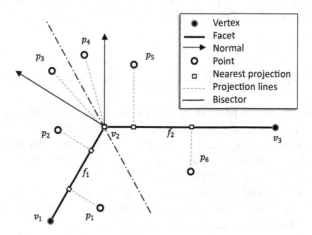

Fig. 1. Lateral view of two neighbour facets (f_1 and f_2) and corresponding nearest projection for six points (p_1 to p_6). Points p_3 and p_4 are equidistant to f_1 and f_2.

3   Proposed Solution

The proposed method can be summarized in two one-time steps, named initialization and refinement, which are described next.

3.1   Initialization

In the first step, an approximate labelling of the pointcloud is generated as follows. The nearest point search strategy is applied on sample points from the triangulated surface, rather than on its vertices. A homogeneous sampling of the surface can warrant that the nearest point is attached to the nearest facet or its neighbours of up to a given order. Random points on the surface are generated through random barycentric coordinates using the reflection method as follows.

Let u_1 and u_2 be two independent random variables uniformly distributed in the interval $[0, 1]$, then define two first barycentric coordinates as:

$$\alpha_k = \begin{cases} u_k & \text{if } u_1 + u_2 \leq 1 \\ 1 - u_k & \text{if } u_1 + u_2 > 1 \end{cases} \quad \text{for } k = 1, 2 \tag{3}$$

and the third barycentric coordinate as $\alpha_3 = 1 - \alpha_1 - \alpha_2$. Random points on the surface are then generated using the convex combination of corresponding vertices as in Eq. (2).

In order to achieve a constant point density δ_S, up to $\delta_S A(f)$ points must be generated for a facet f with area $A(f)$. Of course, the density δ_S of the random pointcloud must be as low as possible to save computation time, but large enough to warrant at least one point is generated inside the smallest triangle area A_{min} or otherwise stated:

$$\delta_S \geq \frac{1}{A_{min}} \tag{4}$$

Furthermore, if the pointcloud density δ_P is known, then it is also advisable to meet $\delta_S < \delta_P$.

The sample points so generated are labelled with the facet used to generate it and then transferred to the nearest point in the input pointcloud through the nearest neighbour search method in $O(m \log(n))$ time. Because the average number of sample points is proportional to the number of facets, the complexity of the labelling is the same up to a constant.

Although the initial labelling is already an approximate solution of the labelling problem, with most errors appearing around the edges, in must situations one may require refining that solution.

3.2   Refinement

In the second step we must further search for the nearest facet on a neighbourhood, up to a given neighbour order, of previously selected facet. For that matter, the facet adjacency matrix $A = [A_{i,j}]$, where $A_{i,j}$ is the number of vertices shared between f_i and f_j, must be used. The adjacency matrix is given by $A = BB^T$, where $B = [B_{i,j}]$ is the face-vertex incidence matrix of order $l \times m$, with $B_{i,j} = 1$ if facet f_i contains the vertex v_j, and 0 otherwise. The incidence matrix is an alternate way of expressing the triangulation, that is $B = B(T)$, where each row of B contain exactly tree ones. The adjacency matrix is combined with the preliminary labelling to find the facet-point neighbour matrix $C^{(1)} = [C_{i,j}^{(1)}]$ in which $C_{i,j}^{(1)} = 1$ facet f_i is a neighbouring facet to point p_j, and 0 otherwise. This matrix is useful to find higher-order neighbours through $C^{(k+1)} = A^k C^{(1)}$, where $C_{i,j}^{(k+1)} \neq 0$ if f_i is in the k-th neighbourhood of a neighbour facet to point i, and 0 otherwise. Hence, $C^{(k+1)}$ provides a quick selection of facets on the neighbourhood of f_i up to an order k, on which the nearest facet can be searched. From our tests, we found that the first-order neighbourhood ($k = 1$) was sufficient to reach the nearest facet.

We define the optimal point labelling function as:

$$L(p_j) = \arg \min_{j | C_{i,j}^{(k)} \neq 0} \{2|d_{i,j}|^2 - |d_{i,j} \cdot n_i|^2\} \quad \text{for } j = 1, \ldots, n \qquad (5)$$

where $d_{i,j} = p_j - q_i$ is the displacement vector, q_i is the nearest point to p_j on facet f_i and n_i is the normal vector of plane containing facet f_i. The second term of the objective function corresponds to the squared projection of the error vector onto the normal, which is $|d_{i,j}|^2$ if q_i is interior to the triangle because the displacement vector and the normal are parallel. If the nearest point is on the edges or vertices of the triangle, then the label of the triangle with maximum projection is assigned, thus solving the problem of equidistant points to shared edges or vertices, except for the points laying along the bi-/trisectors (see Fig. 1).

The complexity of refinement step is $O(n)$ because the number of facets tested is fixed (7 facets per point for a first-order neighbourhood) with the the hidden constants provided by the computation of the point-facet distance. Note that the computation time for matrix C is $O(l^2)$ given the sparsity of the matrices, but this is generally a low burden provided that $n >> l$.

Point-Facet Distance. There are several methods to compute the 3-d distance between a point and a triangle [1,4]. Here we used the approach in [10], where the general problem of finding the closest d-dimensional point to facets of lower dimensions was solved in the context of spectral unmixing problem. As is the case, the fully-constrained spectral unmixing problem is equivalent to the problem of finding the barycentric coordinates of the nearest projection q of a query point p onto a facet f.

Fortunately, an explicit solution can be written for 2- and 3-facets. In particular, the optimal barycentric coordinates on a 3-facet with vertices (v_1, v_2, v_3) have the following explicit form:

$$\alpha_k = \begin{cases} (\mu_{k,1} \vee \mu_{k,2}) \wedge \mu_{k,3}, & \text{for } \lambda_k < 0 \\ \mu_{k,2} \wedge \mu_{k,3} \wedge \mu_{k,1}, & \text{for } 0 \leq \lambda_k \leq 1 \\ (\mu_{k,3} \vee \mu_{k,2}) \wedge \mu_{k,1}, & \text{for } 1 < \lambda_k \end{cases} \qquad (6)$$

where $\mu_{k,l} = \mu(w_{k,l} \cdot (p - v_k))$ are half-space memberships defined in terms of a saturating function $\mu(s) = ((1 - s) \wedge 1) \vee 0$ and the vectors

$$w_{k,l} = \frac{u_{k,l} - v_k}{|u_{k,l} - v_k|^2}, \quad u_{k,l} = \begin{cases} v_l', & \text{for } k = l \\ v_l, & \text{for } k \neq l \end{cases} \tag{7}$$

and v_k' is the projection of v_k onto the opposite line segment. More explicitly,

$$v_1' = v_2 + \lambda_1(v_3 - v_2), \quad \lambda_1 = \frac{(v_1 - v_2)\cdot(v_3 - v_2)}{|v_3 - v_2|^2} \tag{8}$$

$$v_2' = v_3 + \lambda_2(v_1 - v_3), \quad \lambda_2 = \frac{(v_2 - v_3)\cdot(v_1 - v_3)}{|v_1 - v_3|^2} \tag{9}$$

$$v_3' = v_1 + \lambda_3(v_2 - v_1), \quad \lambda_3 = \frac{(v_3 - v_1)\cdot(v_2 - v_1)}{|v_2 - v_1|^2} \tag{10}$$

Equations (6)–(10) will contribute to the overall computational time by a constant factor, which can be lowered if they are applied for computing only two barycentric coordinates, and the third is computed from the sum-to-unit constraint. Hence, the point-facet distance is given by

$$D(p, q) = |p - \alpha_1(v_1 - v_3) - \alpha_2(v_2 - v_3) - v_3| \tag{11}$$

4   Assessment Results

In order to test performance of the proposed method, an experimental analysis was carried out on simulated data and real data. The simulated data was based on a model of a single storey building composed of four primitives with hipped and gabled rooftypes (Fig. 2-A).

In order to test how pointcloud quality can impact the performance of the method, tree pointclouds where simulated by uniform sampling the building model ($\delta = 20$ pts/m^2) and adding Gaussian noise of $N(0, \sigma)$, for $\sigma = 0.5$, 1.0 and 5.0. Figure 2-B shows the case $N(0, 5)$, where the point color represents the facet index used for point generation. Figures 2-C and D show the nearest projection colored by the facet index and by the barycentric coordinates as RGB color scheme, respectively.

Mesh registration errors were simulated through translation ($T_x = T_y$) and rotations (θ) of individual primitive as indicated in Table 1. The labelling method was then applied to each pointcloud with each altered building model (M0-M6) and the percent of correctly labelled points was counted for the initial and refinement steps.

Fig. 2. Visualization of simulated dataset: A. Building geometry, B. Random point-cloud with $N(0; 5)$, C. Nearest projection of pointcloud onto corresponding building facet, and D. Same as C. But colored with barycentric coordinates as RGB. (point density in B and C was reduced for clarity.)

For an appropriate selection of sampled point density required for the initialization step, we used the pointcloud $N(0, 1)$, together with the model M0, and plotted the number of mislabeled points $Err(\delta_S)$ and its slope $(\Delta Err(\delta_S)/\Delta \delta_S)$ as a function of sample point density (δ_S). Figure 3-top shows that slope saturate after $\delta_S > 2$ points/m^2 indicating small relative improvements for larger sample density values, and so we selected $\delta_S = 10$ points/m^2 for all subsequent tests. Figure 3-bottom compares the results for all the combination of pointcloud noise level and model misregistratios. It was observed that the noise level of pointcloud was not as important as the model translation and rotation for determining the labelling errors, that the performance seemed more sensitive to translation than to rotation values, and that the refinement step was able to correct up to 2–4% of the point labels, most of which were observed to occur around break lines of the model.

Table 1. Transformation parameters applied to test models.

Model	M0	M1	M2	M3	M4	M5	M6
θ (deg)	0.0	0.1	0.5	1.0	0.0	0.0	0.0
$T_x = T_y$ (m)	0.0	0.0	0.0	0.0	0.1	0.5	1.0

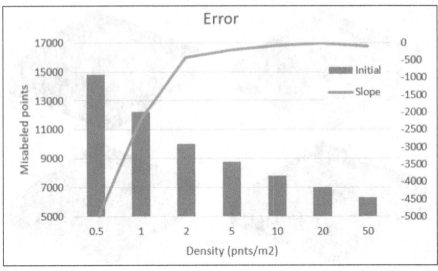

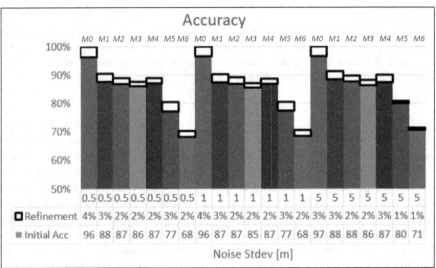

Fig. 3. Top: number of mislabeled points with its slope for pointcloud $N(0, 1)$ and model M0 as function of sampled point density of the initial step. Bottom: percent of correctly labelled points by the initialization and refinement steps for the original (green bars), rotated (blue bars) and translated models (red bars) (Color figure online)

The real dataset was based on a pointcloud of around ($n =$) 2.2 million points generated from low oblique aerial photography collected over the CentroGeo building complex from a drone (DJI Phantom 4 Advance), flying at 50 m above ground and along a double scan grid. The pointcloud was generated in Pix4d software using standard photogrammetric procedures that incorporated three ground control points (GCP) collected with a high precision GPS, with nominal errors of one centimeter. A building model was manually edited on the pointcloud using custom developed tools in MATLAB software. The model consisted of an aggregated of 20 building primitives of rectangular base and predefined roof shapes. The models were converted to a triangular mesh with custom-developed functions in MATLAB, which resulted in $m = 40$ vertices and $l = 56$ triangles.

The labelling method was then applied 1) to estimate the minimum distance between the pointcloud and the mesh, 2) to produce a projected pointcloud for points at $d < 0.5$ m from the mesh and 3) to label pointclouds according to nearest building primitive. Figure 4 provides visualizations for the polyhedral model (A), the pointcloud colored by the minimum distance (B), the pointcloud colored by the nearest building primitive label (C) and the projected pointcloud (D). Estimated distance was compared to that given by that point-mesh distance tool available in CloudCompare software and no significant difference was observed (data not shown). However, the nearest and projections could not be assessed by independent means as the CloudCompare software does not provide such information. Nonetheless, a visuall inspection revealed a correct labelling of the points.

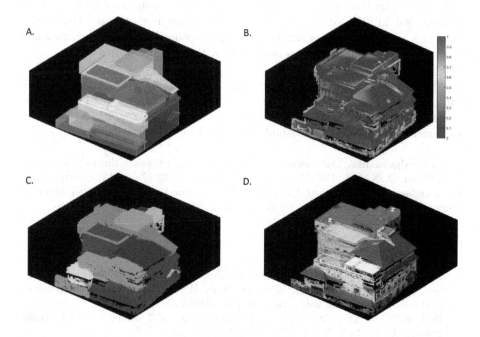

Fig. 4. A. Building model, B. Pointcloud colored by point-mesh distance, C. pointcloud colored bye nearest building primitive and D. Projected pointcloud onto nearest facet

5 Conclusions

The labelling of a pointcloud with nearest facet of a triangular mesh is a basic operation that is currently overlooked by current pointcloud processing software. The operation is particularly useful for model parameter optimization in which the mesh is an intermediate product of a parameterized model of the objects embedded in the pointcloud. While some global registration methods can be used for mesh registration, going back from mesh to models may not always be possible and, therefore, labelling the pointcloud with the nearest primitive can enable a direct link between models and points that is required for parameter adjustment without relaying on the registered geometry. In this paper, such a labelling procedure was formalized, and a method was developed and assessed using simulated and real data sets.

Overall, it was observed that displaced models can have a much more significant effect on the labelling errors than rotations and noise level in pointclouds. Based on this observation, it is advisable to apply a global registration method, such as the ICP algorithm, before the labelling method described in this paper. The latter may be useful for local registration and model parameter optimization (e.g., building height, roof slopes, etc.). The computational burden of method is dominated by the optimization with a linear time complexity $O(n)$, and the initialization in $O(m \log(n))$ time. The contribution from the point-facet distance is a constant factor, which may be easily optimized as the computation of barycentric coordinates involves operations with 0's and 1's.

Future work shall take advantage of the labelling for a quick selection of points needed to optimize parameters of a particular building primitive. Noise filtering from pointclouds cab be also enabled through the projected points, and it should be further exploited for noise characterization, as well as for accuracy assessment of segmentation methods, as well as for visualization purpose.

Acknowledgements. Data used in this study was made possible through the financing from the CONACyT-INEGI Sectorial Fund (Project 268773) and the participation of researchers and students of CentroGeo. Special thanks to José Manuel Madrigal Gómez and Roberto Hernández, for the collection of ground control points.

References

1. Aspert, N., Santa-Cruz, D., Ebrahimi, T.: Mesh: measuring errors between surfaces using the hausdorff distance. In: Proceedings. IEEE International Conference on Multimedia and Expo, vol. 1, pp. 705–708. IEEE (2002)
2. Besl, H.D., McKay, P.: A method for registration of 3-D shapes. IEEE Trans. Pattern Anal. Mach. Intell. **14**(2), 239 (1992)
3. Ji, S., Ren, Y., Ji, Z., Liu, X., Hong, G.: An improved method for registration of point cloud. Optik **140**, 451–458 (2017)
4. Jones, M.W.: 3d distance from a point to a triangle. Department of Computer Science, University of Wales Swansea Technical Report CSR-5 (1995)
5. Kibriya, A.M.: Fast algorithms for nearest neighbour search. Ph.D. thesis, The University of Waikato (2007)

6. Li, H., Hartley, R.: The 3D–3D registration problem revisited. In: 2007 IEEE 11th International Conference on Computer Vision, pp. 1–8. IEEE (2007)
7. Murtagh, F.: A review of fast techniques for nearest neighbour searching. Compstat **1984**, 143–147 (1984)
8. Rusinkiewicz, S., Levoy, M.: Efficient variants of the ICP algorithm. In: Proceedings Third International Conference on 3-D Digital Imaging and Modeling, pp. 145–152. IEEE (2001)
9. Segal, A., Haehnel, D., Thrun, S.: Generalized-ICP. In: Robotics: Science and Systems. vol. 2, p. 435. Seattle, WA (2009)
10. Silván-Cárdenas, J.L., Wang, L.: Fully constrained linear spectral unmixing: analytic solution using fuzzy sets. IEEE Trans. Geosci. Remote Sens. **48**(11), 3992–4002 (2010)
11. Tarsha-Kurdi, F., Landes, T., Grussenmeyer, P., Koehl, M.: Model-driven and data-driven approaches using lidar data: analysis and comparison. In: ISPRS Workshop, Photogrammetric Image Analysis (PIA07), pp. 87–92 (2007)
12. Wang, C., Shu, Q., Yang, Y., Yuan, F.: Point cloud registration in multidirectional affine transformation. IEEE Photonics J. **10**(6), 1–15 (2018)
13. Wang, Y., Solomon, J.M.: Deep closest point: learning representations for point cloud registration. In: Proceedings of the IEEE/CVF International Conference on Computer Vision, pp. 3523–3532 (2019)
14. Xie, Y., Tian, J., Zhu, X.X.: Linking points with labels in 3D: a review of point cloud semantic segmentation. IEEE Geosci. Remote Sens. Magaz. **8**(4), 38–59 (2020)
15. Zhu, L., Barhak, J., Srivatsan, V., Katz, R.: Efficient registration for precision inspection of free-form surfaces. Int. J. Adv. Manuf. Technol. **32**(5), 505–515 (2007)

Dust Deposition Classification on the Receiver Tube of the Parabolic Trough Collector: A Deep Learning-Based Approach

Alan Brian Díaz Reyna[1] , Luis M. Valentin-Coronado[1,2(✉)] ,
and Manuel I. Peña-Cruz[1,2]

[1] Centro de Investigaciones en Óptica, Aguascalientes,
20200 Aguascalientes, Ags., Mexico
{alanbriandr,luismvc,mipec}@cio.mx
[2] Consejo Nacional de Ciencia y Tecnología, 03940 Ciudad de México, Mexico

Abstract. The parabolic-trough collectors are emergent technology that solves thermal energy problems because they take advantage of solar energy, however, those systems are outdoor, making it easy to become dirt. Currently, the inspection of dirt is performed manually. In this work, a system able to detect different dust deposition levels on the receiver tube of the parabolic-trough collector (PTC), using a CNN model, has been proposed. The proposed system has shown a very good performance, achieving an overall accuracy of 0.91 and F1-measure of 0.91 ($\sigma = 0.04$), making it a good alternative for dust classification in PTCs.

Keywords: Computer vision · Convolutional neural network · Parabolic-trough collector · Solar energy

1 Introduction

Renewable energies are becoming a very important alternative to mitigate gas emissions produced mainly by fossil fuels. Applications such as electric power generation, heat generation, refrigeration, to name a few, have begun to be implemented through the use of these clean energies. Although there are various renewable sources, solar energy is the most abundant, besides been available in any location of the Earth. For this reason, many countries, including Mexico, have been promoting research and technological development in the solar energy field. One of the most developed technologies in the use of solar energy are parabolic trough collectors (PTC). PTCs have the capability to capture the solar radiation to transform it into heat, which is transfered to a working fluid. Since a collector works with solar energy, it must be installed outdoors for what they are more susceptible to become dirt, thus undermining its performance.

Centro de Investigaciones en Óptica, A.C.

O. O. Vergara-Villegas et al. (Eds.): MCPR 2022, LNCS 13264, pp. 280–290, 2022.
https://doi.org/10.1007/978-3-031-07750-0_26

Currently in this situation, a visual inspection is performed by persons in order to determine if a cleanness is need or not, which is impractical because the judgment is based on the own experience and perception of each individual, in other words, the assessment criterion is not standardized. To address this problem, it is proposed a system capable to detect different levels of dust deposition in the receiver tube of the parabolic trough collector (autonomously) by analyzing images, taken from a camera mounted on an unmanned aerial vehicle (UAV), based on a deep-learning approach. Figure 1 illustrates the proposed system.

Fig. 1. Unmanned Aircraft vehicle taken images of PTC

2   PTC and the Problem of Dust

For harnessing solar energy on Earth, in general have been created two kinds of technologies: the photovoltaic conversion technologies and photothermal conversion technologies. Regarding the photothermal conversion technologies, the parabolic trough collector is the most mature technology so that it generates the majority of the total global concentrating solar thermal power. Thus, it is of the utmost importance that this type of equipment operates always in optimal conditions.

2.1   Parabolic-Trough Collectors

The photothermal solar collectors are a kind of heat exchanger that turn the solar energy into thermal energy. In them, the energy transfer is performed from a distant source of radiant energy (the Sun) to a fluid. Without optical concentration, the flux of the incident solar energy radiation is, at best, of $1100\,\text{W/m}^2$ approximately [11]. With these radiative fluxes, can be designed solar flat plate collectors for applications that use fluid temperatures up to $100\,^\circ\text{C}$ higher than ambient temperature, however, exists many other applications in which is required higher temperatures than the normally reached by the flat plate collectors. These higher temperatures can be obtained by lodging an optical device between the sun and the energy absorbent surface with the purpose of increasing the density of the incident radiative flux in the absorber. These devices (optical system and absorber) are called solar collectors [8].

A parabolic-trough collector is an integrated system made up of two main elements, i) parabolic-shaped mirrors and ii) a receiver tube placed along the focal axis of the parabola.

This geometry allows to the solar radiation that parallel impinges on the system to be concentrate in the focus, as illustrated in Fig. 2. The focus of the parabola spreads like a focal line along the canal. Over this line is placed a receiver tube which contains the thermal fluid (usually oil) that is heated when the tube absorbs the solar radiation. In Fig. 3 some solar collectors in which is possible to observe the concentrated energy in the receiver tube are shown [15].

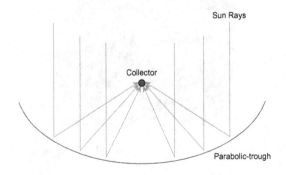

Fig. 2. Diagram of operation of a parabolic-trough collector.

The parabolic-trough collector tend to work over $100\,^\circ\text{C}$ and can be coupled to a Rankine cycle of water-steam to produce electricity.

Currently, the largest commercial complex worldwide is located in Mojave Desert in Kramer Junction (California, USA) and consists of eighth PTC plants with an installed capacity of 340 Mwe (Megawatt electric), however, the cost of the produced electricity in this kind of plants still been too high for achieving a commercial expansion [2].

On the other hand, making the installation of solar energy technologies is only the beginning, for at this point important needs araise. One of these needs is to guarantee, whenever possible, the proper operating of the system, condition that is affected if the required maintenance are not carried out.

Fig. 3. PTC Kramer Junction (California, USA) [6]

2.2 Dust Deposition Effect

The use of solar energy and consequently the production of thermal energy, are directly related to the optical properties of the collector. Then, properties like the reflectivity of mirrors or transmissivity of the glass cover in the receiver tube, are extremely affected by the amount of dust cummulated on these zones. Considering this, some power plants have tried to implement strategies to reduce the effect that the dust produces on the power plant performance. To assess how much the presence of dust affects, different studies have been carried out; for instance, in the work presented in [12], the authors have observed a reduction of between 10% to 60% in the transmittance of the glass plates of several photovoltaic modules. As expected, an increase in the amount of dust produces a drop in the transmittance, which consequently leads to a drop in the power generated,as in the work presented in [3], where the authors have reported a decrease of up to 60% of the energy produced. Given this problem, some strategies have been proposed to determine the level of dust, in such a way that it is possible to take actions that avoid significant drops in energy production. A clear example is the work presented in [16], in which the level of dust in a photovoltaic module is determined based on the analysis of an image by means of a digital image processing approach. In this work, a total of 60 images have been analyzed, among which were images with clean modules as well as images with different levels of dust. Even though several studies related with the detection of dust presence in solar systems have been performed, few of them have focused on the parabolic trough collectors systems of solar thermal power plants.

3   Methods

In this section, the proposed methodology to address the dust classification problem is presented. As Fig. 4 shows, the methodology is divided in five stages. In the first stage, images of different dust levels of the parabolic-trough collector are obtained using the UAV. Whereas in the second stage, a region of interest (ROI) selection as well as a perspective transformation are performed; with this, it is assured that only relevant information is used and that the images are the same size in terms of pixels (487 × 125). In the third stage, the dust level of each image is manually labeling and then, divided in two groups: training images and test images. The model has been trained, using the set of labeled training images in stage fourth. Finally in the last stage, the classification results are obtained.

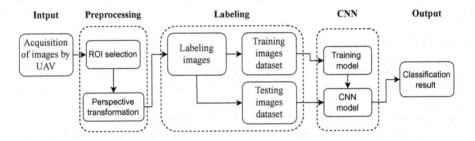

Fig. 4. Methodology used during the realization of this work

A more detailed explanation of each stage is presented in the following sections.

3.1   Input

As a first step, the acquisition of 3,500 images with different levels of dust and at different moments of the day was carried out. The images were acquired with a digital camera mounted on a UAV. The camera used was a DJI-Zenmuse Z3 with 3.5× optical zoom and 12 megapixels of image resolution. Figure 5 shows some of the images acquired with the UAV.

3.2   Preprocessing

Once the images were acquired, a ROI selection (in this case the receiver tube) was performed, this is done to obtain only the relevant information from the PTC; as in most cases the images obtained are not rectangular, thus, a manual perspective transformation is performed; with this, it is ensured that the set of

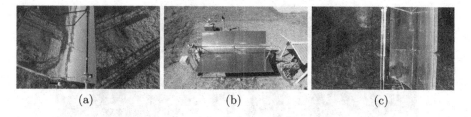

(a)   (b)   (c)

Fig. 5. Example of images taken by UAV.

images (that will be used in the next process) have the same size in terms of the number of pixels (487 × 125). In Fig. 6 the ROI as well as the perspective transformation can be appreciated.

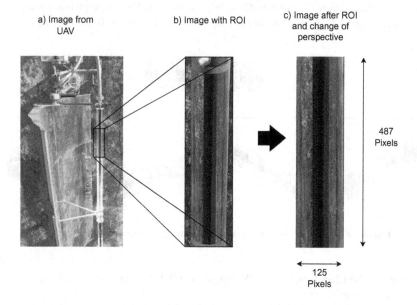

Fig. 6. Preprocessing of the parabolic-trough collector images

3.3 Labeling

To train the classifier, all the images were manually labeled according to a level of dirt (amount of dust). For doing this, four levels of dust were defined, i) clean, ii) middle1, iii) middle2, and iv) dirt. Then, images were separated into training and test groups; this so as to test the classifier with images that would not have seen before and being able to make a correct validation. Characteristic images of each class are shown in Fig. 7.

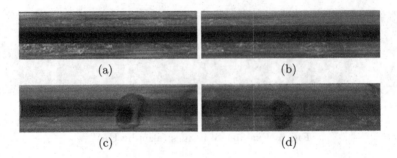

Fig. 7. Example of imagenes labeled. Each image corresponds to each of the four classes (clean, middle1, middle2, and dirt)

To achieve a better trained model, a data augmentation process was carried out, generating "new" images with some rotation and movement both lengthwise and widthwise [13]. Figure 8 shows some images resulting from this process.

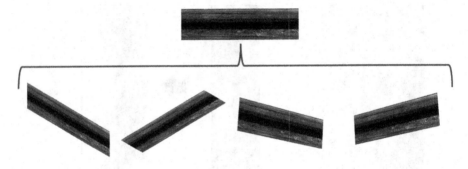

Fig. 8. Example of images resulting from data augmentation process.

The resulting dataset is made up of 3,100 images, in which there are 775 images per class.

3.4   Convolutional Neural Network

A neural network (NN) is a simplified model that emulates the way in which the human brain processes the information. Works by combining a significant number of interlinked processing units that look like abstract versions of neurons [5].

The neural network learns by examining the individual records, generating a prediction for every record and making adjustments to the weightings whenever such prediction is wrong. This process is performed repeatedly and the network still improving its predictions until reaches one or several stopping criteria [5]. Nevertheless, although a NN may be used to address the classification of the dust it is needed to define a set of features, to then extract them, this could not be the best option since a 2D object (image) is mapped into a 1D, which would have some drawbacks, for instance, the spatial information of the image could be lost. Another way to solve the classification problem is by using a Convolutional Neural Network (CNN). CNNs have proven to be a very good tool especially for dealing with image-related problems. The applications in which they have been used are image classification, image semantic segmentation, object detection in images, to name a few. This is because its architecture is designed to work with three-dimensional objects, as is the case of color images, where each channel can be understood as one of these dimensions.

As a classification model, the use of an approach based on deep learning was proposed, particularly a CNN.

This because, since it is optimized for the learning of images [1], solves the problematic related to the dust level classification.

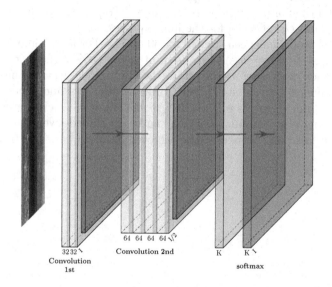

Fig. 9. Architecture of the proposed CNN.

The proposed CNN (see Fig. 9) is made up of an input layer of 514,650 flat neurons (this corresponds to the number of pixels that each of the images has), followed by a layer of convolution ([7]. This layer creates a kernel that convolves with the input of the layer to produce a outputs tensor and create a skew vector that is added to the outputs [7]). Then, it is followed by a third layer called *Max-polling*, which is used to obtain the most important information of each image but keeping it in a smaller size, since the application travels in a 2×2 pixel neighborhood preserving the highest value [4]. Subsequently, there is one more layer of convolution but at this time with 64 kernels and another of *Max-polling*, this with the purpose of reduce the images even more and obtain only the most important information optimizing the training in the hidden layers (there are two hidden layers of 100 neurons each) [4]. The optimization model used is *Adam* [10] since it allows an efficient computing in terms of memory and it is optimized on solving issues with large amounts of data as the images are. Finally, as output a *softmax* layer is implemented.

The softmax function takes as input a vector z of K real numbers, and normalizes it into a probability distribution consisting of K probabilities proportional to the exponential of the input numbers, in this case $K = 4$.

As mentioned, all the images used to train the CNN model must be of the same size in terms of the number of pixels. Additionally, the images are converted to floating-point and normalized for better learning [10].

3.5   Experiments and Results

The proposed method has been implemented using Python as the programming language,and the libraries used were *Tensorflow* [14] for the Convolutional Neural Network and *OpenCV* [9] for the image processing.

The CNN model has been trained for 60 epochs. For the training stage, 3000 labeled images (750 by class) were used, of which 80% of the instances (2,400 images) of each class were used to train the CNN model leaving the remaining ones (600 images) to validate. Figure 10 shows the loss and accuracy graphs during the training process of the CNN model. As it can be seen (Fig. 10(a)), a good learning rate is obtained, which can be concluded given the exponential shape of the loss plot. Moreover, the achieved accuracy over the training data was 0.9183.

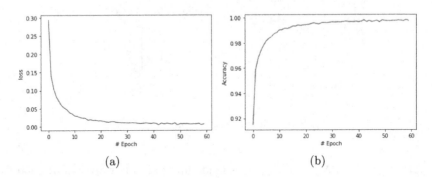

(a)   (b)

Fig. 10. Training stage behavior of the CNN. (a) Loss vs #Epochs. (b) Accuracy vs #Epochs

Once the model has been trained, the set of the 100 remaining images of the dataset, has been used to assess the model's performance. In Table 1 the classification report is presented. From this table it can be seen that the overall accuracy is 0.91. Furthermore, as F1-measure shows, the proposed CNN model can be considered both precise and robust in classifying among instances of the classes.

Table 1. Classification report of the CNN model.

Class	Precision	Recall	F1-measure	Support
Clean	0.960	0.960	0.960	25
Middle 1	0.913	0.840	0.875	25
Middle 2	0.821	0.920	0.868	25
Dirt	0.958	0.920	0.938	25
Accuracy			0.91	100

To visually summarize the performance of the proposed CNN model, the confusion matrix shown in Fig. 11 has been created. From this matrix, it can be observed that mostly misclassified instances of "Middle 1" were predicted as "Middle 2". This can be improved by increasing the database, or by better selecting the elements that make up each class.

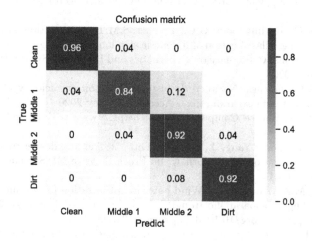

Fig. 11. Confusion matrix obtained

4   Conclusions and Future Work

As has been observed in this work, significant progress has been made on the development of a dust classification system, since there is a functional convolutional neural network model capable to determine the different levels of dirt on the Parabolic-trough collector which has a very good performance as evidenced by the 0.91 of accuracy achieved. This will help to maintain in good conditions the PTC for keeping its optimal performance, thereby contributing to take advantage of natural resources, in this case, solar thermal energy. As future work, an embedded system will be built in which it is integrated the proposed convolutional neural network, besides the development of a user-friendly graphical interface.

References

1. Abu, M.A., Indra, N.H., Rahman, A., Sapiee, N.A., Ahmad, I.: A study on image classification based on deep learning and tensorflow. Int. J. Eng. Res. Technol. **12**(4), 563–569 (2019)
2. AlZahrani, A.A., Dincer, I.: Energy and exergy analyses of a parabolic trough solar power plant using carbon dioxide power cycle. Energy Conver. Manag. **158**, 476–488 (2018). https://doi.org/10.1016/j.enconman.2017.12.071
3. Ghazi, S., Sayigh, A., Ip, K.: Dust effect on flat surfaces-a review paper. Renew. Sustain. Energy Rev. **33**, 742–751 (2014)
4. Hussain, M., Bird, J.J., Faria, D.R.: A study on CNN transfer learning for image classification. In: Lotfi, A., Bouchachia, H., Gegov, A., Langensiepen, C., McGinnity, M. (eds.) UKCI 2018. AISC, vol. 840, pp. 191–202. Springer, Cham (2019). https://doi.org/10.1007/978-3-319-97982-3_16
5. IBM. www.ibm.com/knowledgecenter/neuralnet_model.html. Accessed 19 Nov 2020
6. Instituto Nacional de Electricidad y Energias Limpias (INEEL) antes IIE/Brumen, MC R.: http://www.fordecyt.ier.unam.mx/html/colectorDeCanalParabolico_1. html
7. Kembuan, O., Rorimpandey, G.C., Tengker, S.M.T.: Convolutional neural network (CNN) for image classification of Indonesia sign language using Tensorflow. In: 2020 2nd International Conference on Cybernetics and Intelligent System (ICORIS), pp. 1–5. IEEE (2020)
8. LACYQS Laboratorio Nacional de Sistemas de Concentracion y Quimica Solar. http://concentracionsolar.org.mx/. Accessed 19 Nov 2020
9. Library, Open Source Computer Vision: https://www.python.org/. Accessed 19 Nov 2020
10. Meng, C., Sun, M., Yang, J., Qiu, M., Gu, Y.: Training deeper models by GPU memory optimization on Tensorflow. In: Proceedings of ML Systems Workshop in NIPS, vol. 7 (2017)
11. Moghimi, M.A., Ahmadi, G.: Wind barriers optimization for minimizing collector mirror soiling in a parabolic trough collector plant. Appl. Energy **225**, 413–423 (2018). https://doi.org/10.1016/j.apenergy.2018.05.027
12. Şahin, A.D.: A new formulation for solar irradiation and sunshine duration estimation. Int. J. Energy Res. **31**(2), 109–118 (2007)
13. Taqi, A.M., Awad, A., Al-Azzo, F., Milanova, M.: The impact of multi-optimizers and data augmentation on tensorflow convolutional neural network performance. In: 2018 IEEE Conference on Multimedia Information Processing and Retrieval (MIPR). pp. 140–145. IEEE (2018)
14. TensorFLow. https://www.tensorflow.org/. Accessed 20 June 2021
15. Usamentiaga, R., Fernández, A., Carús, J.L.: Evaluation of dust deposition on parabolic trough collectors in the visible and infrared spectrum. Sensors (Switzerland) **20**, 1–20 (2020). https://doi.org/10.3390/s20216249
16. Yfantis, E., Fayed, A.: A camera system for detecting dust and other deposits on solar panels. Adv. Image Video Process. **2** (2014). https://doi.org/10.14738/aivp. 25.411

Cable-Driven Parallel Robot Controlled by Servo-Vision System

Andrés García-Vanegas[1,3(✉)], Camilo Leiton-Murcia[1], Manuel G. Forero[2(✉)] ⓘ,
Antonio Gonzalez-Rodríguez[3], and Fernando Castillo-García[3(✉)] ⓘ

[1] Semillero MEC-AUTRONIC, Facultad de Ingeniería, Universidad de Ibagué,
Tolima, Colombia
jorge.garcia@unibague.edu.co
[2] Semillero Lún, Facultad de Ingeniería, Universidad de Ibagué, Tolima, Colombia
manuel.forero@unibague.edu.co
[3] Universidad de Castilla-La Mancha, Toledo, Spain
Fernando.Castillo@uclm.es

Abstract. This work proposes the implementation of a control system based servo-vision in a cable-driven parallel robot with four degrees of freedom. In the first instance, a servo-vision based position control system is designed for a correct positioning of the mobile platform (end-effector) within the working space of the fixed platform (frame). Also, this part integrates the application of techniques for object detection in images. The second part verifies the system by tracking trajectories and positioning of the end-effector in the workspace. Moreover, seedling monitoring will be performed in a seedbed located inside the robot, which consists of taking real-time video of the robot's end-effector, for the location and monitoring of the seedlings.

Keywords: Servo-vision · Vision-based control · Computer vision · Cable-driven parallel robot · Cable robot · Parallel robotic

1 Introduction

The use of computer vision for robot motion control is called servo vision (visual servoing). These systems have two ways of acquiring images: the first one by means of a camera attached to the end effector, called EIH (Eye-In-Hand) configuration, and the second one by means of a camera located somewhere in the workspace pointing towards the end effector, called ETH (Eye-To-Hand) configuration [2,3].

Servo vision systems have four control schemes. The first has a hierarchical control structure and the vision system provides the reference to the robot controller (Indirect visual servoing). The second, known as Direct visual servoing, implements a visual controller that directly provides the response to the robot actuators. The third one calculates the pose of the end effector to generate the error signal and is known as Pose based visual servoing (PBVS).

O. O. Vergara-Villegas et al. (Eds.): MCPR 2022, LNCS 13264, pp. 291–302, 2022.
https://doi.org/10.1007/978-3-031-07750-0_27

The fourth, called Image-based visual servoing (IBVS), obtains the error between the expected image and the current image [1,8].

Robots are programmable machines, whose fundamental purpose is to generate defined motions for a specific task. Research on cable-driven parallel robots focuses on improving their precision and accuracy for trajectory tracking. Cable-driven parallel robots (CDPR) are characterized by controlling the position of a moving platform, known as an end-effector, by collecting or releasing cables, strategically distributed on a fixed platform (frame). The length of the cables is defined by the angular position of actuators that form the cable collection system. The number of degrees of freedom of the End-Effector depends on the number and spatial configuration of the cables [7]. The study of the CDPR is focused on improving its precision and accuracy for trajectory tracking, through kinematic and dynamic modeling with control and calibration system based on the measurement of cable tensions, computer vision and inertial sensors [4,5].

These robots can be controlled in open or closed loop. The first one has the advantage of being simpler, however, the reference pose of the end-effector must be calibrated in an initial position, called Home, every time the robot is going to start its tasks, this implies that, if an external factor causes it to lose this position, the model will not work and positioning failures will occur. The second one is more complex to implement, however, it is more robust in the positioning of the end-effector. There are several ways to perform the feedback of the control loop, being computer vision one of the most used in the field of robotics. In the literature, the control schemes that use it are referred to as servo-vision systems. The latter provide the possibility for the end-effector to interact with objects that are present in the workspace.

This paper is organized as follows: Sect. 2 details the materials used in this works. Section 3 describes the servo-vision system developed. Section 4 presents the results and discussions. The paper concludes with some remarks and suggestions for future works.

2   Materials and Method

In this study, a servo-vision system was developed to control a spatial cable-driven parallel robot, called AgroCableBot, to automate small-scale indoor crops, as shown in Fig. 1. The robot has four degrees-of-freedom, three of translation in the Cartesian axes and one of rotation in the vertical axis. The prototype was built with aluminum profiles and 3D printed parts with polylactide (PLA). Its specifications are given in Table 1. As can be seen, the positioning system consists of eight reference circles, four of red color located on the corners of the frame and the other four of blue color located in the end-effector (EE). The robot video input signal is acquired using a Logitech HD Pro C920 webcam with 1080p resolution, located on top 1 m from the end-effector.

The software was developed in Python 3.8 using the OpenCV and PyQt5 libraries, on an Intel(R) Core(TM) i7-4720HQ CPU @ 2.60 GHz 2.59 GHz computer with 16 GB RAM, running in a Windows 10 environment.

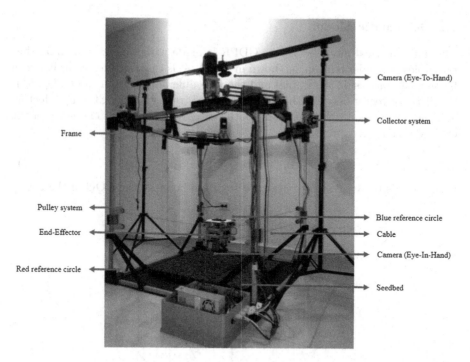

Fig. 1. Experimental prototype of the AgroCablebot indoor robot with 4 degrees of freedom, three of translation in the Cartesian axes and one of rotation in the vertical axis, together with the servo-vision system for the calibration and tracking of the end-effector.

Table 1. Indoor-AgroCableBot specifications.

Parameter	Value/Component	Unit
Stepper motors (NEMA 23)	4	-
Number of cable	8	-
Gear ratio	30:1	-
Drum diameter	66	mm
Cable type	Spider cable	-
Cable diameter	0.6	mm
Degrees-of-freedom	4	-
Size of the robot frame	1.0×1.0	m
Size of the mobile platform	100.0×100.0	mm

2.1   Kinematic Model

The mathematical modeling of the CDPR is made with vectors, assuming that the cables are under tension, as shown in Fig. 2. A_i is the distance vector between home position (inside the frame) and the ith cable output from the pulley, b_i is the distance vector between the COG (center of gravity) of the EE (end-effector) and the ith cable attachment point, both vectors are constant. The norm of the cable vector L_i is expressed as:

$$||\mathbf{L_i}|| = ||\mathbf{b_i} + \mathbf{Cp} - \mathbf{A_i}|| \tag{1}$$

where, C_P is the cartesian position vector from home to the COG of the EE.

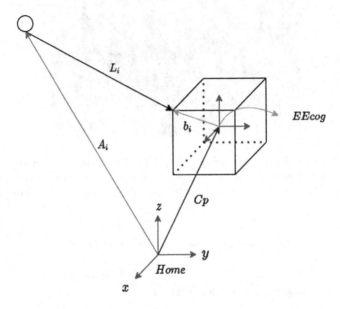

Fig. 2. Schematic of a CDPR with two cables.

Equation (1) relates the current position (C_P) of the COG of the EE with the length of each cable. It is possible to define the angular position of each actuator taking the length of the ith cable as an arc length as is shown in (2).

$$\theta_i = \frac{||\mathbf{L_i}||}{r} - \frac{L_0}{r} = \varphi^{IK}(\mathbf{Cp}) \tag{2}$$

where r is the radius of the cable recollecting system and L_0 is the length of each cable in home position.

Equation (2) is the solution of the inverse kinematic problem of the CDPR, it maps one point in the Cartesian space to the joint space. In order to control the motion of the EE with this close loop application, the First-Order Differential Kinematics are needed. Deriving (2) with respect of the time, one has:

$$\frac{d||\mathbf{L_i}||}{dt} = \frac{d||\mathbf{L_{i(x)}}||}{dx}\dot{\mathbf{x}}, \frac{d||\mathbf{L_{i(y)}}||}{dy}\dot{\mathbf{y}}, \frac{d||\mathbf{L_{i(z)}}||}{dz}\dot{\mathbf{z}} \tag{3}$$

$$\begin{bmatrix} \dot{\theta}_1 \\ \dot{\theta}_2 \\ \dot{\theta}_3 \\ \dot{\theta}_4 \end{bmatrix} = \frac{1}{r} \begin{bmatrix} \frac{d||\mathbf{L_1}||}{dx} & \frac{d||\mathbf{L_1}||}{dy} & \frac{d||\mathbf{L_1}||}{dz} \\ \frac{d||\mathbf{L_2}||}{dx} & \frac{d||\mathbf{L_2}||}{dy} & \frac{d||\mathbf{L_2}||}{dz} \\ \frac{d||\mathbf{L_3}||}{dx} & \frac{d||\mathbf{L_3}||}{dy} & \frac{d||\mathbf{L_3}||}{dz} \\ \frac{d||\mathbf{L_4}||}{dx} & \frac{d||\mathbf{L_4}||}{dy} & \frac{d||\mathbf{L_4}||}{dz} \end{bmatrix} \begin{bmatrix} \dot{\mathbf{x}} \\ \dot{\mathbf{y}} \\ \dot{\mathbf{z}} \end{bmatrix} = \frac{1}{r}\mathbf{J}\begin{bmatrix} \dot{\mathbf{x}} \\ \dot{\mathbf{y}} \\ \dot{\mathbf{z}} \end{bmatrix} \tag{4}$$

where $\mathbf{J}$ is the inverse kinematic Jacobian Matrix. Solving the derivates in 4, the following is derived:

$$\mathbf{J} = \begin{bmatrix} \frac{\mathbf{L_1x}}{||\mathbf{L_1}||} & \frac{\mathbf{L_1y}}{||\mathbf{L_1}||} & \frac{\mathbf{L_1z}}{||\mathbf{L_1}||} \\ \frac{\mathbf{L_2x}}{||\mathbf{L_2}||} & \frac{\mathbf{L_2y}}{||\mathbf{L_2}||} & \frac{\mathbf{L_2z}}{||\mathbf{L_2}||} \\ \frac{\mathbf{L_3x}}{||\mathbf{L_3}||} & \frac{\mathbf{L_3y}}{||\mathbf{L_3}||} & \frac{\mathbf{L_3z}}{||\mathbf{L_3}||} \\ \frac{\mathbf{L_4x}}{||\mathbf{L_4}||} & \frac{\mathbf{L_4y}}{||\mathbf{L_4}||} & \frac{\mathbf{L_4z}}{||\mathbf{L_4}||} \end{bmatrix} \tag{5}$$

Equations (4) and (5) map the Cartesian velocity of the EE, depending on its current position, into angular speed of the actuators.

2.2   Vision System

Workspace Calibration: This is the implementation of geometric transformations in the image with the objective of separating the pixels belonging to the workspace, allowing an easy three-dimensional relationship with the image and corrections of perspective errors attributed to camera positioning as is shown in Fig. 3. Prior to calibration, four red reference circles are placed on the robot frame so that they coincide with as many of the robot's construction factors as possible. In this case, these are fixed at the minimum height of the system and vertically co-linear to the cable sheaves, coinciding with the width, length and height of the workspace.

The perspective transform is used to separate the pixels of the workspace from the rest of the image applying translation, rotation and escalation form 4 points of the source image to 4 points of the destiny image using the Eq. 6. The source points (u, v) are the centroid of the red reference circles and the destiny points are the corners of the output image.

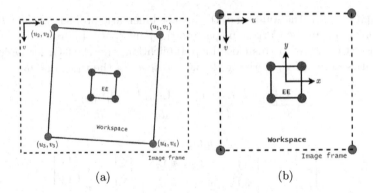

Fig. 3. Workspace calibration of the CDPR with geometric transform. (a) Theoretical image capture performed by the EIH camera. (b) Geometric perspective transformation.

$$\begin{bmatrix} t_i u' \\ t_i v' \\ t_i \end{bmatrix} = \begin{bmatrix} a_1 & 2 & b_1 \\ a_3 & a_4 & b_2 \\ c_1 & c_2 & 1 \end{bmatrix} \begin{bmatrix} u \\ v \\ 1 \end{bmatrix} \tag{6}$$

The reference circles are detected using a HSV threshold filter and morphological operations, specifically dilations and erotions. It results in a binary image with the contours of the circles and their centroid are calculated using the moments of each contour with the Eqs. (7) and (8).

$$M_{ij} = \sum_u \sum_v u^i v^j I(u, v) \tag{7}$$

$$(u, v) = \left(\frac{M_{10}}{M_{00}}, \frac{M_{01}}{M_{00}} \right) \tag{8}$$

Computing Position: In order to compute the height of the EE refereed to a reference plane, the pinhole model of the camera, as shown in Fig. 4, are implemented to obtain a mathematical expression which defines the height of the EE with image features.

This model relates the physical dimension of an object **B** with an image feature i using the relation of the similar triangles as follows:

$$\frac{Z_t}{f} = \frac{B}{i_x} \tag{9}$$

$$\frac{Z_t - Z}{f} = \frac{B}{i'_x} \tag{10}$$

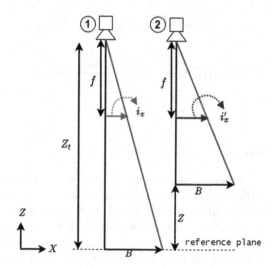

Fig. 4. Spatial relationships of the images obtained by the ETH camera for End-Effector position measurement. Pinhole model of the camera for End-Effector height calculation.

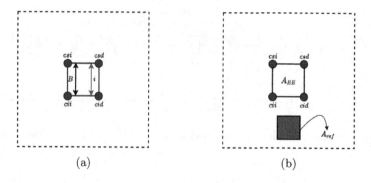

Fig. 5. (a) Relationship between pixels and physical length of the EE for the calculation of the horizontal x and y coordinates. (b) Graphical scheme of the measurement of A_{ref}.

$$i'_x(Z_t - Z) = i_x Z_t \tag{11}$$

$$Z = Z_t(1 - \frac{i_x}{i'_x}) \tag{12}$$

$$Z = Z_t(1 - \sqrt{\frac{A_{ref}}{A_{EE}}}) \tag{13}$$

$$REP = \sqrt{\frac{B^2}{A_{EF}}} \tag{14}$$

$$x = REP(\frac{csd_u + csi_u + cii_u + cid_u}{4}) \tag{15}$$

$$y = REP(\frac{csd_v + csi_v + cii_v + cid_v}{4}) \tag{16}$$

$$\mathbf{Cp} = (x, y, Z - Z_0) \tag{17}$$

2.3   Control System

The closed-loop control is realized from the geometric location of the root. It consists of a proportional controller (C_1) and an open-loop controller (C_2), as illustrated in Fig. 6. The first one corresponds to the control of the EE position in the Cartesian space, whose response or control action is mapped to the joint space by means of first-order inverse kinematics to, subsequently, be the setpoint of the second controller. The latter is in charge of controlling the angular velocity of the actuators, which consequently implies the variation of the cable lengths adjusting the position of the end-effector.

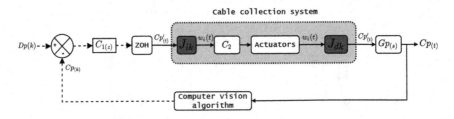

Fig. 6. Block diagram of the servo-vision system implemented in the robot.

3   Results and Discussions

The workspace calibration is presented in Fig. 7a. In this, the vision system detects the red circles, for the calibration of the workspace, and the red reference box for the adjustment of the height Eq. 13. Once the perspective transformation matrix is calculated, it is applied on the image, detecting the end-effector by means of the blue circles attached to the top of it, and its dimensions and position are obtained, as illustrated in Fig. 7b.

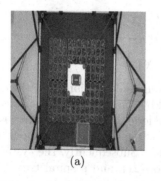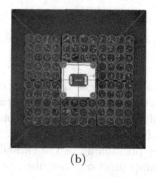

(a)   (b)

Fig. 7. Result obtained from workspace calibration and end-effector detection. (a) Detection of the reference circles and calibration table of the height equation. (b) Perspective transformation, end-effector detection and measurement (L = 150 mm).

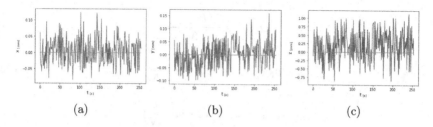

(a)   (b)   (c)

Fig. 8. Result of the end-effector position measurement at Home (0,0,0). (a) X-axis measurement. (b) Y-axis measurement. (c) Z-axis measurement.

The end-effector position measurement is calculated with respect to the robot's home position. For this, the workspace and the height measurement must be previously calibrated. The end-effector is positioned at Home without moving and the readings obtained by the computer vision algorithm are recorded, as shown in Fig. 8. Subsequently, the precision (**P**) and accuracy (**E**) as defined in ISO 5725-1 [6], with the expressions (19) and (18) respectively, are calculated. In these, **VR** represents the desired or reference value, **X** represents one of the coordinates $(\mathbf{x}, \mathbf{y}, \mathbf{z})$ and "$\mathbf{X} - \sigma(\mathbf{X})$ is the standard deviation of the set of readings obtained on the axis. The results obtained for the precision and accuracy for each of the Cartesian axes are presented in Table 2.

Table 2. Accuracy and precision of servo-vision at home position.

Measured axis	Accuracy (mm)	Precision (mm)
x	0.003145	0.041318
y	0.003803	0.050383
z	0.192700	0.444768

$$E = VR - \bar{X} \tag{18}$$

$$P = \sigma(X) \tag{19}$$

The validation of the trajectory tracking and positioning of the end-effector with the servo-vision system is performed by comparing the theoretical response with that obtained from the closed control loop. Initially, the system is subjected to the step function, described in Eq. 20, as the control loop setpoint in order to validate the positioning of the end-effector. Subsequently, the system is tested with the ramp function, described by Eq. (21), and a spiral trajectory, whose expressions are (22), (23) and (24), to validate the trajectory tracking.

$$Dp_{(k)} = \begin{cases} \text{si } kT >= t_1 & B \\ \text{si } kT < t_1 & A \end{cases} \tag{20}$$

$$Dp_{(k)} = \frac{k(B - A)}{N} \tag{21}$$

$$Dp_{x(k)} = r_c cos(2 * pi * \frac{k}{N}) \tag{22}$$

$$Dp_{y(k)} = r_c sin(2 * pi * \frac{k}{N}) \tag{23}$$

$$Dp_{z(k)} = k\frac{Z_{min}}{N} \tag{24}$$

In these expressions, $\mathbf{Dp_{(k)}}$ is the desired position vector or setpoint of the control system, $\mathbf{k}$ is the iteration of the system, $\mathbf{T}$ is the sampling time, $\mathbf{A}$ is the initial position of the EF, $\mathbf{B}$ is the final position, $\mathbf{r_c}$ is the radius of the spiral trajectory and $\mathbf{N}$ is the total number of points of the trajectory to be executed.

The response to the ramp function shows that servo-vision system changes proportionally with time, which translates into straight trajectories. In this case, 6 trajectories, which describe a square, are performed in a single test starting from Home and ending at this same point. The result of this test is shown in Fig. 9. In this it can be seen that the servo-vision system has a very similar response to the theoretical one, presenting an excellent performance in trajectory tracking.

Finally, the results obtained from the performance of the robot in other trajectories are shown. For this test, the servo-vision system is subjected to the elaboration of a cylindrical spiral trajectory, whose result is shown in Fig. 10. Here it can be seen that the servo-vision system is capable of performing this trajectory and whose response is also very similar to the theoretical one.

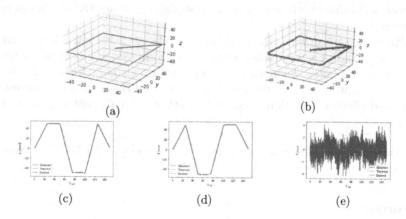

Fig. 9. Response of the servo vision system for tracking a square trajectory: (a) 3D view of the desired trajectory, (b) 3D view of the trajectory described by the end-effector, (c) Response of the motion in x. (d) y motion response, (e) z motion response.

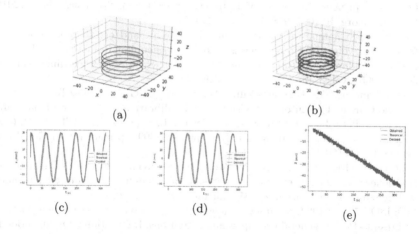

Fig. 10. Response of the servo-vision system for tracking a spiral cylindrical trajectory. (a) 3D view of the desired trajectory (b) 3D view of the trajectory described by the end-effector. (c) Response of the motion in x. (d) Response of the motion in y. (e) Response of the motion in z.

4   Conclusions

In this work, a new method was presented for the position control of a cable-driven parallel robot with 4 degrees of freedom, using a single video camera for the location of the end-effector and stepper motors, obtaining a precision and accuracy of less than 1 mm in the positioning within its workspace, very close to the values obtained with multi-camera systems, which use DC motors of much higher cost.

The vision system was integrated as part of the cascade control loop, allowing to adjust the position of the robot without using other sensors as usually happens in this type of robots. The method decomposes the video into frames and detects the reference circles in blue and red, which improved the accuracy of the robot's frame and effector detection compared to other methods that employ instead squares.

Acknowledgment. This work was supported by project #17-462-INT Universidad de Ibagué.

References

1. Bayani, H., Masouleh, M.T., Kalhor, A.: An experimental study on the vision-based control and identification of planar cable-driven parallel robots. Robot. Auton. Syst. **75**, 187–202 (2016)
2. Chaumette, F., Hutchinson, S., Corke, P.: Visual Servoing. In: Siciliano, B., Khatib, O. (eds.) Springer Handbook of Robotics, pp. 841–866. Springer, Cham (2016). https://doi.org/10.1007/978-3-319-32552-1_34
3. Flandin, G., Chaumette, F., Marchand, E.: Eye-in-hand/eye-to-hand cooperation for visual servoing. In: Proceedings 2000 ICRA. Millennium Conference. IEEE International Conference on Robotics and Automation. Symposia Proceedings (Cat. No. 00CH37065). vol. 3, pp. 2741–2746. IEEE (2000)
4. García-Vanegas, A., Liberato-Tafur, B., Forero, M.G., Gonzalez-Rodríguez, A., Castillo-García, F.: Automatic vision based calibration system for planar cable-driven parallel robots. In: Morales, A., Fierrez, J., Sánchez, J.S., Ribeiro, B. (eds.) Pattern Recognition and Image Analysis, pp. 600–609. Springer International Publishing, Cham (2019)
5. Gonzalez-Rodriguez, A., Castillo-Garcia, F., Ottaviano, E., Rea, P., Gonzalez-Rodriguez, A.: On the effects of the design of cable-driven robots on kinematics and dynamics models accuracy. Mechatronics **43**, 18–27 (2017)
6. ISO: ISO 5725–1: 1994: accuracy (trueness and precision) of measurement methods and results-Part 1: general principles and definitions. International Organization for Standardization (1994)
7. Pott, A.: Cable-Driven Parallel Robots. STAR, vol. 120. Springer, Cham (2018). https://doi.org/10.1007/978-3-319-76138-1
8. Taherian, A., Mazinan, A.H., Aliyari-Shoorehdeli, M.: Image-based visual servoing improvement through utilization of adaptive control gain and pseudo-inverse of the weighted mean of the jacobians. Comput. Electr. Eng. **83**, 106580 (2020)

Medical Applications of Pattern Recognition

OSLeD-wA: A One-Stage Lesion Detection Method with Attention Mechanisms

Sebastián Rascón-Cervantes[1], Graciela Ramírez-Alonso[1(✉)] (ID),
Juan Ramírez-Quintana[2] (ID), Manuel Montes-y-Gómez[3] (ID),
and Roberto López-Santillán[1] (ID)

[1] Facultad de Ingeniería, Universidad Autónoma de Chihuahua, Chihuahua, Mexico
{p281831,galonso,jrlopez}@uach.mx
[2] PVR Lab, Tecnológico Nacional de México/IT, Chihuahua, Chihuahua, Mexico
juan.rq@chihuahua.tecnm.mx
[3] Instituto Nacional de Astrofísica Óptica y Electrónica, Puebla, Mexico
mmontesg@inaoep.mx

Abstract. The detection of lesions from computed tomography scans is an important and nontrivial task in medical diagnosis. The difficulty of this task is related to the medical data where the appearance of different organs and lesions is not easily distinguished from the background. This paper proposes a One-Stage Lesion Detection method named OSLeD-wA. OSLeD-wA is based on the EfficientDet detector incorporating attention mechanisms to enhance the feature maps activations by combining channel and spatial information in different parts of the detector. In addition, the Cut-and-Paste data augmentation strategy was considered in the training of OSLeD-wA, demonstrating that contextual image information is not crucial in detecting lesions; it is more relevant to implement strategies where new lesions could be generated. OSLeD-wA achieves competitive results on the DeepLesion dataset when compared against recent strategies developed to deal with incomplete annotated datasets.

Keywords: One-stage-detector · Medical lesion · Attention mechanism · Cut-and-paste

1 Introduction

Although there is a large volume of research related to convolutional neural networks (CNNs) in image object recognition, the task of automatically detecting medical lesions from computed tomography (CT) scans is still very challenging [6]. Small lesion size, slight inter-class variation, and similarity appearance between the object of interest and background are some of the issues that may affect the correct detection of lesions [11]. It is well known that this medical task demands extensive clinical expertise [14]. For a radiologist, it is customary to

O. O. Vergara-Villegas et al. (Eds.): MCPR 2022, LNCS 13264, pp. 305–315, 2022.
https://doi.org/10.1007/978-3-031-07750-0_28

analyze different CT scans of a patient to find lesions and describe these findings in a radiological report [4]. This task is often tedious and time-consuming, especially, detecting small lesions is one of the most laborious processes for clinicians. Lesions areas are often inconspicuous and cannot be seen clearly with a visual inspection. Moreover, the characteristics of lesions at different human organs are disparate and vary from person to person. The idea behind computational automatic lesion detection methods is to alleviate radiologists workload in locating abnormal findings [1,6].

Most of the CNN methods that automatically detect lesions from CT scans are based on two-stage detectors [7]. The first stage is trained to identify different region proposals, commonly known as the Region Proposal Network (RPN). The second stage is trained to detect and recognize the objects in the previously identified image regions. On the other hand, one-stage detectors do not have the RPN structure, they directly predict all the bounding boxes in one pass of the network. As a result, the two-stage strategy has demonstrated to obtain high accuracy results outperforming one-stage detectors at the cost of high computational complexity with a non-real-time application [7].

In order to develop a computational method that can help radiologists with their daily workload, it is preferred to propose faster and better one-stage detectors with the aim to meet near real-time performance. For this reason, we focus our investigation on using one-stage detectors but at the same time taking care of achieving competent results. In this sense, EfficientDet [10] is a family of one-stage object detectors ranging from EfficientDet-D0 to EfficientDet-D7 that reports state-of-the-art performance with natural images and a reduced computational complexity, which also employs much fewer parameters compared with other methods. However, as far as we know, EfficientDet has not been used in medical tasks. For this reason, we consider important to analyze how it behaves in the automatic detection of lesions from CT scans.

One of the main problems to tackle in medical datasets is that the annotation labels are incomplete; not all the lesions on the CT scans were enclosed by a radiologist, only the most remarkable ones. Because this is not a trivial task, the correct way to have more annotations in the dataset is by consulting a certified radiologist. Unfortunately, this is not easy. A common strategy to increment this annotation information is by using data augmentation strategies such as random flip, random scaling, cropping, and color jittering, achieving improvements on detection tasks [6].

In this paper, we propose a novel one-stage lesion detection neural network architecture named OSLeD-wA based on EfficientDet. This network was enhanced by incorporating channel and spatial attention mechanisms to improve the discriminant capability of the feature maps. OSLeD-wA was validated with DeepLesion, the largest dataset for universal lesion detection tasks. A very interesting finding is that the performance of our proposal increased by using a non-contextual data augmentation strategy based on the Cut-and-Paste mechanism. That means that maintaining the context of the lesion is not as important as generating more data for this particular computer vision task.

2 Related Work

The neural network structure of one-stage detectors is commonly defined by four basic elements: *input, backbone, neck,* and *head.* The *input* refers to the image input processing. The *backbone* is commonly composed of a CNN model pre-trained with ImageNet used to extract features at different scales. Then, the *neck* comprises a set of layers with a combination of top-down and bottom-up connections to fuse features on different scales. Finally, the *head* element is the object detection module that determines the class of objects in an image and predicts their location.

There are few works related to one-stage methods focused on detecting medical lesions in images. Take for instance the work of Lung et al. in [7], where they proposed ROSNet, a nested structure of neural networks that uses the VGG16 network as the backbone. It is worth noting their feature fusion module combined with six nested U-shape neural modules and a multi-level feature pyramid network, which are coupled as the *neck* to extract detailed information. Finally, a re-weighting module improves an initial detection and produces the final result. ROSNet achieved a mean average precision (mAP) of 0.627 with the DeepLesion dataset. Another example is the study of Cai et al. [1], which presented a 3D Context Feature Fusion network, 3DCFF. First, the 3DCFF uses as backbone the Darknet-53 network and different residual layers are integrated to extract features at three different resolutions. Then, the non-maximum suppression algorithm analyzes these outputs and defines the prediction. 3DCFF was trained with the DeepLesion dataset on an NVIDIA 1080Ti GPU, achieving a mAP of 0.649. Finally, MLANet [6] is another one-stage detector trained with the DeepLesion dataset. MLANet combines three Mixed Hourglass Networks as backbones, a Multi-Scale Feature Pyramid Network as *neck*, and a Center-to-Corner transformation as output *head.* Each Hourglass Network is a fully convolutional neural network with an encoder-decoder architecture and residual blocks that extracts information at different scales. MLANet was trained on two NVIDIA GTX 2080Ti with a batch size of 10, achieving 0.883 in the sensitivity metric and 0.65 in mAP.

As can be observed, a common strategy implemented on one-stage detectors is the increasing of the depth of the network by coupling or nesting many times similar modules. On the contrary, EfficientDet proposes a compound scaling method that scales uniformly the resolution, depth, and width of its neural architecture [10]. EfficientDet-D0 is the base detector of this family, and it was designed to combine particular features extracted in the backbone with a new weighted bi-directional feature pyramid network (BiFPN) used as the *neck.* Because EfficientDet-D0 is the network architecture with fewer parameters in this family, we based our research on it.

3 OSLeD-wA Method Description

Our one-stage lesion detector method, OSLeD-wA, incorporates attention mechanisms on the EfficientDet architecture to increase the network's capability of selecting relevant features responses for lesion detection tasks. Channel attention resolves "what" to focus on, whereas spatial attention resolves "where" to focus on [5]. In total, five channel and spatial attention mechanisms were incorporated in the input of the BiFPN layer by considering the work in [9]. In order to reduce false positive detections, three spatial attention mechanisms were also included in the classification head branch. A 3D context approach is used in the input layer to consider a multi-resolution scheme. Also, the Cut-and-Paste data augmentation strategy was implemented in order to increase the number of data in our experiments. Figure 1 shows the block diagram of our method proposal, OSLeD-wA.

3.1   Input Processing: 3D Context Fusion

A CT study is composed of a set of images or slices per patient. The set of slices is defined as $s = \{s_1, s_2, ..., s_n\}$, where the value of n is related to the number of images and may be different for each study. In a medical database used to validate object detector methods, the slice that contains the annotation information (position and type of the lesion) varies in the volume of slices; that is, it could be in the extremes s_1 or s_n, or in any intermediate s_{n-i}. In OSLeD-wA, a 3D context fusion is used on the input stage. This process consists of taking the neighboring images closest to the lesion that contains the annotation as follows:

1. Given an image on the database that contains the annotation information s_i, the anterior s_{i-1} and posterior s_{i+1} images are selected.

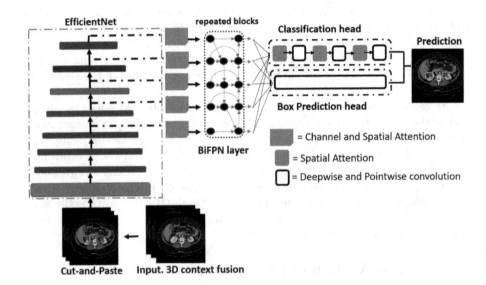

Fig. 1. OSLeD-wA. Block diagram of our proposal.

2. If the image with the annotation information is at the beginning or the end of the CT, it would only have one neighbor, so the image with the annotation is considered twice. That is, if $s_i = s_1$ or $s_i = s_n$, then $s_{i-1} = s_i$ or $s_{i+1} = s_i$.
3. These 3 images are merged as $[s_{i-1}, s_i, s_{i+1}]$

3.2 Data Augmentation: Cut-and-Paste

Horizontal flip is the most common strategy found in literature when performing data augmentation in medical imaging [15]. In the horizontal flip strategy, the pixels are reflected in the y-axis, making it necessary to modify the annotation file that defines the bounding box coordinates of the objects.

Cut-and-Paste is a strategy that has been used successfully in segmentation and classification tasks [3]. This method mainly consists of taking the space of the bounding box that contains the lesion and placing it in another region of the image. The process that we followed is described below:

– For each image, the original coordinates of the bounding box (x_1, y_1, x_2, y_2) that enclose the lesion are located.
– Three possible movements for lesions are established: movement in x, movement in y and movement in x, y in such a way that the new positions of the lesions are inside the body region.
– Each image has a 40% probability of moving in x, 40% of moving in y and 20% of moving in x, y.
– According to the type of movement, one section of the original scan is replaced with the pixel information of the lesion. In addition, the corresponding annotations are generated.

Figure 2 shows an example of this process. The red rectangle encloses the original lesion, and the new positions are defined by the blue rectangles depending on the movement in x, y or x, y. For this particular case, the new coordinates of the bounding boxes are described in Table 1.

Table 1. Cut-and-Paste implementation.

x movement	y movement	x, y movement
$x_1^{new} = c - x_2$	$x_1^{new} = x_1$	$x_1^{new} = c - x_2$
$x_2^{new} = c - x_1$	$x_2^{new} = x_2$	$x_2^{new} = c - x_1$
$y_1^{new} = y_1$	$y_1^{new} = r - y_2$	$y_1^{new} = r - y_2$
$y_2^{new} = y_2$	$y_2^{new} = r - y_1$	$y_2^{new} = r - y_1$

$x_{1,2}^{new}$ and $y_{1,2}^{new}$ correspond to the new bounding box positions, c and r represent the number of columns and rows in the original image. We consider this strategy non-contextual because the lesion can be positioned in a different part of the body not preserving the original contextual information. For example, if a lesion is originally located on the abdomen, this Cut-and-Paste strategy will use the same original image, but the lesion could be positioned in the stomach, spleen, or liver.

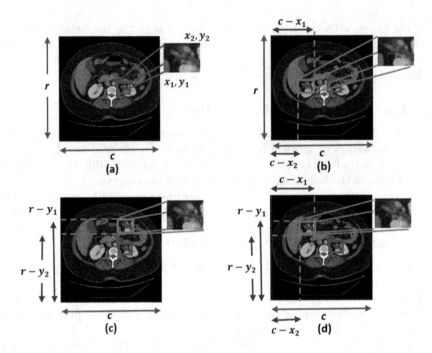

Fig. 2. Cut-and-paste exemplification. (a) Original image. (b) x movement. (c) y movement. (d) x, y movement.

3.3　Attention Mechanisms

Our proposal employs channel and spatial attention mechanisms in the input of the BiFPN layer and in the classification head branch. Eqs. 1 and 2 define them formally.

$$Ch_A(F) = \sigma(MLP(AvgPool(F)) + MLP(MaxPool(F)) \tag{1}$$

$$Sp_A(F) = \sigma(f^{7\times7}([AvgPool(F); MaxPool(F)])) \tag{2}$$

where Ch_A and Sp_A is the channel and spatial attention respectively, σ denotes the sigmoid activation function, F represents an intermediate feature map, MLP denotes a multi-layer perceptron network with one hidden layer, $+$ represents element-wise summation, and $f^{7\times7}$ represents a convolution operation with a filter size of 7×7 [12].

4　Experimental Settings and Results

The DeepLesion dataset, published by the National Institutes of Health (NIH), contains 32,120 axial CT slices from 10,594 CT scans of 4,427 unique patients. It has 27,289 train and validation slices and 4,831 test ones. DeepLesion includes eight types of lesions: lung, mediastinum, liver, soft tissue, pelvis, abdomen, kidney, and bone. One inconvenience of DeepLesion is that not all lesions in every slice were annotated; this is because radiologists generally only identify one representative lesion in each scan in their routine work [14].

Our proposal was implemented in PyTorch. We employed an NVIDIA Titan RTX GPU with 24 GB of memory. A batch size of *one* was considered for training. The *Adamw* solver was used with an initial learning rate of 1e–4 and an early stopping strategy. Finally, the EfficientNet backbone was initialized with an ImageNet pre-trained model. After data augmentation, the total number of annotations to train and validate the method increase to 54,578, a new annotation was created for each original slice. Nine different implementations were tested to evaluate whether or not attention mechanisms and contextual data augmentation strategies were useful. We also experimented with specific data-partitions where only small, hardest-to-detect, or lesions with few samples are used. Table 2 presents the results by considering the sensitivity metric defined by $sensitivity = TP/(TP + FN)$. TP stands for True Positive and FN for False Negative detection. A TP detection is produced when the Intersection over Union is greater than 0.5 ($IoU \geq 0.5$), whereas a FN is produced when the method could not detect a lesion. The sensitivity metric is commonly used in medical analysis because it refers to the method's ability to correctly detect lesions in patients who do have the condition.

The best configuration of Table 2 is EfficientDet-D0 with channel and spatial attention mechanisms in five levels of the backbone and spatial attention mechanisms in the classification *head*. A general *Cut-and-Paste* data augmentation strategy obtained the best performance; that is, it is not necessary to emphasize on specific data. Even when the *Cut-and-Paste* strategy does not preserve context information, for a computer vision perspective, this information might not be as relevant as having a higher number of images to train on.

Table 2. Sensitivity results of the different implementations.

Experiment	Sensitivity
EfficientDet-D0 + Attention Mechanisms + Cut-and-Paste	0.73
EfficientDet-D0 + Cut-and-Paste	0.70
EfficientDet-D0 + Cut-and-Paste + horizontal Flip	0.70
EfficientDet-D0 + horizontal Flip	0.68
EfficientDet-D0 + Attention Mechanisms + Cut-and-Paste in small, abdomen, pelvis, bone, and soft tissue lesions	0.66
EfficientDet-D0 + Attention Mechanisms + horizontal Flip	0.63
EfficientDet-D0 + Attention Mechanisms + Cut-and-Paste in small, abdomen, and pelvis lesions	0.60
EfficientDet-D0 + Attention Mechanisms + horizontal Flip + Cut-and-Paste in small, abdomen, pelvis, bone, and soft tissue lesions	0.55
EfficientDet-D0	0.52

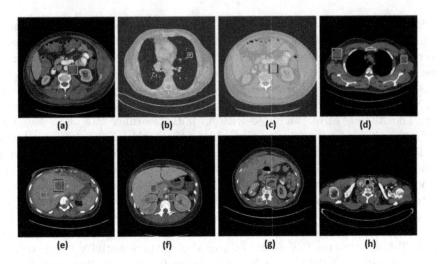

Fig. 3. Detection results of OSLeD-wA. (a) and (b) show lesions correctly detected. (c), (d), (e), (f), and (g) present a correct and incorrect detection. (h) shows an example of an incorrect detection.

Some qualitative results obtained with OSLeD-wA, are shown in Fig. 3. The blue rectangles indicate the bounding box annotations, and the green rectangles show the predictions of OSLeD-wA. Figure 3(a) and (b) show detections that overlap with the bounding box, (c), (d), (e), (f), and (g) present a correct detection accompanied by an incorrect one, and (h) shows an incorrect detection. By carefully analyzing these predictions, it is possible to observe that some regions predicted as lesions have a very similar appearance to those containing the annotated lesion, which could indicate that it may be a lesion, but it was not the most significant one.

Table 3 presents sensitivity results of OSLeD-wA and state-of-the-art methods with the DeepLesion dataset. The FPs column refers to the False Positive detections per image considered by the authors, and the GPU column indicates the hardware used on their implementations.

As previously stated, MLANet achieved the best mAP performance reported by one-stage detectors with the DeepLesion dataset. MLANet, also reported a sensitivity of 0.883. Therefore, MLANet obtained better performance than

Table 3. Sensitivity results of OSLeD-wA-D0 and state-of-the-art methods.

Author	FPs	Sensitivity	GPU
MLANet [6]	4	0.883	2 GTX 2080Ti
OSLeD-wA	**7**	**0.73**	Titan RTX
Lesion Harvester [2]	8	0.74	3 RTX6000
Lyu et al. [8]	8	0.698	Not specified

OSLeD-wA. An important difference between these two implementations is the batch size used on the training, MLANet uses a batch size of *ten*, and OSLeD-wA has a batch size of *one* because of hardware limitations. This hardware capability is directly related to the metric performance. Unfortunately, the other one-stage detectors do not report their sensitivity results. OSLeD-wA was also compared with recent detectors developed to deal with incomplete annotated datasets [2] and [8]. Cai et al. [2] proposed a Lesion-Harvester strategy with the collaboration of a certified radiologist. Their proposal uses a combination of the CenterNet and, the best published two-stage medical detector method to date, MULAN [13] by using a 9-slice volume of images as inputs. Lyu et al. [8] presented a neural architecture where a semantic segmentation branch improves the detection results. In both implementations, the data partition was reduced because of the extra annotated information from a board-certified radiologist. The sensitivity results achieved with OSLeD-wA surpass one of the detectors and is very close to the other one.

5 Conclusions

In this study, we presented a one-stage lesion detection method named OSLeD-wA. OSLeD-wA incorporates channel and spatial attention mechanisms on the original EfficientDet detector with a non-contextual data augmentation strategy. The attention mechanisms improved the capability to select relevant features that helps in the identification of medical lesions by automatically selecting "what" and "where" to focus on. With the implementation of the non-contextual Cut-and-Paste strategy, our proposal increase in 18% the sensitivity results.

The qualitative results obtained with OSLeD-wA, show that the detection of lesions is fairly accurate in applications where a possible lesion must be detected. It also indicates where the doctor must pay attention to analyze in detail these regions and confirm or discard them. Particularly in this dataset, the false positive detections may correspond to lesions.

By comparing OSLeD-wA with state-of-the-art methods, it was found that it could not surpass the best one-stage detector, but this could be directly related to the hardware capability; an increase in batch size can improve the training and detection results. A fair comparative study must consider the same GPU hardware. When comparing with recent strategies developed to deal with incomplete datasets, OSLeD-wA surpasses one of them. The non-contextual Cut-and-Paste strategy was of great importance to achieve these results.

In the future, we will further our research by analyzing in more detail the feature maps and possibly reduce the number of parameters without affecting the sensitivity performance. None of the methods developed to detect lesions on images reported the number of parameters of their proposal. It would be interesting to perform a comparison of methods considering this criterion instead of classifying them on one or two-stage detectors if they are intended for use by the medical community.

314   S. Rascón-Cervantes et al.

Acknowledgements. The authors would like to thank CONACYT for scholarship No. 745939.

References

1. Cai, G., Chen, J., Wu, Z., Tang, H., Liu, Y., Wang, S., Su, S.: One stage lesion detection based on 3D context convolutional neural networks. Comput. Electr. Eng. **79**, 106449 (2019)
2. Cai, J., Harrison, A.P., Zheng, Y., Yan, K., Huo, Y., Xiao, J., Yang, L., Lu, L.: Lesion-harvester: iteratively mining unlabeled lesions and hard-negative examples at scale. IEEE T. Med Imaging **40**(1), 59–70 (2021)
3. Dwibedi, D., Misra, I., Hebert, M.: Cut, paste and learn: surprisingly easy synthesis for instance detection. In: IEEE ICCV, pp. 1301–1310 (2017)
4. Jin, D., Harrison, A.P., Zhang, L., Yan, K., Wang, Y., Cai, J., Miao, S., Lu, L.: Artificial intelligence in radiology. In: Artif. Intell. Med., pp. 265–289. Elsevier (2020)
5. Li, W., Liu, K., Zhang, L., Cheng, F.: Object detection based on an adaptive attention mechanism. Sci. Rep. **10**(1), 1–13 (2020)
6. Liu, Z., Xie, X., Song, Y., Zhang, Y., Liu, X., Zhang, J., Sheng, V.S.: MLANet: multi-layer anchor-free network for generic lesion detection. Eng. Appl. Artif. Intell. **102**, 104255 (2021)
7. Lung, K.Y., Chang, C.R., Weng, S.E., Lin, H.S., Shuai, H.H., Cheng, W.H.: ROS-Net: robust one-stage network for CT lesion detection. Pattern Recogn. Lett. **144**, 82–88 (2021)
8. Lyu, F., Yang, B., Ma, A.J., Yuen, P.C.: A segmentation-assisted model for universal lesion detection with partial labels. In: de Bruijne, M., Cattin, P.C., Cotin, S., Padoy, N., Speidel, S., Zheng, Y., Essert, C. (eds.) MICCAI 2021. LNCS, vol. 12905, pp. 117–127. Springer, Cham (2021). https://doi.org/10.1007/978-3-030-87240-3_12
9. Shao, Q., Gong, L., Ma, K., Liu, H., Zheng, Y.: Attentive CT lesion detection using deep pyramid inference with multi-scale booster. In: Shen, D., Liu, T., Peters, T.M., Staib, L.H., Essert, C., Zhou, S., Yap, P.-T., Khan, A. (eds.) MICCAI 2019. LNCS, vol. 11769, pp. 301–309. Springer, Cham (2019). https://doi.org/10.1007/978-3-030-32226-7_34
10. Tan, M., Pang, R., Le, Q.V.: EfficientDet. scalable and efficient object detection. In: 2020 IEEE CVPR, pp. 10778–10787 (2020)
11. Tao, Q., Ge, Z., Cai, J., Yin, J., See, S.: Improving deep lesion detection using 3D contextual and spatial attention. In: Shen, D., Liu, T., Peters, T.M., Staib, L.H., Essert, C., Zhou, S., Yap, P.-T., Khan, A. (eds.) MICCAI 2019. LNCS, vol. 11769, pp. 185–193. Springer, Cham (2019). https://doi.org/10.1007/978-3-030-32226-7_21
12. Woo, S., Park, J., Lee, J.-Y., Kweon, I.S.: CBAM: convolutional block attention module. In: Ferrari, V., Hebert, M., Sminchisescu, C., Weiss, Y. (eds.) ECCV 2018. LNCS, vol. 11211, pp. 3–19. Springer, Cham (2018). https://doi.org/10.1007/978-3-030-01234-2_1
13. Yan, K., Tang, Y., Peng, Y., Sandfort, V., Bagheri, M., Lu, Z., Summers, R.M.: MULAN: multitask universal lesion analysis network for joint lesion detection, tagging, and segmentation. In: Shen, D., Liu, T., Peters, T.M., Staib, L.H., Essert, C., Zhou, S., Yap, P.-T., Khan, A. (eds.) MICCAI 2019. LNCS, vol. 11769, pp. 194–202. Springer, Cham (2019). https://doi.org/10.1007/978-3-030-32226-7_22

14. Yan, K., et al.: Deep lesion graphs in the wild: relationship learning and organization of significant radiology image findings in a diverse large-scale lesion database. In: 2018 IEEE CVPR, pp. 9261–9270 (2018)
15. Zhang, H., Chen, Y., Song, Y., Xiong, Z., Yang, Y., Wu, Q.J.: Automatic kidney lesion detection for CT images using morphological cascade convolutional neural networks. IEEE Access **7**, 83001–83011 (2019)

Detection of Pain Caused by a Thermal Stimulus Using EEG and Machine Learning

Rogelio Sotero Reyes-Galaviz[(✉)] [ID], Omar Mendoza-Montoya [ID], and Javier M. Antelis [ID]

School of Engineering and Sciences, Tecnologico de Monterrey, 64849 Monterrey, NL, Mexico
a00834264@tec.mx

Abstract. Pain is a subjective feeling difficult to explain since it depends on the history, sexuality, cultural and social context of each person, and worsens its communication in cases of people with certain motor or language diseases. In this research the pain response of 6 healthy participants is studied using an electroencephalographic device. To have a first approach to the problem and a clearer understanding of the pain response, a non-traumatic thermal stimuli is used, which simulates phasic pain that is known for being gradual. The use of machine learning is important to find a discrimination model among 3 conditions proposed (pre-stimulus, beginning of the stimuli and intolerance to the stimuli) and the EEG data recorded. Different machine learning models found a solid distinction between the 3 different conditions in the case of the 4 males. Females could not be classified since the stimulus does not generate any kind of pain to them.

Keywords: Electroencephalography · Machine learning · Pain · Bandpower · Qualia

1 Introduction

Pain is known for being a vital but unpleasant sensation that demands immediate attention, disrupts ongoing behavior and distortions the thought [14]. The traditional theory used to call it an affective quale [5,7] for the affective and sensory behavior when it is perceived [20]. Qualia are defined as subjective experiences linked to the believes of the subject about some stimulus instead of the real experiencing of it, some examples are pain, the taste of some beverage/food or the definition of the color of the sunset [3,9,10]. This means that the same qualia applied to different subjects will provoke a completely different response. This said, it is interesting how pain affects each of us taking in count the history, sexuality, and sociocultural context besides the physiological response [13], but this increases the problem of how to detect or quantify it.

O. O. Vergara-Villegas et al. (Eds.): MCPR 2022, LNCS 13264, pp. 316–327, 2022.
https://doi.org/10.1007/978-3-031-07750-0_29

Nowadays the most common way to assess if a person is experiencing pain is with self-report pain scales, which are pretty unreliable [2]. For people with communication problems or specific disabilities, it is complex to communicate it and almost impossible to quantify it. This is a big opportunity for computational novel methods to detect and quantify pain using biosignals and machine learning methods as a solution. Knowing that pain behavior triggers a series of biochemical reactions that go from the damaged tissues or organs to the spinal cord and culminate in the brain to give a rapid alarm response to the whole body, it is of interest to record the brain signal and observe brain behavior in response to pain stimuli. Currently, there are many articles demonstrating that it is possible to obtain useful information with electroencephalography to detect pain and quantify this biosignal using machine learning techniques [8,15,19,23,24,26,28]. In contrast, this research uses another type of phasic pain stimulus, due to the lack of a pain response using some thermal stimulus described in the articles and for complications with the controlled temperature of the stimulus.

Electroencephalography records the electrical activity of the brain caused from the neuronal interaction, these signals are obtained with electrodes positioned in certain zones of the scalp and due to its non-invasive nature it is used widely in medical and engineering research fields [17,18,22].

2 Materials and Methods

The current study has the intention to find a significant relation among 3 conditions related to the pain response caused by a controlled non-traumatic thermal stimulus in healthy participants. If it is possible to discriminate between the 3 conditions, a broader analysis of these signals is intended to find out what is happening in the brain when going through such an experience. This study was held in the Neuro Technology Laboratory (NTLab) at the Instituto Tecnológico de Estudios Superiores de Monterrey. Before each experiment an informed consent letter was given to the participants and all the protocol was explained clearly.

2.1 Experimental Protocol

The experiment has been carried out with the support of 6 healthy subjects (2 females and 4 males with an average age of 23) who were exposed to a controlled and non-invasive pain stimulus. This stimulus is similar as the Cold Pressure Test (CPT) used by many researches [1,6,8,16] but instead of using cold water as a stimulant, an ice block was applied.

A thermal stimulus was used since the pain to be studied is of the phasic type, which is usually gradual over time while the stimulus is present, as opposed to tonic pain, which is felt as stabbing and disappears even if the stimulus continues affecting. This change was done because the lack of pain response using the normal CPT with the participants due that water can vary its temperature over time when the hand is in it, the use of a block of ice allows to have a better control of its temperature, that must be bellow $0\,^{\circ}C$. When the block of ice is starting to melt this one is changed for a new one. The subjects were asked to sit in front of a screen which showed the instructions for the experiments. There were 3 instructions:

- **+:** This cross is used to advice the participant to focus on it and try to relax before the experiment begins. This task lasts 10 s and is done to obtain the prestimulus response of the brain.
- **On Ice:** The hand is placed on the ice block and is retired whenever the subject wants. This instruction lasts 40 s for men and 2 min for women.
- **Rest:** After the On Ice instruction, this is the last advice. Here, the participant rests for 10 s and then the experiment ends.

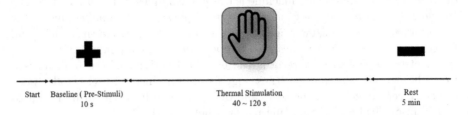

Start	Baseline (Pre-Stimuli)	Thermal Stimulation	Rest
	10 s	40 ~ 120 s	5 min

Fig. 1. Time lapse of experimental protocol that was applied 5 times per hand for each subject.

This is the example of one trial of EEG recording. Each subject repeats this procedure 5 times per hand. Between trials there is a resting time of 2–5 min depending of the subject response to low temperatures. In this resting time, a verbal questionnaire is applied to each subject to know if they are feeling a pain. If subjects are not responding to pain, as is the case for most women, the signals are discarded. A time lapse explaining this experimental protocol can be found in Fig. 1.

This experiment has the intention to cause a response to pain with gradual behavior, which allows to take different segments of the EEG signal from the moment the experiment begins until the hand is removed from the ice to have enough information and be able to discriminate between the 3 proposed conditions (prestimulus, beginning of stimulus, end of stimulus).

Most subjects do not last the 40 s of the On-Ice window, so they withdraw their hand earlier and can use the remaining time to rest. This is due to the fact that each subject has a different reaction time to the stimulus.

To have a controlled time of the events, a camera is recording all the experiment and a UNIX timestamp is running on the video to synchronize all the events as shown in Fig. 2.

2.2   Data Collection

For data collection, a high-performance neuroscience research system was used, the g.USBamp by g.Tec. This device is USB enabled and supports 16 simultaneously sampled bio-signal channels and a total of 4 independent grounds guarantee that there is no interference between the recorded signals. 16 channels were placed following the 10/20 international protocol around the scalp (Fp1, Fp2, F3, Fz, F4, T7, C3, Cz, C4, T8, P3, Pz, P4, PO7, PO8, Oz). This architecture is used because it is not clear which areas act on pain responses and is important to have a general overview of the brain. 16 channels are used to short the time of application of the sensor. The sampling rate was set to 256 Hz and a notch filter of 60 Hz is used to avoid electrical artifacts.

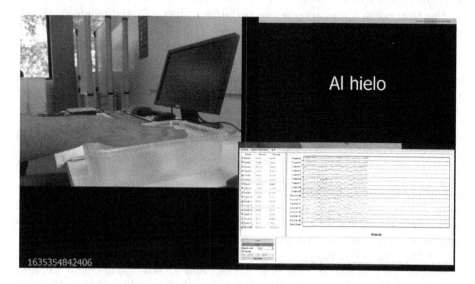

Fig. 2. Example of the photographs recorded while the experiment was going on. These photographs contain the images of the webcam recording the experiment, the screen of the tasks, the unix timestamp and the signal recorded.

For the pre-processing and feature extraction sections MATLAB R2021a was used.

2.3 Pre-processing

As mentioned before, each subject recording is composed of 10 repetitions of the experiment, 5 per hand. Every trial has the information of the 16 channels recorded. The process explained in this section is applied to every channel of every trial recorded.

Pre-processing is applied to the raw data to clean it and to prepare the data for the feature extraction section. In this step a Butterworth bandpass filter from 2 to 80 Hz is applied. This frequency range is defined in order to have the information of all the frequency bands of interest. The frequency bands of interest are Delta (2–4 Hz), Theta (4.1–8 Hz), Alpha (8.1–12 Hz), Beta (12.5, 31) and Gamma (31.1–80 Hz).

The filtered data is now prepared to be sectioned into 3 conditions. Due to the nature of the experiment, each sampled subject has different duration times with the hand on ice, but all have the same 10 s of pre-stimulus. It is of interest to have the 3 conditions to extract characteristics. These are the first 5 s of pre-stimulus as condition 0 (when the cross is on the screen) the first 3 s that the hand is placed on the ice as condition 1 and the last 3 s before removing the hand due to intolerance to the pain generated as condition 2 as shown in Fig. 3. For this procedures it is necessary to watch the videos recorded and take note of the time when these actions are performed. Specially the condition 1 and condition 2.

Even when the raw data was filtered, some noise or artifacts (how they are known in the signal processing field) are still present. To solve this problem and at the same time have more information for classification, every condition is divided into 0.5 s windows and every window will be analyzed to known if that section of the signal is an artifact or not as shown in the Eq. 1 and 2.

$$V_e^{(pp)} > 100 \tag{1}$$

$$\sigma_e > 50 \tag{2}$$

where Eq. 1 means that the voltage peak-to-peak of each electrode (channel) must not exceed 100 mV and the Eq. 2 means that the standard deviation of each electrode should be below 50. If this 2 conditions are true, the window is tagged as an artifact and discarded.

At the end of the pre-processing stage, there should be a 3D matrix of 16 channels, 128 samples (0.5 s of information) and a certain number of windows without artifacts which is variable depending of the quality of the recording. The ideal number of windows should be 10 for condition 0 and 6 for condition 1 and 2.

Fig. 3. Three conditions of interest. On the left the pre-stimulus state (0). In the middle the first 3 s of the hand on ice (1). On the right the last 3 s before removing the hand of the ice (2).

2.4   Feature Extraction

The power band summarizes the contribution or appearance of a specific frequency band in the overall frequency band. This is done by calculating the power spectral density, a specific number which is useful for machine learning applications where one wishes to extract key features that summarize a particular aspect of the data [27]. A band-pass filter is used on the signal to obtain a frequency band of interest, then the resulting filtered signal is squared to obtain an estimate of the power spectral density (PSD) of the signal and finally averaging it over time, in windows of 0.5 s or 10 s windows depending on the study [11].

The MATLAB command *bandpower* decomposes the area under the periodogram curve (PSD) into multiple rectangles and then adds them. This function allows us to know the absolute power of each of the frequency bands that we want to obtain. In Fig. 4 the whole process is summarized.

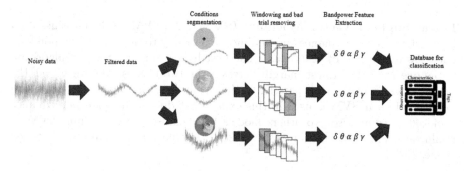

Fig. 4. Protocol of the data processing including pre-processing and feature extraction. All the processes described are applied to every channel of all the hand repetitions recorded.

For this work, the power of 5 frequency bands is calculated for every window. Delta (2–4 Hz), Theta (4.1–8 Hz), Alpha (8.1–12 Hz), Beta (12.5–31) and Gamma (31.1–80 Hz). Having a matrix of 80 components, 5 per channel by a certain number of trials.

2.5   Classification

At the end of the data processing stage, the features extracted are organized in a matrix of 80 characteristics (5 features for each one of the 16 channels) by a certain number of observations (trials) depending on how many were removed in the bad trial removing step. So, the last database has 80 columns of characteristics and 1 column of tags numbered by the type of condition (0, 1, 2) by a certain number of rows which are composed by all the good trials of the hand repetitions (left, right or together). These structures are for each subject recorded.

To achieve a discrimination between the 3 conditions, the Classification Learner application of MATLAB is used. It contains predefined models to train and classify the data using supervised machine learning, statistics and a Machine Learning Toolbox. The databases for each subject are between 180–200 observations for both hands and between 90–100 for each hand. This said, a cross-validation of 5 folds is used. The different models used for this database are:

Linear Discriminant Analysis (LDA). Discriminant analysis a classification algorithm widely used because of its easy interpretation, precision and speed. For big data sets is very functional. A Linear Discriminant Analysis is used in the present work. LDA makes the assumption that nonidentical Gaussian distributions are generated by different classes. The process to train these classifiers is that the fitting function calculates the parameters of a Gaussian distribution for each class and build linear boundaries between classes [25].

Linear Support Vector Machines (SVM). An SVM model classifies data by constructing hyperplanes and finding the best way to segregate data points of one class from those of other class. The best hyperplane in the SVM algorithm is the one with the largest margin between the two classes. Margin means the maximal width of the slab parallel to the hyperplane that has no interior data points. A Linear SVM is used in this experiment due to the good performance achieved in comparison to others models like Quadratic SVM, Cubic SVM or nonlinear SVM. This Linear SVM makes a simple linear separation between classes [12].

k-Nearest Neighbours (kNN). Nearest neighbor classifiers have good classification accuracy in low size dimensions. MATLAB includes a model called Fine kNN, which is used for the experiment, this one categorizes query points based on their distance to points (or neighbours) in a training dataset. In this case the number of neighbours is set to 1 [21].

Neural Network Classifiers (NNs). Neural network models have good classification accuracy and can be used for multiple classes classification. For this work, a narrow neural network is used, which has just 1 fully connected layer. This due to the good performance of the algorithm in comparison with others. Each model in the app is a feedforward fully connected neural network [4].

3   Results and Discussion

In this first approach to distinguish between 3 proposed conditions of the pain response, the results for the 4 male subjects (subject 1, 3, 4 and 6) were absolutely successful which is going to be explained in this section. In the case of the 2 females recorded (subject 2 and 5) the thermal pain stimuli used was not effective at all and the signals recorded are not useful for this experiment. The stimuli did not generate any discomfort or pain to them for almost 2 min. This was applied on different girls before being recorded (almost 8) and the response was the same. They informed to feel cold in their hand but that was it.

For classification, the data extracted from each hand were tested with the different models mentioned above as well as the data from both hands together. The best accuracy values obtained are presented in this paper.

Subject 1. This participant was 27 years old and right handed, the pain response on him was very fast. His tolerance to the stimuli had an average of 7 s becoming him the subject with less time of this experiment. For the left hand the linear SVM model obtained the best accuracy value with a 64.8%. For the right hand, a narrow neural network model with 1 fully connected layer obtained an accuracy of 69.4%. Testing both hands together, an 68.5% of accuracy was achieved by the same SVM model. These results show that the classification with the data from the right hand had better results than using the data from the left hand and even better than with the database of both hands together.

Subject 3. For this participant with 21 years old and left handed the signals showed more activity when it was approaching its maximum tolerance to the stimulus. He had a mean of 13 s with the hand on the ice. For the left hand an 87.2% of accuracy was achieve using a narrow neural network. For the right hand a 82.1% of accuracy resulted with the same neural network model. Finally, for both hands an 82.9% of accuracy obtained the linear SVM model. Similar to the performance of the subject 1 is presented here. The left hand got the best accuracy.

Subject 4. Subject 4 was 23 years old and right handed. The signals increase steadily as time passes, once the participant puts his hand in contact with the ice. He had a mean of 13 s with the hand on the ice. For the left hand an 80.6% of accuracy resulted with the linear SVM model. For the right hand he got an 77.1% using narrow neural networks. In the case of both hands linear SVM model got 79.4% of accuracy. Left hand obtained the best value of classification.

Subject 6. Subject 6 was 22 years old and right handed. This participant lasted the longest under the stimulus with an average time of 30 s. With the left hand, narrow neural networks performed better with a 71.7%. The right hand was not that good obtaining a 69.4% of accuracy with the narrow neural network. For both hands he got a 74% of accuracy with lineal SVM model. In this case the left hand obtained better classification accuracy.

For a better understanding of the results in Table 1 the true positive rates of the best models applied to the data are shown. Table 2 documents the performance of all the models applied.

Table 1. True positives rates of the models with best performance applied to each subject.

Subjects	Cond 0	Cond 1	Cond 2	Accuracy	Model
1 (Left)	82.2%	53.3%	50%	64.8%	SVM
1 (Right)	65.8%	86.7%	56.7%	69.4%	NNs
1 (Both)	89.2%	63.3%	45%	68.5%	SVM
3 (Left)	78.6%	96.4%	86.7%	87.2%	NNs
3 (Right)	75%	89.3%	80%	82.1%	NNs
3 (Both)	58.3%	98.2%	88.3%	82.9%	SVM
4 (Left)	82.1%	75.9%	83.8%	80.6%	SVM
4 (Right)	70.3%	89.7%	73.7%	77.1%	NNs
4 (Both)	73.7%	82.8%	83.3	79.4%	SVM
6 (Left)	78%	85.7%	50%	71.7%	NNs
6 (Right)	63.4%	77.8%	70%	69.4	NNs
6 (Both)	77%	85.7%	60%	74%	SVM

Table 2. Accuracy value of each model applied to all the subjects.

Subjects	LD	SVM	KNN	NNs	SVM (nL)
1 (Left)	46.7%	64.8%	57.1%	58.1%	57.4%
1 (Right)	50%	63.3%	58.2%	69.4%	66.8%
1 (Both)	65.5%	68.5%	63.1%	63.5%	63.2%
3 (Left)	60.5%	76.7%	72.1%	87.2%	82.4%
3 (Right)	52.6%	76.9%	73.1%	82.1%	79.5%
3 (Both)	67.7%	82.9%	72.6%	80.5%	79.6%
4 (Left)	46.9%	80.6%	68.4%	77.6%	73.3%
4 (Right)	37.5%	70.8%	62.5%	77.1%	75.8%
4 (Both)	69.1%	79.4%	62.9%	79.4%	79.1%
6 (Left)	42.4%	69.7%	62.6%	71.7%	65.2%
6 (Right)	36.7%	60.2%	56.1%	69.4%	64%
6 (Both)	62.1%	74%	66.1%	67.8%	67.4

4   Conclusions

The experiments allowed to have a first approach to pain detection with EEG and using machine learning to classify among 3 different conditions. As can be seen in the results, the best performing models were neural networks and SVM.

In the case of subject 3, the classification accuracy was the highest obtained while Subject 1 had the lowest percentage. This may be due to the exposure time and the quality of the recording.

For all participants, having an accuracy percentage higher than 70% is satisfactory as a first experiment and motivate us to continue with this research. Most of the works focused on EEG and pain is limited to identifying or classifying between pain and non-pain. In a future work, the intention is to go beyond this and to be able to analyze the signal in depth. Also the use of power bands as a feature for classification, make this work distinctive in comparison to others.

In the case of the women, there remains a lot of curiosity as to why a stimulus like this does not affect them. For them it only causes cold in the hand and no matter how much we extended the sampling window up to 2 min, the only thing that happened was that the ice melted.

On the other side, this project is an experiment prior to a larger research work where we will try to find this type of gradual pain (phasic) in amputees. The goal in this type of research is to create a Brain-Computer Interface capable of detecting pain in real time, that is where all this research field is heading. The results obtained were better than expected and stimulate to continue with this work.

References

1. Bonotis, P.A., et al.: Automated assessment of pain intensity based on EEG signal analysis. In: Proceedings - 2019 IEEE 19th International Conference on Bioinformatics and Bioengineering, BIBE 2019, pp. 583–588 (2019). https://doi.org/10.1109/BIBE.2019.00111
2. Vimont, C.: Numbers Don't Tell the Whole Story: Experts Say Better Pain Assessment Measures Needed, May 2019. https://www.practicalpainmanagement.com/patient/resources/understanding-pain/numbers-dont-tell-whole-story-experts-say-better-pain
3. Chaparro Gómez, C., Damasio, A.: The Feeling of What Happens Body and Emotion in the Making of Consciousness, 386 p. Harcourt Brace & Company, New York (1999). Persona: Revista de la Facultad de Psicología, ISSN: 1560-6139, No. 3, p. 188–192 (2000). https://dialnet.unirioja.es/servlet/articulo?codigo=6170884
4. Chester, M.: Neural Networks: A Tutorial. Prentice-Hall Inc., Hoboken (1993)
5. Dallenbach, K.M.: Pain: history and present status. Am. J. Psychol. **52**(3), 331 (1939). https://doi.org/10.2307/1416740
6. Elsayed, M., Sim, K.S., Tan, S.C.: A novel approach to objectively quantify the subjective perception of pain through electroencephalogram signal analysis. IEEE Access **8**, 199920–199930 (2020). https://doi.org/10.1109/ACCESS.2020.3032153
7. Gilman, B.I., Marshall, H.R.: Pain, pleasure, and aesthetics. Philos. Rev. **3**(3), 342 (1894). https://doi.org/10.2307/2175978. https://philpapers.org/rec/MARPPA-22
8. Hadjileontiadis, L.J.: EEG-based tonic cold pain characterization using wavelet higher order spectral features. IEEE Trans. Biomed. Eng. **62**(8), 1981–1991 (2015). https://doi.org/10.1109/TBME.2015.2409133
9. Koch, C.: The Feeling of Life Itself: Why Consciousness is Widespread But Can't Be Computed, p. 257 (2019)
10. Kriegel, U.: Current Controversies in Philosophy of Mind, pp. 1–250 (2013). https://doi.org/10.4324/9780203116623

11. Lotte, F.: A tutorial on EEG signal-processing techniques for mental-state recognition in brain–computer interfaces. In: Miranda, E.R., Castet, J. (eds.) Guide to Brain-Computer Music Interfacing, pp. 133–161. Springer, London (2014). https://doi.org/10.1007/978-1-4471-6584-2_7

12. Ma, Y., Guo, G.: Support Vector Machines Applications, vol. 649. Springer, Cham (2014). https://doi.org/10.1007/978-3-319-02300-7

13. O'Keefe, M.: Pain Depends on Context (2021). https://www.painrevolution.org/blog/pain-depends-on-context

14. Melzack, C.: Sensory, motivational and central control determinants of chronic pain: a new conceptual model. Skin Sens. 1, 423–443 (1986)

15. van der Miesen, M., Lindquist, M., Wager, T.: Neuroimaging-based biomarkers for pain: state of the field and current directions. Pain Rep. 4(4), e751 (2019). https://doi.org/10.1097/PR9.0000000000000751

16. Nezam, T., Boostani, R., Abootalebi, V., Rastegar, K.: A novel classification strategy to distinguish five levels of pain using the EEG signal features. IEEE Trans. Affect. Comput. 12(1), 131–140 (2021). https://doi.org/10.1109/TAFFC.2018.2851236

17. Panavaranan, P., Wongsawat, Y.: EEG-based pain estimation via fuzzy logic and polynomial kernel support vector machine. In: BMEiCON 2013–6th Biomedical Engineering International Conference, pp. 1–4 (2013). https://doi.org/10.1109/BMEiCon.2013.6687668

18. Ramirez, R., Planas, J., Escude, N., Mercade, J., Farriols, C.: EEG-based analysis of the emotional effect of music therapy on palliative care cancer patients. Front. Psychol. 9, 254 (2018). https://doi.org/10.3389/fpsyg.2018.00254

19. Rissacher, D., Dowman, R., Schuckers, S.A.: Identifying frequency-domain features for an EEG-based pain measurement system. In: Proceedings of the IEEE Annual Northeast Bioengineering Conference, NEBEC, pp. 114–115 (2007). https://doi.org/10.1109/NEBC.2007.4413305

20. Sherrington, C., Sharpey-Schäfer, E.: Cutaneous sensations. In: Text-Book of Physiology, 1 edn., vol. 2, pp. 920–1001. Pentland, Edinburgh (1898)

21. Steinbach, M., Tan, P.N.: kNN: k-nearest neighbors. In: The Top Ten Algorithms in Data Mining, pp. 151–162 (2009)

22. Subhani, A., Xia, L., Malik, A.: EEG signals to measure mental stress. In: 2nd International Conference on Behavioral, Cognitive and Psychological Sciences - BCPS 2011, p. 10 (2011). http://www.iedrc.org/bcps/

23. Sun, G., Wen, Z., Ok, D., Doan, L., Wang, J., Chen, Z.S.: Detecting acute pain signals from human EEG. J. Neurosci. Methods 347, 108964 (2021). https://doi.org/10.1016/j.jneumeth.2020.108964

24. Tayeb, Z., Bose, R., Dragomir, A., Osborn, L.E., Thakor, N.V., Cheng, G.: Decoding of pain perception using EEG signals for a real-time reflex system in prostheses: a case study. Sci. Rep. 10(1), 4–8 (2020). https://doi.org/10.1038/s41598-020-62525-7

25. Tharwat, A., Gaber, T., Ibrahim, A., Hassanien, A.E.: Linear discriminant analysis: a detailed tutorial. AI Commun. 30(2), 169–190 (2017)

26. Tiemann, L., et al.: Distinct patterns of brain activity mediate perceptual and motor and autonomic responses to noxious stimuli. Nat. Commun. (2018). https://doi.org/10.1038/s41467-018-06875-x

27. Vallat, R.: Bandpower of an EEG signal (2018). https://raphaelvallat.com/bandpower.html
28. Worley, A., Fabrizi, L., Boyd, S., Slater, R.: Multi-modal pain measurements in infants. J. Neurosci. Methods **205**(2), 252–257 (2012). https://doi.org/10.1016/j.jneumeth.2012.01.009

A Lightweight Convolutional Neural Network for Breast Cancer Diagnosis with Histology Images

Juan Ramirez-Quintana[1][(✉)] [ORCID], Ivan Acosta-Lara[1],
Graciela Ramirez-Alonso[2] [ORCID], Mario Chacon-Murguia[1] [ORCID],
and Alma Corral-Saenz[1]

[1] PVR Lab, Tecnologico Nacional de Mexico/I.T, Chihuahua, Chihuahua, Mexico
{juan.rq,m19060581,mario.cm,alma.cs}@chihuahua.tecnm.mx
[2] Facultad de Ingenieria, Universidad Autonoma de Chihuahua, Chihuahua, Mexico
galonso@uach.com

Abstract. A Breast cancer diagnosis provides prevention and treatment to save lives or improve the life quality of patients, and a recent tool with good performance for this diagnosis is deep learning methods to process breast histology images. However, these methods are based on Convolutional Neural Networks (CNN) with a high computational cost that reduces usability. Therefore, this paper proposes an optimized CNN for breast cancer diagnosis named Lightweight CNN for Histology Image Processing (LCIP). LCIP is based on the MobileNet V2 architecture adapted with four inverted residual convolutions to find cell features. LCIP was validated with the BreakHis database, reporting an accuracy of 99.73%, the best result in the literature. Additionally, LCIP is the Histology Image Processing Deep learning method with fewer parameters than recent state-of-the-art methods. These results demonstrate that LCIP is a method that can be used as a feasible, portable, and accessible method to develop novel tools for breast cancer diagnosis.

Keywords: Convolutional Neural Networks · Histology image processing · Breast cancer diagnosis

1 Introduction

According to the World Health Organization (WHO), there exist 2.3 million people with breast cancer and 685,000 deaths related to this disease in 2020. Therefore, the early diagnosis is essential for patients, correct treatment, and care. The first stage of diagnosis is breast self-examination, and the second stage is the analysis with ultrasound, mammography, or magnetic resonance. The final stage is the biopsy, which is a histologic tissue sample analyzed with an expert [1].

Many deep learning methods for histology image processing have been proposed to develop novel breast cancer analysis methods. According to the literature, these methods achieve good results, and they are novel methodologies to prevent breast tumor growth [2]. Regard to histologic image processing with deep learning, different CNN architectures achieve accuracies higher than 90% like Inception-ResNet [3,4] and Xception [5,6]. However, these CNN have high computational costs, and they can be implemented into expensive computational platforms [7]. Therefore, this paper proposes a novel CNN with low computational cost named Lightweight CNN for Histology Image Processing (LCIP). LCIP classifies breast tissue on benign or malignant cells and is based on the MobileNet V2 architecture presented in [8] and inverted residual convolutions layers to analyze histological images with different magnifications and cell features. The architecture of LCIP brings a tool to analyze histological breast tissue with embedded machine learning systems. This tool is useful to reduce clinical costs and supports telemedicine for fast breast cancer diagnosis. According to [9,12], developing tools for telemedicine and breast cancer diagnosis is a paramount topic for health in the next years.

The rest of the paper is organized as follows: Sects. 2 and 3 present the BreakHis dataset and the LCIP proposed method. Section 4 reports the results, and finally, Sect. 5 presents the conclusions.

2   Dataset

There are many breast histologic image datasets to propose tissue analysis algorithms for the literature. Some of them are Grand Challenge on Breast Cancer Histology Images (BACH) [13], Breast Histopathology Images [11], Breast Cancer Histopathological Annotation and Diagnosis (BreCaHAD) [10], and Breast Cancer Histopathological Database (BreakHis) [14]. We select BreakHis because it is the most popular in literature. Also, this database has histologic samples with different magnification levels, which is helpful to train networks with different feature sizes. This aspect is important because the histologic analysis is developed with different magnification observations to diagnose the tissue characteristics.

BreakHis was designed to evaluate the different histologic processing methods. This database is composed of 7,909 microscopic images of breast tumor tissue collected from 82 patients using various magnification factors (40X, 100X, 200X, and 400X). It contains 2,480 benign and 5,429 malignant samples of color images with 700×460 pixels, 8-bit resolution, and PNG format. Table 1 shows the sample distribution according to magnification and the classes of benign and malignant cells.

3   Lightweight CNN for Histology Image Processing

Figure 1 shows a general scheme of the proposed method, where the input is an RGB histological image, $I(x,y)^{RGB}$. The first stage is preprocessing, which consists of color normalization. The next stage is the deep CNN, which analyzes the properties of the image to classify the tissue as Benign or Malignant cells. The deep CNN is based on a MobileNet V2 network, but we add four inverted residual convolutions to generate features with different magnification levels.

Table 1. Sample distribution of BreakHis

Magnification	Benign	Malignant	Total
40X	652	1,370	1,995
100X	644	1,437	2,081
200X	623	1,390	2,013
400X	588	1,232	1,820
Total of images	2,480	5,429	7,909

Then, the feature extraction of LCIP has a convolution layer and inverted residual block composed of parallel dilation convolutions to find features in different magnification levels. The following average pooling and convolution layers are placed to reduce the feature dimension. The classification stage of LCIP is based on two fully connected and a convolution layer of 1×1. The next subsections explain each layer.

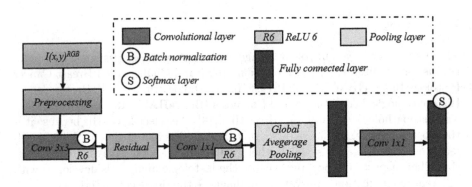

Fig. 1. General scheme of LCIP method.

3.1 Preprocessing

The input of LCIP is $I(x,y)^{RGB}$, which is an image variant to color respect other histological images due to the staining and the acquisition protocol. Then, it is necessary to normalize the images $I(x,y)^{RGB}$ with the method of Macenko [15], which is the most popular in literature for staining normalization. The output of the Macenko method is an image $I_M(x,y)^{RGB}$. The following step is to normalize $I_M(x,y)^{RGB}$ regarding color level intensity with:

$$M(x,y)^{RGB} = \frac{m_{max} - m_{min}}{m_{max} + m_{min}} \tag{1}$$

where m_{max} is the maximum value of the image and m_{min} is the minimum.

3.2 First Convolutional Layer

This layer finds the abstract properties of the cells with the convolution given by:

$$F_\rho(x,y) = f(W_{\tau,\rho,l}(x,y) * F_{\rho-1}(x,y) + \beta_\rho), \rho = 1, \tau = 32, l = 3 \times 3 \quad (2)$$

where ρ is the layer of the network ($\rho = 1$ means the first layer), τ is the depth of the kernels, $F_{\rho-1}(x,y)$ is the feature map of the last layer. The input $F_0(x,y)$ is $M(x,y)^{RGB}$. The activation function $f(.)$ is ReLU 6 [16] because this function generate best generalization results than other activation functions. This layer has a batch normalization to accelerate the deep training by reducing internal covariate shift [17].

3.3 Residual Block

This layer has seven Inverted Residual blocks that consist of a set of convolutions with kernel sizes of 1×1, 3×3, 5×5, and 7×7. These kernels find features of the cells from different magnification images.

Figure 2 shows the scheme of this block, where the first layer of this block is a convolution given by (2), where $\rho = 2$, $\tau = 3$, $l = 1 \times 1$. This layer reduces the computational cost by combining the color image in one channel but preserving the information. The next layer is a set of parallel convolutions given by:

$$F_\rho(x,y) = W_{\tau,\rho}(x,y) \otimes_l F_{\rho-1}(x,y) + \beta_\rho, \rho = 3, \tau = 1 \quad (3)$$

where $\otimes_l$ is a depth separable convolution with dilation l. Figure 2 shows that this block has three convolution given by (3) with a dilation factor of $l = 1 \times 1$, $l = 3 \times 3$, $l = 5 \times 5$, and $l = 7 \times 7$ to find properties and features of tissue cells from different magnification levels. In parallel to the dilation convolutions, there are an average pooling [18] and a convolution given by (2), $\rho = 3$, $\tau = 1$, $l = 1 \times 1$ to find global features. The convolutions of (2) and the next parallel line of the average pooling with the convolution of 1×1 are concatenated to generate a tensor feature map $F_\rho(x,y,k)$, $k = 1, ..., 4$ where from $k = 1$ to $k = 3$ are the dilation convolution outputs $\otimes_l$, $\rho = 4$ $l = \{1,3,5,7\}$, and $k = 4$ is the average pooling [18] with the 1×1 convolution.

The next step is a convolution 3 of $F_\rho(x,y,k)$ where $\rho = 5$, $l = 1 \times 1$, and the input is the concatenated map $F_4(x,y,k)$. Finally, the feature maps are added to fuse the features and find the patterns of the tissue cells. The addition is defined as follows:

$$F_\rho(x,y) = \sum_l [F_{\rho-1}(x,y,k)], \rho = 5 \quad (4)$$

The result in this layer is a set of abstract properties that map tissue composition of different magnification levels. This composition is based on texture, cell corpuscles, and cell nucleus features.

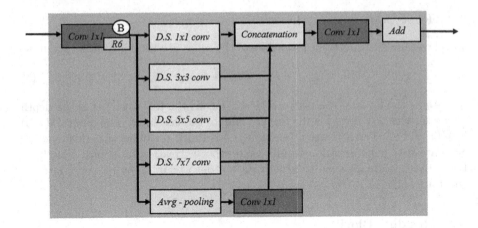

Fig. 2. Inverted residual block.

3.4 Convolutional Layer for Feature Compression

The next layer is a Convolutional layer defined by (2), where $\rho = 6$, $l = 1 \times 1$, and the activation function is ReLU 6. This layer has Batch normalization to normalize the data of all the layers within the same dynamic range. The abstract tissue features are normalized in a single map with this layer.

3.5 Global Average Pooling

This layer compresses the information of the features as possible but keeps the tissue properties. The average pooling is defined as follows:

$$F_\rho(n,m) = \frac{1}{N} \sum_{x=(p-1)\nu, y=(q-1)\mu}^{x=p\nu, y=q\mu} [F_{\rho-1}(x,y)], \rho = 7 \tag{5}$$

where N is the number of windows, (ν, μ) is the size of each windows that compress the features, (P, Q) is the number of windows, $p = 1, ..., P$ and $q = 1, ..., Q$. This layer is the output of the feature extraction stage of LCIP.

3.6 First Fully Connected Layer

This is the first layer of the classification stage of LCIP, and it is defined as follows:

$$F_\rho(n,m) = W_{\tau, \rho, l}(n,m) F_{\rho-1}(n,m) + \beta_\rho), \rho = 8 \tag{6}$$

where $\tau = 1$, $l = \nu \times \mu$, and $W_{\tau, 8, l}(n,m)$ is a set of weights that learns the benign properties of the compress tissue features. Equation 6 is the dot product between the weights and the features $F_7(n,m)$. If $I(x,y)^{RGB}$ has information of benign cells, $F_8(n,m)$ generates a vector with values close to zero, but if $I(x,y)^{RGB}$

has information of malignant cells, $F_8(n, m)$ generate values also close to one, and they surround the feature vectors generated by benign cells. Then, $F_8(n, m)$ generates a nonlinear classification subspace.

3.7 Convolutional Layer for Classification

The next layer is a Convolutional layer that separates the vector values of both classes and works as a new feature map with linear separation. This layer is defined by the Eq. 2, where $\rho = 9$, $\tau = 1$, $l = 3 \times 3$.

3.8 Second Fully Connected Layer

This layer classifies $I(x, y)^{RGB}$ on benign or malignant cells with the following expression:

$$F_\rho(n, m) = f(W_{\tau, \rho, l}(n, m) F_{\rho-1}(n, m) + \beta_\rho)), \rho = 10 \tag{7}$$

where $\tau = 1$, $l = \nu \times \mu$, and $W_{\tau, 10, l}(n, m)$ is a the prototype that represent the pattern of benign cells. Equation 7 represents the dot product between this prototype and the features $F_9(n, m)$. Then, if the result is positive, $I(x, y)^{RGB}$ has information of benign cells, but if the result is negative, $I(x, y)^{RGB}$ has information of malignant cells. In this case, $f(.)$ is a softmax activation function defined in [19]. This activation function generates two magnitudes that represent the classes of benign or malignant tissue.

4 Results

This section presents information about the implementation of LCIP, a comparison of LCIP with the most popular methods in the literature, and a brief Cross-Validation explanation to understand the learning of LCIP.

4.1 Training and Computer Platform

LCIP was trained with backpropagation by considering 1000 epochs with early stopping (the training was stopped in 70 epochs). The BreakHis dataset was divided into 70% of images for training, 15% for the test, and 15% for validation. LCIP was implemented in Python 3.7.0, and the computer has an i7-8750H Intel processor and an NVIDIA GPU GeForce GTX 1060 with a Max-Q design.

4.2 Comparison of LCIP with Other State of the Art Methods

The metrics used to compare LCIP with the state-of-the-art methods were accuracy (Acc), F measure (F1) [20], and Number of parameters (Np). Np is the number of variables that the network processes during the inference. The networks selected for the comparisons have the best results in literature in Acc and Np. These methods are the ResNet-50 [5] network published in 2020, a Capsule Neural Network (CapsNet)[21], and two Inception ResNet published in 2019 [3,4]. Also, we added the MobileNet V2, which is the foundation of our proposed model. Other CNNs were not considered in this comparison because they have low accuracy or the number of parameters is complicated to calculate due to their architecture. Next, we describe the networks used in the comparisons.

Table 2. Sample distribution of BreakHis

Network	Acc	F1	Np
MobileNet V2	54.18%	58.76%	14,056,513
CapsNet [21]	86%	Not available	31,893,908
Inception ResNtet 2 [4]	92.4%	Not available	64,823,657
Inception ResNtet 1 [3]	97.9%	98.47%	55,911,649
Xception [5]	99%	95%	39,737,897
LCIP	**99.73%**	**99.59%**	**6,655,587**

The MobileNet V2 [8] is a CNN for mobile devices or embedded systems. This network has an inverted residual structure with shortcut connections between the bottleneck layers. The intermediate layers use lightweight depthwise convolutions. According to Table 2, MobileNet V2 has the lowest performance because the histologic images have patterns that are not processed adequately with linear operations. However, MobileNet V2 has significantly fewer parameters than ResNet or Inception-ResNet.

CapsNet [21] presents an Acc of 86% but does not report F1. CapsNet has capsules, which are vector structures generated from the outputs of the neuron group. The capsules generate invariant features to spatial and orientation, which help find the nucleus and other cell properties. However, the performance is lower than ResNet or Inception ResNet.

Inception-ResNet [3,4] is an architecture widely used for histologic image processing. The architecture of [3] extracts features constructed with a new autoencoder network that transforms the features to a low dimensional. The model of [4] is an ensemble of VGG19, MobileNet, and DenseNet. This ensemble generates a model similar to the Inception-ResNet network. However, the result is 92.4% with BreakHis, and the Np is the highest.

ResNet-50 presents an Acc of 99% in [5]. This network has pre-trained kernels with ImageNet and was trained with BreakHis, but the Np is high compared to other networks.

LCIP achieves the best results with the highest Acc and the lowest Np. These results are because LCIP combines the architecture of MobileNet with a block that extracts abstract features according to the magnification level. LCIP finds the necessary features describing the cells with the first convolutional layer and the inverted residual block. The following convolutional layer and the average pooling reduce the dimension of the features. Finally, the classification stage generates the hyperplanes to find the subspace where the images can be separated into benign or malignant cells.

4.3   Cross Validation

The methods of ResNet, Inception-ResNet, and LCIP report accuracies higher than 90%, but it is essential to know if a result higher than 90% is due to the network learns. However, none of the articles reported in the literature present an analysis to validate the obtained accuracy, like Cross-Validation (CV). For this reason, this subsection presents the average results of a CV analysis of LCIP, ResNet, and MobileNet V2. The CV was developed with 70 epochs and five k-folds because these parameters were enough to know the generalization capability of the networks. Table 3 shows the average of the five k-folds of the networks. LCIP achieves the best Acc and F1 metrics. ResNet has low F1, which is very different than the result shown in Table 2. On the other hand, MobileNet V2 achieved better results in the CV than the results reported in Table 2. Inception-ResNet 1 and 2 do not generate conclusive results because the CV reports lower performance than MobileNet V2.

Table 3. Average CV of MobileNet V2, ResNet, and LCIP

Network	Average Acc	Average F1
MobileNet V2	63.55%	45.91.76%
Xception [5]	84.75%	76.33%
LCIP	**86.66%**	**80.23%**

5   Conclusion

This paper presents a novel method named Lightweight CNN for Histology Image Processing (LCIP), a network for benign and malignant cell detection in histological breast tissue samples obtained from digital images. LCIP is based on the architecture of MobileNet V2 and a block with dilated convolution in parallel to extract cell features of different magnification levels. The second convolutional layer and the average pooling reduce the dimension of the features. Finally, the classification stage generates the subspaces where the images can be separated into benign or malignant cells. According to the results, LCIP achieves the best accuracy and F1 measure, with fewer parameters in the BreakHis dataset compared to network models reported in the literature. LCIP has a low computational cost architecture that includes a set of layers that find cell features in the different magnification levels. The accuracy of LCIP was 99.73% with 70 epochs, and the average of the five k-folds in CV was 86.66% with 70 epochs. On the other hand, the average accuracy of Xception falls from 99% to 84.75% in the CV, and MobileNet V2 increases its performance from 54.18% to 63.55%.

These results mean that the performances obtained with the backpropagation generate overfitting in all the networks due to $M(x,y)^{RGB}$ do not distinguish features at different magnification levels. However, LCIP achieves better results in the CV than any other method reported in the literature. Furthermore, the number of parameters of LCIP is significantly fewer than MobileNet V2, CapsNet, Inception-ResNet, and Xception-50. These LCIP results are because in the case of images with different magnifications levels, the increase in the number of parallel operations, the network extracts descriptive features of the histological tissue with fewer parameters. Then, based on the accuracy results of LCIP, the CV validation, and the number of parameters, we conclude that LCIP is a feasible network for histologic image processing. Future work will test LCIP in embedded GPU devices to generate embedded machine learning technology for telemedicine.

Acknowledgements. This work was supported by the Tecnologico Nacional de Mexico under grants TecNM. The number of funding support is TecNM 14044.22-P.

References

1. Breast Cancer (2021). https://www.who.int/news-room/fact-sheets/detail/breast-cancer
2. Shen, L., Margolies, L.R., Rothstein, J.H., Fluder, E., McBride, R., Sieh, W.: Deep learning to improve breast cancer detection on screening mammography. Nature **9**(12495), 1–12 (2019)
3. Xie, J., Liu, R., Luttrell, J., Zhang, C.: Deep learning based analysis of histopathological images of breast cancer. Front. Genet. **10**(80), 1–19 (2019)
4. Kassani, S.H. Wesolowski, M.J., Schneider, K.A.: Classification of Histopathological biopsy images using ensemble of deep learning networks. In: 29th Annual International Conference on Computer Science and Software Engineering, pp. 92–99. ACM, Toronto (2019)
5. Al-Haija, Q.A., Adebanjo, A.: Breast cancer diagnosis in histopathological images using ResNet-50 convolutional neural network. IEEE International IOT, Electronics and Mechatronics Conference, pp. 1–8. IEEE, Vancouver (2020)
6. Bhowalm, P., Sen, S., Velasquez, J.D., Sarkar, R.: Fuzzy ensemble of deep learning models using choquet fuzzy integral, coalition game and information theory for breast cancer histology classification. Expert Syst. App. **190**(1), 116167 (2022)
7. Bianco, S., Cadene, R., Celona, L., Napoletano, P.: Benchmark analysis of representative deep neural network architectures. IEEE Access **6**(1), 64270–64277 (2018)
8. Akay, M., et al.: Deep learning classification of systemic sclerosis skin using the mobilenetv2 model. IEEE Open J. Eng. Med. Biol. **2**(1), 104–110 (2021)
9. Wang, Y., et al.: Improved breast cancer histological grading using deep learning. Ann. Oncol. **190**(1), 89–98 (2022)
10. Aksac, A., Demetrick, D.J., Ozyer, T., et al.: BreCaHAD: a dataset for breast cancer histopathological annotation and diagnosis. BMC Res Notes **12**, 82 (2019)
11. Janowczyk, A., Madabhushi, A.: Deep learning for digital pathology image analysis. A comprehensive tutorial with selected use cases. J. Pathol. Inform. **7**(29), 1–10 (2016)

12. The Lancet Rheumatology: Telemedicine: is the new normal fit for purpose? Lancet Rheumatolol. **4**(1), e1 (2022)
13. Aresta, G., Araujo, T.: BACH Grand challenge on breast cancer histology images. Med. Image Anal. **56**(1), 122–139 (2019)
14. Spanhol, F., Cavalin, P., Oliveira, L., Petitjean, C., Heutte, L.: Deep features for breast cancer histopathological image classification. In: International Conference on Systems, Man, and Cybernetics, pp. 1868–1873. Banff, IEEE (2017)
15. Macenko, M., et al.: A method for normalizing histology slides for quantitative analysis. In: International Symposium Biomedical Imaging From Nano to Macro, pp. 1107–1110. IEEE, Boston (2009)
16. Duan, C., Zhang, T.: Two-stream convolutional neural network based on gradient image for aluminum profile surface defects classification and recognition. IEEE Access **81**, 172152–172165 (2020)
17. Kalayeh, M.M., Shah, M.: Training faster by separating modes of variation in batch-normalized models. IEEE Trans. Pattern Anal. Mach. Intell. **42**(6), 1483–1500 (2020)
18. Theodoridis, T., Loumponias, K., Vretos, N., Daras, P.: Zernike pooling generalizing average pooling using Zernike moments. IEEE Access **9**(1), 121128–121136 (2021)
19. Gao, F., Li, B., Chen, L., Shang, Z., Wei, X., He, C.: A softmax classifier for high-precision classification of ultrasonic similar signals. Ultrasonics **112**(1), 1–8 (2021)
20. Liu, M., Xu, C., Luo, Y., Xu, C., Wen, Y., Tao, D.: Cost-sensitive feature selection by optimizing F-measures. IEEE Trans. Image Process. **27**(3), 1323–1335 (2018)
21. Anupama, M., Sowmya, V., Soman, K.P.: Breast cancer classification using capsule network with preprocessed histology images. In: International Conference on Communication and Signal Processing (ICCSP), pp. 1–8. IEEE, Chennai (2019)

Efficient Methodology Based on Convolutional Neural Networks with Augmented Penalization on Hard-to-Classify Boundary Voxels on the Task of Brain Lesion Segmentation

Gustavo Ulloa[1]([🖂]), Alejandro Veloz[2], Héctor Allende-Cid[3], Raúl Monge[1], and Héctor Allende[1]

[1] Universidad Técnica Federico Santa María, Av. España 1680, Valparaíso, Chile
gustavo.ulloa@usm.cl
[2] Universidad de Valparaíso, Blanco 951, Valparaíso, Chile
[3] Pontificia Universidad Católica de Valparaíso, Av. Brasil 2950, Valparaíso, Chile

Abstract. Medical images segmentation has become a fundamental tool for making more precise the assessment of complex diagnosis and surgical tasks. In particular, this work focuses on multiple sclerosis (MS) disease in which lesion segmentation is useful for getting an accurate diagnosis and for tracking its progression. In recent years, Convolutional Neural Networks (CNNs) have been successfully employed for segmenting MS lesions. However, these methods often fail in defining the boundaries of the MS lesions accurately. This work focuses on segmenting hard-to-classify voxels close to MS lesions boundaries in MRI, where it was determined that the application of a loss function that focuses the penalty on difficult voxels generates an increase in the results with respect to the Dice similarity metric (DSC), where the latter occurs as long as the sufficient representation of these voxels as well as an adequate preprocessing of the images of each patient. The methodology was tested in the public data set ISBI2015 and was compared with alternative methods that are trained using the binary cross entropy loss function and the focal loss function with uniform and stratified sampling, obtaining better results in DSC, reaching a $DSC > 0.7$, a threshold that is considered comparable to that obtained by another human expert.

Keywords: Loss function · Convolutional Neural Networks · Multiple sclerosis · Lesions segmentation · Magnetic Resonance Imaging

1 Introduction

Multiple sclerosis (MS) is a chronic autoimmune, inflammatory neurological disease affecting the Central Nervous System (CNS), in which the autoimmune system attacks the myelin sheath, myelin producing cells and the axons present

O. O. Vergara-Villegas et al. (Eds.): MCPR 2022, LNCS 13264, pp. 338–347, 2022.
https://doi.org/10.1007/978-3-031-07750-0_31

in the white matter brain tissue [6]. This can produce progressive loss of sensor, visual, motor and cognitive brain functions in people that suffer this type of condition. Magnetic Resonance Imaging (MRI) is used to detect MS white matter lesions, in particular, employing T1-weighted (T1-w), T2-weighted (T2-w), PD-weighted (PD-w), and fluid attenuated inversion recovery T2 (T2-FLAIR) sequences. MS lesions are expressed in MRI as small hyperintensities regions in T2-w, PD-w and T2-FLAIR MRI sequences, and small hypointensities regions in T1-w MRI sequences [4].

From the point of view of the medical expert, extracting quantitative information about the volume and the amount of MS-related lesions in white matter is important for assisting the diagnosis, for assessing the disease progression, and for testing new drugs [5,11]. In this scenario, image processing techniques such as image segmentation helps radiologists to detect and delineate more accurately MS-related lesions. The MS-related automatic segmentation of lesions also decreases in a great manner the time needed by the radiologist to analyze the progression of this condition. Moreover, it decreases the intra and inter-expert variability in assessing it.

In the last decade, using deep learning architectures based on Convolutional Neural Networks (CNNs), state-of-the-art results have been obtained in most of visual recognition tasks; in particular in image classification, object detection and semantic segmentation. The usual way to perform the segmentation task is by using as input a patch surrounding the interest voxel to classify in one of the defined classes. Typically, the patches correspond to a set of intensities determined by uniform sampling in a square neighborhood centered in the voxel of interest.

The problem of MS-related lesion segmentation is difficult mainly due to the imbalance between voxels that belong to the MS class versus voxels of normal tissues. In the literature this problem is assesed by balancing the majority class by means of a uniform sampling of the non MS-related lesion class [1,10]. Additionally, for segmenting MS-related lesions, some image features, such as partial volume effect, variability of MS lesions intensities and the overlapping between MS lesions and normal brain tissues intensities distributions complicated even more the problem of MS lesion segmentation [4]. Due to this, an accurate segmentation of the MS lesions borders is difficult to determine at glance by radiology practitioners or by using machine learning models. In fact, in these MS lesion domains, i.e. borders, the higher proportion of false positive and false negative errors are concentrated. Although CNNs have obtained prominent segmentation results, they still are not comparable in terms of accuracy to the segmentation that radiologist can produce manually.

In this work, a methodology is proposed that allows addressing the problem of segmentation of multiple sclerosis lesions in an efficient way. A preprocessing of the MRIs is carried out that corrects the excessive truncation of the hyperintensity voxels of the T2-Flair modality used in [1] and [9], since it is in these voxels where the CNN presents the highest false positive rates. Next, a stratified sampling of voxels difficult to classify near the edges is carried out in order to increase their representation in the training set. Finally, the focal loss function is used, which allows the penalty to be focused on the most difficult examples of the training set.

The paper is organized as follows: In Sect. 2 we expose the methodology, where the architecture of the convolutional network used, the improvement in the preprocessing stage together with the application of focal loss are presented. Section 3 presents discussions about the results obtained on the 2015 Longitudinal MS Lesion Segmentation Challenge dataset. Finally, in Sect. 4 conclusions and future works related with the new loss function are presented.

2   Materials and Methods

2.1   Data Set: ISBI2015

We used the longitudinal multiple sclerosis lesion segmentation data set [2], which is a public data set[1]. The training set is conformed by the multi-modality MR images from five patients with 4–5 different image-time points per patient with the corresponding binary masks with manual lesion segmentations. The MRIs were acquired on a 3.0 Tesla MRI scanner, where four modalities were available for each patient, corresponding to T1-weighted, T2-weighted, PD-weighted and T2-FLAIR. Each MR image has a 1 [mm] isotropic cubic voxel resolution.

2.2   Preprocessing

Prior to the extraction of the MR image patches that are used to train the CNN, two preprocessing tasks were applied. Each one consisting in several subtasks that are explained next. The first preprocessing task consists in the standard MRI processing typically made within the medical imaging community and that was also applied for the 2015 Longitudinal MS Lesion Segmentation Challenge dataset [2], i.e. correction of the MR intensity inhomogeneities, skull-stripping, dura mater stripping, and rigid-body registration to a 1 [mm] isotropic MNI template. The second preprocessing task has the following steps: Intensities truncation to the percentiles within the range $[0.01, 0.9996]$, intensities scaling to the range $[0, 1]$, rigid-body registration of the T2-FLAIR images to the ICBM452 probabilistic atlas [7], and, finally, extraction of a subset of supra-threshold voxels. The voxels that belong to this subset are conformed by intersecting the set of voxels that exceeds one threshold on the T2-FLAIR image and another threshold in the probability map of the white matter. This is because MS-related lesions appear as hyper-intense regions on T2-FLAIR images [4] and also are mostly located in the white matter.

2.3   Network Architecture and Training

The CNN used corresponds to a completely convolutional CNN with 7 convolutional layers deep. The input to the network consists of three patches of size

---

[1] https://smart-stats-tools.org/lesion-challenge.

33×33. These patches are extracted from the axial plane of T1-weighted, T2-weighted and T2-FLAIR modalities. Each convolutional layer uses Leaky ReLU with negative slope coefficient $\beta = 0.3$ as activation function, except for the output layer of 1×1 which uses the sigmoidal activation function and not softmax because it was only necessary obtaining a probability map at the output as it is a segmentation problem approached as a voxel-to-voxel binary classification task. The network has 2 layers of MaxPooling of 2×2 with stride 2 and with Dropout after each convolutional layer as regularization method. In order to increase the depth of the network without generating adverse effects such as the problem of the vanishing gradient, the use of a single ResNet block was empirically selected since a greater number of these did not contribute to benefits to CNN training regarding to the evaluated metrics. In Fig. 1 a diagram of the details of the network architecture used is presented. In the image the sampling of the network input patch is highlighted with green squares.

Considering that the CNN has an output of size 1×1, the loss functions used correspond to binary cross entropy and focal loss with parameter values $\gamma = 1.0$, $\gamma = 2.0$ and $\gamma = 3.0$. In order to improve performance in difficult voxels near the edges of the lesions, the non-lesion class, which is the majority, was sampled with a 1:1 balance with the lesion class, where this sampling consisted of a sample stratified considering a proportion p of voxels near the edges of the lesions less than or equal to 2 mm apart and a proportion $1-p$ of voxels randomly sampled from voxels candidates to belong to the classes injury belonging to the non-injury majority class.

Specifically in [9] and [1] a truncation of the quantiles 0.01 and 0.99 was carried out, where we note that the upper quantile truncates on average around 25% of the voxels with higher intensities belonging to the lesion class, voxels where precisely the network concentrates a large percentage of false positives. This situation can be seen in Fig. 2(b). In this work, the truncation procedure was maintained because the results were better compared to the alternative of not performing truncation. The choice of the upper truncation quantile corresponded to the quantile that modifies the intensities of the voxels with the highest intensity to a lesser extent, thus the quantiles 0.01 and 0.9996 were used (Fig. 2(c)).

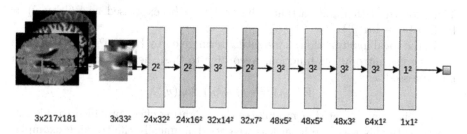

Fig. 1. Blue blocks: convolutional layers and Red blocks: maxpooling layers (Color figure online)

The weights were updated with the stochastic gradient descent. The learning rate selected was 0.01 with decay learning rate of 1×10^{-6}, momentum parameter of 0.9 with Nesterov momentum and batch size of 64. Dropout with probability of 0.1. The implementation and training of the CNN was carried out using Keras Deep Neural Network Library [3] with TensorFlow as backend numerical engine. The model was trained using a NVIDIA GeForce GTX 1080TI Graphic Card.

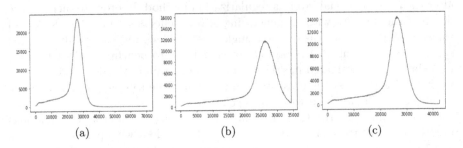

(a)   (b)   (c)

Fig. 2. T2-Flair Histograms: a) Without truncation, b) truncation with quartiles $[0.01, 0.99]$ y c) truncation with quartiles $[0.01, 0.9996]$.

2.4 Focal Loss Function

In [8] the problem of class imbalance is addressed in the task of object detection, specifically when this task is performed by CNNs of a one-stage. This loss function is based on the binary cross entropy loss function, which is given by the expression:

$$BCE(y, \hat{y}) = -y \log \hat{y} - (1 - y) \log(1 - \hat{y}) \tag{1}$$

where $y \in \{0, 1\}$ is the ground truth where $y = 0$ and $y = 1$ correspond to the non-lesion and lesion classes respectively and $\hat{y} \in [0, 1]$ is the probability for the class with label $y = 1$ estimated by the model. For notational convenience, $\hat{y}_t$ is defined as:

$$\hat{y}_t = \begin{cases} \hat{y} & \text{if y=1,} \\ 1 - \hat{y} & \text{otherwise,} \end{cases} \tag{2}$$

Thus, for the t-th input instance the BCE can be expressed as $BCE(y, \hat{y}) = BCE(\hat{y}_t) = -\log(\hat{y}_t)$.

In the focal loss function, a weighting term given by $(1 - \hat{y}_t)^\gamma$ is added to the binary cross entropy loss function. According to this, the focal loss function can be expressed as:

$$FL(\hat{y}_t) = -(1 - \hat{y}_t)^\gamma \log(\hat{y}_t), \tag{3}$$

where γ is a parameter that modulates the weighting effect provided to this loss function. In this way, the focal loss weights dynamically the training examples losses, down-weighting easy-to-classify training examples and assigning higher losses to examples with low prediction accuracy, i.e. hard-to-classify training examples.

3   Experimental Results

3.1   Evaluation

Once the CNN has been trained with the different loss functions, the segmentation masks predicted by the CNN are obtained and their accuracy is evaluated with respect to the masks generated by the expert. The metrics used are the following:

- Dice Similarity Coefficient (DSC) or F_1-score is an overlap measure between two binary label masks:

$$\text{DSC} = \frac{2TP}{2TP + FN + FP}. \tag{4}$$

  where TP, FN and FP correspond to the amount of true positive, false negative and false positive values.
- Sensitivity or True Positive Rate indicates the rate of voxels correctly segmented as lesions:

$$\text{Sensitivity} = \frac{TP}{TP + FN}, \tag{5}$$

- Precision or Positive Predictive Value indicates the rate of segmented voxels from ones estimated as lesions:

$$\text{Precision} = \frac{TP}{TP + FP}, \tag{6}$$

To compare the segmentation performance, we implemented a group cross validation where five identical models were trained. For each fold, the training, validation and test sets were made up of the MR images that were taken over time to the 5 patients. That is, each group was trained with a training set composed of the MRIs of 3 patients, the validation set corresponds to the MRIs of a fourth patient and the test set corresponds to the MRIs of the fifth patient corresponding to a patient along with the MR images that were taken over time. Thus, 5 folds were made, whose details are found in Table 1. Each network was trained until 120 epochs with early stopping of 20 epochs of without diminishing the DSC metric of the validation MRIs, which it was possible to estimate as the model was trained using all the patches from the validation patient's MRIs whose central voxel belongs to the lesion class and most of the voxels candidates to the non-lesion class.

Table 1. Group cross validation sets.

Training		Validation		Testing	
Patients	#MRIs	Patients	#MRIs	Patients	#MRIs
2,3,4	13	5	4	1	4
1,4,5	12	3	5	2	4
2,4,5	12	1	4	3	5
1,3,5	13	2	4	4	4
1,2,3	13	4	4	5	4

Table 2. Results.

LF	p	γ	u	Sensitivity(sd)	Precision(sd)	DSC(sd)
BCE	-	-	0.98	0.7008(0.0173)	0.7153(0.0111)	0.6879(0.0115)
FL	-	1.0	0.90	0.7000(0.0195)	0.7167(0.0135)	0.6884(0.0137)
FL	-	2.0	0.81	0.7009(0.0190)	0.7126(0.0152)	0.6851(0.0106)
BCE	0.1	-	0.94	0.7050(0.0160)	0.7346(0.0180)	0.7003(0.0064)
FL	0.1	1.0	0.83	0.6966(0.0139)	0.7458(0.0112)	0.7033(0.0090)
FL	0.1	2.0	0.74	0.7024(0.0168)	0.7427(0.0145)	0.7046(0.0097)
FL	0.1	3.0	0.68	0.7056(0.0212)	0.7334(0.0154)	0.7005(0.0115)
BCE	0.2	-	0.92	0.6909(0.0171)	0.7397(0.0090)	0.6960(0.0118)
FL	0.2	1.0	0.79	0.6894(0.0165)	0.7357(0.0136)	0.6918(0.0115)
FL	0.2	2.0	0.71	0.6924(0.0162)	0.7393(0.0137)	0.6953(0.0148)
FL	0.2	3.0	0.66	0.6954(0.0126)	0.7364(0.0155)	0.6975(0.0131)

3.2 Results and Discussion

Table 2 presents the results obtained by the network (Fig. 1) using stratified sampling together with the binary cross entropy loss functions (BCE) and focal loss (FL). The parameter p corresponds to the percentage of voxels sampled near the edges of the lesions of the total voxels of the non-lesion class and γ is the focal loss parameter (3). The metrics used correspond to Sensitivity (5), Precision (6) and DSC (4) where the latter is the most used in the segmentation task of medical images.

The best result regarding the precision metric corresponded to 0.7458(0.0112) using $p = 0.1$ and $\gamma = 2.0$. This result shows that this methodology reduces false positives and false negatives, where false positives are reduced more strongly thanks to the application of a stratified sampling of the edges that increases the representation of difficult voxels and the better preprocessing of MRIs. For the sensitivity metric, the best result was obtained using the parameters $p = 0.1$ and $\gamma = 3.0$, which indicates that increasing the γ parameter of focal loss also reduces false negatives.

The best results according to the DSC metric were obtained using $p = 0.1$ and $\gamma = 2.0$, which indicates that for focal loss to have a greater effect on learning for the task of classifying difficult voxels, it is necessary to have a representation in the training set greater than that obtained with uniform sampling, which is approximately 0.026. We note that a larger representation such as $p = 0.1$ implies a decrease in the effect of using focal loss compared to the binary cross-entropy loss function because these difficult voxels are no longer underrepresented in the training set, thus they contribute with similar amplitude in the average penalty within each batch used in updating the network weights.

Some segmentation results are shown in Fig. 3. Figure 3(a) corresponds to an axial view of a T2-Flair MRI of a multiple sclerosis patient. In this modality, the lesions appear as hyperintensities, where the segmentation performed by the expert radiologist is presented in Fig. 3(b). In Fig. 3(c) the results of automatic segmentation of the network are presented where the parameters are $p = 0.0$ and $\gamma = 0.0$ and in Fig. 3(d) with $p = 0.0$ and $\gamma = 1.0$. False positive voxels can be seen in blue and false negatives in green. It can be noticed in Fig. 3(d) that there was a slight decrease in false positives which is due to the application of focal loss.

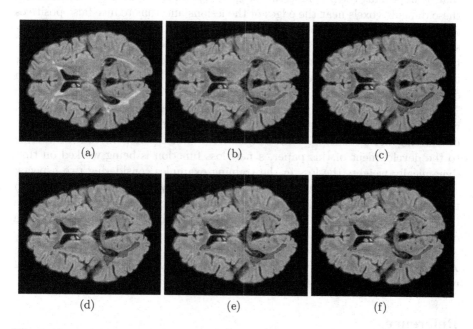

Fig. 3. Automatic segmentations. True positives in red, false negatives in green and false positives in blue. (a) Axial view of T2-FLAIR, (b) T2-FLAIR with expert mask, (c-d) binary cross entropy using uniform sampling with $\gamma = 0.0$ and $\gamma = 1.0$, respectively, and (e-f) stratified sampling with $p = 0.05$ and focal loss with $\gamma = 0.0$ and $\gamma = 1.0$, respectively.

In Fig. 3(e) the results of automatic segmentation are presented using the parameters $p = 0.1$ and $\gamma = 0.0$ and in Fig. 3(f) $p = 0.1$ and $\gamma = 2.0$. In Fig. 3(f) it is possible to observe a decrease in the false positives with respect to all the previous combinations of parameters, which is explained by the use of an stratified sampling of the difficult voxels near the edges and the use of focal loss. Although the false negatives do not decrease what is expected, if a similar value is achieved on average, that is, the gain in precision does not affect the sensitivity of the CNN, which can be seen quantitatively in Table 2.

4   Conclusions and Future Work

This work shows the importance of an efficient design in the task of segmentation of multiple sclerosis lesions, where the application of a loss function that penalizes difficult voxels more extensively can improve the segmentation results. It was empirically verified that the focal loss function requires an adequate representation of the difficult voxels near the edges and that the targeting of the penalty in these improves the results of the DSC metric (Dice). We also conclude that by improving the preprocessing stage it is possible a better representation of these difficult voxels near the edges of the lesions and thus reduce false positives and false negatives, where the best result obtained for the DSC metric corresponded to $DSC = 0.7046$ (0.0097) with the parameters $p = 0.1$ and $\gamma = 2.0$, taking into account that for the medical image segmentation task a value greater than $DSC > 0.7$ is considered comparable to that obtained by another human expert.

As future work, it is proposed to work with non-uniform 3D sampling patches, which is expected to generate an increase in the results in the DSC metric considering the 3D nature of the MRIs. We can also comment that in parallel to the development of this paper, a new loss function is being worked on that dynamically weights the loss in the training examples considering two aspects: 1) The difficulty of classifying the voxel to the injury class or not lesion and 2) the distance from the voxel to the edges of the multiple sclerosis lesions because these voxels are where the highest rate of false positives and false negatives are concentrated.

Acknowledgments. This work was supported in part by Basal Project AFB 1800082 and in part by Project DGIIE-UTFSM PI-LIR-2020-17.

References

1. Birenbaum, A., Greenspan, H.: Multi-view longitudinal CNN for multiple sclerosis lesion segmentation. Eng. App. Artif. Intell. **65**, 111–118 (2017)
2. Carass, A., et al.: Longitudinal multiple sclerosis lesion segmentation: resource and challenge. NeuroImage **148**, 77–102 (2017)
3. Chollet, F., et al.: Keras (2015). https://keras.io

4. Danelakis, A., Theoharis, T., Verganelakis, D.A.: Survey of automated multiple sclerosis lesion segmentation techniques on magnetic resonance imaging. Computer. Med. Imaging Graph. **70**, 83–100 (2018). https://doi.org/10.1016/j.compmedimag.2018.10.002, http://www.sciencedirect.com/science/article/pii/S0895611118303227

5. Giorgio, A., Stefano, N.D.: Effective utilization of MRI in the diagnosis and management of multiple sclerosis. Neurolog. Clin. **36**(1), 27–34 (2018). https://doi.org/10.1016/j.ncl.2017.08.013, http://www.sciencedirect.com/science/article/pii/S0733861917301007

6. Goldenberg, M.M.: Multiple sclerosis review. P&T : a peer-reviewed journal for formulary management **37**(3), 175–184 (2012). https://www.ncbi.nlm.nih.gov/pmc/articles/PMC3351877/,https://www.ncbi.nlm.nih.gov/pubmed/22605909

7. Jenkinson, M., Bannister, P., Brady, M., Smith, S.: Improved optimization for the robust and accurate linear registration and motion correction of brain images. NeuroImage **17**(2), 825 – 841 (2002). https://doi.org/10.1006/nimg.2002.1132, http://www.sciencedirect.com/science/article/pii/S1053811902911328

8. Lin, T., Goyal, P., Girshick, R., He, K., Dollár, P.: Focal loss for dense object detection. IEEE Trans. Pattern Anal. Mach. Intell. **42**(2), 318–327 (2020). https://doi.org/10.1109/TPAMI.2018.2858826

9. Ulloa, G., Veloz, A., Allende-Cid, H., Allende, H.: Improving multiple sclerosis lesion boundaries segmentation by convolutional neural networks with focal learning. In: Campilho, A., Karray, F., Wang, Z. (eds.) Image Analysis and Recognition, pp. 182–192. Springer International Publishing, Cham (2020)

10. Valverde, S., et al.: Improving automated multiple sclerosis lesion segmentation with a cascaded 3d convolutional neural network approach. NeuroImage **155**, 159–168 (2017)

11. Zhou, T., Ruan, S., Canu, S.: A review: deep learning for medical image segmentation using multi-modality fusion. Array **3-4**, 100004 (2019). https://doi.org/10.1016/j.array.2019.100004, http://www.sciencedirect.com/science/article/pii/S2590005619300049

Delimitation of Benign and Malignant Masses in Breast Ultrasound by Clustering of Intuitionistic Fuzzy Superpixels Using DBSCAN Algorithm

Dante Mújica-Vargas[1]([✉])([iD]), Antonio Luna-Álvarez[1], Alberto Rosales-Silva[2], and Andrea Palacios-Cervantes[1]

[1] TecNM-CENIDET, Cuernavaca, Morelos, Mexico
dante.mv@cenidet.tecnm.mx
[2] IPN-ESIME Zacatenco, Ciudad de México, Mexico

Abstract. In this study, we propose a scheme to delimit benign and malignant masses in breast ultrasound images. It consists of two stages: superpixels extraction by an Intuitionistic Fuzzy algorithm, which considers the local information of the image to develop a local segmentation; and clustering the superpixels by means of DBSCAN algorithm. The proposal does not require preprocessing of noise reduction inherent to this type of medical images or enhancement of features. The effectiveness of our proposal is verified by quantitative and qualitative results.

Keywords: Intuitionistic fuzzy clustering · Ultrasound image delimitation · DBSCAN

1 Introduction

Early detection of breast cancer through mammography is essential to reduce mortality among the female population worldwide. Raw mammographic images are complex, since these images are acquired by means of very low dose X-rays, or else ultrasound once the presence of some abnormality is certain [12]. Therefore, computer-assisted analysis techniques based on digital image processing are used to improve visual quality and detect any abnormalities that may be present. Inspection of mammograms for breast tumors is a difficult task that radiologists must perform frequently. Therefore, image analysis methods are needed for the detection and delimitation of breast tumors. Methods have been introduced in the literature to obtain the delimitation of masses in ultrasound images by filtering noise, specifically: alternatives include θ threshold segmentation, preprocessing the image with Max-based filters [15]. In [8] a Gaussian filter is used for spatial smoothing, an Active Contour Model with edge function $E = -|\nabla I(x,y)|^2$ and K-means clustering based on local correntropy. Graph-based models [20], as well as fuzzy clustering [13]. The deep learning methods [3] that do not require denoising or feature enhancement. An Adaptive Fuzzy Filter based on Histogram

O. O. Vergara-Villegas et al. (Eds.): MCPR 2022, LNCS 13264, pp. 348–359, 2022.
https://doi.org/10.1007/978-3-031-07750-0_32

Estimation was proposed. In [7], an Adaptive Interpolation-based Impulse Noise Removal algorithm was proposed, with parametric self-tuning, based on weights Φ calculated from the distance $\Phi_{ij} = \frac{1}{\|(i,j)\|^k}$. A Modified Cascaded Filter [9], consisted of a connection of Decision-based Median Filters and Un-symmetric α Trimmed-Mean Filters.

However, the sharp and sudden variations inherent in ultrasound images in addition to the high density require a robust denoising method in order not to affect the quality of the image f. A clustering algorithm in the crisp domain is effective at up to 2% density [19] and fuzzy at 5 to 10%. Deep learning models adapt better to images with noise and do not require improvement of characteristics, but generate a higher computational cost while they depend on the correct training, adjusting to certain databases. To solve these limitations, this research proposes the extraction of superpixels using Intuitionistic Fuzzy Clustering [14], the over-segmentation performs the delimitation of the different tissues of the image. Then, grouping is performed by means of DBSCAN, which does not require parameter initialization and creates a group for each tissue in globally image.

To understand the complexity of intuitive fuzzy clustering (IFC) and the DBSCAN, Sect. 2 describes the theory. In Sect. 3 the proposed scheme is described and demonstrated in Sect. 4, the conclusion is presented in Sect. 5.

2   Background

Extraction of Intuitionistic Fuzzy Superpixels

As it was established in [14], intuitionistic fuzzy sets were an alternative to oversegment grayscale or color images. Therefore, in this paper they are used to extract superpixels from breast ultrasound. Consider a grayscale image $X = \{x_{mn} \mid m = 1, \cdots, M; n = 1, \cdots, N\}$ expressed in its vector form $\vec{X} = \{\vec{x}_l \mid l = 1, \cdots, L\}$ with $L = M \times N$, its transformation to IFC domain implies:

$$x_l^{IFS} = \left\{ \left\langle \vec{x}_l, \mu(\vec{x}_l), \nu(\vec{x}_l), \pi(\vec{x}_l) \right\rangle \forall \; \vec{x}_l \in \vec{X} | l = 1, \dots L \right\}, \tag{1}$$

where $\mu(\vec{x}_l), \nu(\vec{x}_l)$ and $\pi(\vec{x}_l)$ stand for membership, non-membership and hesitancy degrees, respectively. These parameters can be computed by:

$$\mu(\vec{x}_l) = \frac{\vec{x}_l - \min(\vec{X})}{\max(\vec{X}) - \min(\vec{X})}, \tag{2}$$

$$\nu(\vec{x}_l) = \frac{1 - \mu(\vec{x}_l)}{1 + (e^\lambda - 1) \cdot \mu(\vec{x}_l)}, \; \lambda \in [0,1], \tag{3}$$

$$\pi(\vec{x}_l) = 1 - \mu(\vec{x}_l) - \nu(\vec{x}_l), \tag{4}$$

Constrained by conditions $\mu(\vec{x}_l) + \nu(\vec{x}_l) + \pi(\vec{x}_l) = 1$ and $0 \leq \pi(\vec{x}_l) \leq 1$, for each $\vec{x} \in \vec{X}$. Functions $\min(\vec{X})$ and $\max(\vec{X})$ allow to calculate the minimum and maximum value of $\vec{X}$, respectively. For constant λ, we suggest a value of $\lambda = 0.085$ for better performance on these medical images. The extraction of intuitionistic fuzzy superpixels implies an iterative clustering algorithm that works in a local way; for that purpose next objective function can be stated:

$$\mathcal{J}_m\left(\vec{X}^{IFS}; U, V^{IFS}\right) = \sum_{l=1}^{L}\sum_{k=1}^{K} u_{lk}^{\gamma}\|\vec{x}_l^{IFS} - v_k^{IFS}\|_2^2, \tag{5}$$

where $\vec{X}^{IFS} = \{\vec{x}_l^{IFS} \mid l = 1,\cdots,L\}$ is a vector with l-th pixels stated as intuitionist fuzzy sets. $v^{IFS} = \{v_k^{IFS} \mid k = 1,\cdots,K\}$ is a vector with centroids of the K initial superpixels, with $v_k^{IFS} = \{\mu(\vec{x}_k), \nu(\vec{x}_k), \pi(\vec{x}_k)\}$. $U = \{u_{lk} \mid l = 1,\cdots,L;\ k = 1,\cdots,K\}$ is the cluster partition of $\vec{X}^{IFS}$, u_{lk} is interpreted as the membership of the pixel $\vec{x}_l^{IFS}$ to k-th superpixel. $\gamma \geq 2$ is the fuzzifier parameter. $\|\cdot\|_2^2$ is the square euclidean intuitionistic fuzzy distance, by:

$$\|\vec{x}_l^{IFS} - v_k^{IFS}\|_2^2 = \{(\mu(\vec{x}_l) - \mu(\vec{x}_k))^2 + (\nu(\vec{x}_l) - \nu(\vec{x}_k))^2 + (\pi(\vec{x}_l) - \pi(\vec{x}_k))^2\} \tag{6}$$

It is dealing with a local clustering in K superpixels, for that purpose the input image is split into regular grids with $2R \times 2R$ size, where $R = \sqrt{L/K}$. Figure 1 depicts the graphic representation of the grid, the condition $X = \bigcup_{k=1}^{K} S_k$ must be respected, where S_k is the k-th initial superpixel.

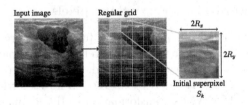

Fig. 1. Grid of initial superpixels.

Objective function (5) exhibits that the variables U and V^{IFS} must be updated iteratively in order to minimize the squared error between the IFC data and the centroids of each cluster. The update formulas can be obtained by setting the partial derivative of $\mathcal{J}_m$ w.r.t. the parameters to optimize equal to zero. Expression to update the lk-th membership degree u_{lk} is stated as follows:

$$u_{lk} = \frac{1}{\sum_{r=1}^{K}\left[\frac{\|\vec{x}_l^{IFS} - v_k^{IFS}\|_2^2}{\|\vec{x}_l^{IFS} - v_r^{IFS}\|_2^2}\right]^{\frac{1}{m-1}}} \tag{7}$$

While the prototypes vector is computed by:

$$v_k^{IFS} = \left\{ \frac{\sum\limits_{l=1}^{L} u_{lk}^{\gamma}\mu(\vec{x}_k)}{\sum\limits_{l=1}^{L} u_{lk}^{\gamma}}, \frac{\sum\limits_{l=1}^{L} u_{lk}^{\gamma}\nu(\vec{x}_k)}{\sum\limits_{l=1}^{L} u_{lk}^{\gamma}}, \frac{\sum\limits_{l=1}^{L} u_{lk}^{\gamma}\pi(\vec{x}_k)}{\sum\limits_{l=1}^{L} u_{lk}^{\gamma}} \right\} \tag{8}$$

Local clustering means that for each k-th superpixel, a segmentation process must be developed taking into account expressions (5), (7) and (8). On the basis of intuitionistic fuzzy clustering, each pixel belongs to all superpixels with a different membership degree, for dealing with this situation current proposal identifies for each x_l, the highest membership degree u_{lk} with respect to K superpixels and assigns it the k-th label.

Clustering of Intuitionistic Fuzzy Superpixels

To delimit masses, it is suggested a clustering process of the intuitionistic fuzzy superpixels by means of Density-Based Spatial Clustering of Applications with Noise (DBSCAN) [21]. This uses local connectivity and density functions to perform clustering, which it is a advantage because it does not require clusters initialization [11]. These can be represented as shown in Fig. 2; in this regard two parameters need to be set: the maximum radius of the neighborhood δ and the minimum number of superpixels in the neighborhood ϑ bounded by δ.

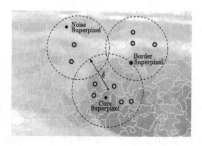

Fig. 2. Representation of superpixel centroids and neighborhood radius.

Core Superpixels are superpixels that are within the δ radius and have at least ϑ neighbors. *Border Superpixels* are superpixels that on the border. *Noise Superpixels* that not correspond to any of the previous types. Algorithm 1 summarizes this algorithm.

Algorithm 1: Intuitionistic Fuzzy Superpixels - DBSCAN

---

    set of superpixels: $S = \{s_1, \cdots, s_n\}$
    states: $core, boder, noise, P_{states}[n]$
    output: Clusters $C = \{c_1, \cdots, c_m\}$

1 $Q \leftarrow P$
2 **while** $Q \neq \emptyset$ **do**
3   pick $p_i \in Q$
4   find all $density - reachable$ superpixels from p_i w.r.t. δ and ϑ
5   **if** p_i *is a core superpixel* **then**
6       $P_{states}[i] \leftarrow core$
7   **else if** p_i *is a border superpixel* **then**
8       $P_{states}[i] \leftarrow border$
9     $c_i \leftarrow core\ superpixel$
10    $Q \leftarrow Q \backslash c_i$
11    $i \leftarrow i + 1$
12 **for** $p_i \in Q\ \forall P_{states}[i] \neq core \wedge P_{states}[i] \neq border$ **do**
13    $P_{states}[i] \leftarrow noise$
14 **return** C

In essence, DBSCAN is an heuristic that analyzes and clusters the superpixels in terms of γ distance. This means that the algorithm includes all core superpixels that are within γ distance of each other in the same cluster, and excludes border and noise superpixels of the interest clusters.

3 Proposed Scheme

Figure 3 shows the proposed scheme. The operation is quite intuitive, the image must be entered into the system, then this is divided into a regular grid. In a full coverage process, on each one of the initial grids is developed in two steps the over segmentation task by means of the IFCM algorithm. First, the local region of the image is transformed into IFC domain via expression (1). The local over clustering is developing via (5), (7) and (8). The result of the DBSCAN (Algorithm 1) to perform a clustering based on local spatial analysis.

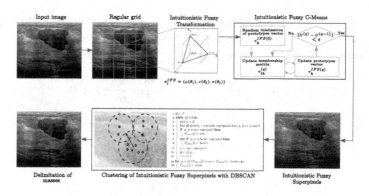

Fig. 3. Proposed scheme.

AOur proposal is made up of two clustering phases, which are developed in a hierarchical manner. It can be guaranteed that the proposal is robust enough to delimit tumors in ultrasound images, without requiring any pre-processing stage. The complexity of this type of images would force us to consider some stage of multiplicative noise reduction. However, it is clear that IFC theory compensates for this requirement. The use of these algorithms can be interchanged, but this does not guarantee similar performance, which supports the strength of IFC sets against vague and corrupted information.

4   Experimental Results

To validate the proposed scheme, the Breast Ultrasound Images Dataset (BUSI) [2] was used. This is composed of three types of samples: ultrasound images with 437 samples of benign masses, 210 malignant masses and 133 without the presence of masses. The images are in png format for 562×471 in grayscale.

For comparison, the experiments with the BUSI Dataset were replicated in: the Salient Attention Contour UNet network (UNet SAC) [18], the Modified Robust Fuzzy C-Means (MFCM) [17] Spatial Guided Self Supervised Clustering (SGSCN) [1], from the MATLAB libraries, the Automatic Nonlinear Filtering and Segmentation for Breast Ultrasound Images (ANFS) [5] from the ICIAR library. Finally, the MATLAB Toolbox for Breast Ultrasound Image Analysis (BUSAT) [16]. All evaluated algorithms and schemes were programmed in Python or MATLAB, using an Intel(R) Core(TM) processor i7-4720HQ CPU @2.60 GHz with 4 cores and 16 GB of RAM memory.

4.1   Metrics

In order to compare with current state-of-art we introduce as first the Hausdorff Distance (HD) such as a contour based accuracy measure is given by:

$$HD(X, Y) = \max\left\{\max(\min(\| X - Y \|_2)), \max(\min(\| Y - X \|_2))\right\}, \quad (9)$$

where $\| \cdot \|_2$ denotes the euclidean distance, X stands for the ground truth (GT) contour, while Y the resulting contour. Region based accuracy measures were also considered. Segmentation accuracy was estimated through MCR:

$$MCR = \frac{misclassified\ pixels}{overall\ number\ of\ pixels} \times 100, \tag{10}$$

the smallest percentage implies the best delimitation. Jaccard Similarity Coefficient (JSC) was used to compare similarity:

$$JSC = \frac{|\,X \cap Y\,|}{|\,X \cup Y\,|}, \tag{11}$$

We also consider the metrics derived from the confusion matrix Sensitivity (SEN), Specificity (SPC) and Precision (ACC) [4].

4.2 Benignant Masses Delimitation

In the first experiment, it is taken a benign mass the cells are not disseminated. Therefore, benign mass is well defined in a specific area. It is possible to interpret this condition as a less complex object for detection compared to a malignant mass. The benign mass located near the upper right border is visibly more opaque than the rest of the tissue, there may be elements that complicate the process of detection [10]. This can be seen in Fig. 4, where the state-of-art algorithms and proposal are evaluated with benign masses.

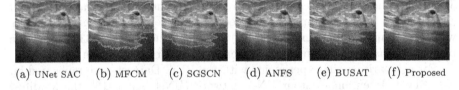

(a) UNet SAC   (b) MFCM   (c) SGSCN   (d) ANFS   (e) BUSAT   (f) Proposed

Fig. 4. Benign mass detection performance, sample 7.

Figure 4 shows that the UNet, ANFS algorithms and the proposed scheme are efficient in approaching the expected delimitation. The rest of the competing algorithms come close to delimiting the expected area, however they are affected by the conditions of the image and detect areas of similar hue to that of the object of interest. In another experiment performed for the benign sample 370, a mass of greater proportion identified in the GT is observed. This mass presents greater variations within the region of interest and outside of it. To observe this, Fig. 5 shows the results obtained from the experimentation.

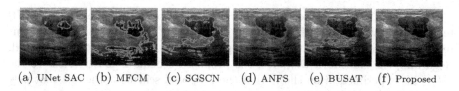

(a) UNet SAC   (b) MFCM   (c) SGSCN   (d) ANFS   (e) BUSAT   (f) Proposed

Fig. 5. Benign mass detection performance, sample 370.

The UNet is less affected by variations in the image in general, however it is the internal variations of the region of interest that affect the segmentation of the mass. It can be identified that the MFCM, BUSAT, SGSCN and the UNet model present the lowest quality delimitation and the proposed scheme, seem more approximate. To be certain of these results, Fig. 6 shows the graphical summary of the region based accuracy metrics.

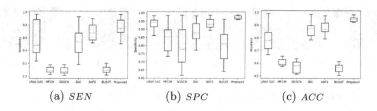

(a) *SEN*   (b) *SPC*   (c) *ACC*

Fig. 6. Average performance by the proposed and competing algorithms.

Figure 6 shows that the MFCM, SGSCN and BUSAT show sensitivity ≈0.2, which is in agreement with what is shown in Figs. 4 and 5 due to erroneous detection in the wrong areas. The proposed scheme obtains an average sensitivity of 0.8 and a ≈0.98, although the UNet model also obtains a maximum of ≈0.98, it obtained an average <0.5 showing that it shows the better performance only for specific cases, this may be due to the training fold. In specificity and accuracy, the proposed scheme obtains the best evaluation with an average of ≈0.95 in both metrics. The accuracy metrics measure the correct delimitation at the pixel level, so the metrics based on contour and region are summarized in Table 1.

Table 1. Contour and region-based metrics obtained for benign mass samples.

Method	Pixel classification		Contour-based	Region-based	
	TP	FP	HD	MCR	JSC
UNet SAC	963	4284	3.70	6.83	0.81
MFCM	2797	2450	14.82	38.41	0.90
SGSCN	3941	1305	14.25	41.44	0.89
ANFS	4137	1110	4.15	1.79	0.27
BUSAT	4347	896	14.70	48.04	0.89
Proposed	**4837**	**410**	**3.36**	**1.36**	**0.91**

In Table 1 it is observed that the UNet model presented the worst TP-FP relationship, which, unlike the other methods, the FP is greater than TP. This result is visible in Fig. 5a, where the region obtained is smaller than expected. Regarding the Hausdorff Distance, the proposed scheme is mostly close to the GT. This experimentation shows that the proposed scheme is the one that performs best delimiting benign masses.

4.3   Malignant Masses Delimitation

For malignant masses, the conditions are different. This type of tumor does not present itself in regular forms, its cells spreading to other tissues, causing isolated cells to be confused by computational methods due to noise captured in ultrasound [6]. A region similar in tone to the one delimited as a malignant mass on one side is observed, so an algorithm can confuse this area as a FP.

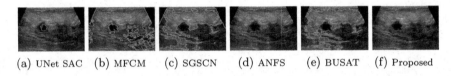

(a) UNet SAC   (b) MFCM   (c) SGSCN   (d) ANFS   (e) BUSAT   (f) Proposed

Fig. 7. Malignant mass detection performance, sample 65.

The SGSCN algorithm seems to delimit a homogeneous area since it has the same hue as the malignant mass. However, when observing Fig. 7 it is easier to identify the malignant mass and that the similar region is actually an affectation of the image during the acquisition.

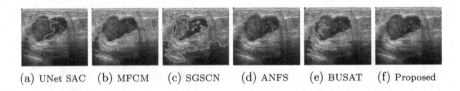

(a) UNet SAC   (b) MFCM   (c) SGSCN   (d) ANFS   (e) BUSAT   (f) Proposed

Fig. 8. Malignant mass detection performance, sample 154.

However, the experimentation is again supported by the region based accuracy metrics. These are summarized graphically in Fig. 9.

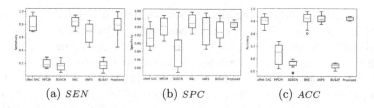

(a) *SEN*   (b) *SPC*   (c) *ACC*

Fig. 9. Average performance by the proposed and competing algorithms.

Unlike the samples with a benign mass, in this experiment the performance of the proposed scheme is diminished, obtaining ≈0.8 of sensitivity, 0.94 of specificity and ≈0.90 of accuracy. Although the metrics indicate a lower performance, the box plots show the proposed scheme with the smallest distribution, which indicates that in general experimentation this is the precision. Similarly, in Table 2 metrics based on contour and region are reported.

Table 2. Contour and region-based metrics obtained for malignant mass samples.

Method	Pixel classification		Contour-based	Region-based	
	TP	FP	HD	MCR	JSC
UNet SAC	4877	5029	8.62	8.09	0.60
MFCM	7742	2164	15.88	34.60	0.71
SGSCN	6439	3466	16.21	45.57	0.32
ANFS	5680	4222	6.78	4.33	0.84
BUSAT	7200	2704	16.17	46.08	0.73
Proposed	**9291**	**614**	**5.16**	**3.98**	**0.84**

As can be seen in Table 2, the proposed scheme presents the best relationship in classification at the pixel level. The UNet model presents a negative balance that is easily observed in Fig. 8a. In the contour-based metric, the proposed scheme continues to obtain the smallest distance. This is observable in Fig. 8f that delimits a slightly larger area that coincides with the GT.

5   Conclusion and Future Work

In this article, a scheme for the delimitation of masses in ultrasound images was presented, this done by oversegmentation of the image by means of Intuitionistic Fuzzy Clustering that delimits each region and later groups those superpixels that belong to the mass group, benign or malignant. The proposed scheme demonstrated to identify a benign mass with an average precision of 95% and 88% for malignant masses, in terms of measurement based on contours it obtained a distance of ≈3.36 for benign and 5.16 for malignant, turning out to be the least among the competing algorithms. For measures based on region, similarity of 91% was obtained for benign cases and 84% for malignant cases. It was observed that the proposed scheme performs better to delimit benign masses. In addition to the reported metrics, the proposed scheme offers the following advantages compared to state-of-art methods: (1) it does not require training or prior adjustment, (2) the number of clusters is self-adjusting, so it does not require start parameters, (3) it can obtain the area of interest without the need for guidance. As future work, it will be considered to implement the scheme to speed up its processing to obtain a delimitation in real time. In addition, it is considered to consider an algorithm based on direction detection in textures and edges, to detect the spread of malignant masses.

Acknowledgements. The authors thank to CONACYT, as well as TecNM-CENIDET for their financial support through the project "Delimitación de masas sólidas malignas en mamografías mediante un algoritmo de nodos conectados con el menor ángulo polar".

References

1. Ahn, E., Feng, D., Kim, J.: A spatial guided self-supervised clustering network for medical image segmentation (2021)
2. Al-Dhabyani, W., Gomaa, M., Khaled, H., Fahmy, A.: Dataset of breast ultrasound images. Data Brief **28**, 104863 (2020)
3. Byra, M., et al.: Joint segmentation and classification of breast masses based on ultrasound radio-frequency data and convolutional neural networks. Ultrasonics, 106682 (2022)
4. Chen, H., et al.: Segmentation of lymph nodes in ultrasound images using u-net convolutional neural networks and Gabor-based anisotropic diffusion. J. Med. Biol. Eng. **41**(6), 942–952 (2021)
5. Elawady, M., Sadek, I., Shabayek, A.E.R., Pons, G., Ganau, S.: Automatic non-linear filtering and segmentation for breast ultrasound images. In: Campilho, A., Karray, F. (eds.) Image Analysis and Recognition, pp. 206–213. Springer International Publishing, Cham (2016). https://doi.org/10.1007/978-3-319-41501-7_24
6. Fayed, L., Seong, J.: Differences between a malignant and benign tumor. verywellhealth.com (2020)
7. Gökcen, A., Kalyoncu, C.: Real-time impulse noise removal. J. Real-Time Image Process. **17**(3), 459–469 (2018). https://doi.org/10.1007/s11554-018-0791-y
8. Joshi, A., Khan, M.S., Niaz, A., Akram, F., Song, H.C., Choi, K.N.: Active contour model with adaptive weighted function for robust image segmentation under biased conditions. Expert Syst. App. **175**, 114811 (2021)
9. Karthik, B., Krishna Kumar, T., Vijayaragavan, S.P., Sriram, M.: Removal of high density salt and pepper noise in color image through modified cascaded filter. J. Amb. Intell. Human. Comput. **12**(3), 3901–3908 (2020). https://doi.org/10.1007/s12652-020-01737-1
10. Magny, S.J., Shikhman, R., Keppke, A.L.: Breast imaging reporting and data system. StatPearls [Internet] (2021)
11. Mao, Y.M., Mwakapesa, D.S., Li, Y., Xu, K., Nanehkaran, Y.A., Zhang, M.: Assessment of landslide susceptibility using DBSCAN-AHD and LD-EV methods. J. Mount. Sci. **19**(1), 184–197 (2022)

12. Meenalochini, G., Ramkumar, S.: Survey of machine learning algorithms for breast cancer detection using mammogram images. Mater. Today Proc. **37**, 2738–2743 (2021)
13. Militello, C.: Semi-automated and interactive segmentation of contrast-enhancing masses on breast DCE-MRI using spatial fuzzy clustering. Biomed. Signal Process. Control **71**, 103113 (2022)
14. Mújica-Vargas, D.: Superpixels extraction by an intuitionistic fuzzy clustering algorithm. J. Appl. Res. Technol. **19**(2), 140–152 (2021)
15. Patra, D.K., Si, T., Mondal, S., Mukherjee, P.: Breast DCE-MRI segmentation for lesion detection by multi-level thresholding using student psychological based optimization. Biomed. Signal Process. Control **69**, 102925 (2021)
16. Rodríguez-Cristerna, A., Gómez-Flores, W., de Albuquerque-Pereira, W.C.: BUSAT: a MATLAB Toolbox for breast ultrasound image analysis. In: Carrasco-Ochoa, J.A., Martínez-Trinidad, J.F., Olvera-López, J.A. (eds.) MCPR 2017. LNCS, vol. 10267, pp. 268–277. Springer, Cham (2017). https://doi.org/10.1007/978-3-319-59226-8_26
17. Song, J., Zhang, Z.: A modified robust FCM model with spatial constraints for brain MR image segmentation. Information **10**(2), 74 (2019). https://doi.org/10.3390/info10020074
18. Vakanski, A., Xian, M., Freer, P.E.: Attention-enriched deep learning model for breast tumor segmentation in ultrasound images. Ultrasound Med. Biol. **46**(10), 2819–2833 (2020)
19. Xu, Y., Wang, Y., Yuan, J., Cheng, Q., Wang, X., Carson, P.L.: Medical breast ultrasound image segmentation by machine learning. Ultrasonics **91**, 1–9 (2019)
20. Zhang, Y., Liu, M., He, J., Pan, F., Guo, Y.: Affinity fusion graph-based framework for natural image segmentation. IEEE Trans. Multimed. (2021)
21. Zhu, Q., Tang, X., Elahi, A.: Application of the novel harmony search optimization algorithm for DBSCAN clustering. Expert Syst. App. **178**, 115054 (2021)

Machine Learning and Symbolic Learning for the Recognition of Leukemia L1, L2 and L3

Rocio Ochoa-Montiel[1,2]([envelope]) [ORCID], Humberto Sossa[1,4] [ORCID], Gustavo Olague[3] [ORCID], and Carlos Sánchez-López[2] [ORCID]

[1] Instituto Politécnico Nacional, Centro de Investigación en Computación, Av. Juan de Dios Bátiz and M. Othón de Mendizabal, 07738 Mexico City, Mexico
ma.rocio.ochoa@gmail.com
[2] Facultad de Ciencias Básicas, Ingeniería y Tecnología, Universidad Autónoma de Tlaxcala, Apizaco, Mexico
[3] EvoVision Laboratory, CICESE Research Center, Ensenada, Mexico
[4] Tecnológico de Monterrey, Escuela de Ingeniería y Ciencias, Av. General Ramón Corona, 2514 Zapopan, Jalisco, Mexico

Abstract. Leukemia is a health problem that affects to world population causing thousands of kills yearly, thus accurate and human-readable diagnostic methods are required. Symbolic learning uses methods based on high-level representations of problems, which is useful to design interpretable models to understand the solutions found to solve a problem. In this work, we analyze the performance of 3 classifiers used frequently in machine learning, which are independently embedded into a model of symbolic learning named brain programming. Results suggest that the classifiers as MLP and SVM are robust to noisy data, with the MLP demonstrating the most stable behavior into the symbolic learning model, which is fundamental in models of evolutionary vision as the brain programming.

Keywords: Symbolic learning · Evolutionary vision · Leukemia recognition

1 Introduction

Artificial vision models offer excellent alternatives for solving major problems in diverse fields [1–3]. Particularly, in the medical area, one of these problems is opportune cancer detection, whose cost of diagnosis is significantly elevated. Acute leukemias (AL) are a type of cancer that requires greater attention due to their indolent course and short evolution, with an average annual lethality of 3 to 5 cases per 100,000 population and with a marked upward trend. In children, AL is the most frequent cause of death due to neoplasia [4]. Morphological classification of LAs is useful in the early stages of diagnosis, however in at

© The Author(s), under exclusive license to Springer Nature Switzerland AG 2022
O. O. Vergara-Villegas et al. (Eds.): MCPR 2022, LNCS 13264, pp. 360–369, 2022.
https://doi.org/10.1007/978-3-031-07750-0_33

least 20% of cases human errors can be made [5], so the use of computer vision techniques is useful to decrease these failures.

There are numerous papers in the literature that address the problem of leukemia classification based on visual analysis, with handcrafted approaches being the most frequently used [2,6–8]. In these approaches, the features of color, shape, distribution of cellular components, and the number of cells are taken into account since they are considered in the medical literature for the recognition of various hematological diseases [9]. Since the feature extraction methods used in handcrafted approaches are driven by human reasoning, some elements of these approaches can be useful in symbolic learning models, in which a certain degree of explainability can be achieved in the learning process. Therefore, in this paper, we propose to use a symbolic learning model called brain programming in which we evaluate the performance of three standard classifiers embedded independently in the model to address the problem of leukemia recognition.

In the next section, the materials and methods are described. Section 3 presents the methodology proposed. In Sect. 4, Experiments and Results are shown. Conclusions are included in Sect. 5.

2 Materials and Methods

2.1 Classical Classifiers in Machine Learning

Support Vector Machine SVM. SVM is a promising nonlinear, nonparametric classification technique, and with strong theoretical foundations based on the Vapnik-Chervonenkis theory [10]. For the SVM a data point is viewed as an m-dimensional vector, and the question is whether such points can be separated with a hyperplane. Many hyperplanes might classify the data. The general idea of SVM is to find the best hyperplane which represents the largest separation or margin between the two classes. In this work, we use an SVM working with the discriminate hyperplane defined by the Eq. 1.

$$f(x) = \sum_{i=1}^{l} \alpha_i y_i K(x_i, x) + b \tag{1}$$

where the training data is $(x_i, y_i), i = 1, ..., l$; 1 for the positive class and -1 otherwise, $y_i \in \{-1, 1\}$, $x_i \in R^p$, and $K(x_i, x)$ is the kernel function.

Random Forest RF. The random forest (RF) algorithm includes several relatively uncorrelated classification models (decision trees) that operate together as an ensemble to produce a nonlinear response that helps to outperform the classification performance of any individual model included in the ensemble, called a forest. The RF is based on the bagging method, in which each tree included in the forest is grown with B independent bootstrap samples, which are randomly chosen with replacement from the original data set. The parameter B refers to the number of trees in the ensemble, which in this work is designated

500 decision trees [11]. The classification of a new pattern in the RF is defined as $\hat{y}(x) = \sum_{j=1}^{B} l_i(\hat{y}_j(x))$, where B is the number of trees, $i = 1, ..., c$, c is the number of classes, and $l_i(.)$ is the indicator function as in Eq. 2.

$$l_i(\hat{y}_j(x)) = \begin{cases} 1 \ \hat{y} = i, \\ 0 \ \hat{y} \neq i \end{cases} \tag{2}$$

Multi-layer Perceptron MLP. An MLP is an artificial neural network composed of basic computing units stacked in multiple layers to form a feedforward network (input, hidden, and output layers). Each neuron receives an input $X = x_1, ..., x_n$, and computes a weighted linear sum of the signal as in Eq. 3.

$$O = \sum_{i=1}^{n} w_i x_i + bias \tag{3}$$

where w_i are the weights associated with the neuron. O from each neuron then passes through an activation function AF to supply the output transmitted by the neuron. In this work, the backpropagation algorithm is used to train the net. We consider one hidden layer with 50 neurons and an AF of sigmoid type. It is important to mention that the parameters used by each classifier were obtained by experimentation.

2.2   Symbolic Learning Through the Brain Programming

In general, symbolic learning analyzes methods based on high-level symbolic representations of problems, logic, and search. Such high-level representations are characterized by being human-readable. Therefore, symbolic learning investigates the implications for research in artificial intelligence [12].

Brain programming (BP) is an evolutionary computer vision paradigm in charge of finding a set of operations through an optimization process. These operations are embedded within a hierarchical process called visual cortex artificial visual cortex (AVC) in which genetic programming (GP) is the method used to discover a set of visual operators (VOs) within the AVC [13]. These visual operators are functions for describing image classes, where for example, the sum operator denoted by $A + B$ in Table 1 indicates the sum between two images.

The problem of image classification from the point of view of data modeling through GP is how the BP performs image recognition. In this way, the BP can be considered as a symbolic learning approach. The learning process of BP is defined since a minimization problem requires finding a solution $P_{min} \in S$ such that $\exists P_{min} \in S : f(P_{min}) \leq f(P)$. Since the direct mapping between the domain and codomain is unknown or not well defined, the model follows several stages. Unlike traditional approaches to finding best-fit parameters, in this case, we fit the data by discovering functions that perform classification within BP. Thus, the classification problem through BP is defined as in Eq. 4.

$$min(y - f(x, \mathbf{F}, \mathbf{T}, \mathbf{a})) \tag{4}$$

Table 1. Functions and Terminals for the evolutionary visual operators.

Functions	Terminals
Orientation (OV_o)	
$A + B$, $A - B$, $A * B$, A/B, $|A + B|$, $|A - B|$, $inf(A, B)$, $sup(A, B)$, $\sqrt{A}$, A^2, $\log(A)$, $thr(A)$, $round(A)$, $\lfloor A \rfloor$, $\lceil A \rceil$, $G_{\sigma=1}(A)$, $G_{\sigma=2}(A)$, $|A|$, $D_x(A)$, $D_y(A)$, $k + A$, $k - A$, $k * A$, k/A	$I_{color} = I_r, I_g, I_b, I_c, I_m, I_y, I_k, I_h, I_s$ I_v, $I_x \in I_{color}$, $G_{\sigma=1}(I_x)$, $D_x(I_x)$, $D_y(I_x)$, $D_{yy}(I_x)$, $D_{xx}(I_x)$, $D_{xy}(I_x)$
Color (OV_c)	
$A + B$, $A - B$, $A * B$, A/B, $k + A$, $k - A$, $k * A$, k/A, $thr(A)$, $round(A)$, $\lfloor A \rfloor$, $\lceil A \rceil$, $\sqrt{A}$, A^2, $\log(A)$, $(A)^c$, $exp(A)$	$I_r, I_g, I_b, I_c, I_m, I_y, I_k, I_h, I_s, I_v$, $Op_{r-g}(I_{rgb})$, $Op_{b-y}(I_{rgb})$
Shape (OV_s)	
$A + B$, $A - B$, $A * B$, A/B, $k + A$, $k - A$, $k * A$, k/A, $thr(A)$, $round(A)$, $\lfloor A \rfloor$, $\lceil A \rceil$, $A \oplus SE_{dm}$, $A \oplus SE_s$, $A \oplus SE_d$, $A \ominus SE_{dm}$, $A \ominus SE_s$, $A \ominus SE_d$, $Sk(A)$, $Perim(A)$, $A \circledast SE_{dm}$, $A \circledast SE_s$, $A \circledast SE_d$, $T_{hat}(A)$, $B_{hat}(A)$, $A \odot SE_s$, $A \odot SE_s$	$I_r, I_g, I_b, I_c, I_m, I_y, I_k, I_h, I_s, I_v$
Mental Maps (OV_{MM})	
$A + B$, $A - B$, $A * B$, A/B, $|A + B|$, $|A - B|$, $\sqrt{A}$, A^2, $\log(A)$, $D_x(A)$, $D_y(A)$, $|A|$, $k * A$, $G_{\sigma=1}(A)$, $G_{\sigma=2}(A)$	CM_d, $D_x(CM_d)$, $D_y(CM_d)$, $D_{xx}(CM_d)$, $D_{yy}(CM_d)$, $D_{xy}(CM_d)$

where (y, x) are the label and the image from dataset, respectively; $f(.)$ represent the classifier, **F**, **T**, and **a** refer to function and terminals sets, and the parameters controlling the evolutionary process. The objective function that measures the model performance in arriving at the desired solution is given in quantitative terms of the multi-class classification through accuracy. Hence, $f(.)$ denotes a label value indicating the degree of class membership given by the classifier, and whose range is $[0, 1]$.

The criterion for minimization in terms of a classification problem allows to discover an optimal solution to the problem. In this work, we study the performance of three classifiers commonly used in machine learning, to learn a mapping $f()$ that associates descriptors d_i created by the AVC to labels y_i in a multi-class classification task.

3   The Proposed Methodology

In the proposed methodology, the leukemia image recognition problem is introduced from the standpoint of data modeling using a symbolic learning model named brain programming. BP is consisting of two stages, in the first, the purpose is to discover functions to optimize complex models adjusting operations within them. In the second stage, the parts (programs) are applied to a hierarchical model for the feature extraction. Figure 1 presents the general scheme of the proposal.

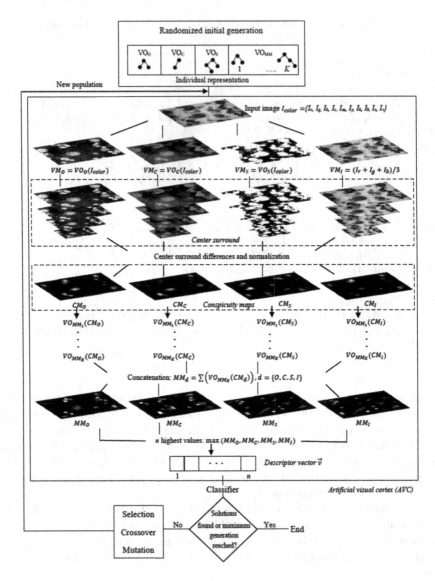

Fig. 1. General flowchart of the methodology

The evolutionary process starts with an initial random population in which an individual represents a program. Each individual (symbolic solution) consists of four types of functions, one for each VO visual operator. These operators are selected from the set of functions and terminals in Table 1. It is important to note that each individual is composed of a variable number of syntactic trees whose range is from 4 to 10, where 3 correspond to the visual operators of orientation, color, and shape; and from 1 to 7 correspond to the visual operators of the MM mental maps shown in Fig. 1.

Feature extraction is performed by the AVC whose hierarchical structure inspired by the human visual cortex, finds salient points in the image to generate an image descriptor that is subsequently used for classification. The set $I_{color} = \{I_r, I_g, I_b, I_c, I_m, I_y, I_k, I_h, I_s, I_v\}$, is created from multiple color channels whose elements refer to the color components of RGB, HSV, and CMYK color spaces.

In the first phase, the decomposition of the image into its relevant features is performed by applying the VOs, the output of which is an image called visual map VM. The next step, called center-surround, consists of the scale-invariant features are extracted and stored in a conspicuity map (CM). The CM is calculated as the difference between the different scales that are obtained through a pyramid of 9 levels: $P_d^\sigma = \{P_d^{\sigma=0}, P_d^{\sigma=1}, P_d^{\sigma=2}, ..., P_d^{\sigma=8}\}$. A Gaussian smoothing filter is used on each VM to calculate each pyramid. This produces an image that is half the size of the input map. The process is repeated 8 times to obtain the 9-level pyramid. In the next step, the differences with respect to each pyramid level in P_d^σ are calculated using Eq. (5) as follows:

$$Q_d^j = P_d^{\sigma = \lfloor \frac{j+9}{2} \rfloor + 1} - P_d^{\sigma = \lfloor \frac{j+2}{2} \rfloor + 1}, \tag{5}$$

where $j = 1, 2..6$. Each level of P_d^σ is normalized and scaled to the dimensionality of the VM using polynomial interpolation. Finally, the six levels are combined into a single map with a summation operation, and a CM is obtained for each dimension. The second phase begins with description and classification. First, a mental map (MM) is built from the CMs using Eq. 6, where d is the dimensionality and k is the cardinality of the set EVO_{MM}. This MM discriminates unwanted information, highlighting the most salient features of the object. VOs are defined through syntactic trees, and the MMs occupy the fourth position of the tree onward.

$$MM_d = \sum_{i=1}^{k} EVO_{MM_i}(CM_d). \tag{6}$$

The generated program is applied to each image from the MMs obtained and concatenated with the rest of the syntactic trees. Then, the n highest values are used to define the descriptor vector $\vec{v}$ for the input image in turn. Thus, the next step is to train a classifier using the feature vectors obtained from the data set. In this paper, SVM, RF, and MLP classifiers are used independently to analyze their model performance. This means that each classifier creates a model $f(\mathbf{x})$ that maps a set of descriptor vectors $\mathbf{x}_i$ to their corresponding labels $\mathbf{y}_i$, thus satisfying Eq. 4.

The selection, crossover, and mutation processes are performed as suggested in [13]. Finally, the stopping conditions are (1) the algorithm reaches a predefined number of generations, or (2) the fitness of the algorithm reaches an optimal value; in this case, all images are correctly classified.

4   Experiments and Results

The experiments were performed on a CPU i9, 64 GB RAM, Windows10, and MATLAB. Initialization values for the algorithm are: (a) Initialization. - Ramped half and half, (b) Tree depth. - Dynamic depth selection, (c) Dynamic max depth. - 50 levels, (d) Maximum length of genes. - 10, (e) Selection. - Roulette wheel, and (f) Elitism. - Keep the best individual. The evolutionary loop ends until the classification rate is 100% or the algorithm reaches the maximum number of generations $N = 30$ using a population size of 30 individuals, and crossover and mutation rate of 0.4 and 0.1, respectively.

The dataset is composed of bone marrow smear images from three subtypes of acute lymphoblastic leukaemia (ALL): L1, L2, and L3. The RGB images are in BMP format with resolutions of 1280 × 1024 pixels, and they were selected from an own dataset [14]. The images are resized to 256 × 320 pixels using bicubic interpolation due to the high computational cost. We used balanced sets of 217 images. Images contain one or more interesting cells that appear with nucleous of irregular purple regions, see Fig. 2. The dataset was divided into three parts: a learning set, a validation set, and a testing set as in previous work [15]. To obtain reliable fitness values, each new individual is estimated by the average classification error rate with the classifier using five-fold cross validation. The learning set is randomly divided into five equal parts, five training cases are evaluated with the MLP on 4 out of 5 of these parts, and the result is computed with the remaining validation set.

To select the best-performing solution, we test the classification error for every fold on validation set. Hence, we select one solution with the best validation error as the (near-) optimal feature descriptor for the final testing result. Finally, the test set is divided five-fold with the aim of computing the statistical results of the best solution discovered in the previous stage. We apply the same process for the learning set, and the overall classification result is calculated as the average of the 5 classifier test accuracies.

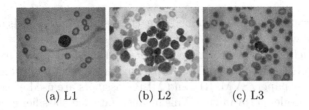

(a) L1   (b) L2   (c) L3

Fig. 2. Types of lymphocytic leukemia cells

4.1   Results

In this work, we propose to analyze the performance of SVM, RF, and MLP classifiers as embedded elements in a symbolic learning model called brain programming, for the recognition of L1, L2, and L3 leukemia.

To evaluate the performance of each classifier, the BP model shown in Fig. 1 was used, in which each classifier was used in independent experiments to control the evolutionary process. For each experiment, 10 runs were performed.

The results obtained for each case are presented in Table 2. For a more robust evaluation, the 3 classifiers are tested in each experiment with the test set, which gives an idea of the quality of the descriptor obtained in each experiment. It is important to note that at the beginning of the learning process, the classifiers use random data obtained from the initial population, and as the evolutionary process immersed in the model progresses, these data are reorganized until the appropriate patterns are found to achieve the expected recognition. Thus, we can observe that the RF classifier obtained an unstable performance with variable standard deviations in its evaluation with other classifiers, as well as the presence of outliers. On the other hand, the SVM shows a slight tendency to overfitting and a relatively high standard deviation. Finally, the MLP, although it did not reach high results in the validation, did show a more stable behavior when evaluated with the rest of the classifiers, as well as a lower standard deviation. The average test set for the 3 classifiers used in the evaluation of each experiment is 81.04% for MLP, 79.76% for RF and 80.48% for SVM.

Table 2. Results of accuracy for selected classifiers

Stat.	Evolution from MLP				Evolution from RF				Evolution from SVM			
	Val.	Test			Val.	Test			Val.	Test		
		MLP	RF	SVM		MLP	RF	SVM		MLP	RF	SVM
1	92.82	84.56	82.87	84.39	95.38	86.38	86.97	86.15	94.87	85.16	83.36	84.31
2	92.30	79.47	83.37	80.75	94.35	85.54	82.89	83.93	94.87	84.96	83.72	84.79
3	92.30	**86.66**	86.43	85.29	93.84	84.74	83.02	84.36	94.87	84.69	83.15	84.57
4	91.28	77.15	84.65	76.61	93.84	74.97	80.06	81.04	94.35	84.01	83.67	84.32
5	90.25	81.73	83.79	84.40	92.82	81.28	84.25	83.70	94.35	84.52	82.87	84.11
6	89.74	77.48	78.89	77.16	90.76	76.59	79.30	80.94	89.23	83.84	84.9	82.90
7	89.74	82.48	84.02	81.42	90.25	<u>51.15</u>	80.73	<u>63.96</u>	87.69	78.25	78.27	78.11
8	88.20	79.94	81.99	77.99	90.25	83.52	84.63	84.03	85.12	75.83	77.76	75.54
9	85.12	74.38	80.33	76.88	87.69	76.06	80.70	77.61	84.61	77.03	76.99	75.40
10	85.12	78.33	80.45	76.31	83.58	74.49	74.95	74.78	81.53	70.75	65.40	71.23
Average	89.69	80.22	82.68	80.12	91.28	77.47	81.75	80.05	90.15	80.90	80.02	80.53
σ	±2.79	±3.69	±2.28	±3.59	±3.59	±10.32	±3.36	±6.62	±5.15	±5.06	±5.88	±5.00
Outliers detected	0	0	0	0	0	<u>1</u>	0	<u>1</u>	0	0	0	0
Critical value Z	2.28	2.28	2.28	2.28	2.28	2.28	2.28	2.28	2.28	2.28	2.28	2.28

Finally, Fig. 3 shows the convergence plot and the structure of the individual obtained for the best solution of Table 2.

$$EVO_o = G_{\sigma=1}(S)$$
$$EVO_c = M$$
$$EVO_s = round(0.36 - K)$$
$$EVO_{MM_1} = D_y(D_y(CM_d))$$
$$EVO_{MM_2} = G_{\sigma=1}(|D_x(D_y(CM_d))|/D_y(CM_d))$$
$$EVO_{MM_3} = D_y(D_y(||||D_x(D_x(CM_d))) + CM_d||||))$$
$$EVO_{MM_4} = G_{\sigma=1}(D_x(CM_d)/D_x(D_x(CM_d)))$$

(a) Individual structure

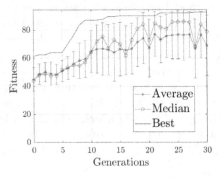

(b) Convergency graph

Fig. 3. Results for the best solution

5   Conclusions and Future Work

In this work, three classifiers used in diverse applications of machine learning were assessment into a model of symbolic learning named brain programming. Since, the task of object recognition requires a clear explanation of the object recognition task for a better understanding of the study object, symbolic learning techniques as helpful. Since BP is an evolutionary vision technique, a suitable classifier to control the optimization process is important to achieve satisfactory performance. As has been shown, the findings demonstrate that of the three classifiers evaluated an MLP is the most suitable for the problem studied. On the other hand, considering that the MLP classifier achieved better model performance (81.04%), this represents an error rate of 18.96%. Although this is not a significant improvement over the 20% error rate that is generally present in medical practice, it does represent an advantage because the information provided by the model during learning can be considered as a form of explainability for the understanding of the visual process that leads to image recognition.

As future work, we intend to analyze and improve the process of generating the descriptors in the model using biologically inspired modeling for more accurate modeling. Furthermore, although the performance of each classifier is susceptible to improvement, working with data that by nature do not have well-defined patterns is an important challenge to cover.

Acknowledgements. Authors would like to acknowledge the support provided by the Instituto Politécnico Nacional under projects: SIP 20200630, SIP 20210788, and SIP 20220226; CONACYT under projects: 65 (Fronteras de la Ciencia) and 6005 (FORDECYT-PRONACES), and CICESE through the project 634-135 to carry out this research. First author thanks the Autonomous University of Tlaxcala, Mexico for the support. Authors also express their gratitude to the Applied Computational Intelligence Network (RedICA).

References

1. Hemaanand, M., Kumar, V.S., Karthika, R.: Smart surveillance system using computer vision and Internet of Things. J. Comput. Theor. Nanosci. **17**, 68–73 (2020)
2. Benomar, L., Chikh, M.A., Descombes, X., Benazzouz, M.: Multi features based approach for white blood cells segmentation and classification in peripheral blood and bone marrow images. Int. J. Biomed. Eng. Technol. **1**, 1–19 (2018)
3. Tian, H., Wang, T., Liu, Y., Qiao, X., Li, Y.: Computer vision technology in agricultural automation-a review. Inf. Process. Agric. **7**(1), 1–19 (2020)
4. Cancer: World Health Organization (2021)
5. Ruiz Argüelles, G.J., Ruiz Delgado, G.J.: Fundamentos de Hematología, 5th edn. Panamericana (2014)
6. Bodzás, A., Kodytek, P., Žídek, J.: Automated detection of acute lymphoblastic leukemia from microscopic images based on human visual perception. Front. Bioeng. Biotechnol. **8**, 1005 (2020)
7. Ghadezadeh, M., Asadi, F., Hosseini, A., Bashash, D., Abolghasemi, H., Roshanpoor, A.: Machine learning in detection and classification of leukemia using smear blood images: a systematic review. Sci. Program. **2021**, 1–14 (2021)
8. Alagu, S., Bagan, K.B.: Acute Lymphoblastic Leukemia diagnosis in microscopic blood smear images using texture features and SVM classifier. In: Alliance International Conference on Artificial Intelligence and Machine Learning (AICAAM), pp. 175–186, April 2019
9. Rodak, B.F., Carr, J.H.: Clinical Hematology Atlas. W. B. Saunders Co. (2016)
10. Vapnik, V.N.: The Nature of Statistical Learning Theory. Information Science and Statistics, 2nd edn. Springer, New York (2000). https://doi.org/10.1007/978-1-4757-3264-1
11. Breiman, L.: Random forest. Mach. Learn. **45**(1), 5–32 (2001). https://doi.org/10.1023/A:1010933404324
12. Haugeland, J.: Artificial Intelligence: The Very Idea. MIT Press, Cambridge (1985)
13. Olague, G., Clemente, E., Dozal, L., Hernández, D.: Evolving an artificial visual cortex for object recognition with brain programming. In: Schuetze, O., et al. (eds.) EVOLVE - A Bridge Between Probability, Set Oriented Numerics, and Evolutionary Computation III. Studies in Computational Intelligence, vol. 500, pp. 97–119. Springer, Heidelberg (2014). https://doi.org/10.1007/978-3-319-01460-9_5
14. Ochoa-Montiel, R., Sossa-Azuela, H., Olague, G.: Dataset_leukemia (2021). Copyright 03-2021-112413373300-01
15. Ochoa-Montiel, R., Sossa, H., Olague, G., Chan-Ley, M., Menendez-Clavijo, J.: Symbolic learning using brain programming for the recognition of leukaemia images. Computación y Sistemas **25**(4) (2021)

Author Index

Printed in the United States
by Baker & Taylor Publisher Services